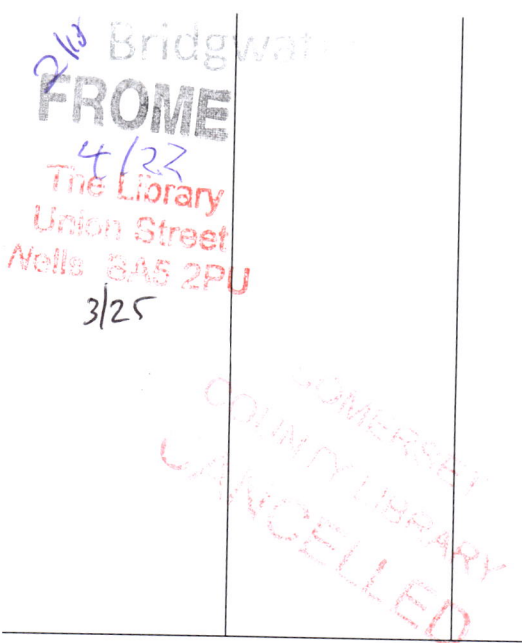

Please return/renew this item by the last date shown on this label, or on your self-service receipt.

To renew this item, visit **www.librarieswest.org.uk** or contact your library

Your borrower number and PIN are required.

Libraries**West**

JOHN R. LEIGH

The
NAÏVE
SHAKESPEAREAN

Edited by Marjorie J. Leigh

Published by Paragon Publishing
© Marjorie J. Leigh 2017

The rights of Marjorie J. Leigh to be identified as the author of this work have been asserted by her in accordance with the Copyright, Designs and Patents Act of 1988.
All rights reserved; no part of this publication may be reproduced, stored in a retrieval system, or transmitted in any form or by any means, electronic, mechanical, photocopying, recording or otherwise without the prior written consent of the publisher or a licence permitting copying in the UK issued by the Copyright Licensing Agency Ltd, www.cla.co.uk

ISBN 978-1-78222-542-3

Book design, layout and production management by Into Print
www.intoprint.net, +44 (0)1604 832140

Front cover photo: Garry Knight (Hark, hark!) [CC BY 2.0 (http://creativecommons.org/licenses/by/2.0)], via Wikimedia Commons
Front cover illustration: Wenceslas Hollar, derived from: The Old Globe.jpg, Public Domain, https://commons.wikimedia.org/w/index.php?curid=20070574
Back cover photo: 'Emma': The quadrangle of Emmanuel College, Cambridge.
Photo courtesy of Martin Brock.

Printed and bound in UK and USA by Lightning Source

CONTENTS

IN MEMORY OF JOHN RAYSON LEIGH 6

AUTHOR'S PREFACE. 7

EDITOR'S NOTE re LINE REFERENCES 13

PART I: INTRODUCTION 15

1. Going to the Play 16
2. On the Writing of Plays. 21
3. Audiences. 29
4. Dialogue 34
5. Character.. 43
6. Analysing Hamlet. 51
7. The Constitutional Background 55
8. How Old is Hamlet? 62
9. The Ghost. 72

PART IIA: HAMLET THE MELODRAMATIC HERO 87

10. Hamlet the Lunatic. 88
11. Hamlet's Soliloquies 96
12. The Murder of Gonzago.. 104
13. The Murder of Gonzago (cont'd) 113
14. After the Gonzago-play 120
15. After the Gonzago-play (cont'd). 133

PART IIB: THE TWO FAMILIES IN HAMLET 143

16. Polonius, Ophelia and Laertes, & Rosencrantz and Guildenstern. 144
17. Gertrude 155
18. Hamlet the Young Man 162
19. Hamlet the Young Man (cont'd) 168
20. Claudius 180

PART IIC: HAMLET—CONSTRUCTION & CRITICAL HISTORY 193

21. What Kind of Play is Hamlet? 194
22. A Short History of the Character-problem in Hamlet 204
23. A Comparison of the First and Second Quartos of Hamlet 214
24. Further Notes on Hamlet. 223
25. An Elizabethan Spoof: Troilus and Cressida 232
26. All's Well That Ends Well 237
27. Measure for Measure 245
28. Emergence of the Theme 249
29. Othello 254
30. The Character of Macbeth 272
31. Macbeth & Lady Macbeth 282

PART III: THEME OF THE LATER PLAYS: FAMILY 291

32. King Lear 292
33. Antony and Cleopatra: Mistress or Wife? 301
34. The Last Plays 316

PART IV: ODDMENTS.. 323
35. Two Jacobean Spoofs .. .. .324
36. A Specimen Synopsis of the Spanish Tragedy. .. .. .328
37. Who was the author of Shakespeare's Plays?.. .. .. .336
BIBLIOGRAPHY. 338
THE PLAYS 342

IN MEMORIAM

Published in honour of my father, John Rayson Leigh (1916–2007), who loved Shakespeare, music, literature, science and mathematics: a true polymath. His collected writings, twenty years in the making (to 2002), are here set out.

AUTHOR'S PREFACE

Of all the remarks which must have been made to me during my time at Cambridge (it began in 1934, when I went up to study Modern Languages), I now remember only three. The first is not relevant to this book but is perhaps worth quoting.

On our first day in College, we newcomers assembled in the College Hall, where we were addressed by the Senior Tutor. After giving us some information on what our life in the College would entail, he said (as well as I remember after sixty-odd years), "From here you will go to the Old Library, where you will meet the Master and Fellows of the College. You will then proceed to the Senate House in a somewhat disorderly body."

We did.

The other two remarks came from my German supervisor. On one occasion he said, "There are only two good reasons for writing a book: One, you have something new to say; Two, you have nothing new to say, but are saying what is already known in a new way which you think will be interesting or significant."

In view of the millions of words which have already been written about Shakespeare, it is extremely difficult to say anything which has not already been said about him, but I have found many things to say which, to the best of my knowledge, have not been said before; otherwise I would not have offered this book for publication. Some of the notions in this book may already have been hinted at, but my approach has been my own. Having come to believe that a completely independent approach was needed, as from an 'innocent' (one reason for the title of this book), I have done my own thing. So, if anyone tells me that something in this book has already been said or hinted at, I shall be interested but not repentant. It is hardly possible to read everything that has been written about Shakespeare; in any case, I have occasionally found that where an opinion has already been hinted at, the critic has not developed his idea as far as he should have.

During my time at Cambridge, a distinguished German critic called Emil Ludwig was writing weighty volumes on individual German authors of the late eighteenth century. I had read one of them, and during my second year when he published another, and I asked my German supervisor (who, of course, had read it) whether we needed to plough through that one as well, he replied: "Don't bother: he has got clean away from his subject, and is playing with concepts". [1]

At the time I thought that the Germans would be more prone to play with concepts than some other nations, perhaps because of the structure of their language, perhaps because of the contributions to philosophy of their great philosophers, but I now know that they are far from unique in that respect. When I began writing this book as a retirement occupation and reading critical works, it seemed to me that the English-speaking critics of Shakespeare must be the world's leaders in the art of playing with concepts, but since then I have accepted that critics in other nations might equal them.

Since my subject at Cambridge was not English, I did not then know that the playing with concepts by the critics of Shakespeare had begun a few years earlier. In 1904, A.C. Bradley had published his *Shakespearean Tragedy*, so thoroughgoing a work that there seemed to be few, if any, further opportunities for originality, but new approaches had to be found if the Shakespeare industry was not to die on its feet.

In 1930, Wilson Knight published a volume of essays called *The Wheel of Fire*, the first

---

[1] Referred to later as 'deconstructuralism'

being "On the Principles of Shakespeare Interpretation". Possibly because he had learned from the astronomers that space and time are interrelated, he decided that there must be a spatial as well as a temporal element in Shakespeare's plays:

> Receiving this whole Shakespearean vision within the intellectual consciousness demands a certain and very definite act of mind. One must be prepared to see the whole play in space as well as time. It is natural in analysis to pursue the steps of the tale in sequence, noticing the logic that connects them, regarding the essentials that Aristotle noted: beginning, middle and end. And yet by giving supreme attention to this temporal nature of drama we omit what, in Shakespeare, is at least of equivalent importance. A Shakespearean tragedy is set spatially as well as temporally in the mind. By this I mean that there are throughout the play a set of correspondences which relate to each other independently of the time-sequence which is the story...Now if we are prepared to see the whole play laid out, so to speak, as an area, being simultaneously aware of these thickly scattered correspondences in a single view of the whole, we possess the unique quality of the play in a new sense. 'Faults' begin to vanish into thin air. Immediately we begin to realise necessity where before we saw irrelevance and beauty dethroning ugliness...

By examining the spatial element and "set of correspondences", Wilson Knight appears to have meant no more than establishing the initial dramatic situation and its background, i.e. the world of the play, and identifying the inter-related details of the plot. And as for not enquiring into "perfect verisimilitude to life", surely it is this verisimilitude which gives such vividness to Shakespeare's plays?

> There is a maxim that a work of art should be criticised according to the artist's "intentions": than which no maxim could be more false... "Intentions" belong to the plane of intellect and memory: the swifter consciousness that awakens in poetic composition touches subtleties and heights and depths unknowable by intellect and intractable to memory. That consciousness we can enjoy at will when we submit ourselves with utmost passivity to the poet's work; but when the intellectual mode returns it often brings with it a troop of concepts irrelevant to the nature of the work it thinks to analyse.

Than this, nothing could have been more perverse, for (a) the artist's intention is the foundation of the creative urge, and to a large extent it is a conscious intention; (b) his care over the composition of his creation (and composition is as important in determining the effect of an artistic creation as its content) is again largely in the intellectual mode; (c) the rest (as is shown in the introductory chapters) is a question of instinct and intuition, in the case of plays the instinct for what is theatre and the intuitive understanding of one's fellow-humans without which the play's personages will lack life; if the play is in verse, the innate ability to write poetry.

At the same time, he was correct in emphasising the need to study the "thickly scattered correspondences" while excluding "troops of concepts" from one's own mind (not that the emphasis had any effect).

After Wilson Knight, L C Knights' essay *How many children had Lady Macbeth?* (1933)—a more correct version of the title would have been "How many children had Lady Macbeth once had?"—expressed the same ideas in his own way:

> For some years there have been signs of a reorientation of Shakespeare criticism. The books that I have in mind have little in common with the majority of those that have been written on Shakespeare, but they are likely to have a decisive influence upon criticism in the future. The present, therefore, is a favourable time in which to take stock of the traditional methods, and to inquire why so few of the many books that have been written are relevant to our study of Shakespeare as a poet. The inquiry involves an examination of certain critical presuppositions, and of these the most fruitful of irrelevancies is the assumption that Shakespeare was pre-eminently a great 'creator of character'...
>
> We are faced with this conclusion: the only profitable approach to Shakespeare is a consideration of his plays as dramatic poems, of his use of plays to obtain a total complex emotional response. Yet the bulk of Shakespeare criticism is concerned with his characters, his heroines, his love of nature or his 'philosophy'—with everything, in short, except the words on the page, which it is the main business of the critic to examine.

Knights did not define total "response". Is it an indivisible unity or does it consist of distinguishable components? His emphasis on examining the words on the page was too inexplicit to help any reader. He later repeated his description of previous character-criticisms as "irrelevancies" (Wilson Knight had called them "false criticism") and described *Macbeth* as a "dramatic poem", when it is a poetic drama and first and foremost a play. He also let fall such profundities as "The theme of *Hamlet* is death", and "Macbeth is a statement of evil". These are ponderous comments calculated to impress the unwary reader, but empty of precise significance. My dictionary gives no fewer than thirteen meanings of 'evil' as noun and adjective; as for 'death', it is the theme of every tragedy of the time, but signifies only that at the end of the play the principals will be dead, the all-important question being: why did the playwright choose to dramatise such a plot?

Neither critic grasped the implication of spatial and temporal: that the first step in the study of a play must be the establishing of the nature, sequence, and consequences of the events of the plot in order to identify the playwright's dramatic purpose.

Academics must publish if they can, and what they publish should be original in some respect; as my German supervisor remarked, there is little point in repeating what has already been said. After Bradley's *Shakespearean Tragedy* (1904), no one appeared to be able to improve on his interpretations, so new approaches of any kind had to be found. These attempts at new approaches took Shakespearean criticism even further astray than it had been.

In 1935 Caroline Spurgeon published her *Shakespeare's Imagery*, a study of his use of metaphor: a very thorough-going study, but without any emphasis on the contribution of the images to the playwright's dramatic intention; it seemed that their purpose was to establish the atmosphere of the play, and that the critic need not pay attention to anything else. Was she inspired by Knights' description of Shakespeare's plays as "dramatic poems"?

Criticism began to depart ever further from the plays as plays, which are always about people and their problems—highly personal problems being the most interesting to audiences—and not about concepts, as Salman Rushdie (1983) says in his novel *Shame*: "Politics empties theatres in old London town."

Attempts to break new ground eventually reached perversity. Apparently the reader must now appreciate Shakespeare by passively letting any kind of poetic association or abstract concept come into his mind, or in the case of recent schools of thought, discuss Shakespeare in terms of some abstract system both remote from and irrelevant to him, and sometimes not detectably relevant to any author. I have in fact come to see much of the contemporary criticism of Shakespeare as acres of verbiage.

From one volume of essays on a single play, I gleaned the following concepts. It is not a complete list:

Universes of thought	Problems of identity
Dimensions of reality	Transcendence of limitations
Conceptions of being	The disjunctive imagination
The weight and density of time	The image-thought of disease process
Corrupting finitude	Shapes of infinite desire
Ceremonies for chaos	Essence and existence
Unconscious tapinosis	The infinite and fathomless
Drive for the absolute	Equilibrium of disillusionment
The literature of preliminary devaluation	

'Tapinosis' is not in any of my three dictionaries, all large ones. From the Oxford English Dictionary, it means 'language demeaning the worth of something'—surely too erudite a word for most readers?

Do playwrights really have such abstractions in their heads when writing plays, or theatregoers when watching them? When I am safely parked in my theatre seat and the curtain has risen, my attention is on the stage; I must follow the things done and said there with the same continuous attention as during a conversation in real life; thoughts of my own may come into my mind, but to let them distract me from what is happening on the stage is less than fair to the playwright, the cast and myself. Since I may miss some significant word or action, I do not need to be told that my response must be total. Plays (I repeat) are not about concepts, doctrines or -isms; they are first and foremost about people, the most interesting aspects of whom are always their most intimate. If we are watching a play on a proscenium stage, we are looking through a window into someone else's private life; if in a theatre-in-the-round, into a goldfish bowl.

I no longer respect the academic critics although there may still be some who keep their feet on the ground. I conclude that their care over detail creates a mist in front of their vision which prevents them from seeing the play as a structured whole.

I bow to their scholarship, in particular to the care with which they have established and annotated the texts, but not to their powers of analysis or interpretation. Some appear to have forgotten that Shakespeare's plays were intended to be acted, not read; that acting is a very precise art; that a play is not a literary but a semi-literary creation which only comes alive when performed, and may come alive in a variety of ways, depending on how it is cast, directed and acted in successive productions.

Sometime after the compilation of the above list I learned that it had been the merest beginning. In his *Preface to Appropriating Shakespeare*, whose title means 'reserving the criticism of Shakespeare exclusively to one's own school', Professor Brian lists over forty headings under which critical articles on Shakespeare are now grouped, and then continues:

> The situation in Shakespeare studies now reflects the general pattern of well-defined groups competing with each other for the reader's attention, alle-

giance, and purchasing power. The annual bibliography of 'Shakespeare Quarterly' now also classifies criticism into categories, and without going into detail we can see the same groups consolidating themselves. Among the newer key-words in the annual index are: allusion, colonialism, culture, deconstruction, discourse, eroticism, female characteristics, feminism, gender, historicism, ideology, Judaism, literary theory, male characteristics, mimesis, naming, patriarchy, post-structuralism, power, psychoanalysis, psychology, reception, representation, self-reflexiveness, sexuality, structuralism, subversion, theatricality, transvestism...Instead of a critical model opening up a field to fresh enquiry, these approaches effectively close it down, recasting it in their own images.

It is not easy to use a concept in a train of reasoning unless one knows the word for it and is clear as to its meaning (in fact, without this condition it may never form part of one's mental processes). As examples, "Sexism", "Racism" and "Feminism" are the headings of three sections of an editor's introduction to *Othello* but, from the O.E.D., these words did not appear in English till the second half of the nineteenth century; how, then, could they have formed part of Shakespeare's creative thinking? Some of the words in Professor Vickers' list did not appear till the second half of the twentieth century; how, then, could they be relevant to Shakespeare or any of his contemporaries?

To borrow a phrase from computer cybernetics, this type of criticism is virtual criticism. The acres of verbiage have become square miles, and the feet of some critics are now above the cirrostratus which—for the non-meteorologist—is a layer of very high cloud, often obscuring the ground to airborne travellers above it!

Such is the present state of the Shakespeare industry. And why has such an industry arisen around Shakespeare but not around Chaucer, Milton, Fielding, Scott, Dickens, or any other great and prolific author? The answer must be: failure to arrive at satisfactory interpretations of his characterisations and dramatic intentions. Books and essays continue to be turned out and lectures delivered on any topic which can be remotely associated with a Shakespeare play, and only too often they are more about the topic than the play. Rarely are they about Shakespeare's dramatic intention, or a play's effect on the stage.

So my approach to Shakespeare has been the reverse of the conventional 'character-first' procedure: 'construction and plot' first in order to establish the playwright's dramatic intention, then character. In fact, if the play is not very complex, character may then seem so obvious as to make character-analysis unnecessary, though not with some of his plays; examining all the words on their pages and identifying their thickly-scattered correspondences (particularly with *Hamlet*) while excluding troops of concepts is not an especially simple operation. From my own experience, it requires long practice; it is a kind of intellectual discipline which no one else (so far as I know) has taken as far as it should have been. If the reader tries it himself, he will eventually realise that Shakespeare's dramatic writing is enormously detailed and enormously explicit; no word may be overlooked.

This book was begun as a retirement occupation in 1982, and has taken since then to complete, off and on, and sometimes more off than on, partly because of unwanted interruptions (some of them long), and partly because I often had to wait while ideas and impressions clarified themselves in my mind. After completing my account of *Hamlet* I had become sufficiently well practised in the method to apply it to the later plays, did so, with equally interesting results, and then realised that I would have to write introductory chapters to explain and justify the method. They are intended to emphasise that writing a play is a practical activity in which any critical playing with concepts is totally out of place; also that when the theatregoer takes his seat in his stall he should have emptied his mind of concepts.

It is a hobbyist's book. However, having read many French and German plays at school and Cambridge, where I also read the complete works of Shakespeare, Sheridan, Shaw, Galsworthy, and some anthologies of plays, I became a reader of plays for pleasure as much as novels, and now regard myself as no longer a hobbyist and more of a professional than most of the academic critics I have read.

It deals only with *Hamlet* and the later plays, the earlier plays being straightforward. I suspect that their straightforwardness has inveigled the academic critics into accepting that the later plays can be regarded as equally straightforward, although some, in particular *Hamlet*, contain far more subtleties.

Before World War II, the general outlook remained heavily Victorian, sex being rarely, if ever, mentioned; hence school pupils read only the 'safe' plays, i.e. those with few or no explicit sexual references. But *Hamlet* (and others of Shakespeare's plays) are now read in sixth forms, so this book is intended as a handbook or manual in play-reading for students of all ages from sixteen upwards—another reason for its title.

Much of my interpretation is based on what I have seen during my own life. After I retired, I had time to remember events which I had noticed in the past and which had stuck in my memory but which I had not understood at the time, and eventually came to understand them. I could not have arrived at my interpretations in my younger days, and I suspect that they are more likely to be accepted by older than by younger readers. Hence my comments include a number of personal interpolations and recollections (yet another reason for its title). Without these recollections I could not have written some sections of the book.

My bibliography should not be taken too seriously. The works I found most useful were works of reference, anthologies of criticisms, and editions of plays, and to these I am much indebted, but the list of the hundred and fifty or so critical works of which I kept a list is something of a fib, for although I began by reading through some of them, I soon found myself merely skimming them, my approach being so different from that of their authors that they were of little use to me, and now have no recollection of most of them. Eventually I decided to read no more.

My interpretations, whether anticipated by anyone else or not, have been my own. Whether the reader will agree with them remains to be seen, but at least my attempts at interpreting Shakespeare have not been flattened under a weight of scholarly reading. A recent edition of *Hamlet* contains: introductory matter—just over 160 pages; the play, with footnotes on each page invariably containing far more words than the text—260 pages; Longer Notes—152 pages—the scholarly edition to end all scholarly editions, in which the commentary and notes displace the play as the prime object of study. It is possible to read Shakespeare for pleasure, but would any student who was compelled to plough through so much editorial exhibitionism ever enjoy him again?

This book, then, is an attempt at a counterblast to present trends in Shakespeare criticism. It is high time that someone outside the Ivory Tower of Academe blew a whistle on these trends, high time Hans Andersen's little child said, "But the emperor has no clothes on!" and high time the plays were recreated—so to speak—in terms not of concepts swarming into the minds of erudite readers, but simply of how they were intended to be watched and heard by the early audiences for whom they were written.

John. R. Leigh (2002)

EDITOR'S NOTE re LINE REFERENCES

Line-references in *Hamlet* refer to the New Swan edition (1968, reprinted 1976), ed. Bernard Lott M.A., Ph.D.; for the other plays, various editions (see Bibliography). Line-numbering varies, particularly in scenes containing passages of prose or when an editor shortens a long scene and creates another, as can be seen in different editions of the same play. Either way, the references will be there to within a few lines, whatever copy is consulted.

PART I
INTRODUCTION

1

GOING TO THE PLAY

What is the theatrical experience?

The theatregoer goes to the theatre not only because he hopes to enjoy it, but because that particular experience cannot be obtained elsewhere.

If he is to have it, the following four conditions must be met:-
1) The play must be well written by a playwright whose intention is to make some kind of dramatic point, i.e. to say or illustrate something which causes his audiences to leave the theatre feeling that they have learned something or, if they are not certain what the point was, at least feeling thoughtful enough to continue thinking about the play. It will then be remembered for a long time; sometimes it is never forgotten.

The theatregoer should have chosen the play in the hope of producing this effect. Of course, much depends on his tastes. If he is young, he will probably choose to be entertained by a musical, a farce, or a bedroom comedy, and will only remember the amusement it gave him, but the older theatregoer may have seen enough in the way of superficially entertaining productions to prefer something with meat in it.

An example of a play intended to give its audiences food for thought is Arthur Miller's *The Last Yankee* (1993).

The play opens in the anteroom of a psychiatric hospital with a conversation between two husbands whose wives are patients there. One is a member of an old and distinguished American family who has elected not to follow some prestigious profession such as that of lawyer or doctor, but to become a carpenter; the other, a successful businessman who has set out to make money, and is so full of his success that he is extremely patronising in his attitude to the carpenter. Evidently the carpenter is happily married, for he and his wife have seven children, whereas the business man has none: "I guess we left it too late."

Why are their wives in the hospital?

The second scene takes place in a ward in the hospital in which there are three beds, in one of which throughout the scene a young woman lies asleep. Either she is unable to face reality, or possibly is in deep-sleep therapy. Most of it is devoted to a conversation between the carpenter and his wife. (Here I must explain that my rule when either reading or watching a play is: go by the words of the play: take them as meaning exactly what they say.) So, while watching, I was hoping to hear some word or phrase which I could latch on to as giving a hint as to the dramatist's meaning, and I found it in a remark by the carpenter to his wife: "You don't have a mental problem; you have an attitude problem!"

During their conversation, the business man's wife enters. She is a small, timorous woman who has devised some little occupation for herself in the hospital; her husband is so over-confident, so authoritative, so patronising, that she abandons all and rushes out.

The play is in fact about the "attitude", and it appears that two, or perhaps three, wives are in a mental hospital because of it. Whose is the fault? Are the wives suffering because their husbands have, so to speak, taken their attitudes home with them? If the carpenter—is he at fault? Has he suffered so much from the patronising attitude that he could not help taking it home with him, so that it has begun seriously to trouble his wife?

The business man has certainly taken his attitude home with him. A small woman, his wife is a gentle retiring soul, but the effect of his dominating pride in his own success, his superiority, his always knowing better than she—has been to crush her.

These reflections came fairly quickly; two others came later.

When the business man says, "We have no children; we seem to have left it too late," is he speaking the truth? Have they had no children because of the psychosomatic effect of his dominance on his wife? (*Psychosomatic effect* means the apparent malfunctioning of some part of the body caused by the mental stress of a severe problem.) Had she been so crushed by her husband at home that she had been unable to bear his children? Not being a doctor, I do not know whether this is likely, but the body is not a machine pure and simple, and I do not think it impossible. (A psychosomatic effect is the specific theme of another Miller play, *Broken Glass.*)

Where did Miller find this idea for a play? It seems unlikely that it was entirely his own invention; more likely that he had actually seen or known of wives having to go into mental hospitals, or at least suffering badly because of the "attitude".

These were my own thoughts; I was not able to learn what thoughts had entered other minds. If a play has caused them to leave the theatre feeling thoughtful, how many theatregoers exchange ideas afterwards?

2) The performance must be good enough to cause the spectators to forget that they are watching actors.

After my wife and I had seen Tennessee Williams' *Cat on a Hot Tin Roof*, she said, "Being American, I knew that the accents were not perfectly authentic, but after a time I forgot that I was watching actors." This was a considerable tribute to the naturalness of the performances. I also forgot it while watching *The Last Yankee* which had a British cast.

3) The spectator must be cooperative in that he should be prepared to forget that he is watching actors and to believe that what he is seeing on the stage is real. Children watch pantomimes, plays, films and television scripts as if they are real; they are naïve. The theatregoer should be prepared to render himself equally naïve and to suspend disbelief.

Some minds cannot do this because they lack imaginative power. Others will not do it because they consider themselves too worldly-wise, too hard-headed (or however they think of themselves) to submerge themselves in what they see on the stage. The habitually sceptical mind is unlikely to have the full theatrical experience.

Here I take issue with those Shakespeare critics who say that his characters are stage characters and not to be regarded as real people; or rather, I do not so much take issue with them as express my wonderment that anyone could make such a comment. Why have his characters fascinated his readers for four hundred years? I interpret the comment as a tacit admission that the critic had not been able to arrive at a satisfactory interpretation of the personages he was discussing.

It is of course possible that the theatregoer does not become caught up in the play because he does not understand its background. Many years ago I began to read Tennessee Williams' *A Streetcar Named Desire*, which I soon abandoned because I could not understand the point of what I was reading. More recently, when it was put on at a local theatre, I decided to see it, and found that its background was explained in a programme note: it is set in the Deep South of the United States where, by convention, the male is all-male—big, crude, and totally *macho*—and the female must continuously pretend to be all-female, butterfly-minded and without a mind of her own.

Not being an American, I could not have understood the play without that programme note, and I suspect that such notes would be useful to the younger members of today's audiences, when old plays are revived that made their impact on previous generations with different outlooks and conventions.

4) Being in an audience caught up in the performance is another requisite. A screened performance in the cinema may produce this also, but a televised performance seen in one's own living room may not, because there is not the same awareness of a community watching together. The awareness of being in a community may amount merely to the knowledge that all the members of the audience have chosen the same evening to watch the play, but it is enough if they have chosen it in the hope of the theatrical experience.

At the same time, it has been said that a play is unthinkable without an audience, even if it is only an audience of one (a point to be remembered by the student of Shakespeare: Shakespeare wrote his plays to be acted, not read).

This awareness of a common interest is obviously more likely to come if the audience is watching not images on a screen but live personages on the stage; the greater degree of immediacy makes it much easier to believe that they are real. The fact that the actors are alive gives the theatregoers the feeling that, unknown to the characters portrayed, they are eavesdropping on their private lives and able to see them in their most intimate moments.

In any case, while a playwright's creation must pass through the interpretative minds of the director and the cast, a screened performance has also passed through the mind of the cameraman, a very important contributor to the production, who can make or mar a film. Now it is well known to all photographers that narrowing the viewing angle and zooming in increases visual impact; this technique is very often used, and I find that it is over-used. As an example, a common practice is to narrow the viewing angle so that the screen shows only the head of the person who is speaking, then the head of the person who replies, both usually wearing suitably emotional expressions. This intensifies the impact of what is being said and of how it is being said; but this is to an unnatural degree compared with a stage performance in which many actors i.e. the speaker, the person being addressed, others present—and their reactions to what is being said, along with their surrounding stageset—remain in full view of the spectators.

In this respect, the stage is (or should be) much more natural than the screen. I have long been annoyed by the practice which, I suspect, is only too often used to increase visual impact in order to conceal poverty of inspiration in the writing of the script. And after a time, too much of it inevitably dulls the viewer's response. A well-written play induces the spectator to watch continuously in order to ensure that he will miss nothing, however quiet, of what is happening on the stage. In effect, should this technique be used to do his watching for him?

A part of the community feeling is the reaction of the audience, a kind of interchange between the audience and the cast of which the actors are always aware. Depending on the moment in the play, the reaction may be anything from a roar of laughter, or a sudden intake of breath, or a shifting in the seat, to complete momentary stillness. Some actors have said that they could manipulate the reactions of their audiences; this would no doubt increase the effectiveness of poor plays, but a good play should hold its audience with the minimum of such manipulation.

The feeling among those present that they constitute a 'we' may occur whenever people have assembled for a common purpose: in church, or in a hall or outdoor venue: for example, the ancient Greek tragedies developed from religious ceremonies and were based on stories from their religion and, since they had choruses, might be roughly compared to the performance of an oratorio; the morality plays which preceded the Elizabethan drama were also based on religious themes; or in the concert hall, provided that they are not attending the service or the concert merely because it is a social occasion or a required formality. The place where the performance is being given may then play its part in arousing the feeling of "we". Given such conditions, a televised performance cannot be the equal of watching and listening in person in the company of others who have come to the same place for the same purpose.

Today, plays are rarely on purely religious subjects, but a kind of community awareness arises from the common interest in the emotional relationships they usually depict; in particular, interest in themes of the timeless and universal family type (of which more will be said later). As an example, I quote the performance of *Cat on a Hot Tin Roof* during which my wife forgot that she was watching actors, as did I and doubtless many others.

The most popular operas are about emotional relationships. Only once have I been to the opera in Italy, and I still remember the occasion in Naples just after the end of World War II. The double bill performance was of the heavenly twins, *I Pagliacci* and *Cavalleria Rusticana*, and I found first, that the crowd scenes were far more natural than anything I had seen before; and second, that the stage crowd appeared to extend itself over the footlights to include the audience! I inferred that although many Italians know their operas backwards, they always *live* them, i.e. their approach is always naïve, which is the best way for the theatrical experience. Possibly those Germans who are fond of Wagner's five-hour operas live their Wagner also. In Britain, perhaps because we are (or were) less overtly emotional than some other nations, we do not have enough native opera, although ladies may sometimes be seen drying their eyes during performances of such operas as *Madame Butterfly*.

How many readers of fiction read plays for pleasure as well as novels? Plays are not so easy to read as novels; where the novelist can describe persons, places and backgrounds at whatever length he wishes, the limited stage-time of a play compels the playwright to be much more concise and taut. So, unless the printed edition includes a large number of descriptive stage directions, the play-reader must use his evocative imagination more than the novel-reader. He must visualise the personages in terms of his own experiences of people, in the hope that they will come alive to him. This leads to a difficulty. The play may come alive in the reader's mind, though his impression of it may not be the same as anyone else's; in fact, if he has formed his impressions by first reading it, he may be surprised, even disappointed, when he first sees it in performance, because actors and actresses all have their own individualities. Since we are all unique individuals, they are unlikely to match what the play-reader has visualised. Directors also have their own ideas on the interpretation of plays.

Playwrights themselves have had this experience. Shaw said that when he went to watch his plays in rehearsal, he was always astonished by what he saw. Oscar Wilde remarked, after seeing *The Importance of Being Earnest* in rehearsal, "Yes, it is quite a good play. I remember I wrote one very like it myself!" According to Diderot, Voltaire, when watching a famous contemporary actress called La Clairon in one of his plays, said, "Did I really write all that?" More recently William Nicholson, playwright and former B.B.C. director, has spoken of "…the intense excitement of actors producing ideas I'd never imagined when I wrote the script."

So, if the theatregoer has already read a play, he should be prepared, when he sees it in production, to forget his own impressions and watch what transpires on the stage as if it were new to him.

Is there, then, a case for not reading plays before seeing them? I do not think so, for if the theatregoer first reads a play, then sees it and is surprised by what he sees, he will at least realise that a play only acquires real existence when staged, and that it may do so in more than one way in successive productions.

On the other hand, many old plays which are rarely staged today remain worth reading because they illustrate the outlooks and social conventions of past generations in a manner rarely equalled by history books.

2

ON THE WRITING OF PLAYS

Who can write plays?

Since many famous authors have written plays which today are rarely staged, the question should be "Who can write successful plays?" The answer must be: fewer people than the number of would-be playwrights.

Who can explain how plays should be written if they are to be successful? Oddly, here the answer is—nobody, not even the successful playwrights.

The ability to write successful plays appears to be something that the playwright must have been born with, and that his interest in drama should have appeared at an early age: perhaps he played with a toy theatre, and even tried writing plays while still a child. Experience of the theatre, of the art of acting and of audiences, eventually causes his early interest to develop into a kind of instinct which is so deep in him and so complex that he cannot analyse or explain it, as the following quotations suggest:

> There are those who from their birth know how to write a play (I do not say that the gift is hereditary); and there are those who do not know at once, and these will never know. You are a dramatist, or you are not; neither will-power nor work has anything to do with it. The gift is indispensable. I think that everyone whom you may ask how to write a play will reply, if he can really write one, that he doesn't know how it is done.
>
> Alexandre Dumas, fils, (1824–1895)

> To see this clearly—how to achieve success in the theatre—you must consider two questions which have no relation to each other:
> 1. How should one set about composing a dramatic work which shall succeed and make money?
> 2. How shall one set about composing a dramatic work which shall be fine and have some hope of survival?
>
> Reply to the first question: Nothing is known about it; for if anything were known, every theatre would earn six thousand francs every evening...
>
> Reply to the second question: to compose a dramatic work which shall be fine and shall live, have genius! There is no other way. In art, talent is nothing. Genius alone lives.
>
> Theodore de Banville (1823–1891)

> You ask me how a play is made, my dear Dreyfus. I may well astonish you, perhaps, but on my soul and honour, before God and man, I assure you that I know nothing about it, that you know nothing, that nobody knows anything, and that the author of a play knows less about it than anyone else...
>
> The author in travail with a play is an unconscious being, whatever he may think about himself; and his piece is the product of instinct rather than of intention.
>
> Eduard Pailleron (1834–1899)

> The information which the dramatist seeks cannot be told, even by those who know. For the gaining of such knowledge is the acquirement of an instinct which enables its possessor automatically to make sure of the effective in playwriting and constructing and devising, and automatically to shun the ineffective. This instinct must be planted and nourished by more or less (more if possible) living with audiences, until it becomes part of the system—yet constantly alert for the necessary modifications which correspond to the changes which the tastes and requirements of these audiences undergo.

William Gillette, intron to "How to Write a play" in *Papers on Playmaking* (1957)

Except for the last, these extracts are from nineteenth-century French playwrights and in this century[2] Terence Rattigan has said much the same thing. In a preface to a volume of his collected plays, he says:

> ...that strange, almost mystical element in the craft of playwriting known as "sense of theatre"...I have a sense of theatre. I am not at all sure what it is, I admit, but I do know that I have it now, that I had it at the age of eleven when I made my first, most unimpressive attempt at writing a play...

Rattigan, who worked for a time as scriptwriter in Hollywood, recounts the following episode:

> A film producer of Central European origin, and with little command of the English tongue, who had commissioned me to 'inject' some comedy into a script, ordered me peremptorily into his office one day and pointed with a furiously shaking finger to a line in a scene I had written for him. 'How', he demanded, 'can this be funny?'
>
> The line he had pointed to consisted of the single word 'Yes'...I could not explain to him why the word 'Yes' in that particular context was funny. I doubt, anyway, if I could have explained it to myself. I could only assure him with youthful and fervent conviction that not only was it utterly hilarious, but that it would get a far better laugh than any of the prettily phrased epigrams that I had laboriously turned for him, and that it had, in fact, been a hundred times more difficult to write...
>
> I can hear the laugh now. It was, happily, by far the biggest in the film.

If a playwright of Rattigan's calibre could not explain why a single word should arouse such a laugh, who else could?

A little thought shows that there is nothing unusual in the requirement of innate ability for high artistic achievement. When we consider, say, such painters as Rembrandt, Velazquez, or Turner, such architects as Wren, or such composers as Bach, Mozart, and Beethoven, it must be obvious that they could only have attained such supreme mastery of their arts if they had been born with such mastery, and that they would have devoted their lives to becoming masters even if for a while they had starved in garrets. Why did Shakespeare leave his family and emigrate, so to speak, to London, where he is said to have supported himself in his early days there by holding horses (naturally, outside playhouses)?

Not many novelists or poets have written good plays. Notable exceptions which come to mind are Victor Hugo, Alexandre Dumas, his son of the same name, and Galsworthy,

---

2   Twentieth century

all of whom were highly successful as both novelists and playwrights, but Wordsworth, Coleridge, Shelley, Keats, Scott, Byron, Tennyson, and Swinburne all wrote dramas which did not establish a reputation for them as dramatists. Generally, the author of fiction is either a novelist or a playwright, but not both.

This is not to say that successful playwrights have never offered hints on how to write plays.

The first important piece of advice is that novels and plays are not written in the same way:

> You ask me how a play is made.
> By beginning at the end.
> A novel is quite a different matter.
>
> I could mention several illustrious novelists who have often started out without knowing where they were going.
>
> Walter Scott, the great Walter Scott, sat down of a morning at his study table, took six sheets of paper, and wrote 'Chapter One' without knowing anything else about his story than the first chapter. He set forth his characters, he indicated the situation; then characters and situation got out of the affair as best they could. They were left to create themselves by the logic of events.
>
> Eugene Sue often told me that it was impossible for him to draw up a plan. It benumbed him...More than once at the end of one of his serial stories he left his characters in an inextricable situation of which he himself did not know the outcome...
>
> George Sand frequently started a novel on the strength of a phrase, a thought, a page, a landscape. It was not she who guided her pen, but her pen which guided her...
>
> But never have Scribe, or Dumas père, or Dumas fils, or Augier, or Labiche, or Sardou, written 'Scene One' without knowing what they were going to put into the last scene.
>
> Ernest Legouve (1807–1903)

Dickens, who wrote his novels in serial instalments, remarked that he sometimes found his characters insisting on behaving in their own way, even doing the opposite of what he had intended for them! I suspect that the best novels are written in that way, the writer being guided by his pen and watching and listening to his characters rather than steering them. A novel written to some previously formulated plan will probably seem too contrived or artificial if the characters move along grooves predestined for them by their author.

> I don't know what's going to happen in a story, just as we don't know what's going to happen with life. Just think how dull it would be if we did know the outcome. The excitement is being curious. That's what keeps me going.
>
> William Trevor, short story writer (1928–2016)

However, Elizabeth Bowen's essay "Notes on Writing a Novel" might have been written by a playwright. It contains such hints as:

> PLOT. ESSENTIAL. THE PRE-ESSENTIAL.
> Plot might seem to be a matter of choice. It is not... He [the novelist] is forced towards his plot... Plot is diction. Action of language, language of action.

Plot is story... Story involves action... Action by whom? The characters... Plot must further the novel towards its object... Plot must not cease to move forward.
CHARACTERS.
Are the characters, then, to be constructed to formula, i.e. the formula pre-decided by the plot?...
No... It would be impossible. One cannot make characters, only marionettes. The manipulated movement of the marionette is not the action necessary for plot... It is the indivisibility of the act from the actor, and the inevitability of that act on the part of that actor, that gives action verisimilitude... The term 'creation of character' (or characters) is misleading. Characters pre-exist. They are found.

In Orion, anthology of prose and verse (1946)

The advice from playwrights is to the same effect. Ernest Legouve's "A play is made by beginning at the end" may be compared with Harold Macmillan's advice to a new M.P. about to make his maiden speech: "Write the end of your speech first!"

Tragedy is thus a representation of an action that is worth serious attention, complete in itself and of some amplitude.

Aristotle (384–322 BC)

See to the connection from the beginning until the action runs down; but do not permit the untying of the knot until reaching the last scene; for the crowd, knowing what the end is, will turn its face to the door and its shoulder to what it has awaited three hours to face; for in what appears, nothing more is to be known...
In the first act set forth the case. In the second, weave together the events, in such wise that in the middle of the third act, one may hardly guess the outcome. Always trick expectancy...

Lope de Vega (1562–1635)

"I used to go through four processes before taking up the construction and final polishing of a play. The first step was the making of the outline with its division into three principal parts: the exposition, the arch of the plot, and the catastrophe. The second step consisted in the apportioning of the action among acts and scenes; the third in the dialoguing of the most interesting incidents, the fourth in the general dialoguing of the whole.

Carlo Goldoni (1707–1793)

When I have no idea, I gnaw my nails and invoke the aid of Providence.
When I have an idea, I still invoke the aid of Providence, but with less fervour, because I think I can get along without it.
It is quite human, but quite ungrateful.
I have then an idea, or I think I have one. I take a quire of white paper, linen paper—on any other kind I can imagine nothing—and I write on the first page:
PLAN
By 'plan' I mean the developed succession, scene by scene, of the whole piece, from the beginning to the end.
So long as one has not reached the end of his play he has neither the begin-

ning nor the middle. This part of the work is obviously the most laborious. It is the creation, the parturition.

As soon as my plan is complete, I go over it and ask concerning each scene its purpose, whether it prepares for or develops a character or a situation, and then whether it advances the action. A play is a thousand-legged creature which must keep on going. If it slows up, the public yawns; if it stops, the public hisses.

Eugene Labiche (1815–1888)

There is only one true method for the conception and parturition of a play—which is, to know quite exactly where you are going and to take the best road that leads there.

Victorien Sardou (1831–1898)

When my story is good, when my scenario is clear and complete, I might have my play written by my janitor! He would be sustained by the situations; and the play would succeed!

A plan is to a play what it is to a house: the first condition of its beauty and stability.

Eugene Scribe (1791–1861)

So the plot must be formulated before any dialogue is written, from which it follows that students of plays should begin by analysing their construction rather than 'character', poetic content, or whatever else.

As a consequence of the need for a preliminary plan, plays are much harder to write than novels:

The art of drama, in its higher forms, is not and can never be easy; nor are such rewards as fall to it out of proportion to the sheer mental stress it involves. No amount of talent, of genius, will, under modern conditions at any rate, enable the dramatist to dispense with a concentration of thought, a sustained intensity of mental effort, very different, if I may venture to say so, from the exertion demanded in turning out an ordinary novel...What attracted him to the drama was precisely the belief that he could turn out a good play with far less mental effort than it cost him to write a good novel; and here he was woefully in error...

Sir Arthur Wing Pinero (1855–1934): lecture on
"Robert Louis Stevenson's Attempts at Plays"

At my school, our Modern Languages teacher told us, "Every word in a well-written play must perform one of three functions: to illuminate a character, elucidate the situation, or advance the action. As I later learned, she was slightly misquoting Eugene Labiche with her substitution of 'word' for 'scene'; however, I consider the substitution an improvement.

I have a volume of parodies which contains a section of self-parodies, passages in which their authors are more like themselves than usual. One of them is the death of Little Nell in Charles Dickens' *The Old Curiosity Shop (1840–1)*. After a couple of pages, there is a gap with a note "Several pages are here omitted", and then Little Nell is allowed to die after another half-page. This was Dickens 'running on'; he was writing a serialised novel for a captive readership, and could run on (in this passage, tear-jerk) as long as he wished. The dramatist cannot run on like this, for he must say all he has to say in the two to three hours of stage time, and some of this must be expended in the initial process called exposition: informing the audience as to who the characters are, what they are, where they are, and how they stand in relation to one another. Now the essence of drama is continuous movement: states Labiche, "A play is a thousand-legged creature which must keep on going." Movement must begin with the opening sentences; hence this information must be conveyed or at least suggested in the opening scenes, and conveyed without interfering with the movement, for which reason the writing of an exposition which both conveys the information and begins the movement with no obvious pauses for narrative or description requires much care. And the movement must not be interrupted in later scenes when new characters enter.

Another important consideration in the writing of a play arises from the fact that plays are always being performed for the first time.

An absurdity? Not in the least; how many members of any audience go to see a play (or the same production of it) a second time? Very few; hence, for the vast majority of theatregoers, every performance of a play will be its first and probably its only performance. Looking back over such plays as I have seen in recent years and remember well enough, I find that in most cases they made their impact well enough to leave me feeling that I did not need to repeat the experience, and I suspect that most other theatregoers find that once is sufficient.

And since plays must move continuously, the writing must be sufficiently sharp and clear, so that the audience can catch and understand all indications of the movement as they come and go. The novel-reader can turn back and re-read previous passages if he wishes, but not the theatregoer.

An essential quality in any would-be playwright is the ability to write theatre. But what is meant by theatre? Not having come across any definition of it in my reading (except from Rattigan) I have attempted my own.

In its broadest definition, it is that which distinguishes a play from a conversation-piece. Stage dialogue normally contains little description or narrative, and sometimes little discussion of opinions or emotions.

Since movement is essential, it must help to keep the action moving.

It follows that it helps to keep audiences continuously watching and listening, without the need to remind themselves that they must do so if they are to miss nothing of the movement.

It may consist of things said or of things done on the stage; also of how or when they are said or done, and sometimes of things not said or done.

Since tension between characters holds the audience's attention, it may either create tension or release it, and since neither tension nor its absence should continue for too long, there should be alternation between the two.

Long, eloquent or loud speeches are not theatre (a mistake made by Marlowe in his *Tamburlaine* plays and by R.L.Stevenson in his attempts to write plays).

Elegant or witty exchanges in the fashion of the time, as in the Restoration comedies and some modern farces, are unlikely to contain any true theatre.

Since movement implies continuous development of the situation, and since changes in the situation may spring from the characters' inner motivations, it should reveal or suggest them.

Discussions and explanations in real life often contain pauses for thought which would slow up movement on the stage; hence conversational exchanges bringing new decisions or changes of attitude in the characters must be relatively rapid compared with real life. This may suggest that the characters have quicker-than-average minds: an important factor in the artificiality of the stage, and one in respect of which it is larger than life. Are slow-minded persons, even those who are apparently slow-minded because they are careful thinkers, likely to hold the audience's attention? Even in kitchen-sink drama, whose characters are at the bottom of the social heap, conversational exchanges must not be slow.

'Theatre' may be overt or it may imply. In the preface quoted earlier, Rattigan considers that implication is much the more effective:

> Sense of theatre does not lie in the explicit. An analysis of those moments in the great plays at which we have all caught our breaths would surely lead to the conclusion that they are nearly always those moments when the least is being said, and the most suggested: 'As kill a king?—Ay, lady, 'twas my word'; 'She'll come no more. Never, never, never, never, never'; 'Cover her face'.etc.
>
> Has not sense of theatre to do with the ability to thrill an audience by the mere power of suggestion, to move it by words unspoken, rather than spoken, to gain tears by a simple adverb repeated five times, or in terms of comedy to arouse laughter by a simple nod? Surely, in comedy as in tragedy, it is the implicit rather than the explicit that gives life to a scene, and, demanding the collaboration of an audience, holds it, contented, flattered, alert, and responsive.
>
> I am sure that this instinct for the use of dramatic implication is in fact a part of the mystique of playwriting, and, in my view, by far the most important part, for it is the very quality that can transform a mere sense of theatre into a sense of drama. I am equally sure that it is, in fact, an instinct, unhappily not to be learned, but only inherited, in that it implies in its possessor a kind of deformity of the creative mind, a controlled schizophrenia which will allow a dramatist to act as audience to his own play while in the very process of writing it. It is this eccentric faculty, and only this, that will enable him to master those vital problems of the whole craft of playwriting—what not to have your actors say, and how best to have them not say it.

These attempts at definition refer more to the general art of writing stage dialogue than to theatre, for a piece of theatre is an effective dramatic stroke which lends special significance to its moment and therefore becomes an important event in the plot, and there must not be too many such moments, or their impact may be weakened. They must be carefully led up to, and the audience's attention must be held as they approach, i.e. the instinct for creating moments of theatre is intertwined with the instinct for choosing or devising a plot which permits such moments—occasional moments—to be built into it.

Here is a famously loud example of theatre. A second quiet one from Shakespeare's *Julius Caesar*, depending for its effect on what is not said, is given in a later chapter.

In Bernard Shaw's *Pygmalion* (1912), Professor Higgins, whose speciality is phonetics and the science of speech, has taken a Cockney flower girl into his house, undertaking to his friend Pickering that he will transform her into a lady by simply teaching her to speak educated English. At one point in the play she has learned the phonetics, but no more:

Eliza [Darkly] My aunt died of influenza: so they said...but it's my belief they done the old woman in.

Mrs Higgins [Puzzled] Done her in?

Eliza Y-e-e-es, Lord love you! Why should she die of influenza? She come through diphtheria right enough the year before. I saw her with my own eyes. Fairly blue

with it, she was. They all thought she was dead, but my father he kept ladling gin down her throat till she came to so sudden that she bit the end off the spoon.
Mrs Hill. [Startled] Dear me!
Eliza [Piling up the indictment] What call would a woman with that strength in her have to die of influenza? What become of her new straw hat that should have come to me? Somebody pinched it; and what I say is, them as pinched it done her in... Well, I must go...So pleased to have met you. Goodbye.
Freddy [Opening the door for her] Are you walking across the park, Miss Doolittle? If so—
Eliza Walk? Not bloody likely. *[Sensation]* I am going in a taxi.

Sensation there would be, in an Edwardian drawing room!

Note:
The only type of education in Shakespeare's time was the classical education in grammar schools and universities. Latin was the "foundation of grammar school Latinity", the authors being Terence, Horace, Plautus, and Cicero. In his *Ars Poetica* Horace had laid down that tragedy should have no more and no fewer than five acts. This idea began to be developed during the Renaissance; in particular, it was eventually realised that there was more to the planning of an effective play than merely writing a string of scenes and dividing them into five sections.

From his advice quoted above, and virtually repeated by Goldoni, Shakespeare's Spanish contemporary Lope da Vega had realised this. His three-act structure was obviously more suited to short plays (since he wrote nearly five hundred plays, they must have been short!) than to the longer plays which were already being written before Shakespeare came to London. His three-act and Shakespeare's five-act plans differ only in that in the longer plan there are two upward steps from the introduction to the climax and two downward steps to the dénouement.

Shakespeare began his playwriting career in 1592; by the end of the decade his increasing intuitive understanding of human motives, his ability to write dialogue which is characteristic and revelatory of the speaker, and his instinctive grasp of effective plot-construction had all ripened to the point where he could write *Hamlet*, the greatest of his plays and perhaps the greatest of all plays.

The essence of this type of plot is continual change or novelty in successive scenes, but not smoothly continuous change, the ideal climax being sudden and unexpected. To what extent was Shakespeare consciously aware of its effectiveness? The question arises from the fact that while the First Folio *Hamlet* (1623) has some act and scene divisions, they die out during the second act, new scenes being indicated only by stage directions for entrances and exits, i.e. the manuscripts sent to his printers could not have contained them. He would have learned of the five-act construction in his grammar school, but it was more probably his innate playwriting genius and his increasing experience of audiences which eventually led him to the above construction.

The names of the five Steps (remembered from this writer's days in his own grammar school) are: Exposition, Development, Climax, Continuation, and Resolution. They are explained in greater detail in Chapter 6.

3
AUDIENCES

The best inspiration for a writer is a mortgage that looks like a telephone number... it may sometimes be appropriate to remember what Raymond Chandler's agent said when asked what was the best form of writing: 'Cheques!'

Lindsey Davis, novelist

Why are plays written?

To make money!

While this may sound mercenary, the playwright always hopes that his plays will make money. After all, if a play folds after a few performances there is heartbreak for all involved in the costly processes of casting, producing and rehearsing. Shakespeare wrote to make money; he was the Elizabethan equivalent of a Hollywood scriptwriter who kept his theatre company in business by turning out a new play approximately every six months for twenty years, and always intending to buy a house and estate in Stratford to which he could eventually retire as a landed gentleman. He bought New Place, the first of his Stratford properties as early as 1597. His scripts must have remained the property of his theatre company, for his will, which is long and detailed, contains no mention of any box of manuscripts brought to Stratford, although it would have been a valuable legacy. He, too, wrote for "cheques".

From whom do plays make money? Obviously—from their audiences—but which audiences?

Always, audiences of their own day and no others! Playwrights do not write plays for past audiences because those audiences are dead, nor for future audiences because their tastes and outlooks are still unknown. Who, alive during the 1950's, could have anticipated the effect on our outlooks and tastes of the Swinging Sixties? Both the general outlook and the current taste in all forms of fiction change unpredictably from generation to generation, so plays must always be written so as to appeal to contemporary audiences.

No apology is offered for these near-truisms, for they have important implications for both the student of old plays and the theatregoer watching the revival of an old play. The student must try to establish the extent to which the outlook or conventions of the audiences for whom the play was written, determined the characterisation or the action of the play. The theatregoer attending a revival must be aware that he is watching a piece of living history of the kind not usually found in history books and provided, of course, that the director has not tried to modernise the play or to translate it from some other country. Such attempts as I have seen have usually missed the flavour of the original and failed to establish a convincing one of their own.

It is true that since human nature changes little, the best plays contain universal elements—yet here a paradox arises: if we are to see any aspect of a personage as universal, he must be alive to us on the stage, and he will seem most alive if he is well individualised and at the same time a person of his own era. As an example, we may all see something of ourselves in Hamlet, but we must not forget that he is both a human being and an Elizabethan hero in an Elizabethan type of play.

Some paradoxes can be shown not to be true paradoxes, though this appears to be one such. It may even be the case that the contemporary aspects of a character's motivation or behaviour are as interesting as any universals; it may, in fact, be necessary to establish them first in order to place the universal elements in their contemporary context. This is the case with *Hamlet*.

All plays date. Some, being topical, date rapidly, others more slowly, but sooner or later it becomes obvious that they belong to their own age. Shaw's *Pygmalion*, Coward's *Brief Encounter*, or Dodie Smith's *Autumn Crocus* may be played as up-to-date plays, perhaps with a few minor changes, but eventually that they are twentieth century plays will become obvious, just as Sheridan's plays soon came to be seen as eighteenth-century plays. Writing in 1822 of *The School for Scandal* (1777), Lamb said, "It is impossible that it should now be acted", which implies that the play was already being seen as dated by 1800, although when it was first put on, the play drew larger houses for some years than any other. Shaw's *Caesar and Cleopatra* and *Saint Joan* are not on contemporary topics and will date more slowly than his other plays, but will eventually be seen as twentieth-century plays, if only because of their spoken idiom.

Since tastes in themes and forms of drama change, playwrights must not use outmoded models. What audience today would be satisfied by a nineteenth-century melodrama, with its villainous seducer from whom the brave and handsome hero rescues the virtuous heroine at the last minute?

> Those who are called 'men of letters' (that is, in plain words, unlettered men who have not studied anywhere but on the stage) have decreed that a man knows the theatre when he composes comedies according to the particular formula invented by M. Scribe. You might as well say that humanity began and ended with M. Scribe...
>
> Théodore de Banville (1823–1891)

The second important fact with respect to theatre audiences is that although they have been exposed to a torrent of entertainment on the stage, the cinema screen and the television, the vast majority of them remain naïve (theatre critics and the members of the acting profession are not, but represent only a tiny minority of the population); the third, that although the play may contain a moral or message, they do not go to the theatre to be lectured to or preached at but to be entertained:

> I write in accordance with that art which they devised who aspired to the applause of the crowd; for since the crowd pays for the comedies, it is fitting to talk foolishly to it to satisfy its taste.
>
> Lope de Vega (1609)

> Puisque nous faisons des poèmes pour être représentées, notre premier but doit étre de plaire à la cour et au peuple, et d'attirer un grand monde à leurs représentations. Il faut, s'il se peut, y ajouter des règles, afin de ne déplaire pas aux savants, et reçevoir un applaudissement universel; mais surtout gagnons la voix publique.
>
> Pierre Corneille (1634)

> We are spectators to a plot or intrigue...and take it all for truth. We substitute a real for a dramatic person, and judge him accordingly. We try him in our courts, from which there is no appeal to the dramatis personae, his peers...What is

there transacting, by no modification is made to affect us in any other manner than the same events or characters would do in our relationships of life. We carry our fireside concerns to the theatre with us. We do not go thither, like our ancestors, to escape from the pressure of reality, so much as to confirm our experience of it.

Lamb *On Artificial Comedy* (1822)

The language that we use in our plays is the language used by the spectators every day; the sentiments that we depict are theirs; the persons whom we set to acting are the spectators themselves in instantly recognised passions and familiar situations. No preparatory studies are necessary; no initiation in a studio or school is indispensable; eyes to see, ears to hear; that's all they need. The moment we depart, I will not say from the truth, but from what they think is truth, they stop listening. For in the theatre, as in life, of which the theatre is the reflection, there are two kinds of truth: first, the absolute truth, which always in the end prevails, and secondly, if not the false, at least the superficial truth, which consists of customs, manners, social conventions; the uncompromising truth which revolts, and the pliant truth which yields to human weakness...

It is only by making every kind of concession to the second that we can succeed in ending with the first. The spectators—like kings, nations, and women—do not like to be told the truth, all the truth. Let me add quickly that they have an excuse, which is that they do not know the truth; they have rarely been told it. They therefore wish to be flattered, pitied, consoled, taken away from their preoccupations and their worries, which are nearly all due to ignorance, but which they consider to be the greatest and most unmerited to be found anywhere, because their own.

This is not all; by a curious optical effect, the spectators always see themselves in the personages who are good, tender, generous, heroic whom we place on the boards; and in the personages who are vicious or ridiculous they never see anyone but their neighbours. How do you expect, then, that the truth we tell them can do them any good?

Alexandre Dumas, fils (1824–1895)

These comments imply a somewhat patronising, perhaps slightly contemptuous attitude to audiences, but since the vast majority of theatregoers are unfamiliar with the conditions and conventions of the stage, go to the theatre to be entertained, and are naïve, there is perhaps some justification for it. How often do we want to be told the truth, when it is often so unpleasant? For the majority, the theatre is an escape from some of the unpleasantnesses of our daily lives. At the same time, being compelled to accept an unpleasant truth is often beneficial! On the stage, of course, it is not happening to us.

In any case, we all need fantasies. As children, we may read fairy tales and animal stories, but the taste for fantasies remains with us until late in our lives. The authors of love-, crime-, action- and spy- stories have learned to cater very accurately not so much for the tastes of their readers as for their need, as have playwrights and script-writers. In a world which is becoming steadily more mechanical and monotonous, the need for escape into fantasy is, if anything, increasing.

What should plays be about?

Obviously, they may be about virtually any subject, provided that they entertain or interest their audience, which implies that their audience must easily understand what they are about and can easily apply Lamb's "moral test".

In sum: past playwrights knew that they must construct their plots before writing any dialogue. They wrote to a plan, with a specific dramatic purpose; they created recognisable characters for audiences who wanted a clearly recognisable resolution of the situation. In Elizabethan times, there was no intermediate genre called, somewhat vaguely, drama; plays were either comedies which ended happily—usually with the uniting of two lovers, or tragedies at the end of which most or all of the principals were dead on the stage. Obviously, such definite resolutions must have been preferred by audiences, and from my own observation, audiences have hardly changed in this respect. Plan can be equated to dramatic purpose; planless plays, such as those of Beckett and Pinter, have no easily recognisable dramatic purpose and merely puzzle audiences.

Note: Some time after the writing of this chapter, an article appeared in *The Times* (17.6.96), headed "Beckett Baffled by His Own Enigma". It is a commentary on both Beckett himself and the academic bien-pensants:

> Samuel Beckett confessed that he did not have "...the ghost of a notion" what his 1949 work *Waiting for Godot* was about, according to previously unpublished correspondence. In two newly disclosed letters written in the 1950's Beckett wrote: "I do not know who Godot is. I do not even know if he exists."
>
> The play, so different from the stage drawing-room murder mysteries of its era, generated a frenzy of textual analysis which continues to this day. Countless academics and critics have claimed that they alone comprehend the symbols, silences and arcane references—from Dublin pipe-shops to Parisian boulevards—which litter the play.
>
> Privately, it seems, Beckett thought they were wasting their time. Writing in 1952 to Michel Polac, a Paris radio producer, he said, "As for wanting to find in all this a broader and loftier meaning to take home after the performance...I cannot see the point in doing so."...
>
> In a letter to Mr. Desmond Smith, a Canadian theatrical producer, Beckett admitted that he intended to befuddle audiences.
>
> "Confusion of mind and of identity," he wrote, "is an indispensable element of the play and the effort to clear up the ensuing obscurities, which seems to have exercised most critics to the point of blinding them to the central simplicity, strikes me as quite nugatory." By this confession, Beckett is a spectacularly successful dramatist: though bien-pensants have claimed to understand it. *Waiting for Godot* has left generations of theatregoers bewildered.

Said the American critic Dorothy Parker after seeing *Waiting for Godot*, "There is less in this than meets the eye."

As for Pinter's plays, I have seen only two. While watching *The Homecoming*, such peculiar things were being said and done on the stage that I began to wonder whether I was watching a spoof of some kind, thereafter watched it as a spoof, found it most amusing and at the end applauded loudly. I was the only member of the audience who did! As for *No Man's Land*: at the end I still did not know who the principal characters were, what they were, where they were, or why they were where they were. I certainly left the theatre feeling thoughtful: "What on earth was it all about?"

Pinter can certainly write stage dialogue which grabs and holds the audience's attention (his critics call it 'menace'), but it can leave audiences unclear as to what the play was about. This is not enough for most theatregoers. Dorothy Parker's comment applies equally to Pinter.

Incidentally, the term 'spoof' was fairly close to the mark, for one critic interprets *The Homecoming* as a satiric commentary on some of the less savoury aspects of family life in the East End of London.

4
DIALOGUE

Dialogue provides means for the psychological materialisation of the characters. It should short-circuit description of mental traits. Every sentence in dialogue should be descriptive of the character who is speaking. Idiom, tempo, and shape of each spoken sentence should be calculated by the novelist towards this end...

There must be present in dialogue—i.e. in each sentence spoken by each character—either (a) calculation, or (b) involuntary self-revelation.

Elizabeth Bowen in *Orion a Miscellany* (1945)

The ear for dialogue may be defined as: first, in the author, the ability to write dialogue as described above i.e. which is exactly what the characters would say and exactly how they would say it, in whatever situation they are in, to the point where it can be heard in the mind's ear, and is therefore instantly revelatory of them; and secondly, in the reader, the ability to hear and appreciate such dialogue.

How many readers have the ear for such dialogue? Very few, it seems, otherwise the pulp novels, whose dialogue often consists merely of what the characters would say to keep the story moving, would be less popular than they are. And 'very few' applies also to the academic population; otherwise the critical appreciation of some of Shakespeare's plays would have been much more penetrating than it has been.

As for authors, it often appears in the greatest, though in varying degree, but in some minor authors to a quite marked degree. I quote a short passage from a 1930s novel in which the speech of a Devon girl is reproduced:

(Cluny Brown is a London girl who has been given a position as housemaid in a Devon country house. Her fellow-maid is Hilda, who has had a baby after a brief love-affair with a sailor.)

> Gary was her infant son, and a source of great pride to her; she wagered that when his Dad came back and saw'n him'd wed she for sure—though whether her'd wed he was another story; him'd have to mend his wild ways, said Hilda sternly, afore her went to church with'n.

Margery Sharp *Cluny Brown*

A triviality? Not in the least, when it occurs in a novel which moves placidly from its beginning to its end (but with a surprising ending), in which the events arise naturally from the characters being what they are and where they are, and whose characters always speak in character. Hilda's remarks might have been reported in Standard English, but the salt of the passage would have been quite lost. Not all the dialogue is such concentrated revelation as too much of it would have made a placid novel approach the farcical at times. (I regard it as a little unfortunate that radio, television, and today's wider educational opportunities are causing local forms of speech to die out and so to give both writers and readers fewer opportunities for such revelation.)

Many of the great writers have it; I quote a passage which alone tells us much of what we need to know about the speaker:

"Did you ever hear the like on't?" said Mr. Tulliver, as Maggie retired. "It's a pity but what she'd been the lad—she'd ha' been a match for the lawyers, she would. It's the wonderfull'st thing"—here he lowered his voice—"as I picked the mother because she wasn't o'er 'cute—being a good-looking woman too, an' come of a rare family for managing; but I picked from her sisters o'purpose, 'cause she was a bit weak, like; for I wasn't agoin' to be told the rights of things by my own fireside. But you see, when a man's got brains himself, there's no knowing where they'll run to; an' a pleasant sort of soft woman may go on breeding you stupid lads and 'cute wenches, till it's like as if the world was turned topsy-turvy. It's an uncommon puzzling thing."

Mr. Riley's gravity gave way, and he shook a little under the application of a pinch of snuff..."

George Eliot *The Mill on the Floss* (chap. 3)

The speech of educated minds is usually less revelatory than that of uneducated people, because they have the wider range of both vocabulary and ideas, their sentences are more grammatical, and their remarks are more considered and less spontaneous. The difference appears in Dickens' novels; compare, for example, the speech of Mark Tapley or Mrs. Gamp with that of Martin in *Martin Chuzzlewit*; as examples from a play, compare Eliza's speech with that of the others present in the passage previously quoted from *Pygmalion*, or her father Alfred Doolittle with Professor Higgins later in the play.

Shakespeare's ear for dialogue developed slowly, the dialogue in his early histories being merely determined by the speakers' political situations and not otherwise revelatory of them (although, as with Dickens, the speech of his commoners is more characteristic of the speaker than that of his noble personages). Consider the opening speeches in his first play, *King Henry VI Part I* where the speakers are the Dukes of Bedford and Gloster:

Bedford Hung be the heavens with black, yield day to night!
 Comets, importing change of time and state,
 Brandish your crystal tresses in the sky,
 And with them scourge the bad revolting stars
 That have consented unto Henry's death!
 Henry the Fifth, too famous to live long!
 England ne'er lost a king of so much worth.

Gloster England ne'er had a king until his time.
 Virtue he had, deserving to command:
 His brandisht sword did blind men with his beams;
 His arms spread wider than a dragon's wings;
 His sparkling eyes, replete with wrathful fire,
 More dazzled and drove back his enemies
 Than midday sun fierce bent against their faces.
 What should I say? his deeds exceed all speech:
 He ne'er lift up his hand, but conquered.

(I.i,1–16)

These speeches are typical of the whole play in that no speech contains any hint as to the speaker's individuality. There are no prose speeches; it is all in blank verse, whose rhythm makes it more suited to the expression of emotional states or the description of a tense situation than the more relaxed because less rhythmic prose, but less characteristic of the speaker.

Eventually Shakespeare realised or was told by a fellow-playwright, that his plays would become more vivid if he made his dialogue more characteristic of his speakers, and was careful to cultivate his 'ear':

> "Ben Jonson and he did gather the humours of men dayly wherever they came."
> John Aubrey *Brief Lives* (1693)

His 'ear' had begun to appear in *Romeo and Juliet* I,iii,12ff.:

Nurse I'll lay fourteen of my teeth—
   And yet to my teen be it spoken, I have but four—
   She's not fourteen. How long is it now
   To Lammas-tide?
Lady Cap. A fortnight and odd days.
Nurse Even or odd, of all days in the year,
   Come Lammas-eve at night shall she be fourteen.
   Susan and she—God rest all Christian souls!—
   Were of an age. Well, Susan is with God;
   She was too good for me:—but, as I said,
   On Lammas-eve at night shall she be fourteen;
   That shall she; marry, I remember it well.
   'Tis since the earthquake now eleven years;
   And she was weaned—I never shall forget it—
   Of all the days of the year, upon that day:
   For I had then laid wormwood to my dug,
   Sitting in the sun under the dovehouse wall;
   My lord and you were then at Mantua: -
[Juliet and Lady Capulet are not fond of her wordy reminiscences, and show it, but she cannot be stopped.]
   Nay, I do bear a brain;—but, as I said,
   When it did taste the wormwood on the nipple
   Of my dug, and felt it bitter, pretty fool,
   To see it tetchy and fall out with the dug!
[She guffaws]
   Shake, quoth the dovehouse: 'twas no need, I trow,
   To bid me trudge;
   And since that time it is eleven years;
   For then she could stand high-lone; nay, by th' rood,
   She could have run and waddled all about;
   For even the day before, she broke her brow;
   And then my husband—God be with his soul!
   A' was a merry man—took up the child:
   "Yea", quoth he, "dost thou fall upon thy face?
   Thou wilt fall backward when thou hast more wit;
   Wilt thou not, Jule?" and, by my holidame,

The pretty wretch left crying and said "Ay".
To see, now, how a jest should come about!
I warrant, an I should live a thousand years,
I never should forget it: "Wilt thou not, Jule?" quoth he;
And, pretty fool, it stinted and said "Ay."
[She guffaws again.]
    Lady Cap. Enough of this; I pray thee, hold thy peace.

This Nurse is a fat, warm, bosomy, loving animal of a woman, a born wet-nurse who has enjoyed every minute of her occupation, and has become very self-important because she well understands its value to the growing infant. She cares nothing for the embarrassment this recital causes to Juliet and her mother.

She has her own man Peter who must accompany her when she goes out into the streets and carry her parasol or fan ("My fan, Peter", II,iii); she has become self-important and fusses at times:

    Nurse An 'a speak anything against me, I'll take him down, an a' were lustier than he is, and twenty such Jacks; and if I cannot, I'll find those that shall. Scurvy knave! I am none of his flirt-gills; I am none of his skains-mates.—And thou *[she turns to Peter her man]* must stand by too, and suffer every knave to use me at his pleasure?
    Peter *[With apparent indignation]* I saw no man use you at his pleasure; if I had, my weapon would quickly have been out...
(Rom. II,iv,151–158)

Ben Jonson (1572–1637) created his humorous personages to satirise his fellow Londoners, but his characterisation is superficial and his dialogue contrived, because he is generally amusing his audiences by merely making his characters speak as people of their humours would. There is occasional depth, but it rarely has the intuitive penetration which causes so many of Shakespeare's characters to be alive to us today.

His ear for dialogue eventually became so highly attuned that he could characterise Iras, the girl of few words in *Antony and Cleopatra,* by giving her few words to say.

She and Charmian always appear together, and from their first appearance it is clear that Charmian is much the more lively and talkative of the two. In fact, in most of their subsequent appearances, Iras enters with Charmian but does not speak. Shakespeare waits until her last appearance before displaying her as she really is.

In Act V,ii,190ff. Octavian assures Cleopatra that he does not intend to lead her in triumph in Rome ("make prize with you"), but she does not believe him:

    Cleo. He words me, girls, he words me, that I should not
      Be noble to myself. But hark thee, Charmian.
                                               [Whispers Charmian.]

Cleopatra is sending Charmian to bring in the clown with the asps: the scheme she has not yet mentioned to either. Iras becomes impatient: "Why whisper so long—and why whisper at all—when we all know what we have to do?":

    Iras. Finish, good lady, the bright day is done,
      And we are for the dark.
[Dolabella enters and informs Cleopatra that Caesar intends to send her and her children ahead through Syria; then leaves:]
    Cleo.   Now, Iras, what think'st thou?

>   Thou, an Egyptian puppet, shall be shown
>   In Rome as well as I: mechanic slaves
>   With greasy aprons, rules, and hammers shall
>   Uplift us to the view. In their thick breaths,
>   Rank of gross diet, shall we be encloued,
>   And forc'd to drink their vapour.
> *Iras*   The gods forbid!
> *Cleo.* Nay, 'tis most certain, Iras: saucy lictors
>   Will catch at us like strumpets, and scald rhymers
>   Ballad us out o' tune. The quick comedians
>   Extemporally will stage us, and present
>   Our Alexandrian revels; Antony
>   Shall be brought drunken forth, and I shall see
>   Some squeaking Cleopatra boy my greatness
>   I'the posture of a whore.
> *Iras*   O the good gods!
> *Cleo.* Nay, that's certain.
> *Iras* I'll never see't; for I am sure my nails
>   Are stronger than mine eyes.
> *Cleo.*   Why, that's the way
>   To fool their preparation, and to conquer
>   Their most absurd intents.

[She orders her two women to bring her royal robes. The Guard enters with the Clown bearing his basket:]

> *Guard*   This is the man.
> *Cleo.* Avoid, and leave him.   *[Exit Guardsman.]*
>   Hast thou the pretty worm of Nilus there,
>   That kills and pains not?
> *Clown* Truly I have him: but I would not be the party that should desire you to touch him, for his biting is immortal: those that do die of it, do seldom or never recover.
> *Cleo.* Remember'st thou any that have died on't?
> *Clown* Very many, men and women too. I heard of one of them no longer than yesterday, a very honest woman, but something given to lie, as a woman should not do, but in the way of honesty, how she died in the biting of it, what pain she felt: truly, she makes a very good report o' the worm; but he that will believe all that they say, shall never be saved by half that they do; but this is most fallible, the worm's an odd worm.
> *Cleo.* Get thee hence, farewell.
> *Clown* I wish you all joy of the worm.
> *Cleo.* Farewell.
> *Clown* You must think this, look you, that the worm will do his kind.
> *Cleo. [In deadly fear that the Guard will return before she and her women have done what they intend.]*
>   Ay, ay, farewell.
> *Clown* Look you, the worm is not to be trusted, but in the keeping of wise people; for indeed, there is no goodness in the worm.
> *Cleo.* Take thou no care, it shall be heeded.

Clown Very good: give it nothing, I pray you, for it is not worth the feeding.
Cleo. Will it eat me?
Clown You must not think I am so simple but I know the devil himself will not eat a woman: I know that a woman is a dish for the gods, if the devil eat her not. But truly, these same whoreson devils do the gods great harm in their women; for in every ten that they make, the devils mar five.
[Her three Farewells having gone unheeded, she now takes him by the arm and leads him to the door.]
Cleo. Well, get thee gone, farewell.
Clown *[Still talking as he goes out]*
Yes, forsooth; I wish you joy o' the worm. *[Exit.]*
[Charmian and Iras re-enter with Cleopatra's robes and jewels and begin to dress her.]

Cleo. Give me my robe, put on my crown, I have
Immortal longings in me. Now no more
The juice of Egypt's grape shall moist this lip.
[Iras who, characteristically, has not spoken after "I am sure my nails are stronger than mine eyes," pauses while dressing her queen, and gets on with what she has to do by taking an asp and applying it to herself, the first to do so.]
Yare, yare, good Iras; quick; methinks I hear
Antony call. I see him rouse himself
To praise my noble act. I hear him mock
The luck of Caesar, which the gods give men
To excuse their after wrath. Husband, I come:
Now to that name, my courage prove my title!
I am fire and air; my other elements
I give to baser life. So, have you done?
Come, then, and take the last warmth of my lips.
Farewell, kind Charmian, Iras, long farewell.

[Kisses them. Iras falls and dies.]

[Cleopatra is only just in time to give her a farewell kiss.]

Such is Iras, characterised to the end by her brevity, and meeting this last and greatest moment of her life not so much by rising to it as by simply being herself: terse, blunt, and utterly loyal to her mistress.

Other silent, loyal personages in Shakespeare who are also characterised by their few words are Horatio in *Hamlet* and Virgilia in *Coriolanus*, whom her husband calls "my gracious silence". They, too, always speak in character.

Incidentally, who is this Clown, what is he, where does he come from? Who else in Shakespeare talks on as unstoppably as he and, in particular, says "Look you"?

Fluellen Captain Macmorris, I peseech you now, will you vouchsafe me, look you, a few disputations with you, as partly touching or concerning the disciplines of the war, the Roman wars, in the way of argument, look you, and friendly communication; partly to satisfy my opinion, and partly for the satisfaction, look you, of my mind, as touching the direction of the military discipline; that is the point.

(*Henry V:* III,ii,96–103)

It is hardly believable, but this Clown is also a Welshman!

How on earth did a Welshman get into Cleopatra's Egypt?

My wife once suggested that Mr. Shakespeare might have received some such letter as: "Dear Will, I am sending you my nephew. He is from the Valleys, and nothing will do for him but he must become an actor. Can you help?", but it is much more likely that Shakespeare, needing a character who would talk on and on at the wrong moment, decided that it must be a Welshman rather than an Englishman or Irishman (and certainly not a Scotsman), and the Clown would be played by the actor who played Fluellen.

How old is he? From his remarks on women, he might be a middle-aged husband who has become disillusioned, but I think that he is a young man and that he is talking in a kind of conventional style which he hopes will prolong the conversation, first with a little dead-pan humour, then by trying to stimulate a response from the ladies by causing them to bridle a little. He is probably something of a ladies' man who, on finding himself in the company of three high-born and handsome women, tries to impress them with his conversational wit, and continues for too long.

This episode is usually called 'comic relief', but while it does give the spectators some relief from the continuous tension of the previous scenes, its purpose is often more subtle than mere comedy.

Scientists and engineers use zero or reference levels for their measurements: the reference level for contours on maps is mean sea level; for temperature, the freezing point of water; for electrical potentials, the potential of earth.

At a climactic moment in the play, when the principal characters are in a highly-charged emotional state, Shakespeare suddenly introduces someone who has nothing in particular on his conscience and no especial problems in his life, and is therefore at the zero-level of emotion. His entry may offer the spectators relief by not requiring them to be absorbed in the high emotional state of the principals for too long, but his real function is to bring them down to earth for a moment by contrasting the relaxed minds of people living their everyday lives with those of the principals in their tragic situation. If he happens to have a sense of humour, he will let it appear as he normally does, for he knows of no reason why he should not, and the effect is to heighten the contrast between his own carefree condition and that of the principals. He may be comic, but not necessarily so; this Clown, the Porter in *Macbeth*, and the two Clowns in the Graveyard scene in *Hamlet*, are not especially comic; 'funny-man' types in such situations would be out of place. On his departure, the tragic atmosphere, momentarily interrupted, returns easily and naturally to its previous level, where an episode which induced loud laughter in the spectators would constitute an atmosphere-destroying break.

Iras's totally matter-of-fact "Finish, good lady, the bright day is done, / And we are for the dark" are among the greatest lines in drama, and the Clown's little dead-pan jokes—"Truly his biting is immortal; those that do die of it do seldom or never recover"—coming at such a moment from a cheerful, quite unsuspecting young countryman, are supreme examples of theatre.

When Bradley published his *Shakespearean Tragedy* in 1904, it was thought to be the last word in character-criticism, and new approaches had to be found, but who can say that character-criticism is dead, when minor characters can be so rewarding?

What is the function of imagery in Shakespeare's dialogue?

While Caroline Spurgeon appeared to have fully covered the subject in her *Shakespeare's Imagery*, in fact she had not, for she failed to distinguish between the functions of imagery in lyric poetry and in dramatic dialogue:

> That time of year thou mayst in me behold
> When yellow leaves, or none, or few, do hang
> Upon those boughs which shake against the cold,
> Bare ruin'd choirs, where late the sweet birds sang.
> In me thou see'st the twilight of such day
> As after sunset fadeth in the west;
> Which by and by black night doth take away,
> Death's second self, that seals up all in rest.
> In me thou see'st the glowing of such fire,
> That on the ashes of his youth doth lie,
> As the death-bed whereon it must expire,
> Consumed with that which it was nourished by.
> > This thou perceivest, which makes thy love more strong,
> > To love that well which thou must leave ere long.
>
> *(Sonnet 73)*

Many such images may be found in the *Sonnets* (although no other contains such a string of them), and their function is always a static one: to establish the mood of the poem. A play must never cease to move; otherwise the attention of the audience may wane. Said a contemporary playwright: "If you lose your audience's attention for a few minutes, you have lost your play." There is usually little time for moods; even brief stasis can be an interruption in drama, and Shakespeare used imagery, among other purposes, to keep the play moving. An image throws a flash of illumination on some stage in the speaker's thinking, after which he continues without pause to the next phase in it; or, if he has only made a brief remark, someone else may speak.

How many children of this age of battery chickens have ever seen a broody hen which has scratched a hollow in the soil under the hen-house, in what it hopes is a safe place, and is now sitting on its clutch of eggs, fiercely defending them against all-comers (except perhaps the familiar hand of its owner, when it comes to insert a china egg in exchange for one of its own)?

> King   There's something in his soul
> > O'er which his melancholy sits on brood:
> > And I do doubt the hatch and the disclose
> > Will be some danger;

Having thus illuminated his thought with an image which would be familiar to his audiences (London was not a large city at the time, and in any case Shakespeare would not have used an image which was not quickly recognisable to his spectators), Claudius does not extend or dwell on it, but immediately moves on to the next phase of his thinking:

> King   ...which for to prevent
> > I have in quick determination
> > Thus set it down: he shall with speed to England,
> > For the demand of our neglected tribute.
>
> *(Hamlet* III,i,166–169)

"Trammel" in Macbeth's soliloquy (I, vii,3) is usually taken as meaning simply *entangle*, but the whole image shows it to be a reference to the trammel-net. This consisted of three vertically-hung layers, the two outer layers being of wide mesh and the inner layer of small mesh, so that a fish encountering it would easily swim through the first outer layer, then push some of the inner layer through the mesh of the second outer layer and form a bag in which it would indeed become trammelled. The best place for such a net would be the shallows in an estuary at low water, the net being hung from stakes, so that fish might be caught both coming in and going out with the tide. On encountering the net, some fish might leap over it:

Macbeth   If th'assassination
   Could trammel up the consequence, and catch
   With his surcease success; that but this blow
   Might be the be-all and the end-all—here,
   But here, upon this bank and shoal of time,
   We'd jump the life to come.

Having illuminated his thinking with an image which again would be familiar to his hearers as the Thames was once a salmon river—as probably were all the rivers in Britain before the Industrial Revolution polluted them—Macbeth does not pause, but moves on to the next stage in his reflections, illustrating it with yet more images:

Macbeth   But in these cases
   We still have judgment here; that we but teach
   Bloody instructions, which, being taught, return
   To plague th'inventor: this even-handed Justice
   Commends th'ingredience of our poison'd chalice
   To our own lips.

(Macbeth I,vii,2–12)

Imagery is not usually a part of the 'ear for dialogue' in the writing of speeches. An image may reveal something of the speaker, but not in the same way as highly idiomatic speech, for, as mentioned earlier, the speech of educated people is much less revelatory of the speaker, less audible than that of uneducated people, and blank verse, in which most of the images occur, is more educated than prose because more formal. Its main functions are (a) to enrich the poetic content of the dialogue; (b) to illuminate, but only briefly, the trends of thought in discussions or soliloquies, and so help to keep the scene moving; c) to play its part in establishing the atmosphere of the play with references which would be immediately understood by the audience.

Although Miss Spurgeon maintains that his images reveal something of Shakespeare the man, they only tell us that he was an encyclopaedic observer of the world around him who noted, understood and remembered phenomena of every kind, then used them to enrich his poetry and, more importantly, to make his speakers' meanings instantly clear.

It should be clear from the previous remarks that although the formulation of a plan is the first and most fundamental step in the writing of a play, it is only a first step, for the playwright must then think himself into his characters' skins and, ideally, 'hear' them speaking as he writes their dialogue. The events of the plot will be influenced or even determined by what they say and how they say it; hence if they are to come alive on the stage, their dialogue must be characteristic of them while keeping the action moving. If their dialogue contains imagery, every image must be an event in the plot.

Since these processes are inextricably intertwined, the playwright in travail of a play will indeed be Pailleron's "unconscious being".

5
CHARACTER

> "The centre of the tragedy, therefore, may be said with equal truth to lie in action issuing from character, or in character issuing in action."
>
> A C Bradley *Shakespearean Tragedy* (Lecture 1)

This reads like a definition of character, which seems to have been accepted as a complete definition; but is not, for character covers a number of possibilities:

1) Moral character: the determination to do what is right in the circumstances, according to what the individual has been taught, or the determination to do the opposite, or the failure to realise that every individual must make a conscious decision to do one or the other.
2) Outlook, which depends on a variety of factors:
    a) Sex, there being a world of difference between the outlooks of the two sexes (not without reason has it been said, "Not another sex, another race!").
    b) Age: our responses to the problems of life change with experience, which only comes with time.
    c) Station in life: in Shakespeare's time, from king to clown.
    d) The effects of education or upbringing.
    e) Occupation, there being considerable differences between the outlooks of generals, lawyers, doctors, engineers, artisans, etc., and corresponding differences between their reactions to any situation.
3) Innate temperament: in Shakespeare's time, humour (choleric, phlegmatic, sanguine, melancholic).

Character may mean any of these, since they may all have their effect on what a personage does, why he does it, or how he does it. Unless it is merely a sad story, in tragedy the first factor *moral character* is usually the most important and the one which we find the most interesting because the most general (moral considerations being independent of individuality). However, other possible factors must not be neglected. Their importance varies from play to play, depending on the dramatist's intention.

In addition to these possibilities, it may be a mistake to examine what a character *is*, for he may change between the beginning and the end of the play, the change in him being often the point of the play:

> "Molière's personages are; Shakespeare's become."
>
> Coquelin *Molière and Shakespeare* (1915)

The large auction houses employ art experts who must be familiar with the works of artists from many nations and many eras. Could they truly be called art experts if they only knew the artists of their own nation and perhaps of one age? Does not this argument apply equally to the study of plays?

Further, all great artistic creations depend for their effect not only on their content but also on that mysterious architectonic or structural quality called composition—mysterious because it is not easy to explain why good structure should be so necessary. All paintings and photographs must be well composed if they are to have pictorial effect; musical pieces are simply called compositions. Anyone hoping to appreciate classical music must begin by learning such compositional elements as counterpoint and sonata form.

As has been shown, while plays must be fully planned before any dialogue is written, is there not a case for beginning the study of such artistic creations by examining their structure, and for comparing Shakespeare's ideas on play-construction with those of other playwrights?

I have yet to come across an English-speaking critic who has seen any point in comparing the plays of Shakespeare with those of the French seventeenth century dramatists. Corneille, Racine and Molière lived two generations after Shakespeare in another country, wrote in a different language, and developed quite different ideas on both the forms and the purposes of drama, but the contrasts make comparisons illuminating.

The French critics—mainly Chapelain—established a number of 'Rules' or principles for the composing of plays based on classical models. Chapelain even went so far as to say that the beauty of a play should be assessed in terms, not of its effect in entertaining audiences, but of its conformity with the 'Rules':

1) For the sake of verisimilitude, the unities must be observed:
   a) Unity of action: there should only be one plot, i.e. no sub-plot.
   b) Unity of time: the events of the plot should take place in one day.
   c) Unity of place: all the events should take place in one spot.
2) All the important events should take place off-stage and then be reported and discussed. Nothing in the way of display, violence, or anything sensational should be shown on the stage.
3) Drama should have a moral or educational purpose, this requirement being most likely to be met, not by the use of moral sentences or maxims, but by the creation of personages who are seen on the stage as alive.
4) The principal characters should be of noble birth and the language should be formal, noble.
5) Comedy must not be mixed with tragedy.

These restrictions had the effect of creating a type of psychological drama in which the action takes place solely in the minds of the personages: 'character-tragedy' in its purest and most intense form. Not everyone agreed with their rigorous application. Corneille, for example, found them unnecessarily restrictive; Dr Johnson later argued against them, but so convincing was their application by Corneille, Racine and Molière that they were almost universally accepted, to the point where they stifled originality in drama till well into the next century.

Plays are always written for audiences of their own day, and the differences between the Elizabethan and French ideas on play-writing reveal the differences between the audiences for whom they were written.

The French theatre audiences soon became the most civilised and sophisticated the world had seen. The contrast between them and the Elizabethan audiences is pointed as much by the contrasts in play construction i.e. the tightness of construction according to the Rules having the effect of intensifying the action, as by the playwrights' concepts of character. The French audiences became content with nothing more than talk from the stage, often in long speeches, and in a single plot with relatively few events of which none took place on the stage, all being reported or described. At the beginning of the century, their tastes had been the same as those of the Elizabethans for variety of character, action, display, passion, and violence, but they civilised themselves fairly rapidly in perhaps twenty years from 1620, whereas the English audiences did not, for the Jacobean plays continued the traditions of the Elizabethan stage.

Thus the principal difference between the Elizabethan and French playwrights and audiences was that the latter were more consciously aware of the meaning of character in drama and of its role in the plot.

Pierre Corneille (1606–1684) was educated at a Jesuit college, where he would become acquainted with the subtleties of disputation for which the Jesuits gained themselves a reputation for prevarication; and he later became a lawyer. Preferring to occupy official positions, he did not practise, though he would remain aware that there are two sides to most issues.

For his plots Corneille chose extreme situations, basing them on history, otherwise his audiences would have found them too improbable. His personages find themselves in situations such that either they are compelled to choose between two courses of action; or that each choice will have a far-reaching, even drastic effect on their lives; and that both choices can be justified, i.e. it is not a question of choosing 'right' or 'wrong' but of choosing between two 'rights': the most difficult of situations. They are therefore compelled to review their personal motives, and do so, usually at some length.

As an example of his method, I have chosen two speeches from his second great play, *Horace* (1640). As Rome and a neighbouring nation, Alba, are at war, they have decided to settle their differences not in battle but by each sending out three champions: the brothers Horace for Rome and the brothers Curiace for Alba. The result of their combat will then settle the war. Only one of each set of brothers appears in the play, Horace for Rome, and Curiace for Alba—but Horace is married to Curiace's sister Sabine, and Curiace is affianced to Horace's sister Camille i.e. the two families are closely linked by friendship and marriage.

Horace is a stiff-necked, bigoted patriot who will sacrifice even close family ties for what he sees as an opportunity for a unique claim to fame, whereas Curiace, no less brave but wider in vision, is horrified by the prospect before him (II,iii,9 ff.):

Horace Fate, which has opened a gateway to honour for us, challenges our resolution with a signal circumstance. It has exhausted all its force in creating a misfortune in order the better to measure itself against our quality, and since it sees in us souls superior to the common run, it offers us an opportunity of an uncommon kind.

To fight an enemy in defence of one's fellows, to expose oneself to the blows of an unknown adversary, is a common enough manifestation of simple courage; thousands have already displayed it, thousands more will do so. To die for one's country is so worthy a fate that many would hope to meet such an end.

But to be willing to sacrifice to the common good something one loves, to face in combat another self, to assail an enemy who might cite as his supporters the brother of one's wife and the affianced bridegroom of one's sister, to ignore these ties and to arm oneself for one's country against a 'blood' which one would otherwise defend with one's own life—firmness of soul of this order was only to be found in us. Few will envy the lustre of such renown, but few hearts have dared to aspire to it.

Curiace Our names, it is true, would never be forgotten; we should welcome such an illustrious opportunity; we shall exemplify a rare nobility of soul. But your resolution is something barbarous—few, even the greatest souls, would be vain of achieving immortality by such a means. No matter how highly such ephemeral fame may be prized, obscurity is to be preferred to renown so gained.

For myself, I venture to say, and you have seen for yourself that it is true, that I have not hesitated; neither our long friendship, nor love, nor family connection, have caused me to waver. And since, in choosing me, Alba has honoured me as much as Rome has honoured you, I may do as much for her as you for Rome.

At heart, I am equally resolute, but in the end I am a man; I realise that your honour requires you to shed my blood; mine, that I drive my sword into you, that I must kill a brother when affianced to his sister, that I must accept such a contrariety in order to serve my country. I haste to my duty without fear, but at heart I am appalled, I shudder with horror.

I pity myself, and envy those who have already died in this war but I do not recoil. This proud, melancholy honour stirs me, but does not shake my resolve; I welcome what it offers, but regret what it may lose for me.

And if Rome demands an even greater dedication, I thank the gods that I am not a Roman, that I may still retain in myself something of what is human.

Horace If you are not a Roman, be worthy of being one, and if you are my equal, let it appear more clearly...

...Alba has chosen you, I no longer know you.

Curiace I still know you, and it is that which slays me.

The last two lines lose their effect in translation: they are an alexandrine couplet in which Curiace's reply follows immediately on Horace's last line and rhymes with it. Voltaire found the couplet, which sums the argument, sublime:

Horace Albe vous a nommé, je ne vous connais plus.
Curiace Je vous connais encore, et c'est ce qui me tue.

Corneille's successor Racine scorned the complexities of his plots, and held that the emotion to be depicted in tragedy should be love. Coming to a crossroads in their lives, his principals succumb to temptation, where Corneille's do not. He has been described as "painter of the will"; his characters have even been described as supermen, but exaggeratedly, for there have always been people prepared to suppress personal desires or resist temptation and act in terms of principle or conscience. For him, love is based not on passion but on high esteem.

He took his plots from history, and since historians record the actions of persons in the public eye far oftener than those of lower rank, the principal personages of his tragedies are of eminent or noble birth. Suggested to us at school, a reason for this was that they are free of the economic motive, yet to the tragedian a much more valid reason is that, being persons of eminence, they could be expected to be better educated, more intelligent, more articulate, and more self-aware than the majority of the population.

Such self-awareness is an essential element in the first meaning of character, *moral* character. If my definition of a good play is accepted, one which causes us to leave the theatre feeling thoughtful (almost synonymous with pointing a moral), we may possibly do so if the principal dramatis personae act merely in terms of inarticulate impulse or instinct, but such crude motivation is unlikely to be as interesting as problems of personal principle which the characters are compelled, and are sufficiently self-aware, to discuss.

Some examples of character in Shakespeare

In *Julius Caesar*, a number of its personages refer to themselves from time to time in the third person, though not in any other play. In this reader's experience, the only people who referred to themselves in the third person were small children.

Children often grow up to become what the grown-ups around them—usually parents, but sometimes others—expect or encourage them to become; sometimes they accept a grown-up who is not their parent as example or role-model. What they eventually become is not necessarily what they would have become under other circumstances. It is possible that at an early age the child senses that the personality which the grown-ups have apparently assigned to him, and to which they have given a Christian name, is not quite the same as what he feels to be 'himself'. He does not as yet know who 'himself' is, but the grown-ups seem to know, so he may call this personality by this name as if it were distinct from 'himself'. He may even regard his body as something distinct from 'himself'.

The characters in *Julius Caesar* are no longer small children, and should have grown out of this habit, but some of them have grown into it. Do they have two selves? Are they aware that they have, or may have, two selves and can they assume either self at will? One of the selves is that of the public self, the traditional Roman republican whose ancestors drove out King Tarquin. To what extent do they (or can they) drop it when not in public?

Says the Doctor in Act II of Luigi Pirandello's (1922) *Henry IV*:

> It is necessary to understand the social psychology of the madman. It gives him a peculiar keenness of observation. He can, for instance, quite easily detect the true identity of anyone who appears before him in disguise...He can, in fact, clearly distinguish it as a disguise and yet at the same time believe in it. Just as children do. For them, dressing up is not only play, it is reality too. But the thing is extremely complicated. It is complicated in this sense...He must be perfectly conscious of being himself...In his own eyes he must inevitably be an Image, a picture in his own imagination.

The personages in *Julius Caesar* are not mad, but they are certainly dressing up at times, they act in terms of their republican/Roman images. They do not see themselves as having a problem of identity; it is not a case of not knowing who they really are, but of knowing too well who they are supposed to be!

[Caesar refers to himself in the third person immediately in his first appearance:]

    Caesar   I hear a tongue, shriller than all the music,
       Cry "Caesar!" Speak; Caesar is turned to hear.

                                                                                 (I,ii,16–17)

He has evidently intended to create a public image of Caesar, and speaks in terms of this image in the Capitol (III,I,39ff.):

Caesar   Be not fond
    To think that Caesar bears such rebel blood
    That will be thawed from the true quality
    With that which melteth fools...
    ...I am constant as the northern star
    Of whose true-fixed and resting quality
    There is no fellow in the firmament.

[However, his behaviour in private shows that the image sometimes takes over the whole

man. Decius Brutus has seen through Caesar:]
>Cassius It may be, these apparent prodigies,
>   The unaccustomed terror of this night,
>   And the persuasion of his augurers,
>   May hold him from the Capitol today.
>Decius Never fear that: if he be so resolved,
>   I can o'ersway him; for he loves to hear
>   That unicorn may be betrayed with trees,
>   And bears with glasses, elephants with holes,
>   Lions with toils, and men with flatterers;
>   But when I tell him he hates flatterers,
>   He says he does, being then most flattered.
>   Let me work,
>   For I can give his humour the true bent,
>   And I will bring him to the Capitol.
>
>   (II,I,197–210)

In II,ii,42ff. when Calpurnia kneels to beg him not to go to the Capitol, his reply is from Caesar:
>Caesar Caesar should be a beast without a heart
>   If he should stay at home today for fear.
>   No, Caesar shall not...

[Eventually, he decides to humour her, speaking as 'I':]
>Caesar Mark Antony shall say I am not well,
>   And, for thy humour, I will stay at home...
>   I will not come today,—tell them so, Decius.

[Decius, knowing his man, now does exactly what he has promised, by appealing to the Image in the third person lines 91ff.:]
>Decius I have, when you have heard what I can say:
>   And know it now,—the senate have concluded
>   To give, this day, a crown to mighty Caesar.
>   If you shall send them word you will not come,
>   Their minds may change. Besides, it were a mock
>   Apt to be rendered, for some one to say
>   "Break up the senate till another time,
>   When Caesar's wife shall meet with better dreams".
>   If Caesar hide himself, shall they not whisper,
>   "Lo, Caesar is afraid?"
>   Pardon me, Caesar, for my dear dear love
>   To your proceeding bids me tell you this;
>   And reason to my love is liable.

[And Caesar agrees to go to the Capitol.]

Brutus thinks of himself in the third person. In his reply to Cassius in I, ii, he says:
>Brutus Till then, my noble friend, think upon this:
>   Brutus had rather be a villager

>Than to repute himself a son of Rome
>Under these hard conditions...
>
> (I,ii,170–173)

In II,i, Brutus considers his position:
> *Brutus* It must be by his death; and for my part,
> I know no personal cause to spurn at him,
> But for the general. He would be crowned;
> How that might change his nature, there's the question;
> It is the bright day that brings forth the adder,
> And that craves wary walking...
> ... The abuse of greatness is, when it disjoins
> Remorse from power; and, to speak truth of Caesar,
> I have not known when his affections swayed
> More than his reason...
> ... And, since the quarrel
> Will bear no colour for the thing he is,
> Fashion it thus: that what he is augmented,
> Would run to these and these extremities:
> And therefore think him as the serpent's egg,
> Which, hatched, would, as his kind, grow mischievous,
> And kill him in the shell.
>
> (II,i,10–34)

While Brutus is the noblest of them all, in that his motives contain no trace of self-interest, he is also the most muddle-headed of them all. He is the traditional Republican Roman whose ancestor drove out Tarquin, and little else; his vision includes nothing outside his Image of himself.

Conscience plays no part in his reflections; he does not consider the morality of political assassination, or reflect that conspiracies are necessarily furtive affairs and that furtiveness is good for no one. Courts of justice condemn accused persons for what they have done, not for what they might do, but Brutus condemns Caesar because he might accept the crown and become a tyrant, even though he admits that Caesar's affections sway him less than his reason and that he will not necessarily "disjoin remorse from power."

Why does he not consider offering Caesar some advice on the wisdom or otherwise of accepting the crown? He is a friend of Caesar's, and admired by him; surely Caesar would listen to him?

He is so narrowly upright as to be no politician. Politicians must often trim their sails, or compromise, or accept the least of the available evils. Brutus makes no attempt to consider who or what might follow Caesar at the head of Rome, or what will happen to the body of the snake after its head has been chopped off.

In Aesop's *Fables* (c.620–560 BC), the frogs ask Jupiter to send them a king: he sends them a log. When they discover that it is a lifeless object and ask him to send them another king, he sends them a stork—which then eats them. Caesar, who intended to proscribe some of his opponents, was something of a King Stork, but the Triumvirs were certainly much more of one than he. They proscribed and executed more Romans than Caesar was intending, including wealthy but otherwise inoffensive Romans, merely to annex their wealth. But Brutus' reflections contain no thought of what form of government might fill the vacuum after Caesar's death, or of the risk of a civil war. He is the virtuous Republican Roman—and nothing more.

In the example of theatre previously referred to, Cassius turns against Caesar not because he is envious, but for another reason.

Caesar Who is it in the press that calls on me?
   I hear a tongue, shriller than all the music,
   Cry "Caesar!" Speak; Caesar is turned to hear.
Sooth. Beware the Ides of March.
Caesar What man is that?
Brutus A soothsayer bids you beware the Ides of March.
Caesar Set him before me; let me see his face.
Cassius Fellow, come from the throng; look upon Caesar.
Caesar What say'st thou to me now? Speak once again.
Sooth. Beware the Ides of March.
Caesar He is a dreamer; let us leave him; pass.

(I,ii,15–24)

Cassius, realising that Caesar intends to become the sole ruler of the Roman empire, has decided, being an old friend of Caesar's, to renew the acquaintance in the hope of becoming one of the great man's intimates. So when Caesar says, "Set him before me," he seizes the opportunity to remind Caesar of his existence by taking the Soothsayer by the arm and leading him before him. But Caesar looks at him, sees immediately what he is after, decides that he wants none of him, and ignores him, speaking only to the Soothsayer and ignoring Cassius without acknowledging his action.

Suppose that the episode had gone differently:

Cassius Fellow, come from the throng; look upon Caesar.
Caesar Why, it is my old friend Cassius! What a long time since we last met! We must meet again and talk over old times. Dine with me tonight—see that you do not fail me!

There might still have been a conspiracy against Caesar, which we can be sure that Cassius would not have joined! He is the Epicurean, the pleasure-lover, who has always given his emotions free rein, and he turns against Caesar, not from envy, but from acute pique at not being invited to join the great man's inner coterie. He is not a role-player; his motives stem entirely from his outlook.

According to Plutarch, Mark Antony had studied the art of eloquence in Greece during his youth, and when he delivers his "Friends, Romans, countrymen" speech to the Roman mob, he puts on an act very skilfully indeed—but he is not a role-player in the same sense as Caesar and Brutus.

Note:
Among Shakespeare's principal characters, the clearest example of an eminent personage who has never analysed his personal motives is Macbeth, but since this play requires a fuller treatment, one is given later in chapter 30.

6
ANALYSING HAMLET

Since the terminations of cart*wright*, wain*wright*, ship*wright* and play*wright* indicate that they construct something, the first step in studying a play must be an examination of its construction or plot:

1) <u>Act I</u>: Exposition, in which the audience is introduced to all or most of the principal characters and their situation; for example, their relationships within their own group and to their external circumstances. Every detail in the opening is intended to be remembered by the audience as having a bearing on the play's subsequent events. Ideally, the opening scene grabs the attention of the audience, and thereafter never allows it to relax.

<u>Act II</u>: Development; the action has begun to move.

<u>Act III</u>: Climax; an event occurs which introduces tension into the situation or increases any tension already present and implies a change in the situation, its effects being uncertain.

<u>Act IV</u>: Continuation or Descending Action; further developments, the consequences of the Climax.

<u>Act V</u>: Resolution or Dénouement; if the play is a comedy—happy ending; if a tragedy—catastrophe, which is always a definite result indicating the playwright's dramatic intention.

2) Remembering that the writing of a play must be more economical than that of a novel, and that every word must carry its due weight, examine each word and determine its significance with respect to situation, motive, or action. No word in a well-written play is superfluous; each word has been carefully placed where it is.

The words of the play are the principal medium through which the playwright conveys his meaning, and since the play must move continuously, their significance must be clear enough to be grasped quickly by the audience as they come and go: this is necessary because plays are almost always staged before they are published. Early audiences have not read them and are seeing them for the first time and, as pointed out earlier, even if a play has a long run the majority will see it only once— which is an important reason for explicitness in the writing. The Elizabethan audiences for whom the play was written were naïve, more so even than present-day audiences because many of them were illiterate. Because of the more limited range of theatrical experiences open to them, they could only go by the words they heard.

Therefore, regard yourself as not free to use your scholarly mind, your command of abstractions, your vivid imagination, or your warm sympathies. Before you use your supposed powers of interpretation, study the words of the play, taking them as meaning exactly what they say. Treat every word as a contribution to the playwright's intention, remembering that his intention must always be instantly clear to his audiences. You should then realise that Shakespeare's writing is extremely explicit as well as extremely detailed.

At the same time, look for any undertones; I find that they are more likely to occur in Shakespeare than in other playwrights of the time. Remember Rattigan from Chapter 2 and consider not only what has been said but also whether something significant may have been left unsaid.

If after this approach you are still uncertain as to your interpretation, admit that you are!

3) The rhythm of Shakespeare's blank verse and the richness of his language when, at times, even the sound of it can have a lulling effect on the mind. Therefore, read *under* the poetry; read it as if it were prose. Remember that no matter how rich the language may be, *under* it is simply someone talking. Will this approach reduce your appreciation of the poetry? It will not; why should it? It may even increase your admiration of the combination of richness and explicitness in Shakespeare's style.
4) If you have the ear for dialogue, an approximate synonym is 'sense of style". Use it. If not, cultivate it.
5) Remembering that plays are always written for contemporary audiences, and that their personages must be comprehensible to them, recreate the Elizabethan outlook (the world of the play) in whichever of its aspects affect situation, motivation, or action. It was very different from ours.

One approach is through the statutes of the time, since they prescribe the conduct of the population and therefore to some extent determine its outlook. Several proved to be relevant to *Hamlet*.

As an example: in his soliloquy at the priedieu, Claudius speaks of "buying out the law." Which law of those in force at the time?

As another:

King How dangerous is it that this man goes loose!
    Yet must not we put the strong law on him,
    He's loved of the distracted multitude.

(IV, iii 2–4)

Prosecutions are always brought under a particular law, i.e. no one can be prosecuted for being a bad lot but only under some specific law; e.g. for murder, fraud, arson, burglary, or whatever else. Hence, when Claudius talks of putting the "strong law" on Hamlet, he must again have in mind an offence under a specific law. Which law—the same or another?

Contemporary laws relevant to the play are topicalities which help contemporary audiences to grasp the dramatic situation quickly. Can you identify any other topicalities?
6) The dramatic situation consists of a group of personages of both sexes, different ages, different outlooks, and in a particular set of external circumstances. Be sure you understand it. Examine the details of these circumstances, partly because they give the play realism, partly because factors in the personages' external circumstances may influence their speech and actions. In most plays it is straightforward, but not in Hamlet.
7) Since character in the sense of outlook and behaviour changes considerably with age, estimate the ages of the play's principals as plausibly as you can.
8) Dramatic situation starts in one condition and ends in another. Be sure that you understand the precise nature of, and reasons for, the events of the plot which cause it to change. Consider also whether changes in the situation produce changes in the personages. The most effective approach is to write out a scene-by-scene synopsis of the play. The synopsis of Thomas Kyd's *The Spanish Tragedy*, given at the end of the book, proved to be an eye-opener. Determine the development of the main plot and of the sub-plot, if any, and establish their relationship. If there are episodes or passages which are apparently irrelevant, or at least not closely relevant to the main plot, the question then is: for what purpose did the playwright insert them? To stablish the time-scale of the plot.
9) A well-written play may be compared to an architect-designed building in which every detail contributing to its function or appearance has been carefully chosen and placed where

it should be. When you have got this far, consider whether the structure's details are all interrelated. Is it consistent or are there any apparent inconsistences or irrelevancies?

While you are about it, do not conclude (as have some critics of *Hamlet* and some modern directors of his plays) that some of the play's minor characters are unnecessary. Do not claim that you know more of the art of playwriting than Shakespeare!

10) Do not pay too much attention to sources. Your intention should be to determine Shakespeare's own dramatic purpose. First examine the play as a completely original creation.

Then, when considering the source or sources of the play, decide in which respects the playwright adhered to them or departed from them, for in some of Shakespeare's plays the departures are as important as the adherences as pointers to his dramatic intention. He created his own personages for his own dramatic purpose.

11) Only now do you consider character, being clear as to which of its meanings apply.

Read your characters sympathetically; do not assume any of them to be all-white or all-black. We are all a mixture of the good and the less-than-good; read your characters as fellow-humans who have their own viewpoint. A favourite saying of the trade unions is or was: "Every man is right in his own eyes." Shakespeare saw all his characters from their own standpoint.

If persons of different temperaments or outlooks might react in the same ways if placed in a particular situation (as in the Greek tragedies), *character* in the sense of individuality is unimportant. On the other hand, it will be important if the events of the plot are due to the personages doing what they do because they are what they are. In *Macbeth* and *King Lear*, for example, *character* is at the core of the play; how important is it in *Hamlet*?

The essence of some plays is that the principal personages change: in comedies—for the better; in tragedies—for the worse. Macbeth, for example, changes drastically. Of those critics that I have read, and I have read more of them than I can remember, the mistake of all these critics of Hamlet has been to discuss Hamlet as he 'is'.

Hamlet is a melodrama with an improbable plot, but is this important if the personages seem alive and real? In the opinion of some critics (Poe, Stoll), Hamlet should be seen as a stage character, not as a real person; do you agree?

You should now be clear as to the play's dramatic intention or purpose.

Perhaps I should have begun this account with 'Rid your mind of preconceptions'. I will admit to two when studying Hamlet: I had never accepted the conventional view that *Hamlet* is an excessively reflective or hesitant young man, because I did not believe that such a hero in an Elizabethan revenge tragedy would have had the slightest appeal to its audiences. Imagine a type of action-film still popular, the Hollywood Western, and give it a dreamy cowboy hero who dallies and reflects and hesitates before riding off in pursuit of his father's murderer! Would it really go down with fans waiting to see the bad man biting the dust? And what appeal would a dreamy Hamlet have had to audiences who numbered bearbaiting, bullbaiting, cockfighting, public executions and including the hanging, drawing, and quartering of convicted traitors, and watching lunatics among their entertainments?

Nor had I accepted that Claudius is merely a plain, evil-minded villain.

If, therefore, you have read critical accounts of any play you are studying, do not let them bias you; do your own thing; do not merely tack together hints from other minds.

After over twenty years in my retirement, and with many unwanted interruptions of developing and applying this method, do I claim to have correctly assessed the significance of every little detail in *Hamlet*?

I wish I could be sure that I have.

And this leads to a difficulty. There is so much detail in the play that I have constantly been faced with the problem of where to insert the explanation, and in the end decided to build up the picture gradually. So, if the reader comes upon some statement which he does not understand, or with which he finds himself disagreeing, he should read on to the end without pausing anywhere for very long. He may disagree with my overall view of the play, but at least he should eventually agree that it is coherent.

7

THE CONSTITUTIONAL BACKGROUND

CLAUDIUS the KING

"Hamlet, Prince of Denmark, his Tragedy. I know not whether this story be true or false; but I cannot find in the list given by Dr. Heylin, such a King of Denmark, as Claudius."

Gerald Langbaine *An Account of the English Dramatick Poets* (1691)

(i)

The 'historical' situation is a collection of elements assembled by Shakespeare to suit his own purpose, and not another sea-coast of Bohemia, city in Illyria or other imaginary location. He created what to his audiences would have been a familiar Renaissance court as a setting which would also be familiar to his audiences. Since he devoted well over a hundred lines to the constitutional and diplomatic situations, it is necessary to decide how he envisaged them and which of their elements are of prime importance in his dramatic scheme. While some are important and others less so, they prove to form a detailed and consistent picture. Though in some of his plays Shakespeare departed from his sources, in *Hamlet* he did not so much change history as adapt it for his dramatic purpose, as described in the following section.

(ii)

The capital is Elsinore, where it has never been. Since the opening scene displays sentries on an elevated platform (i,ii, 211 and I,iv,70), the Royal court is set in the Castle at Elsinore. Note that Kronborg Castle had been sumptuously rebuilt on the same site during the reign of Frederick II (1534–1588) as a replacement for the old Krogen Castle: originally it was a fortress, placed to enforce a toll on ships passing through the Sound in return for the maintenance of peace on the sea, and now was eminently suitable as a sumptuous royal residence as much as a strategic fortress.

A number of characters bear such names as Claudius, Bernardo, Francisco, Marcellus, Polonius, Laertes, Reynaldo, Fortinbras—none of which has a Scandinavian ring.

At the same time, the play contains a number of other topicalities, such as a fencing match with foils, the universities of Paris and Wittenberg (both cities resembling London in having theatres and highly professional theatre companies) and—a topicality of extreme importance in the play's dramatic scheme—an elective monarchy.

Ophelia refers to Hamlet's doublet (II,i,77), a garment which did not become fashionable till the Renaissance. Shakespeare's productions of the play were therefore in Elizabethan costume, i.e. in modern dress to his audiences. He did not so much change history as adapt it to his purpose.

What is Denmark at the time of the play, a kingdom or an empire? Young Fortinbras "claims the conveyance of a promised march / Over his kingdom" (IV,iv,3–4), and at the end states that he has "some rights of memory in this kingdom" (V,ii,371), but Claudius calls

Gertrude "our imperial jointress" (I,ii,9), and Hamlet calls him "a cutpurse of the Empire" (III,iv,100).

In Shakespeare's picture Denmark's empire comprises Denmark, Norway, a part of Southern Sweden, and England, i.e. a loose federation of independent kingdoms originally four in number but now three:
1) The kingdom of Denmark, comprising the Jutland peninsula, the Baltic islands to the east, and a part of Southern Sweden. This last-named territory was once ruled by an independent monarch, Old Fortinbras, who lost his life and his lands to the Elder Hamlet some time before the beginning of the play.
2) The kingdom of Norway
3) The newly conquered kingdom of England (IV,iii,59–60). As an example of Shakespeare's adaptation of history, Canute was king of England, Norway and Denmark from 995 to 1035.

The principal monarch of this federation is the King of Denmark whose position is not hereditary; he is elected. A number of questions at once arise.

Whence did Shakespeare derive his inspiration for the idea of an elective monarchy? There is no need to cite, as does Dover Wilson, the election of James VI of Scotland to succeed Elizabeth since she herself named him on her deathbed as her successor. Elective monarchies had been the rule rather than the exception throughout Central Europe for some centuries before Shakespeare's time. Kings were elected in the medieval German Empire, Poland, Denmark, the medieval Austrian Empire, and the later Holy Roman Empire. Denmark's monarchy was elective from 1250 until 1660.

Who are the possible candidates in a Danish election? From Hamlet's giving his 'dying voice' to Young Fortinbras (V,ii,338) they appear to be any of the members of the three Royal families.

Shakespeare appears to have envisaged the following small family tree:

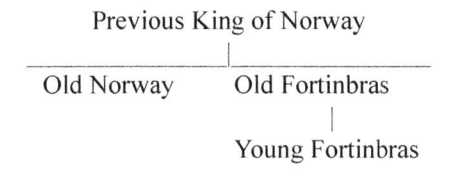

```
              Previous King of Norway
         _____|_____
        Old Norway         Old Fortinbras
                                 |
                           Young Fortinbras
```

Since Young Fortinbras is the son of Old Fortinbras (now dead) and also the nephew of Old Norway (I,ii,28–30), Old Fortinbras and Old Norway were either brothers or brothers-in-law.

Old Fortinbras is referred to as "th'ambitious Norway" (I,i,61) and "Fortinbras of Norway" (I,i,82). In those days kings and nobles were often referred to by the names of their kingdoms or estates. Gertrude, for example, says to Hamlet, "Let thine eye look like a friend on Denmark" (I,ii,69), and Claudius says, "Do it, England" (IV,iii,64); in both cases the speaker is referring to the king, not the country. Hence "Norway" may be taken as being Old Fortinbras' family name, i.e. he had been another member of the Norwegian Royal family, and had in fact been Old Norway's brother.

They ruled separate territories, for when Old Fortinbras lost his life and his lands to the Elder Hamlet, Old Norway did not lose his.

Young Fortinbras is not Old Norway's heir. He has nothing to inherit; his father had lost "all those lands / Which he stood seized of" (I,i,88–89) to the Elder Hamlet, and he is hoping to recover them by raising a mercenary army ("a list of lawless resolutes") in his uncle's kingdom. He is a landless prince who may nevertheless be elected to the Danish throne by virtue of his birth. Whether Old Norway has an heir who could also be a candidate we do not know.

It is easy to infer that the two brothers had quarrelled and divided the Norwegian kingdom between them. Even the reason for the quarrel can be inferred: differences of temperament causing differences of opinion over policy. The four kingdoms constituted a powerful federation which Old Norway did not want to see disrupted. When Old Fortinbras, the more aggressive of the two, attempted to enlarge his domain at the expense of Denmark, Old Norway must have disapproved, for he displays no sympathy towards his nephew's hope of recovering the lost lands.

While Old Norway retained the western part of the Scandinavian Peninsula which is now Norway, Old Fortinbras took that part of Southern Sweden which lies opposite the Danish island of Zealand. His attempt at enlarging his kingdom at the expense of the Elder Hamlet failed, and Old Norway evidently feels that his lands should remain part of Denmark, for he makes his nephew swear to abandon any thought of recovering them by force of arms (II,ii,71).

Who are the members of the Electoral College? Apparently they are the members of the three Royal families (from Hamlet's giving his 'dying voice' to Young Fortinbras—V,ii,338), together with, perhaps, some other nobles.

If a non-Danish king is elected, as Young Fortinbras may be, what territories will he rule and from which country? The play does not say.

Much more important is the question: what were Gertrude's rights as the widow of the Elder Hamlet? Claudius refers to her as "our imperial jointress", but the phrase is never elucidated. Was she really an "imperial jointress", i.e. had she had the right to continue to rule by herself but, as will be seen, totally uninterested in state affairs. Had she married Claudius in order to ensure that Denmark had a strong head of state and thereby protect her own position? Or, as the widow of an elected monarch, did she have no rights, and did she marry Claudius in order to retain her position as queen and perhaps improve her son's prospects? Or did she marry him for some other reason?

Not one of these questions can be answered from explicit statements in the play, and the fact that they are not answered leads to two questions of even more fundamental importance: why did Shakespeare choose a kingdom having an elective monarchy, and why did he then leave its constitutional details unelucidated?

Although he is not, most critics regard Claudius as a usurper. Since he has come to his throne through a murder, he is in that sense a usurper, but no one knows that he is a murderer; to everyone around him, including Hamlet, he is a legitimately elected monarch who has not deprived Hamlet of an inheritance. While evidence supporting this statement is mainly negative evidence, it is very strong.

At the beginning of the play the Ghost demands revenge on him as a murderer and an "adulterate beast" and not as a usurper. The duties it lays on Hamlet are to avenge his father's death and to put an end to the "luxury" in the Royal bed of Denmark, which Hamlet is expected to carry out with no thought of personal gain in the form of a recovered inheritance; otherwise the Ghost would certainly urge him to recover it. Hamlet would express the resentment of a dispossessed heir if he felt it, and speak of his rights if he had any.

Even in his soliloquies, he never does. These are the passages which have given rise to the great 'character-problem' of the play. Before he sees the Ghost, he only hopes to return to Wittenberg (I,ii,112–113).

As will be seen, at no time does either he or Horatio, who are both law students, refer to his hereditary rights. His friends Rosencrantz and Guildenstern challenge him to admit that his madness is due to frustrated ambition (II,ii,249), and after the Gonzago-play Rosencrantz reminds him that "You have the voice of the king himself for your succession in Denmark" (III,ii,318). When he calls Claudius "A cutpurse of the empire, and the rule / That from a shelf the precious diadem stole" (III,iv,100–102), he is referring to the murder of his father. At no time does he suggest that the diadem was stolen from him; he merely describes Claudius as having "popp'd in between th'election and my hopes" (V,II,65). No other dispossessed heir would have announced his return from such a sea voyage as Hamlet's by polite letters to the King and Queen, and apparently submissively then returned to the Castle, but Hamlet does. And he never calls Claudius a usurper. In fact, the terms usurp, usurper and usurpation are never spoken by anyone in the play.

As confirmation that the monarchy is elective, the Danes who burst into the Castle shout, "Choose we; Laertes shall be king!" (IV,v,102), and at the end of the play Hamlet gives his "dying voice" to Young Fortinbras, the landless son of a former provincial ruler who, only a few months before, has been threatening to make war on Denmark.

Hamlet's apparent lunacy is described by the King as "turbulent and dangerous" and later by Laertes as "crimeful and capital" (III,i,4 and IV,vii,7). At the end of the Nunnery scene Polonius suggests that he should be confined as a lunatic as an alternative to sending him to England (III,i,185). If Claudius feared Hamlet as a rival, would he not welcome his nephew's lunacy as a good reason to have him put away? Yet as will be seen later from the time-scale of the play, he postpones taking a decision with respect to his mad nephew for two-and-a half months, until just before the Gonzago-play. His decision is not to confine him but to send him to England.

When he hears of Polonius' death (IV,i,12ff.) he says:

King   O heavy deed!
   It had been so with us, had we been there.
   His liberty is full of threats to all,
   To you yourself, to us, to everyone.
   Alas, how shall this bloody deed be answered?
   It will be laid to us, whose providence
   Should have kept short, restrained, and out of haunt
   This mad young man. But so much was our love,
   We would not understand what was most fit...

He had refrained from having Hamlet confined because he was hoping to see his nephew cured. Evidently he did not fear Hamlet as the rightful heir to the throne.

It is clear that Shakespeare chose the elective monarchy to eliminate any fear of a dispossessed heir in Claudius, and any resentment of a usurper in Hamlet, as factors in the relationship between the two men; equally clear that he left all the other constitutional and dynastic details unexplained because they were irrelevant to his central theme.

What is this theme?

The play depicts a King, a Queen, and a Prince.[3] If political and dynastic factors are irrelevant, the theme must be their family relationship. And that is what it turns out to be: a study of an intimate relationship from which political factors were excluded because they would have been complicating or contaminating elements.

(ii)

At the beginning of the play Shakespeare devotes some little time to displaying Claudius as a capable and authoritative ruler. This, in fact, is the dramatic purpose of the ambassador scene s (I,ii and II,ii), which can only be understood in the context of a federation or empire.

From the beginning of his reign, Claudius is faced with two problems which he very astutely solves simultaneously.

In I,i we learn from Marcellus that Denmark is being hastily rearmed, and since he mentions the rearming with some surprise, we infer that it was initiated by Claudius and not by the Elder Hamlet. Horatio explains one reason for it: Young Fortinbras, smarting under the simultaneous loss of his father and his lands, has "sharked up a list of lawless resolutes" (I,i,98) with the intention of recovering the lost territories by force of arms (I,i,80–107). A second reason is the presence of the Poles.

At an earlier time, the Poles had held about half the southern coast of the Baltic lands. While on a previous occasion they had attempted to enlarge their dominion at the expense of Denmark, they had been defeated by the Elder Hamlet when he "smote the sledded Polack on the ice" (I,i,63). They have reappeared, and have occupied some small enclave of land in Danish territory: "To give five ducats, five, I would not farm it" (IV,iv,20).

Where the Elder Hamlet would have challenged Young Fortinbras to single combat again, Claudius does better. He has seen some fighting (in IV,vii,83 he mentions to Laertes that he has "served against the French"), but, being a "moor" to the Elder Hamlet's "mountain" (III,iv,67–68), is too short in stature to be able to match his heroic brother's prowess on the battlefield. Probably Young Fortinbras has chosen this moment to recover his father's lands because he will not have to face such a warrior as the Elder Hamlet.

Having learned that Young Fortinbras is raising his mercenaries in his uncle's kingdom (II,ii), and "out of his subject" (I,ii,33), he sends Cornelius and Voltimand to inform Old Norway of the fact, at the same time forbidding them to do more than convey the information (I,ii,36–38). We infer that they may not discuss the possibility of joint action against Young Fortinbras, or even convey Claudius' displeasure at the news. Young Fortinbras is Old Norway's nephew, and Claudius, as head of the empire, naturally does not want dissension within it and will not be a party to it. Being sure that Old Norway does not want it either, he is relying on him to discourage his nephew from attacking Denmark.

The mission is entirely successful. On their return (II,ii,60–80) the ambassadors tell him that Old Norway has risen from his sickbed, summoned his nephew to his presence, rebuked him, and made him swear never to attack Denmark again; further, since his nephew's energies must be given some scope, that he has promised him three thousand ducats annually if he will lead his mercenaries against the "Polack".

Elsinore is situated in the northeast corner of Zealand, the most easterly of the Danish islands. Southern Sweden, recently become a part of the kingdom of Denmark, lies only a few miles away across the Sound. Young Fortinbras will need permission to march through

---

3   King, Queen, Prince and Royal Family are capitalised in order to suggest how the play's contemporary audiences would see such high-born personages.

it from Norway, make the short sea passage, and come past Elsinore to meet the Poles. The spot where they have landed is not stated, but it is probably on the southern shore of Zealand, their intention being to threaten Elsinore.

Well, the Poles are going to be driven out, and at no cost to Claudius, for Young Fortinbras will do the fighting while Old Norway provides the finance! "It likes us well," says the King (II,ii,80), who evidently prefers diplomacy to the cruelties of war.

Of Claudius the King it is not necessary to say more, except that his shrewdness as a diplomat is matched by the dignity and authority he displays in all his appearances. He is respected by everyone as a conscientious and capable king.

Claudius the man will be examined later; until then it is only necessary to remember two points: firstly, he is a constitutionally elected monarch, who is perfectly secure on his throne (his interest in probing the cause of Hamlet's madness is therefore not motivated by suspicion of a possible rival or fear of a dispossessed heir); and secondly, Gertrude's rights are never mentioned, nor—an important point—is her descent. In those days, royal marriages were always arranged for political or dynastic reasons; surely, as queen, she would come of another royal, or at least a high-ranking noble, family? If no information is given on either of these points, they must be of no consequence in the dramatic situation.

This deduction is confirmed by Hamlet's first soliloquy (I,ii,129–159) in which he registers his shock at his mother's sudden and complete transfer of her affections to her new husband. If her early second marriage had been justified by some reason of state, Hamlet would be aware of it and would mention it. It would be a mitigating factor to him but nowhere in the play does he do so.

We therefore infer that when Claudius wooed and won Gertrude, he did not do so for political or dynastic reasons.

(iii)

Shakespeare's exposition proceeds: the Ghost and Young Fortinbras, the Hamlet family, and the Polonius family in that order, i.e. he introduces the Ghost and Young Fortinbras simultaneously, then devotes eighty-one lines to Young Fortinbras: Marcellus' "Why is Denmark re-arming?", Horatio's reply, Claudius' despatch of his ambassadors, and Voltimand's report on his return in II,ii. Since he is introduced so early and at such length, Shakespeare intended him to be remembered by the audience; the threat of invasion was to be felt as hovering over Elsinore as much as the spirit, seen or unseen, of the Ghost. To the play's early audiences, the threat would have had a high degree of topicality, for none of them could have forgotten the protracted dispute with Spain which for many years had caused much "impress of shipwrights" and "daily cast of brazen cannon", that reached momentary peaks in the Armadas of 1588 and 1597, and did not end till after the writing of *Hamlet*.

Young Fortinbras is regarded by some as peripheral to the play's main theme, but the references to him have this and other purposes. They display Claudius as a capable and authoritative king: how, for example, does he know that Old Norway not only is "bedrid" but also "scarcely hears" of his nephew's activities in his own kingdom, those activities being hostile to Denmark? He evidently has an efficient intelligence service, and knows how to use it.

We are reminded of him again in Act II when Voltimand makes his report, and again when he is briefly displayed in person in IV,iv, partly to remind us of his existence and partly to revive Hamlet's drive to revenge as indicated by "How all occasions do inform against me"; and, as will be seen, to revive it at the wrong moment; and then at the end of the play, to tell us that life will go on much as it did before, as it always does even after such a tragedy. As might be expected of a character that is described so early and at such length, he proves to have an important effect on the play's events.

Note:
The eldest son, Eric IV Plovpenning, who had long since been crowned as consort, was soon in dispute with the church and with his brothers about royal prerogatives. His brother, Duke Abel of Schleswig, proclaimed himself king, and had Eric murdered (1250). He was then elected king...Thus was the hereditary principle broken...

    The estates met in Copenhagen in Sept. 1660...The church representatives...constrained the rigsraad and the nobles to confer on Frederick III and his family the hereditary succession to the throne.

(*Encyc. Brit.* (1957 edn.), article Denmark: History, pp 205, 20)

8

HOW OLD IS HAMLET?

"It being my luck to meet with a sort of drolling workmen upon all occasions."
Samuel Pepys *Diary,* 28 September (1660)

I once saw the Gravediggers' scene (Act V,i) played by two young men who entered dressed in unbelievably ragged garments and with arms and faces smeared with red and black make-up, then bawled all their conversation in a heavily rustic Devon-cum-Dorset accent. Evidently the director had failed to realise that a First Clown who can so easily defeat Hamlet in their little battle of conceits cannot be as rustic as all that; further, that the two Clowns are of quite different ages, although this should be evident from the authoritative, often condescending, manner in which the First Clown speaks to the Second. The First Clown is in fact the Sexton and the Second Clown his Assistant or Apprentice. Strictly, *apprentice* only referred (and refers) to a boy learning a skilled trade, which the Sexton's occupation was not, though I shall call him that because he talks so much like the apprentices I have known.

It has long been traditional to play jokes of one kind or another on apprentices, the theory being that their wits are thereby sharpened, and the scene suggests that this tradition is very old, for the Sexton jests as the expense of his Apprentice from beginning to end of their conversation. The version of the Hales v. Petit case of 1554 which the Sexton quotes to his Apprentice is deliberately and not accidentally garbled in order to puzzle him. He repeatedly passes off on the boy what must have been the ancient chestnuts of his occupation: "wilfully seeks her own salvation", "drowned herself in her own defence", "se offendendo". The Sexton is in fact something of a wit (if he can hand out the gibberish of his opening remarks with such a perfectly straight face, he must be!) and the scene is as amusing and subtle as any in Shakespeare. Certainly it is the best of the so-called comic relief scenes and at the same time somewhat less comic than its surface suggests.

Enter the Sexton and his Apprentice, returning to the churchyard to finish a job they have started, and chatting as they go. The Apprentice seems to be indignant about something, while the Sexton seems surprised.

Sexton Is she to be buried in Christian burial that wilfully seeks her own salvation?

App. I tell thee she is; and therefore make her grave straight. The crowner hath sat on her and finds it Christian burial.

Sexton How can that be, unless she drowned herself in her own defence?

App. Why, 'tis found so.

Sexton It must be "se offendendo", it cannot be else. *[Weightily]* For here lies the point: if I drown myself wittingly, it argues an act. And an act hath three branches: it is, to act, to do, to perform. Argal, she drowned herself wittingly.

App. Nay, but hear you, goodman delver—

Sexton Give me leave. Here lies the water; good. Here stands the man; good. If the man go to this water and drown himself, it is, will he, nill he, he goes—mark you that; but if the water come to him, he drowns not himself. Argal, he that is not guilty of his own death shortens not his own life.

App. *[Annoyed by this mumbo-jumbo]* But is this law?

Sexton Ay, marry is't; crowner's quest law.

App. [*Angrily*] Will you ha' the truth on't? If this had not been a gentlewoman, she should ha' been buried out o' Christian burial.

Sexton [*Solemnly, "One law for the rich and another for the poor" not being news to him.*] Why, there thou say'st. And the more pity that great folk should have countenance in this world to drown or hang themselves, more than their even Christian. [*He climbs down into the grave.*] Come, my spade...

[*The boy hands it to him, and thereafter passes spade, shovel or mattock as required, also tidying the earth as it is thrown out. As he works, the Sexton continues with the education of his Apprentice:*]

...There is no ancient gentlemen but gardeners, ditchers, and gravemakers. They hold up Adam's profession.

App. Was he a gentleman?

Sexton A' was the first that ever bore arms.

App. Why, he had none.

Sexton What, art a heathen? How dost thou understand the Scripture? The Scripture says, Adam digged. Could he dig without arms? I'll put another question to thee: if thou answerest not to the purpose, confess thyself—

[*..."and be hanged", he is going to say, but the Apprentice interrupts with the Elizabethan equivalent of "Come on!"*]

App. Go to!

Sexton What is he that builds stronger than either the mason, the shipwright, or the carpenter?

App. [*Thinks; then, triumphantly*] The gallows-maker, for that frame outlives a thousand tenants.

Sexton I like thy wit well, in good faith; the gallows does well—but how does it well? It does well to those that do ill; now thou dost ill to say the gallows is built stronger than the church; argal, the gallows may do well to thee. To't again, come.

App. Who builds stronger than a mason, a shipwright, or a carpenter?

Sexton Ay, tell me that, and unyoke.

App. [*Delighted to hear that he is to be given a break*] Marry, now I can tell!

Sexton To't.

App. [*Doesn't think for long; he wants to get away.*] Mass, I cannot tell.

[*Enter Hamlet and Horatio, at a distance. Hamlet is wearing a sea-cloak which envelops his other garments.*]

Sexton Cudgel thy brains no more about it, for your dull ass will not mend his pace with beating; and when thou art asked this question next, say "a gravemaker". The houses that he makes last till Doomsday. Go, get thee to Yaughan; fetch me a stoup of liquor.

[*Exit Apprentice, the Sexton having given him the price of their 'elevenses'.*]

Sexton [*Now working alone; sings what little he remembers of a popular song to keep himself company.*]

   In youth, when I did love, did love,
    Methought it was very sweet
   To contract (O) the time for (Ah) my behove,
    O, methought there was nothing meet.

Hamlet Hath this fellow no feeling of his business, that he sings at gravemaking?

Horatio Custom hath made it in him a property of easiness.
Hamlet 'Tis e'en so; the hand of little employment hath the daintier sense.
Sexton [*Sings*] But age with his stealing steps
                Hath clawed me in his clutch,
                And hath shipped me intil the land
                As if I had never been such.

                                                              [*Throws up a skull.*]

Hamlet That skull had a tongue in it, and could sing once. How the knave jowls it to the ground, as if it were Cain's jawbone, that did the first murder! It might be the pate of a politician, which this ass now o'erreaches; one that would circumvent God, might it not?

[*At "this ass" the Sexton momentarily pauses, raises an eyebrow, then continues working. Hamlet, occupied with the skull, does not notice him.*]

Horatio It might, my lord.
Hamlet Or of a courtier, which could say, "Good morrow, sweet lord! How dost thou, good lord?" [*Holding the skull at arm's length, he bows courteously to it.*] This might be my lord Such-a-one, that praised my lord Such-a-one's horse, when he meant to beg it, might it not?
Horatio [*Smiling*] Ay, my lord.
Hamlet Why, e'en so, and now my Lady Worm's, chapless, and knocked about the mazzard with a sexton's spade. Here's fine revolution, and we had the trick to see it. Did these bones cost no more the breeding, but to play at loggats with 'em? Mine ache to think on't.
Sexton [*Sings*]

                A pickaxe and a spade, a spade,
                For and a shrouding sheet;
                O, a pit of clay for to be made
                For such a guest is meet.

                                                       [*Throws up another skull.*]

Hamlet There's another; why may not that be the skull of a lawyer? Where be his quiddits now, his quillets, his cases, his tenures, and his tricks? Why does he suffer this rude knave now to knock him about the sconce with a dirty shovel, and will not tell him of his action of battery? Hum! ...

[*Hamlet coughs to hide the urge to laugh at his own pun. He continues in the manner of a lawyer in court, holding out the skull in one hand and grasping a lapel with the other.*]

    ...This fellow might be in's time a great buyer of land, with his statutes, his recognisances, his fines, his double vouchers, his recoveries: is this the fine of his fines and the recovery of his recoveries: to have his fine pate full of fine dirt? Will his vouchers vouch him no more of his purchases, and double ones too, than the length and breadth of a pair of indentures? The very conveyances of his lands will hardly lie in this box, and must the inheritor himself have no more, ha?
Horatio [*Much amused*] Not a jot more, my lord.
Hamlet [*Still orating*] Is not a parchment made of sheepskins?
Horatio Ay, my good lord, and calfskin too.

Hamlet They are sheep and calves which seek out assurance in that.—I will speak to this fellow. *[To the Sexton]* Whose grave's this, sirrah?

Hamlet's intention is to continue in the same vein at the expense of the Sexton, but he has chosen the wrong man for his purpose. The Sexton is quite unperturbed; despite that the young man may have a pretty wit, he is a much older hand at the game. His manner contains no hint of sarcasm or resentment; on the contrary, it suggests only the courtesy due to a stranger.

Sexton [As if surprised] Mine, sir.
[He continues working as before, singing to himself as he works; he will let Hamlet make the running.]
          O a pit of clay for to be made
          For such a guest is meet.
Hamlet I think it be thine indeed, for thou liest in't.
Sexton You lie out on't, sir, and therefore it is not yours; for my part, I do not lie in't, and yet it is mine.
Hamlet Thou dost lie in't, to be in't, and say it is thine; 'tis for the dead, not for the quick; therefore thou liest.
Sexton 'Tis a quick lie, sir; 'twill away again, from me to you.
[Unable to think of any further possibilities from "quick" and "lie", Hamlet is forced to repeat his question.]
Hamlet What man dost thou dig it for?
Sexton For no man, sir.
Hamlet What woman, then?
Sexton For none, neither.
Hamlet [His patience beginning to crack] Who is to be buried in't?
Sexton One that was a woman, sir; but, rest her soul, she's dead.
Hamlet [Defeated; letting his exasperation show] How absolute the nave is! We must speak by the card, or equivocation will undo us. By the Lord, Horatio, this three years I have taken note of it: the age is grown so picked, that the toe of the peasant comes so near the heel of the courtier, he galls his kibe……
[He tries yet another approach.]
    …How long hast thou been a gravemaker?
Sexton [After a little thought] Of all the days i'th'year, I came to't that day that our last King Hamlet o'ercame Fortinbras.
Hamlet [Pretending not to know] How long is that since?
Sexton Cannot you tell that? Every fool can tell that: it was that very day that young Hamlet was born—he that is mad and sent into England.
Hamlet Ay, marry, why was he sent into England?
Sexton Why, because a' was mad. A' shall recover his wits there; or, if a' do not, 'tis no great matter there.
Hamlet Why?
Sexton 'Twill not be seen in him there; there the men are as mad as he!
Hamlet [Persisting; he wants to hear all the gossip about himself.]
    How came he mad?
Sexton Very strangely, they say.
Hamlet How strangely?

Sexton Faith, e'en with losing his wits.
Hamlet [*Still persisting*] Upon what ground?
S*exton* Why, here in Denmark!

He smiles at last, and looks briefly up at Hamlet. And now something dawns on Hamlet; his face clears; the two men understand one another. The Sexton's next remark is a tacit invitation to Hamlet to continue the conversation in a normal vein. This Hamlet does in the way of Royal personages conversing with their subjects by asking him questions about his occupation. The Sexton is pleased to answer them.

Sexton I have been sexton here, man and boy, thirty years.
Hamlet How long will a man lie i'th'earth ere he rot?
Sexton I'faith, if a' be not rotten before a' die—as we have many pocky corses now-a-days that will scarce hold the laying in—a' will last you some eight year or nine year. A tanner will last you nine year.
Hamlet ...he more than another?
Sexton Why, sir, his hide is so tanned with his trade that a' will keep out water for a great while; and your water is a sore decayer of your whoreson dead body. Here's a skull now hath lain you i'th'earth three and twenty years.
Hamlet Whose was it?
Sexton A whoreson mad fellow's it was: whose do you think it was?
Hamlet Nay, I know not.
Sexton A pestilence on him for a mad rogue!—a' poured a flagon of Rhenish on my head once. This skull, sir, was Yorick's skull, the King's jester.
Hamlet This?
Sexton E'en that.
Hamlet Let me see. [*Takes the skull*] Alas, poor Yorick!—I knew him, Horatio: A fellow of infinite jest, of most excellent fancy; he hath borne me on his back a thousand times; and now, how abhorred in my imagination it is!—my gorge rises at it. Here hung those lips that I have kissed I know not how oft. Where be your gibes now? Your gambols? Your songs? Your flashes of merriment, that were wont to set the table on a roar? Not one now to mock your own grinning? Quite chopfallen? Now get you to my lady's chamber, and tell her, let her paint an inch thick, to this favour she must come; make her laugh at that.—Prithee, Horatio, tell me one thing.
Horatio What's that, my lord?
Hamlet Dost thou think Alexander lookt o'this fashion i'the earth?
Horatio E'en so.
Hamlet And smelt so? Pah! [*He puts down the skull.*]
Horatio E'en so, my lord.

No stage direction of *[Exit First Clown]* appears in the text, but while Hamlet is reminiscing of Yorick and orating of Alexander, the Sexton will have made everything tidy and doubtless removing the skulls from sight! He will have collected his tools, and either left the stage or moved off to one side, his departure being acknowledged by Hamlet.

This scene is beautiful theatre, its subtleties lying more in its undertones than in what is actually said.

When the Sexton hears himself called "this ass" and listens to Hamlet exercising his wit at the expense of the skull, he knows what he may expect. As a commoner replying to a lord, he must remain respectful; moreover, he can act the simpleton who is not so simple as all that. Hamlet is never given a straight answer to any of his questions except "How long hast thou been a gravemaker?"

He is given an apparently straightforward answer for a reason. The graveyard will not be far from the Castle; the Sexton has worked in it many years and has long known all the Castle's residents by sight; so, when Hamlet appears, the Sexton at once recognises him. However, knowing that his Prince is under a cloud and even seems to be in disguise (the tradition that Hamlet enters in sailors' clothes is probably correct), he is careful to address him only as "Sir", never as "Your Royal Highness" or even "My Lord".

On "Why, here in Denmark…", Hamlet suddenly understands that the Sexton had deliberately introduced his name into the conversation, i.e. "That very day young Hamlet was born", in order to convey to him: first, that he had recognised Hamlet from the start; second, that he would not betray his young Prince's incognito even though Hamlet was reputed to be "mad and sent into England".

The tone of the conversation then changes completely. Up to this point, their conversation has been a verbal fencing match, but they now understand one another and stop fencing. Hamlet continues in a much more courteous vein by chatting with the Sexton about his trade. The atmosphere becomes so relaxed that the Sexton drops into workman's language, letting fall a couple of "whoresons", which were the Elizabethan equivalent of the word which Kipling later called "The Adjective". He can also reveal that he had known Yorick. Quite possibly the episode with the flagon of Rhenish had taken place in the Castle's cellars.

There is an even deeper undertone in their first exchange. Sextons know all the gossip because they inevitably must: who is going to be buried, where the family grave is and who is going to be buried in it, who may soon need to be buried, who is going to be married, whose baby will soon be christened. The Danes who break into the Castle know of Polonius' death, which the Sexton will also know. Probably he buried Polonius. The interest of the public in Royal families being what it is, it may even have got out that Hamlet was in love with Ophelia, and if it has, the Sexton will have heard the rumour.

Sextons must obviously possess some tact. Can the Sexton possibly reply to Hamlet's "Whose grave's this, sirrah?" with "This grave, sir, is for the Lady Ophelia, the girl they say you were in love with and whose father you killed"?

Hamlet's age has long remained a mystery, yet from evidence in this scene it is possible to deduce the ages of all its characters with reasonable accuracy.
The Sexton makes three statements:
1) "Here's a skull now hath lain you i'th'earth three and twenty years." He is speaking of Yorick's skull. Since Hamlet remembers Yorick, he must be older than twenty-three.
2) "I came to't... that very day that young Hamlet was born". He does not say how long ago this was because Hamlet obviously knows his own age.
3) "I have been sexton here, man and boy, thirty years."

He now gives the time interval, because if he did not, Hamlet would not know how long it was. Apparently the two time intervals are not the same.

Although it does not refer to Hamlet, his last statement has been taken to mean that Hamlet is thirty years old. But thirty is not a plausible figure; it does not fit Hamlet's behaviour throughout the play; he is not quite mature enough for thirty. How old would a young man be who (a) at the beginning of the play has been a student at Wittenberg, perhaps for five years if he went there when he was twenty; (b) on his return is so smitten by the sight of Ophelia that he starts sending her posies of the kind read out by Polonius in II,ii? Other aspects of his behaviour suggest that he has not reached the relative maturity of thirty.

Today, if you ask a skilled man how long he has been working in his trade, he will count the years from the day when he "came out of his time". This is a phrase I have often heard; it means: "When I completed my apprenticeship and became a fully-fledged skilled man." A boy had and perhaps still has to serve as apprentice from fourteen to twenty-one if he wishes to hold a skilled man's union card and draw a skilled man's wage. Semi-skilled and unskilled occupations do not require an apprenticeship.

The Statute of Artificers and Apprentices 1563 ('artificer' being the Elizabethan equivalent of 'skilled man') was passed to codify and regulate the terms of training and employment in a large number of trades, since an apprenticeship then lasted from fourteen to twenty-four years of age. It names about sixty trades, including the all-important trade of husbandry, but the occupation of sexton is not among them. From this it may be inferred that sextons were not considered to be artificers or husbandmen and that their assistants could not properly be called apprentices, although, as previously stated, I have called the Second Clown 'Apprentice' because he talks like an apprentice. For this reason the duration of their assistantship was not specified, and in any case it could not have been: there would only be one sexton per parish, and while an assistant might become full sexton after a few years if his sexton died or moved to another parish, he might be compelled to wait many years if he did not.

"Thirty years" includes the Sexton's time, boy as well as man. It is reasonable to interpret him as meaning that he had worked some years as a boy before he "came to't", i.e. became full sexton, Hamlet being born on the day when he "came to't".

If he was "boy" for four or five years, Hamlet is now twenty-five or twenty-six, and when Yorick died, was between two and three, or three and four years old. Many people remember the events of their childhood as far back as that (and one's knowledge of lively small boys suggests that Hamlet would only have kissed Yorick on the lips when he was very small). Hamlet is older than twenty-three, but not by much.

This estimate is apparently, though not necessarily, inconsistent with other indications in the play. He is referred to as Young Hamlet, probably to distinguish him from his father the Elder Hamlet. Laertes speaks of his love for Ophelia as "a violet in the primy youth of nature", which suggests that Hamlet is barely out of his adolescence. How long have he and Horatio been at Wittenberg (or Laertes at Paris), when children in Shakespeare's time matured earlier than today, and boys went up to a university at fourteen or fifteen? Would Hamlet have been sent to a university as distant from Elsinore as Wittenberg, and in a foreign country where a foreign language is spoken, when he was as young as that? At the beginning of the play Laertes is returning to Paris, probably after a year or two there; I put him at about twenty.

The Sexton may have started his own assistantship at fifteen or sixteen, in which case he is now forty-five or forty-six. His boy is perhaps seventeen or eighteen, for he already knows enough about his occupation to argue over the circumstances of Ophelia's burial, i.e. he is old enough to have learned that there is one law for the rich and another for the poor, and still young enough to feel indignant about it!

Horatio is about as old as Hamlet. And incidentally, what were these two studying at Wittenberg? Here the reader is reminded of a rule mentioned in a previous chapter: in a well-written play every word must either tell the audience something of the dramatic situation; or tell the audience something of the speaker; or advance the action. Now Hamlet's "quillets and quibbles" speech (V,I,90) tell us nothing new about the situation, nor does it advance the action; hence it must have been inserted to tell us something of Hamlet.

So both he and Horatio, whom Hamlet addresses as "fellow-student" (I,ii,176), were studying law! How else could Hamlet be so familiar with so many legal terms, and Horatio appreciate them? And are not Hamlet's somewhat unfeeling speeches to the skulls the kind of performance a student might put on for the amusement of a fellow student?

For a moment Hamlet and Horatio are students again—until Ophelia's cortege appears.

In this scene Shakespeare achieves much more than comic relief. He reminds us via the Sexton of the zero-level of ordinary life for a moment. He introduces an undercurrent of profound pathetic irony, for while Hamlet is amusing himself at the expense of the skulls, he does not know that the girl he had loved more than "forty thousand brothers" is dead; and, most important of all from the standpoint of his hero's character, Shakespeare displays Hamlet for the only time in the play as his true self, as the cheerful and high-spirited young man he would have remained if his father had not been murdered. Since the conversation up to the entry of Ophelia's funeral cortege does not advance the action in any way, this must be its purpose.

The song the Sexton sings is worthy of remark because it makes its little contribution to the zero-emotion level of the scene (his occupation has certainly developed a "property of easiness" in him!) and because it exemplifies Shakespeare's observation, not merely of the deeper aspects of human behaviour, but also of the superficial ones. The Sexton sings to keep himself company because people have always done so. Wordsworth's solitary Highland lass sang to herself; a child playing by itself will sing to itself, as does Ophelia in her mad scenes. (The decorator who came to repaper two rooms while this book was being written also sang to himself!)

The Sexton's singing to himself neither advances the action nor tells us anything of importance about the Sexton, yet the scene would be a little poorer without it. It is an apparently casual, yet completely natural, touch which brings life to the scene, although it is something which people do habitually, even unconsciously. It is one of the reasons why Shakespeare was praised for his naturalness, although his critics appear to have admired the naturalness of his characters rather than of the writing which makes them natural. I have not come across any critic who noticed such apparent trivialities.

In his *Shakespeare's Workmanship* (1918), Sir Arthur Quiller-Couch records an interesting reminiscence:

> Again, when an actor takes a benefit, what is the piece most commonly chosen?—Hamlet. Why? "Because," it may be answered, "Hamlet himself is notoriously a 'star' part, with plenty of soliloquies, with plenty of what I believe is called 'fat' in the profession; and invested by tradition with a certain aura of greatness and crowned as with a halo". I applaud the answer; it is an excellent one as far as it goes. But why does the gentleman who enacts the First Gravedigger also choose Hamlet for his "benefit" night? Now that question happens to be more searching than for a moment it may seem. I was once assisting at a dress rehearsal of Hamlet, when the First Gravedigger came off the stage in a passion. "Why", he wished to know, "should I be treated like a dog by that conceited fool?"—meaning our Hamlet, of course. "His temper gets viler at every rehearsal. Surely, after airing his

vanity through four acts, he might be quiet while I have my little say!" "Bless you, sir," answered an old dresser, "it's always like that. In these forty years I've helped dress (I dare say) that number of Hamlets: and Hamlet and the First Gravedigger always fall out. It's a regular thing. I've known 'em come to blows." The old man allowed that he could not account for it at all.

In forty years of *Hamlet* productions the actors playing Hamlet must have met too few "drolling workmen"!

An anonymous eighteenth century critic whose mind was dominated by the French 'Rules' who seems also to have been a somewhat disillusioned man, was even wider of the mark:

> Though this scene is full of Humour, and had not been amiss in low Comedy, it has not the least business here...To mix Comedy with Tragedy is breaking through the sacred Laws of Nature, nor can it be defended...This incoherent Absurdity will for ever remain an indelible Blot on the Character of our Poet; and warn us no more to expect Perfection in the Work of a Mortal, than Sincerity in the Breast of a Female.

Unsigned essay *Miscellaneous Observations on the Tragedy of Hamlet* (1752)

The apparently late indication that Hamlet and Horatio are law students is actually the confirmation of an early hint. In I,i Horatio's law student's scepticism with respect to the Ghost immediately appears: "Horatio says 'tis but our fantasy". He delivers his account of the Old Fortinbras episode in the detailed, pedantically accurate style of a lawyer opening his case in court, quoting such phrases as "stood seized of", "a moiety competent" and "well ratified by law and heraldry", which are terms not normally used by a non-lawyer. Most of his later remarks are in character as law-student, as both are obviously familiar with quiddits, quillets, fines, vouchers, double vouchers, and actions of battery. This facet of Hamlet was adopted and adapted by Shakespeare from Thomas Kyd's *The Spanish Tragedy*, in which the central character Hieronimo is a Marshal of Spain and a judge or magistrate. Because of its relevance to Hamlet in other respects, this play will be referred to later.

Everyone who undergoes a highly specialized professional training acquires the outlook peculiar to that profession, and since no word in a play is in it by accident, it must be assumed that Hamlet's law studies have created the lawyer's outlook in him, and that that outlook will play a part in his thoughts and actions. It is not entirely essential to make him a law student if he is to think and act as he does, but Shakespeare made him so in order to reinforce or confirm his motivation at various moments in the play, of which the two most important are his first encounter with the Ghost, and his slaying of Polonius.

He has been described ad nauseam as a young man excessively given to reflection or speculation. Yet do not law students very soon learn that they must rely on facts: i.e. hard evidence, rather than on speculation or reflection? Solicitors and barristers must establish the facts supporting their client's plea; the duty of juries is to find the facts, i.e. to decide how much of the evidence may be taken as factually reliable and how much should not. Hamlet's "prophetic soul" impels him to accept the Ghost's story as true, while at the same time he is immediately aware as law-student that he will have the greatest difficulty in proving the murder against Claudius. It is a necessary condition of the plot that it should not be openly provable, and that public justice should never be obtainable. We, the audience, learn that Claudius is a murderer from his soliloquy at the priedieu, while no one in the play hears it.

How, then, is Hamlet to proceed? How can he possibly obtain satisfactory proof that Claudius murdered his father, or even (forensic medicine being then far in the future) that his father had died by murder? And although, as his first soliloquy reveals, he dislikes his uncle acutely, must he not, as law-student, adopt the detached, unprejudiced approach necessary in the investigation of a crime—should he not be equally prepared to find his uncle guilty or innocent?

In fact, he is; he more than once confirms that he is, but emotion later overcomes his detachment at the wrong moment.

Note: The Hales v. Petit case of 1554:
1. Hales committed suicide by walking into a river at Canterbury.
2. The counsel for the defence argued that "the act of self-destruction consists of three parts. The first is the imagination, which is a reflection or meditation of the man's mind whether or no it be convenient to destroy himself and in what way it may be done; the second is the resolution, which is the determination of the mind to destroy itself and to do it in this or that particular way; the third is the perfection, which is the execution of what the mind has resolved to do. And this perfection consists of two parts, viz. the beginning and the end. The beginning is the doing of the act which causes the death, and the end is the death, which is only a sequel of the act.
3. There was much discussion as to whether Hales was the 'agent' or the 'patient', in other words whether he went to the water or the water came to him; and the verdict was:

"Sir James Hale was dead. And how came he by his death? It may be answered by drowning. And who drowned him? Sir James Hales. And when did he drown him? In his lifetime. So that Sir James Hales being alive caused Sir James Hales to die, the act of the living was the death of the dead man. And for this offence it is reasonable to punish the living man, who committed the offence, and not the dead man."

Quoted by Dover Wilson in his *Notes to The New Shakespeare Edition* of the play.

9

THE GHOST

But there is nothing which delights and terrifies our English Theatre so much as a Ghost, especially when he appears in a bloody Shirt. A Spectre has very often saved a Play, though he has done nothing but stalked across the Stage, or rose through a Cleft of it, and sunk again without speaking one Word. There may be a proper Season for these several Terrours, and when they only come in as Aids and Assistances to the Poet they are not only to be excused but to be applauded...The appearance of the Ghost in "Hamlet" is a Masterpiece in its kind, and wrought up with all the Circumstances that can create either Attention or Horrour. The Mind of the Reader is wonderfully prepared for his Reception by the Discourses that precede it. His dumb Behaviour at his first Entrance strikes the Imagination very strongly; but every Time he enters he is still more terrifying. Who can read the Speech with which young Hamlet accosts him without trembling?

Joseph Addison, *The Spectator*, No. 44 (20 April 1711)

(i)

That the action of Hamlet turns upon the Ghost was acknowledged by the play's early critics; then it began to be supposed that the action turns upon the 'character' of its hero. Hamlet is a contemporary play; it was written, as all plays are, to appeal to contemporary audiences whose outlook was naturally that of their own age, and its hero was necessarily an Elizabethan, otherwise he would have been a stranger to his audiences. It is therefore necessary to recreate the Elizabethan outlook in those of its aspects which are relevant to the play, and of these one of the most important is the religious element.

Beginning with the Ghost, a strong religious but not sectarian vein runs through Hamlet, reappearing in various aspects to the end of the play. In Kyd's *The Spanish Tragedy,* Hieronimo quotes "Vengeance is mine, saith the Lord" to himself, then decides to be his own avenger. Hamlet does not quote it, but must be well aware of what he is doing when he spares Claudius at prayer. He later reveals that he has seen himself as "scourge and minister", and eventually accepts that he must wait on the will of Providence.

The age was at once highly religious and highly superstitious. There was no clear dividing line between religion and what we now regard as superstition, and belief was fervent, even fanatical. The age did not think of itself as superstitious. Heretics were burnt at the stake because it was accepted as fact that if the sufferer was destined for Purgatory before going to Heaven, the flames of the stake would shorten his time therein; if for Hell, the flames of the stake would be a mild introduction to the far hotter flames of Hell, in which he would in any case spend the rest of eternity.

Partly in order to illustrate the degree to which such beliefs dominated the majority of contemporary minds, partly because of the connection between the Witchcraft Acts of 1563 and 1603, the *Daemonologie of King James*, the writing of *Hamlet,* and in particular, the characterisation of its Ghost, and the subsequent fortunes of Shakespeare's theatre company, some time must be spent on witchcraft.

The following extracts from Oswald Spengler's *The Decline of the West* (1923) tell the reader more about the Middle Ages than some entire volumes:

The Father-godhead men felt as force itself, eternal, grand, and ever-present activity, sacred causality, which could scarcely assume any form comprehensible by human eyes. But the whole longing of this "young" race, the whole desire of this strongly-coursing blood, found its expression in the figure of the Virgin and Mother Mary, whose crowning in the heavens was one of the earliest motifs of Gothic art. She is a light-figure, in white, blue, and gold, surrounded by the heavenly hosts. She leans over the new-born child; she feels the sword in her heart; she stands at the foot of the cross; she holds the corpse of the dead Son...

But this world of purity, light, and utter beauty of soul would have been unimaginable without the counter-idea, inseparable from it, an idea that constitutes one of the maxima of Gothic, one of its unfathomable creations—one that the present day forgets, and deliberately forgets. While she there sits enthroned, smiling in her beauty and tenderness, there lies in the background another world that throughout nature and throughout mankind weaves and breeds ill, pierces, destroys, seduces—namely, the realm of the Devil. It penetrates the whole of creation, it lies ambushed everywhere. All around is an army of goblins, night-spirits, witches, werewolves, all in human shape. No man knows whether or not his neighbour has signed himself away to the Evil One. No one can say of an unfolding child that it is not already a devil's temptress. An appalling fear, such as is perhaps only paralleled in the early spring of Egypt, weighs upon man. Every moment he may stumble into the abyss. There were black magic, and devils' masses, and witches' sabbaths, night feasts on mountain-tops, magic draughts and charm-formulae. The Prince of Hell, with his relatives—mother and grandmother, for his very existence denies and scorns the sacrament of marriage, he may not have wife or child—his fallen angels and his uncanny henchmen, is one of the most tremendous creations in all religious history. The Germanic Loki is hardly more than a preliminary hint of him. Their grotesque figures, with horns, claws, and horses' hoofs, were already fully formed in the mystery plays of the eleventh century; everywhere the artist's fancy abounded in them, and, right up to Durer and Grunewald, Gothic painting is unthinkable without them. The Devil is sly, malignant and malicious, but yet in the end the powers of light dupe him. He and his brood, bad-tempered, coarse, fiendishly inventive, are of a monstrous imaginativeness, incarnations of hellish laughter opposed to the illumined smile of the Queen of Heaven...

It is not possible to exaggerate either the grandeur of this forceful, insistent picture or the depth of sincerity with which it was accepted...Man walked continuously on the crust of the bottomless pit. Life in this world is a ceaseless and desperate contest with the Devil, into which every individual plunges as a member of the Church Militant, to do battle for himself and to win his knight's spurs.

...Every man knew the world to be peopled with angel and devil troops. The light-encircled angels of Fra Angelico and the early Rhenish masters, and the grimacing things on the portals of the great cathedrals, really filled the air. Men saw them, felt their presence everywhere...They were glimpsed without being seen. They were believed in with a faith that felt the very thought of proof as a desecration.

For the Devil gained possession of human souls and seduced them into heresy, lechery, and the black arts. War was waged against him on earth, and waged with fire and sword upon those who had given themselves up to him...It was not only the love-glowing hymns to Mary, but the cries from countless pyres as well that rose to heaven. Hard by the Cathedral were the gallows and the wheel. Every man lived in those days in the consciousness of an immense danger, and it was hell, not the hangman, that he feared. Unnumbered thousands of witches genuinely imagined themselves to be so; they denounced themselves, prayed for absolution, and in pure love of truth confessed. Inquisitors, in tears and compassion for the fallen wretches, doomed them to the rack in order to save their souls.

King Henry VI: Part II,I,iv,23ff. would have fascinated its audiences as much as the Ghost in *Hamlet*. The persons present are: aloft, the Duchess of Gloster and John Hume, a priest; below: Roger Bolingbroke, a conjurer; Robert Southwell, another priest; and Margery Jourdain, a witch:
[Here do the ceremonies belonging, and make the circle Bolingbroke *or* Southwell *reads* "Conjuro te", *etc. It thunders and lightens terribly; then the Spirit riseth.]*
　Spirit　Adsum.
　Margery J.　Asmath,
　　By the eternal God, whose name and power
　　Thou tremblest at, answer that I shall ask;
　　For, till thou speak, thou shalt not pass from hence.
　Spirit　Ask what thou wilt;—that I had said and done!
　Roger B. *[Reading out of a paper]*
　　"First of the King: what shall of him become?"
　Spirit　The duke yet lives that Henry shall depose;
　　But him outlive, and die a violent death.
[As the Spirit speaks, Southwell writes the answer.]
　Roger B.　"What fates await the Duke of Suffolk?"
　Spirit　By water shall he die, and take his end.
　Roger B.　"What shall befall the Duke of Somerset?"
　Spirit　Let him shun castles.
　　Safer shall he be upon the sandy plains
　　Than where castles mounted stand.
　　Have done, for more I hardly can endure.
　Roger B.　Descend to darkness and the burning lake!
　　False fiend, avoid!
[Enter the Duke of York and the Duke of Buckingham, with their guard, and break in.]

(I,iv,23–40)

All the participants are arrested. In II,iii, King Henry condemns the two men to be hanged and the witch to be burnt; the Duchess of Gloster, being a great lady, to be "despoiled of her honour" during her life, undergo three days' open penance, then be banished to the Isle of Man.The medieval and Elizabethan view of witches and spirits was evidently a collection of contradictions. Why did priests as well as witches take part in such ceremonies? Pagan superstitions and practices had not yet died out, even among the clergy. Why is Asmath so uncomfortable on earth, away from the sulphurous flames of the burning lake? In particular, why were conjurers, who supposedly possessed powers of control over the minions of the Evil One and could compel them in the name of the Lord to perform such services as predicting the future, condemned to death for doing so?

In his History of English Law, Sir William Holdsworth mentions statutes of 1549 and 1563 in which prophecies were first made felonies, then misdemeanours:

> "The reason for the enactment of these two latter statutes...was the fact that these prophecies were made for the purpose of stirring up rebellion."

There were more general reasons: first, that human nature is notoriously frail, and such powers might be used for purposes detrimental to one's fellow humans; second, that all commerce with spirits was considered dangerous to one's immortal soul even in the absence of illicit intentions, and was therefore forbidden; and third and probably most important of all, every one of the innumerable and apparently undeserved calamities and misfortunes which afflicted humankind could be ascribed, and in the absence of anything resembling the scientific approach, was ascribed either to direct Satanic intervention or to the machinations of persons who had dedicated themselves to the service of the Evil One. As for spirits, they came from either Purgatory or Hell itself, and unless their provenance could be established—which it never could—were to be acutely distrusted.

This was the medieval outlook, which persisted until a century or more after Shakespeare's death. Spengler continues:

> Puritanism, not in the west only, but in all cultures, lacks the smile that illumined the religion of the spring—every Spring—the moments of profound joy in life, the humour of life...Deadly earnest broods over the Jansenist mind of Port Royal, over the meetings of the black-clothed Roundheads, by whom Shakespeare's Merry England was annihilated in a few years. Now for the first time the battle against the Devil, whose bodily nearness they all felt, was fought with a dark and bitter fury. In the seventeenth century more than a million witches were burnt—alike in the Protestant North, the Catholic South, and even the communities in America and India...Witches were burnt because they were proved, and not because they were seen in the air o'nights.

If Coleridge had lived in the seventeenth century, it is to be doubted whether he could have written his "Rime of the Ancient Mariner" (1798) as he did, for the spirit-figures in the tale would have been as real to him as were the angels and demons of "Paradise Lost" to Milton.

The first Witchcraft Act, the *Bill against Conjurations & Witchcrafts and Sorcery and Enchantments (33º HEN. VIII. c. 8)* was passed in 1542:

> If any person or persons, after the first day of May next coming, use, devise, practise or exercise, or cause to be used, devised, practiced or exercised, any invocations or conjurations of spirits, witchcrafts, enchantments or sorceries, to the intent to get or find money or treasure, or to waste, consume, or destroy any person in his body, members or goods, or to provoke any person to unlawful love, or for any other unlawful intent or purpose, or by occasion or colour of such things or any of them, or for despite of Christ, or for lucre of money, dig up or pull down

any cross or crosses, or by such invocations or conjurations of spirits, witchcraft, enchantments or sorceries take upon them to tell or declare where goods stolen or lost shall become [happen to be], That then all and every such offence and offences, from the said first day of May next coming, shall be demyde [deemed], accepted and adjudged felony.

In all cases upon conviction the punishment was to be "pains of death" and forfeiture of possessions without benefit of clergy or sanctuary.

Why was this Act passed?

Henry had been weakening the power and authority of the Church, partly because of its corrupt condition, partly in the hope of obtaining the divorce from Katharine of Aragon for which Rome was withholding its approval. In 1534 the Act of Supremacy had transferred the supreme authority over the Church from Rome to the Sovereign; between 1535 and 1540 Henry had dissolved the smaller, followed by the larger monasteries, and the transference of the responsibility for prosecuting witches from the Church to the lay authorities may have been a part of his policy. Possibly the authority of the Church had by then been reduced to the point where too few witches were being prosecuted, and it was felt that a gap should be filled. Parliament, of course, would welcome any extension of its authority.

The effect was disastrous. The Papal Bull "The Witches' Hammer" of 1487 had enjoined the ecclesiastical authorities to be diligent in the prosecution of witches but at the same time to exercise care in the examination of the accused and their accusers. No such injunction was included in this Witchcraft Act of 1542 or its successors. The concern of the Church had always been the welfare of the immortal souls of its parishioners. Burning at the stake was the punishment for heresy, i.e. deviation from Christian doctrine, not for offences under lay statutes; and the function of the lay magistrates was simply to administer statute law. The law of evidence did not exist; fear of witchcraft dominated their minds to the extent that supposed witches were tortured and executed on the mere accusation of witchcraft. The courts did not hang a man because someone said he had stolen or killed; they required proof of such charges, but they condemned supposed witches on mere allegation by almost anyone, even children.

The prosecutions of witches increased with the rise of Puritanism:

> On the whole, the Calvinists, generally speaking, were of all the contending sects the most suspicious of sorcery, the most undoubting believers in its existence, and the most eager to follow it up with what they conceived to be the due punishment of the most fearful of crimes.
>
> Sir Walter Scott, *Letters on Demonology and Witchcraft* (1830)

Immediately after the accession of Edward VI in 1547, this Act was repealed and the responsibility for prosecuting witches restored to the Church. In 1563 another Witchcraft Act was passed (*5° ELIZ. c. 16*) which was in much the same terms as the original Act, except that the punishment for certain offences, such as invoking spirits to discover buried treasure or to provoke unlawful love, was reduced to a year's imprisonment with six hours' imprisonment in the pillory every quarter on market days or fairs; however, depending on the offence, second convictions brought death or life imprisonment. It also introduced a phrase which had not been in the original Act, which stated that many fantastical and devilish persons had devised and practiced invocations of evil and wicked spirits "to the peril of their own souls." In both acts, the prohibition was on invoking or conjuring up spirits, i.e.

neither act mentioned spirits which might appear of their own accord.

In 1604, very soon after James' accession, another *Act against Conjuration, Witchcraft and dealings with evil and wicked Spirits* (1º JAC.I. c. 12) replaced it. In the first paragraph it stated that the earlier act was "utterlie repealed", then continued in its second:

> AND for the better restraining the said offences, and more severe punishing the same, be it further enacted by the authority afore-said, That if any person or persons, after the said Feast of Saint Michael the Archangel next coming, shall use, practise or exercise any Invocation or Conjuration of any evil and wicked Spirit, or shall consult, covenant with, entertain, employ, feed, or reward any evil and wicked Spirit to or for any Intent or purpose; or take up any dead man, woman, or child out of his, her or their grave, or any other place where the dead body resteth, or the skin, bone or any other part of any dead person, to be employed or used in any manner of Witchcraft, Sorcery, Charm, or Enchantment; or shall use, practise or exercise any Witchcraft, Enchantment, Charm or Sorcery whereby any person shall be killed, destroyed, wasted, consumed, pined or lamed in his or her body, or any part thereof; that then every such Offender or Offenders, their Aiders, Abetters and Counsellers, being of any the said Offences duly and lawfully convicted and attainted, shall suffer pains of death as a Felon or Felons, and shall lose the privilege and benefit of Clergy and Sanctuary.

Its third paragraph repeated the other provisions of the previous act.

Why was an Act rephrased that had apparently been satisfactory for the previous forty years? The earlier Acts had merely prohibited the invoking or conjuring of evil and wicked spirits for various unlawful purposes. Why did this act now repeat the ban on such invocations, and then extend it to consulting with all evil and wicked spirits, including any which might have appeared without being invoked?

Since the change was made well within the first year of James' reign, it may have been at his instigation. He was a convinced believer in witchcraft, having become persuaded of its existence when a supposed witch, who was later executed, told him of something he had said to his bride, Princess Anne of Denmark, on their wedding night when no one else had been present. He was a lover of the theatre, for he became the patron of Shakespeare's theatre company almost immediately on his accession, and it seems likely that he had the Act rephrased after seeing *Hamlet*. It is difficult to see why else a previously satisfactory act should have been replaced.

James had studied the subject to the point where he considered himself an authority, and in 1597 published his views in his *Daemonologie*. His "Preface to the Reader" begins:

> The fearfulle aboundinge at this time in this countrie, of these detestable slaues of the Deuill, the Witches or enchaunters, hath moued me (beloued reader) to dispatch in post, this following treatise of mine, not in any wise (as I protest) to serue for a shew of my learning & ingine, but onely (mooued of conscience) to pre-asse thereby, so farre as I can, to resolue the doubting harts of many; both that such assaults of Sathan are most certainly practized, & that the instrumentes thereof, merits most severly to be punished: against the damnable opinions of two principally in our age, wherof the one called SCOT an Englishman, is not ashamed in publike print to deny, that ther can be such a thing as Witchcraft: and so mainteines the old error of the Sadducees, in denying of spirits.

A Kentish man, Reginald Scot had studied some law, become a justice, and been sickened by the numbers of starving, short-tempered but otherwise harmless old women who, accused of witchcraft, were being condemned. In 1584 he had published his *Discoverie of Witchcraft* and gave his reasons in his "Epistle to the Reader":

> First, that the glorie and power of God be not so abridged and abased, as to be thrust into the hand or lip of a lewd old woman: whereby the worke of the Creator should be attributed to the power of a creature. Secondlie, that the religion of the gospell may be seene to stand without such peevish trumperie. Thirdlie, that lawfull favour and christian compassion be rather used towards these poore soules, than rigor and extremitie. Bicause they, which are commonlie accused of witchcraft, are the least sufficient of all other persons to speake for themselves; as having the most base and simple education of all others; the extremitie of their age giving them leave to dote, their povertie to beg, their wrongs to chide and threaten (as being void of anie other waie of revenge), their humor melancholicall to be full of imagination, from whence cheefelie proceedeth the vanitie of their confessions...
>
> For the world is now at that stay... that even as when the heathen persecuted the christians, if anie were accused to beleeve in Christ, the common people cried "Ad leonem"; so now, if anie woman, be she never so honest, be accused of witchcraft, they cry "Ad ignem".

He remained a believer in witchcraft, ghosts and spirits (the last part of his book was devoted to "Divells and spirits") and in other superstitions such as the magical properties of precious stones. One part of his book was devoted to the "detection" of many of the sleight-of-hand tricks practised on ignorant onlookers by conjurers and "couseners", such as how to swallow a dagger, how to pass a ring through one's cheek, how to perform various card-sharping tricks, even how to cut off one's head and lay it on a platter! Nevertheless, James decided that he must be refuted, and after his accession to the English throne had as many copies as possible of the book collected and publicly burned.

The *Daemonologie* is in three parts, each in the form of a dialogue between Philomathes who asks questions, and Epistemon who answers them. The first book is a description of "Magie in speciall", the second of "Sorcerie and Witchcraft in speciall", the third of "All these kindes of Spirites that troubles men or women", including those appearing of their own accord. The Thirde Booke begins:

Chap. 1. ARGV.

The division of spirites in foure principall kindes. The description of the first kind of them, called Spectra & Vmbrae Mortuorum. What is the best way to be free of their trouble.

PHILOMATHES: I pray you now then go forward in telling what ye thinke fabulous, or what may be trowed in that case.

EPISTEMON: That kinde of the Deuils conuersing in the earth, may be diuided in foure different kindes, whereby he affrayeth and troubleth the bodies of men: for of the abusing of the soule, I have spoken alreadie. The first is, where spirites troubles some houses or solitarie places: The second, where spirites followes upon certaine persones, and at divers houres troubles them: The thirde, when they enter within them and possesse them: The fourth is these kind of spirites that are called vulgarlie the Fayrie. Of the three former kindes, ye harde alreadie, how they may artificiallie be made by witchcraft to trouble folk: Now it restes to speak of their naturall comming as it were, and not raysed by Witchcraft.

But generally I must fore-warne you of one thing before I enter this purpose: that is, that in my discourseing of them, I deuide them in diuers kindes, yee must notwithstanding there of note my Phrase of speaking in that: for doubtleslie they are in effect, but all one kinde of spirites, who for abusing the more of mankinde, takes on these sundrie shapes, and vses diuerse formes of outward actiones, as if some were of nature better then other.

Nowe I returne to my purpose: As to the first kinde of these spirites, that were called by the auncients by diuers names, according as there actions were. For if they were spirites that haunted some houses, by appearing in diuers and horrible formes, and making great dinne: they were called Lemures or Spectra. If they appeared in likenesse of anie defunct to some friends of his, they wer called umbrae mortuorum: and so innumerable stiles they got, according to their actiones, as I have said alreadie. As we see by experience, how manie stiles they have given them in our language in the like manner: Of the appearing of these spirites, wee are certified by the Scriptures, where the prophet Esay 13. and 34. cap. threatening the destruction of Babell and Edom: declares, that it shall not onlie be wracked, but shall become so great a solitude, as it shall be the habitackle of Howlettes, and of ZIIM and IIM, which are the proper Hebrewe names for these Spirites. The cause why they haunt solitarie places, it is by reason, that they may affraie and brangle the faith of suche as them alone hauntes such places. For our nature is such, as in companies we are not so soone mooued to anie such kinde of fear, as being solitare, which the Deuill knowing well inough, hee will not therefore assaile us but when we are weake: And besides that, G O D will not permit him so to dishonour the societies and companies of Christians, as in publicke times and places to walk visiblie among them. On the other parte, when he troubles certaine houses that are dwelt in, it is a sure token either of grosse ignorance, or of some grosse and slanderous sinnes amongst the inhabitantes thereof: which God by that extraordinary rod punishes...

PHI. But by what way or passage can these Spirites enter in these houses, seeing that they alledge that they will enter, Doore and Window being steiked?

EPI. They will choose the passage for their entresse, according to the forme that they are in at that time. For if they have assumed a deade bodie, whereinto they lodge themselues, they can easely enough open without dinne anie Doore or Window, and enter in thereat. And if they enter as a spirite onelie, anie place where the aire may come in at, is large inough for an entrie for them: For as I said before, a spirite can occupie no quantitie.

PHI. And will God then permit these wicked spirites to trouble the reste of a dead bodie, before the resurrection thereof? Or if he will do so, I think it should be of the reprobate onely.

EPI. What more is the reste troubled of a dead bodie, when the Deuill carries it out of the graue to serve his turn for a space, nor when the Witches takes it up and joyntes it, or when as Swine wortes vppe the Graues?...

PHI. And what meanes then these kindes of spirites, when they appear in the shaddow of a person newlie dead, or to die, to his friendes?

EPI. When they appeare vpon that occasion, they are called Wraithes in our language. Amongst the Gentiles the Deuill used that much, to make them beleeue that it was some goode spirite that appeared to them then, ether to forewarne them of the death of their friend; or else to discouer vnto them, the will of the defunct, or what was the way of his slaughter, as is written in the booke of the histories Prodigious.

In Chapter II, speaking of "the next two kindes of spirites, whereof the one follows outwardlie, the other possesses inwardlie, the persons that they trouble", he says:

EPI. It is to obtaine one of two thinges thereby, if he may: The one is the tinsell ["vital spark"] of their life, by inducing them to such perilous places at such time as he either follows or possesses them, which may procure the same...The other thing that he preasses to obteine by troubling of them, is the tinsell of their soule, by intising them to mistruste and blaspheme God.

James' book is much inferior to Scot's. It is too short, making no attempt to refute Scot point by point; if anything, Scot's book is too long and comparison of their styles shows that Scot was much the more matter-of-fact thinker. James was described as "the wisest fool in Christendom", which presumably meant "convinced of the comprehensiveness of his learning, but not clear-headed." Scot's approach was largely factual, while that of James in lay in terms of Biblical doctrines. Further, James completely ignored Scot's main complaint, that many perfectly harmless, penniless, sometimes cold and starving old women were being accused and condemned without any attempt to verify the charges against them. This was simply not justice, but the point escaped James.

Shakespeare may have decided to dramatise the Amleth legend because it contained a ghost which, with a little ingenuity, could be tailored to suit James' views.

The Elder Hamlet's Ghost, which comes without being invoked, appears in a solitary place where there are few to see it; a sin has been committed in the house; it reveals how it was "slaughtered"; it has apparently usurped the form of the Elder Hamlet; it has "no quantitie" ("For it is as the air, invulnerable") Horatio asks whether it knows of "buried treasure in the womb of earth"; it entices Hamlet to a dangerous place; it discovers its will to him; it would be taken by the audience as endangering the "tinsell" of his soul (as it does after the Gonzago-play).

Where there are so many points of resemblance, they are unlikely to be purely coincidental.

In his *Miscellaneous Observations on the Tragedy of Macbeth* (1745) Dr. Johnson remarked:

> This book was, soon after his Accession, reprinted at London, and as the ready way to gain K. James's favour was to flatter his speculations, the system of "Daemonologie" was immediately adopted by all who desired either to gain preferment or not to lose it.

That James would accede to the English throne must have been apparent for some years before Elizabeth's death, for the uniting of the kingdoms would eliminate what had been the ever-present threat of invasion from Scotland, particularly in the event of an alliance between Scotland and England's old enemy, France. In 1558, French troops had been sent to Scotland; war was not declared, but an English fleet was sent to the Forth, where it besieged and captured Leith, on the doorstep of Edinburgh. In the subsequent Treaty of Edinburgh 1560, the French force was required to withdraw. Shakespeare, always the man of business, would be concerned to remain in favour with the Court, the more so because King James was known to be fond of the theatre.

He succeeded. Until 1603 his theatre company was under the patronage of the Lord Chamberlain and was known as The Chamberlain's Men. Then, on the 19th of May 1603 and two months after his accession, King James became its patron, after which it was known as The King's Men. It was frequently called upon to perform before him, which was almost four times as often as under Elizabeth. Its members received a small annual stipend as Grooms of the Chamber, receiving occasional gifts from the Sovereign. Court performances were well paid.

The name at the head of the list of members of the company on the Royal licence is that of Lawrence Fletcher, who had acted in Edinburgh in the 1590s and become "comédiane to his Majesty". It is likely, therefore, that Shakespeare read the *Daemonologie* on Fletcher's advice in anticipation of James' accession, and, when he came to write *Hamlet*, was careful to create a Ghost whose behaviour accorded precisely with James' doctrines; equally likely that the Ghost inspired James to have the Witchcraft Act amended so as to emphasise the prohibition on commerce with all spirits, whether invoked or not.

James later became more sceptical. In 1618 he interviewed the Laicester Boy, whose accusations had sent eight supposed witches to their deaths, and persuaded him to admit that his accusations had all been invented and doubtless from schoolboy malice. He should now have had a clause added to the Witchcraft Act requiring judges to establish the truth or otherwise of allegations by careful examination of the witches' accusers but did not, no doubt because he remained convinced of the "fearfulle aboundinge" of witches and witchery; the witch-hunts continued with even greater ferocity. The Puritans appointed a lawyer, one Matthew Hopkins, as prosecutor of witches; he called himself "Witchfinder General", was paid 20 shillings for each visit to places where there were supposed witches, and 20 shillings for each conviction, and in 1646 lost his position because of his greed.

Such, then, was the fear of witches, ghosts and spirits which pervaded all but a very few minds, and would have caused the Ghost in *Hamlet* to be seen, not as an effective and skilfully used dramatic device, but as a living, frightening figure whose menacing presence, whether visible or not, would be felt as brooding over the play from its beginning to its end.

Among the general populace, belief in witchcraft, ghosts and spirits did not begin to die out until the second half of the eighteenth century. Opinion in the more highly educated had become more enlightened somewhat earlier, the last Witchcraft Act of 1603 having been repealed in 1736, but in 1754 Arthur Murphy wrote:

> This nation has in all ages been much more addicted to folly and superstition than any other whatever. The belief of ghosts and apparitions is at present as strongly implanted in the minds of the major part of the inhabitants of this kingdom as it was in the days when ignorance and want of knowledge and experience blinded the eyes of men."

As late as 1765, Sir William Blackstone wrote in his *Commentaries on the Laws of England*:

"To deny the possibility, nay, actual existence, of witchcraft and sorcery is flatly to contradict the revealed word of God."

Still, the theatre critics, being among the better educated, had earlier begun to forget the effect of the Ghost on Elizabethan minds. All of them, it appears, had forgotten the living fear which the thought of ghosts and spirits had induced in the minds of an earlier age, to the point where supposed witches were tortured, then burnt or hanged on mere allegation; none of them remembered that Hamlet, for the safety of his immortal soul, would be bound to distrust the Ghost even though it appeared in the very semblance of his father and claimed to have come from Purgatory to tell him its story, and that a good half of the interest of the play to the Elizabethan spectators would be dependent on his response to the fact that it was a ghost, i.e. that no matter what story it told, its intentions were probably malicious. At the end of the play they would all note—King James among them—that its story, though true, had brought about the deaths not only of the guilty party but also of a number of innocent ones: the annihilation of two entire families.

(ii)

Examination of the play shows that the Ghost inspires acute fear and distrust in all who see it, from its first appearance to its last.

In I,i, Bernardo is about to describe its last appearance when it enters:
Bernado In the same figure, like the King that's dead.
Marcellus Thou art a scholar; speak to it, Horatio.
Bernado Looks it not like the King? Mark it, Horatio.
Horatio Most like.—It harrows me with fear and wonder.
Bernado It would be spoke to.
Marcellus   Question it, Horatio.
Horatio What art thou, that usurp'st this time of night
   Together with that fair and warlike form
   In which the majesty of buried Denmark
   Did sometimes march? By heaven, I charge thee, speak!

(I,i,41–48)

For all the Ghost's resemblance to the Elder Hamlet, Horatio believes that it is "usurping" that warlike form. Has he been truly harrowed? He has; summoning his courage to speak to it has cost him something.
Bernardo How now, Horatio! You tremble and look pale.

(I,i,53)

Horatio thinks it is no more than "a mote to trouble the mind's eye", and, as a hint to the audience to expect exciting events, gives a long list of omens which had been "harbingers preceding still the fates". It then re-enters: "I'll cross it, though it blast me". We learn in the next scene that the sentries had been equally afraid when they first saw it:
Horatio   Thrice he walked
   By their oppressed and fear-surprised eyes
   Within his truncheon's length, while they, distilled
   Almost to jelly with the act of fear,
   Stand dumb and speak not to him.

(I,ii,200–204)

[Hamlet questions Horatio closely, and is equally aware of the danger; like Horatio, he will "cross it though it blast me":]

> *Hamlet*   If it assume my noble father's person
> I'll speak to it, though hell itself should gape
> And bid me hold my peace.
>
> (I,ii,242–244)

[When it appears to him, his first words are a prayer for celestial protection:]
> *Hamlet*   Angels and ministers of grace defend us!
> Be thou a spirit of health or goblin damned,
> Bring with thee airs from heaven or blasts from hell,
> Be thy intents wicked or charitable,
> Thou comest in such a questionable shape
> That I will speak to thee.
>
> (I,iv,39–44)

[In the hope that it will reply he even adds, as a kind of concession:]
> *Hamlet*   I'll call thee Hamlet,
> King, Father, Royal Dane. O, answer me!

[But he too is harrowed with fear:]
> *Hamlet*   What may this mean?
> That thou, dead corse, again in complete steel
> Revisits thus the glimpses of the moon,
> Making night hideous, and we fools of nature
> So horridly to shake our disposition
> With thoughts beyond the reaches of our souls?
>
> (I,iv,44–56)

After the Ghost has vanished, he begins his soliloquy with "O all you host of heaven", and immediately adds "And shall I couple hell?"

When its voice is heard from the cellar, he has recovered his courage; further, he must affect to treat the whole episode lightly so as to divert his companions' curiosity. And apart from the fact that the Ghost's communication was of a highly private nature, he has more than one reason for swearing his companions to secrecy: he would not wish it to be known that he had been speaking to a ghost!

His next reference to the Ghost comes at the end of his Hecuba soliloquy:
> *Hamlet*   The spirit that I have seen
> May be the devil. And the devil hath power
> T'assume a pleasing shape; yea and perhaps
> Out of my weakness and my melancholy
> Abuses me to damn me. I'll have grounds
> More relative than this.—The play's the thing
> Wherein to catch the conscience of the King.
>
> (II,ii,573–580)

The first five of these lines are virtually repeated in *Macbeth*. Macbeth allows him to be led on by witches who know that he is both ambitious and vulnerable to temptation, and does not pause to reflect on the intentions which may lie behind their prophecies. Banquo is wiser:
> *Banquo*   And oftentimes, to win us to our harm,
> The instruments of darkness tell us truths,

Win us with honest trifles, to betray's
In deepest consequence.

(*Macbeth*: I,iii,123–126)

Hamlet's "weakness and melancholy" are his grief for his dead father and his shock at his mother's early second marriage. He remains aware that the Ghost may be playing on them in order to tempt him into killing an innocent man and so damning his soul for ever; hence he must establish the truth of its story before considering any action against Claudius.

He repeats his distrust to Horatio before the Gonzago-play:

Hamlet   If his occulted guilt
Do not itself unkennel in one speech,
It is a damned ghost that we have seen,
And my imaginations are as foul
As Vulcan's stithy.

(III,ii,76–80)

Being a law student, he knows that he cannot possibly rely on a ghost's tale as proof of anything; he is prepared to admit that his suspicion of his uncle may be unfounded. As mentioned earlier, it is not essential to make him a law student if he is to require more definite proof of the Ghost's story, but he is one and thinks as one. The Elizabethan spectator, aware of the danger that Hamlet is stepping into, would be pleased to note that he asks Horatio, also a law student, to observe the King's reactions during the Gonzago-play as an independent witness. The Ghost's last appearance is in the closet scene. In his furious tirade against his uncle, Hamlet has already described him as a murderer, and the Ghost apparently enters to prevent him from revealing too much to his mother, whom it had enjoined him to spare. Now the Gonzago-play has convinced Hamlet that the Ghost spoke the truth; yet the first words he utters are the same prayer for celestial protection as that of the first act, "Angels and ministers of grace defend us!"

Hamlet   Save me and hover over me with your wings,
You heavenly guards!

(III,iv,103–104)

Although he has accepted that it is "honest", he remains afraid of it as a spirit.

In sum: when Hamlet expresses the need to be cautious with respect to the Ghost, he means what he says. Both as an Elizabethan and as law-student, he has good reasons for meaning what he says, and his reasons for hesitating and delaying would be obvious to his Elizabethan audiences. He certainly reveals emotional undertones which must be accounted for, though to Shakespeare's spectators the question would be not "What kind of young man is Hamlet?" but simply "How is he going to find a method of testing its story?" He remains aware that the Gonzago-play will be as much a test of the Ghost as of the King. To the Elizabethan spectators he would be in as much danger from the other world as from any enemies in this one.

It is of course pertinent to ask: if Hamlet distrusts the Ghost as much as that, why does he not reject its story out of hand; why does he elect to "wipe away all trivial fond records" and devote himself solely to the verification of its story?

He himself gives the answer: "O my prophetic soul!" Does he have a prophetic soul? He does indeed: he has a premonition during the voyage to England: "Sir, there was in my heart a kind of fighting / That would not let me sleep" (V,ii,4–5), and another immediately before the fencing match: "Thou wouldst not think how ill all's here about my heart" (V,ii,194–5).

A trivial point? Not in the least; to the Elizabethan spectator it would explain the conviction with which Hamlet undertakes a spiritually dangerous task, one which might imperil his immortal soul.

And perhaps his prophetic soul explains "The time is out of joint; O cursed spite / That ever I was born to set it right": he somehow knows what the end will be for him, and undertakes his duty in despair.

After hearing the Ghost's story, then, Hamlet feels that it is true, but cannot possibly act upon it until he is satisfied of its truth. By what means can he satisfy himself? Only after a considerable time does the arrival of the Players suggest a method to him.

Part IIA

HAMLET THE MELODRAMATIC HERO

10

HAMLET THE *LUNATIC*

(i)

Lunatics were a source of amusement to the Elizabethans. Not till the advent of medical psychology in the nineteenth century did they become objects of pity: "The pretended madness of Hamlet causes much mirth."

Dr. Johnson *Preface* to *Shakespeare* (1765)

Ghosts, poisonings, stabbings, incest, adultery, lunacy, and violence were among the sensational plot elements of the day, which the playwrights used to attract their audiences— as do scriptwriters today—the main sensational elements now being explicit violence and explicit sex.

In Thomas Kyd's *The Spanish Tragedy*, Hieronimo becomes distracted by grief when his son is murdered; his wife Isabella runs mad and eventually hangs herself. Ben Jonson later lengthened two scenes and added another long scene merely to extend the display of Hieronimo in his madness. These additions contribute nothing to the action; they actually hold it up, and can only have been inserted as additional entertainment for the spectators.

In Fletcher and Shakespeare's *The Two Noble Kinsmen* (1634) the Gaoler's Daughter runs mad; she is shown in no fewer than six scenes, occasionally singing children's songs, as does Ophelia, of whom she appears to have been an extended copy.

In Middleton and Rowley's *The Changeling*, Dr. Alibius takes in lunatics and undertakes to cure them; Antonio the "Changeling" and Franciscus counterfeit madness in order to be admitted to the establishment, both having designs on the doctor's wife Isabella. The doctor is asked (III,ii) to arrange an entertainment to be performed by his lunatics on the third night of a wedding's revels. At one point Isabella counterfeits madness. The scenes in the asylum, which constitute a sub-plot, must have been intended to offer a comic, and perhaps blackly comic, contrast to the main action.

John Webster (1621) used lunatics in *The Tragedy of the Duchess of Malfi*. At the beginning of IV,ii, a "hideous noise" is heard, from madmen placed around the Duchess's lodging:

> *Servant*   I am come to tell you
> Your brother hath intended you some sport.
> A great physician, when the Pope was sick
> Of a deep melancholy, presented him
> With several sorts of madmen, which wild object
> Being full of change and sport, forc'd him to laugh,
> And so the imposthume broke; the selfsame cure
> The Duke intends on you.

The madmen enter, sing a melancholy song to a "dismal kind of music", indulge in wild and whirling conversation for a while, perform a dance, and sing another song. The Duchess and her maid are then strangled on the stage (an extreme of sensation), apparently with the madmen still present. There is no stage direction *[Exeunt Madmen]*. The point of introducing madmen into such a scene, who also hold up the action, is difficult to see. Why pad out such an episode, even if lunatics were a form of audience-entertainment? No doubt they add atmosphere, but the scene is quite long and horrifying enough without them.

To Shakespeare's spectators, Hamlet's lunacy would be doubly amusing: they were watching a lunatic, and they would know that the lunacy was being skilfully simulated. Since on hearing the Ghost's story Hamlet can instantly decide to put on the "antic disposition", then carry it off so well as to deceive the entire court, he too must have spent some time watching lunatics!

(ii)

In III.iii, Claudius kneels to pray, yet finds that he cannot pray. He has decided to have Hamlet secretly executed in England; the length of his agonised soliloquy suggests that he is uncertain whether he should have done so. In the course of his soliloquy he says:

King May one be pardoned and retain th'offence?
In the corrupted currents of this world
Offence's gilded hand may shove by justice,
And oft 'tis seen the wicked prize itself
Buys out the law.

(III,iii,56–60)

In 1534 an Act (26º HEN. VIII. c. 13) was passed, the "strong law" referred to by Claudius in IV,iii,3, "whereby divers offences be made high treason, and taking away all sanctuaries for all manner of high treasons":

> Forasmuch as it is most necessary, both for common policy and duty of subjects, above all things to prohibit provide restrain and extinct all manner of shameful slanders perils or imminent danger or dangers which might grow happen or rise to their Sovereign Lord the King the Queen or their Heirs...Be it therefore enacted...that if any person or persons after the first day of February next coming, do maliciously wish will or desire by words or writing, or by craft imagine invent practise or attempt, any bodily harm to be done or committed to the King's most royal person, the Queen's or their heirs apparent, or to deprive them or any of them of the dignity title or name of their royal estates, or slanderously and maliciously publish and pronounce, by express writing or words, that the King our sovereign Lord should be heretic schismatic tyrant infidel or usurper of the crown...
>
> ...Then such persons should suffer pains of death and such other penalties as were customary in cases of high treason.

After the numerous civil wars over the succession to the throne, kings were naturally nervous of "seditious words", and this was the fourth in a long series of acts prohibiting "slanders", the first in 1275 and the last well before *Hamlet* in 1581. The first three had merely prohibited slanders of "great men" and required the offender to bring to court the person from whom he had heard the slander, but this act now designated slander of the monarch as high treason bringing severe punishment. Other acts followed under Philip and Mary, though they stipulated lesser punishments such as loss of the right hand and a heavy fine. (They did not explicitly repeal the act of 1534, though they may have intended to supersede it.)

The Act of 1581 (23º ELIZ. c. 2), probably aimed at those supporters of Mary, Queen of Scots, who believed her to be the legitimate occupant of the English throne, was more comprehensive than the previous Acts:

a) anyone convicted of speaking seditious words and rumours against "our most natural sovereign Lady the Queen's Majesty" should be set upon the pillory, lose both his ears or pay a fine of two hundred pounds, and be imprisoned for six months;
b) anyone convicted of repeating such seditious or slanderous "news" should be pilloried, and lose one ear or pay a fine of two hundred marks, and be imprisoned for three months;
c) any second offence would on conviction be punishable by death;
d) anyone publishing any book, rhyme, ballad, letter or writing against the Queen or encouraging insurrection or sedition should suffer "pains of death" as a felon;
e) casting nativities or prophesying as to how long the Queen would live or who should succeed her, or desiring her death, was also punishable with death.

The rest of the Act defined the powers of Mayors and Justices to commit and try offenders, required its proclamation in all counties, stipulated that two witnesses be brought face to face with the accused, repealed previous Acts of the reigns of Philip and Mary and Elizabeth, and stated that this Act would only remain in force during the Queen's reign.

The comprehensiveness of its prohibitions on slanders and libels suggests that there was, if not a stream, at least a continuous trickle of them; its provision that it must be proclaimed in all counties, that all members of the population (including Shakespeare's audiences) would be aware of it.

The Gonzago-play, which contains not only a satire on the royal marriage but also the suggestion that Claudius is a usurper of the crown by murder, is therefore a treasonable slander, and will compel Claudius to take the decision with respect to his lunatic nephew which he has been postponing for some time. Hamlet may be a Prince of the Royal Family, but in putting on the Gonzago-play he is sticking his neck out a long way (literally, since noble offenders were customarily beheaded!), and his spectators would be aware that he is.

The law of lunacy is relevant to and mentioned at three points in *Hamlet*. Criminals who had committed a crime, even murder, were not (and are not) necessarily punished; if found by medical psychologists to be lunatics and not responsible for their actions, they were (and are) confined. In Shakespeare's time, and for over two centuries afterwards, a panel of ecclesiastics—who were the best psychologists of the time—since in their work they would learn much of the subtleties and vagaries of human nature, examined them after indictment by the magistrates to decide whether they were or were not lunatics. The example of this procedure, which is the most apt for the present purpose, is taken from the contemporary history of France.

Henry IV of France, who had been brought up as a Protestant, became king in 1589. Only after he had won battles against his Catholic opponents and accepted conversion to Catholicism did he pacify all opposition. In 1598 he promulgated the Edict of Nantes, which gave a large measure of religious and civil liberty to his Protestant subjects. While proceeding to Mass on May 14 1610, he was stabbed to death by one François Ravaillac, a fervent Catholic who did not believe that Henry's conversion had been sincere. (Henry is reputed to have said "Paris is worth a Mass".)

Ravaillac's examining panel consisted of three cardinals, an archbishop, and four bishops[4]. The Church was extremely careful, these being the most able, the most learned and the

---

4   From *Procès, Exament, Confessions et négations du meschant et execrable parricide François Ravaillac* (1611)

most experienced of churchmen. They soon decided that although he might be a religious maniac, he was not a lunatic.

He was then returned to the lay authorities and tortured to make him reveal the names of any accomplices; he had none. Then he was executed by being broken on the wheel, which was a form of punishment in which the executioners strapped the victim to a wheel, and then broke his bones with hammers. They could have killed him quickly, but regicide-murder of the king's most sacred person was the worst of all treason crimes, so they spread the punishment over a whole day, watched by a dense crowd. Had he been found to be lunatic, he would merely have been confined and no doubt for life. However, Ravaillac's treatment illustrated the practice of Shakespeare's time.

While kneeling at the priedieu after the Gonzago-play, Claudius is well aware that he should have his lunatic nephew arrested and examined. As he later admits to Laertes (IV,vii,17), he should certainly have ordered a "public count", i.e. an examination followed by confinement, especially after the slaying of Polonius, Hamlet's attempt at regicide. If he decides to have Hamlet executed, his prizes, his crown and his queen, will have tempted him to "shove by justice" and "buy out the law", i.e. to evade the law. The execution will have to be carried out in secret and in some place remote from Denmark, the vassal "tributary" kingdom of England being convenient for the purpose. For this reason, Shakespeare, careful of detail in his play construction, made England a dependent kingdom in his picture of the Danish empire. Claudius is able to decide to send Hamlet to England "For the recovery of our neglected tribute" (III,i,169), then change his intention into something more malign, knowing that "England" will obey him.

Hence, the commission to the King of England is both secret and full of threats. Its import is revealed in a soliloquy (IV,iii,57–67) that is heard only by the audience, for Claudius cannot reveal its content to any of his court.

Similarly, when he later excuses himself to Laertes, he might defend himself further by mentioning his attempt to have Hamlet executed, but dares not do so since, as King, he should set an example by obeying the law.

(iii)

Convinced as he is that the Ghost's story is true, Hamlet is sure that he must abandon all his dearest hopes in life:

Hamlet [Aside] The time is out of joint.—O cursed spite
   That ever I was born to set it right!
   [Aloud] Nay, come, let's go together.

(I,v,189–191)

Even if he lives on after killing Claudius in the character of a lunatic, he will have no further hope of coming to the throne, nor will he be able to marry Ophelia:

Ophelia My lord, as I was sewing in my closet,
   Lord Hamlet, with his doublet all unbraced,
   No hat upon his head, his stockings fouled,
   Ungartered and down-gyved to his ankle;
   Pale as his shirt, his knees knocking each other,
   And with a look so piteous in purport
   As if he had been loosed out of hell
   To speak of horrors—he comes before me.

Polonius Mad for thy love?
Ophelia My lord, I do not know,
   But truly I do fear it.
Polonius What said he?
Ophelia He took me by the wrist and held me hard.
   Then goes he to the length of all his arm,
   And with his other hand thus o'er his brow,
   He falls to such perusal of my face
   As he would draw it. Long stayed he so.
   At last, a little shaking of mine arm,
   And thrice his head thus waving up and down,
   He raised a sigh so piteous and profound
   That it did seem to shatter all his bulk,
   And end his being. That done, he lets me go;
   And with his head over his shoulder turned,
   He seemed to find his way without his eyes,
   For out o'doors he went without their help,
   And to the last bended their light on me.

(II,i,76–99)

This is Hamlet's farewell to Ophelia. He cannot explain his reasons to her; it must be a silent farewell.

An outward sign of mental disturbance is neglect of the sufferer's appearance; in a woman, for example, neglect of her hair is often a revealing sign. In their first appearances, Gertrude and Ophelia will be well soignées. After the closet scene, when Gertrude's conscience becomes tortured, her appearance will be less so; Ophelia's, in her mad scenes, very much less so.

Hamlet knows that if he is to play the lunatic convincingly, he must look the part. Ophelia's description of his irruption into her father's house in II,i prepares the audience for his appearance when he next comes on stage. In his opening scenes he is dressed with care in his solemn black mourning clothes; when he next enters in II,ii, reading a book, he is as Ophelia has described him, still in the same clothes, which are now in a dreadfully neglected state. The King confirms the change in his appearance:

King   Something you have heard
   Of Hamlet's transformation; so call it,
   Since nor th'exterior nor the inward man
   Resembles that it was.

(II,ii,4–7)

As part of his simulation of lunacy he is careful not to change his clothes, and he continues in this state of neglect until his return from the sea voyage.

When in II,ii, Hamlet greets Rosencrantz and Guildenstern with pleasure, and eventually asks, "What make you at Elsinore?", they do not answer immediately. When he presses them to answer, they withdraw to confer before answering, so making him suspicious and sealing their ultimate fate. Why do they hesitate to answer? Because of his appearance, which is totally unlike that of the Prince Hamlet they had known!

After his return from the sea voyage he no longer affects lunacy, so, whether in sailors' clothes according to the tradition or otherwise, he will be tidily dressed again.

In his stage appearances as lunatic we only see Hamlet behave as a young man who has become harmlessly mad. At other times he must be quite violent, for the King describes him as "Grating so harshly all his days of quiet / With turbulent and dangerous lunacy" (III,i,3–4), and, at the end of III,iii, when he rushes out after ranting at Ophelia, Polonius suggests that he should be confined as an alternative to sending him to England (III,iii,185). In IV,vii, Laertes is rightfully angry with Claudius:

Laertes   It well appears—but tell me
   Why you proceeded not against these feats,
   So crimeful and so capital in nature,
   As by your safety, wisdom, all things else
   You mainly were stirred up.
                                             (IV,vii,5–9)

"Crimeful and capital" are even stronger than "turbulent and dangerous"; the plural "feats" implies that the wanton slaying of Polonius was merely the last of a series of turbulent feats and should have been anticipated by an earlier "public count".

Why does Hamlet occasionally make his lunacy turbulent and dangerous? He is preparing the ground! Any such violent act as the slaying of Claudius must not appear to have been premeditated; it must be attributable to his lunacy and to nothing else.

(iv)

His simulation of lunacy is perfectly convincing to Polonius, who has known him since birth but less so to Claudius, who at the end of the Nunnery scene would not otherwise decide to send him to England in the hope that he would be cured by the sea voyage; and, as remarked, must at times be worse than anything seen on the stage. How is it that he can put on so convincing a performance, as we shall see, for more than two months?

Not only is he quick-witted and fertile enough to ad-lib his way out of any situation, and familiar with the behaviour of lunatics, he is also an accomplished actor, as Shakespeare makes clear in II,ii,425ff.:

Hamlet   *"The rugged Pyrrhus, like th'Hyrcanian beast"*
   —'tis not so—it begins with Pyrrhus:
      "The rugged Pyrrhus, he whose sable arms,
      Black as his purpose, did the night resemble...
      ...Roasted in wrath and fire,
      And thus o'ersized with coagulate gore,
      With eyes like carbuncles, the hellish Pyrrhus
      Old grandsire Priam seeks."—
   —So, proceed you.
Polonius   'Fore God, my lord, well spoken, with good accent and good discretion.
   First Player   *"Anon he finds him*
         Striking too short at Greeks...
         ... The instant of clamour that she made—
         Unless things mortal move them not at all—
         Would have made milch the burning eyes of heaven,
         And passion in the gods."...
Polonius [Aside] Look whe'er he has not turned his colour, and has tears in's eyes!—
   [To the First Player] Pray you, no more.

In his aside, while Polonius is speaking of the First Player, who has brought tears to his eyes, he may also be watching Hamlet and perhaps says "Pray you, no more", because he fears that too much emotion may be aroused in the mad Prince. Possibly both have tears in their eyes since Hamlet will shortly speak his Hecuba soliloquy, though in any case Polonius is informing the audience that they have been watching a first-class actor. Now, how is it that Hamlet can know and deliver the speech so well? He later addresses the First Player as "old friend". Is there not a suggestion that he has been coached in it by, and perhaps on occasion acted alongside, these excellent professionals, "the best actors in the world"? He has certainly absorbed some of their skills.

(v)

After speaking to the Ghost, Hamlet immediately sees all the implications of his position:

Hamlet Here, as before, never, so help you mercy,
How strange or odd soe'er I bear myself—
As I, perchance, hereafter shall think meet
To put an antic disposition on—
That you, at such times seeing me, never shall,
With arms encumbered thus, or this headshake,
Or by pronouncing of some doubtful phrase,
As "Well, well, we know", or "We could an if we would",
Or "If we list to speak", "There be, an if they might",
Or such ambiguous giving out, to note
That you know aught of me; this not to do,
So grace and mercy at your most need help you,
Swear.

(I,v,169–181)

The comprehensiveness of Hamlet's instructions to his friends, and their proof of his ability to 'think forward' instantly, hardly bear out the suggestions that he is hesitant by nature or suffering from real madness.

He decides to affect lunacy because, as an Elizabethan, he cannot accept a ghost's story and, as law-student, must first obtain proof of the accusation of murder. The task seems impossible, but from loyalty to his dead father he is ready to devote his whole time to devising a means of proving it. He does not wish to be diverted from his self-imposed task by the King, who will naturally wish to employ him as "our chiefest courtier" (I,ii,117) in such state duties as "the demand of our neglected tribute" from England (III,i,169) and other assignments; he wishes to be left in idleness and solitude for as long as may be necessary.

As law-student he is well aware that if he kills Claudius he cannot possibly cite the Ghost's story as the reason for killing him since he will certainly not be believed. He will be a regicide, and may be "put to the question" to make him reveal his motives and the names of any accomplices or fellow conspirators. However, if he can assume and sustain the appearance of lunacy, he will escape such a fate. He will be confined, perhaps for life, perhaps not; although if he is released after a time, his hopes in life will have vanished. He alone will be the avenger because he alone must be, and no one will ever know why he has killed Claudius.

But what precisely are Hamlet's intentions with respect to his mother?

The Ghost enjoins him to spare her, and repeats the injunction:

Ghost But howsoever thou pursuest this act,

> Taint not thy mind, nor let thy soul contrive
> Against thy mother aught. Leave her to heaven,
> And to those thorns that in her bosom lodge,
> To prick and sting her.
>
> (I,v,84–88)

To what does "thorns" refer? To her guilt over her "o'erhasty" second marriage or to something worse? After the Ghost has left him, his "O most pernicious woman!" indicates the suspicion that has immediately entered his mind. The thought naturally comes to him as law-student that the speed of her second marriage and her happiness in it lay her open to the suspicion of having had a part in the murder, or at least of having been privy to it. Thus although he should spare her, is he to spare her to the point of leaving the suspicion unresolved?

He preserves privacy in one respect: he describes to Horatio the "circumstance...of my father's death" (III,ii,72–73) but not, it seems, the whole of the Ghost's story. It has required him to avenge its murder and to end the "lust and luxury in the royal bed of Denmark". Hamlet would hardly speak of this aspect of his mother's behaviour even to his close and loyal friend. The Gonzago-play turns out to be as much a test of his mother's conscience as of the King's; he only asks Horatio to observe the King during its performance and reserves the task of watching his mother to himself.

To what extent does he wish to keep the whole affair as private as possible? If he is to spare her completely, since the Ghost justifies its injunction when it appears in her closet by describing her as a "weakest body", she must never realise that she has married her first husband's murderer. That thought would horrify her if she were innocent and, being a "weakest body", she may well be innocent. If Hamlet kills Claudius in the character of a lunatic, the world will never know that she has married her first husband's murderer—nor will Gertrude herself—and will never suspect her of complicity. She and all around her will regard her son's lunacy and the loss of her second husband as a double misfortune.

Thus Hamlet instantly sees a number of good reasons for playing the lunatic, and leaving his mother to Heaven should be one of them; but how far does he actually obey the Ghost's injunction?

11
HAMLET'S SOLILOQUIES
(i)

[Hamlet's self-reproaches] ...I cannot but feel, are not meant to hurt him in our opinion, are merely to explain and justify the story. Here we are at the heart and core of the character; and even if Shakespeare had desired it, he could scarcely, on the contemporary stage, have introduced so fundamental an innovation as, in the place of a popular heroic revenger, a procrastinator, lost in thought and weak of will. Thereby he would have both disappointed and bewildered the company and audience he had undertaken to please...

If at any other time [Hamlet] had shown himself a procrastinator, Horatio or Laertes, the King or the Queen, would have said or hinted as much; and by the laws of dramatic technique, both in that day and this, they were under a heavy necessity of saying it, and not the contrary, now...

Whatever may be thought of him, such an heroic but pathetic Hamlet as...I have been presenting, has the advantage over the morbid one of being stage-fit and fairly intelligible, which the psychologists have never made him, and being in keeping with the text, the times and the dramatic tradition and the theatrical favour of two centuries...

E.E.Stoll *Art and Artifice in Shakespeare* 1933

Hamlet's soliloquies are taken as indications of 'character', although they are spoken at different moments in the play and express emotions corresponding to those moments. Hamlet is in one mood when he says, "O that this too, too solid flesh would melt"; in another when he says, "O what a rogue and peasant slave am I"; in another when he says, "To be or not to be". As events cause the play to progress from its initial situation, Hamlet produces responses appropriate to each moment; each soliloquy describes his response, not in order to suggest that he is excessively given to soliloquising, but to inform the audience as to his feelings or intentions at that moment. If the soliloquies tell us anything about Hamlet, it is that he is a young man who, though normally given to action, is frustrated because he cannot act.

The soliloquies can only be correctly interpreted when placed in the play's time-scale. Establishing it offers no difficulty; any indications of the passage of time must be such that the audience can easily catch them as the play's events come and go.

In *Hamlet* they are:
- Hamlet's "A little month" (I,ii,147)
- Ophelia's "Nay, 'tis twice two months, my lord [since your father's death"] (III,ii,120)
- Hamlet's instruction to the Players to put on the Gonzago-play "tomorrow night" (II,ii,513)
- The King's "The sun no sooner shall the mountains touch / But we will ship him hence" (IV,i,29–30)

When the Elder Hamlet is found dead and since the nation must not lack a monarch, an election is held immediately; Claudius wins it before Hamlet can return from Wittenberg and within "a little month" he marries Gertrude; soon afterwards Hamlet says, "O that this too, too solid flesh would melt."

There is no reason to suppose that this soliloquy proceeds from an over-reflective nature, for it expresses a perfectly natural emotion: disgust with his mother's all-too-apparent disloyalty to his dead father. Its style, which is full of exclamations, interjections and broken sentences, shows that it is an outburst and not a meditation. "To be or not to be" is a meditation, but among the soliloquies it is the only quiet meditation. All the others either are or contain outbursts of strong emotion.

The same evening when Hamlet talks to the Ghost, he decides to affect an "antic disposition" in order to be left alone while he ponders its story; after a considerable interval he hits on the Gonzago-play as a means of testing its truth. Thus the elapsed time between his conversation with the Ghost and the Gonzago-play is about two-and-a-half months, allowing about a fortnight between his mother's second marriage and his meeting with the Ghost.

The climactic events of the play take place on three consecutive days, but within a shorter time than three whole days.

On Day One during the afternoon or evening, Rosencrantz and Guildenstern arrive, closely followed by the Players (II,ii). After the First Player has delivered the "rugged Pyrrhus" speeches Hamlet says:

Hamlet Dost thou hear me, old friend; can you play "The Murder of Gonzago"?
First Pl. Ay, my lord.
Hamlet We'll ha't tomorrow night.

(II,ii,510–513)

When all but Hamlet have left the stage, he continues, "O what a rogue and peasant slave am I," in the middle of which he furiously accuses himself of cowardice, although he is no coward:

Hamlet   Am I a coward?
   Who calls me villain? breaks my pate across?
   Plucks off my beard, and blows it in my face? ...
                  ... For it cannot be
   But I am pigeon-livered, and lack gall
   To make oppression bitter.

(II,ii,545–552)

At the beginning of the third act (Day Two) the King asks Rosencrantz and Guildenstern whether they have been able to discover the cause of Hamlet's "turbulent and dangerous" lunacy. They have not, but mention that the Players "already have order / This night to play before him" (III,i,20–21). A little later in the same scene, Hamlet voices his "To be or not to be". This soliloquy is therefore spoken during the morning of Day Two (Rosencrantz and Guildenstern have only a little time in which to attempt to "probe" Hamlet). Again Hamlet accuses himself of cowardice:

Hamlet Thus conscience does make cowards of us all.

(III,i,83)

III,ii begins with Hamlet's speeches on acting, and ends with the presentation of *The Murder of Gonzago*.

After the presentation has come to its sudden end, Hamlet says: " 'Tis now the very witching time of night", i.e. it is now midnight, the traditional time when graves yawn and witches fly. The mood of this soliloquy is black rage:

Hamlet   Now could I drink hot blood?
And do such bitter business as the day
Would quake to look on.

(III,ii,364–366)

Shortly afterwards he steals upon the King at his prayers and says, "Now might I do it" (which, strictly, is an "aside" rather than a soliloquy, Claudius being also present on the stage).

Within the first half-hour of Day Three he kills Polonius; a little later the King hears of the slaying and says:

King The sun no sooner shall the mountains touch
But we will ship him hence.

(IV,i,29–30)

On his way to the ship Hamlet sees Young Fortinbras' army marching by and says "How all occasions do inform against me". Again it contains self-castigation for cowardice:

Hamlet   Now, whether it be
Bestial oblivion, or some craven scruple
Of thinking too precisely on th'event—
A thought which, quartered, hath but one part wisdom
And ever three parts coward—I do not know
Why yet I live to say, "This thing's to do."

(IV,iv,39–44)

In the early hours of Day Three he then takes ship for England.

Thus all the soliloquies except the first are spoken within a time which may be no more than thirty-six hours, from the afternoon of Day One to the early morning of Day Three.

The facts emerging from this study of the time-scale are:
1) Hamlet's simulation of lunacy has gone on for two-and-a-half months, and has been "turbulent and dangerous", "crimeful and capital".
2) All the soliloquies except the first two "O that this too, too solid flesh" and "O all you host of heaven" are spoken within a very short space of time at the end of the two-and-a-half months, during which Hamlet's mood has changed.
3) Except for " 'Tis now the very witching time of night", the later soliloquies all contain the same self-accusation of cowardice; all but "To be or not to be" contain outbursts of strong emotion, and "To be or not to be" obviously stems from acute depression.

Hence Hamlet has not spent his time mooning about the Castle and muttering to himself with a faraway look in his eyes. The "turbulent and dangerous" lunacy, the close spacing of the soliloquies at the end of the two-an-a-half months, and their content, suggest that during the long period of enforced idleness and simulated lunacy, something has been slowly boiling up in Hamlet.

When he steals upon the King at his prayers, he restrains his feelings from boiling over; in his mother's closet he lets them do so, with disastrous effect.

The remaining events of the play take place within an unspecified but relatively brief time, long enough for Hamlet to encounter the pirates and be put ashore, for Laertes to hear of his father's death and return from Paris, for Ophelia to be buried, and for the fencing match.

(ii)

One of the prime aspects of tragedy is the possibility of 'character' becoming changed under the pressure of situations and events, and Hamlet does change; he loses his judgment and even becomes callous; his soliloquies reveal this change. And it must be remembered that they were intended for audiences, not readers; i.e. they had a specific theatrical purpose.

In his first soliloquy he explains why he, a solitary figure in black, is remaining aloof from the general rejoicing over his mother's second marriage. It is anything but a reflective soliloquy, for it is an outburst, the interjections and broken sentences emphasising his difficulty in expressing himself adequately. His emotion is not in the least unnatural; since his father's death and his mother's rapid second marriage are recent and disturbing events in his life, it cannot be taken as typical of him.

His Hecuba soliloquy (II,ii,523–580) is in three parts. It begins with self-castigation:

Hamlet O, what a rogue and peasant slave am I!
   Is it not monstrous, that this player here,
   But in a fiction, in a dream of passion,
   Could force his soul so to his own conceit,
   That from her working, all his visage wanned,
   Tears in his eyes, distraction in's aspect,
   A broken voice and his whole function suiting
   With forms to his conceit? And all for nothing!
   For Hecuba!

The self-castigation develops into a burst of fury, in which there is an element of rage at the fate which has placed him where he is and at which he cannot strike back:

Hamlet   Am I a coward?
   Who calls me villain? breaks my pate across?

Is he (the audience wonders) losing the self-control he has displayed so far? No, he recovers it and rebukes himself for his momentary lapse:

Hamlet Why, what an ass am I! This is most brave,
   That I, the son of a dear father murdered,
   Prompted to my revenge by heaven and hell,
   Must, like a whore, unpack my heart with words,
   And fall a-cursing, like a very drab,
   A stallion.
   Fie upon't! Foh! About, my brain!
[And he forces himself to state his plan calmly:]
                        ... I have heard
   That guilty creatures sitting at a play
   Have by the very cunning of the scene
   Been struck so to the soul that presently
   They have proclaimed their malefactions;
   For murder, though it have no tongue, will speak
   With most miraculous organ. I'll have these Players
   Play something like the murder of my father

>Before mine uncle. I'll observe his looks;
>I'll tent him to the quick. If he but blench,
>I know my course...

The audience have just heard Hamlet request the Players to put on *The Murder of Gonzago*; without this explanation they would not know why, nor would they understand Hamlet's behaviour when it is eventually presented. They now know that they must watch him as well as the King during its performance.

He also reassures his audience that he remains aware of the danger of trafficking with spirits, and of the need for proof of the murder:

Hamlet ...The spirit that I have seen
>May be the devil. And the devil hath power
>T'assume a pleasing shape; yea and perhaps,
>Out of my weakness and my melancholy,
>As he is very potent with such spirits,
>Abuses me to damn me. I'll have grounds
>More relative than this.—The play's the thing
>Wherein I'll catch the conscience of the King.

His next soliloquy, "To be or not to be", follows a similar pattern except that it has no central spasm of rage. Such an outburst would now be out of place, for both the situation and the mood have changed. No doubt generals who have made the dispositions for a battle and are waiting for zero-hour know Hamlet's mood better than anyone else. He has been inspired to put on the Gonzago-play and written the lines which the Players are to study, has yet to rehearse them in their parts, and is now in the waiting-time which must elapse between the planning of a project and its putting into execution. He has nothing to do but to pace the hall, his mind given up to whatever thoughts may come into it.

It is to be noted that he begins by virtually repeating the first three lines of his first soliloquy "O that this too, too solid flesh would melt". Has his mother's "o'erhasty" second marriage to Claudius, whom he dislikes, thrown him into such shock that, though now calmer, he is still in shock? It seems so, for he is so abstracted that for a while he does not see Ophelia (III,i,56ff.):

Hamlet To be, or not to be—that is the question:
>Whether 'tis nobler in the mind to suffer
>The slings and arrows of outrageous fortune,
>Or to take arms against a sea of troubles,
>And by opposing end them?

Some of his audience would now begin to worry about their hero. Is he really contemplating ending his life?—Yet he pulls himself out of his mood again:

Hamlet Thus conscience does make cowards of us all,
>And thus the native hue of resolution
>Is sicklied o'er with the pale cast of thought.

(III,I,83–85)

These lines mean, not "Conscience has inhibited my will to act", but "I must beware lest it do so". They are another brief self-reproach in which he once more assures his audience that he remains firm in his purpose.

He now sees Ophelia, who is apparently so deeply immersed in a religious book that she has not noticed him. He walks over to her, but she does not look up. She is aware that he is there, and he knows that she is aware of him. When two people who are or have been in love enter the same room, each usually knows immediately that the other is there!

She does not wish to speak first. For one thing, he is older than she, and much cleverer; for another, she has been ordered to return his "remembrances", which had become precious to her. After a pause, during which she still does not look up, he says in lines 90–91:

Hamlet   Nymph, in thy orisons
    Be all my sins remembered.

The remark is gently sarcastic, with the emphasis on "my": i.e. if you must remain so intent on your pious exercise, spare a prayer for me!

Forced to answer, she delivers her prepared speech to which he replies, "I never gave you aught", implying that he is no longer the man he was. Ophelia has not realised that his irruption into her closet was a silent farewell, and he is now saying, more forcibly, "For reasons that I cannot explain, we can no longer mean anything to one another." An older mind than hers might suspect something hidden behind his behaviour, as does Claudius, but she does not.

Suddenly he realises that she has been 'planted'. Polonius has his own house (III,i,133), and the normal place for such a devotional exercise would be the privacy of her own chamber. And how does such a young girl[5] come to be in the Castle by herself, apparently unescorted?

He throws a question at her: "Where's your father?" She answers hesitantly, with a transparent lie: "At home, my lord." Now he is sure that they are not alone, begins to rant more wildly for the benefit of the hidden listeners, twice says "Farewell" and goes to the door, and finally rushes out.

Is he more brutal to Ophelia than he needs to be? He seems to feel that he must be cruel to be kind; he is at first gentle, inventing disillusionment with himself; then he begins to rave for the benefit of the eavesdroppers; at the same time. The emotions expressed in his first soliloquy are too strong to be suppressed ("Frailty, thy name is woman!"), and he actually betrays himself with "Those that are married already, all but one, shall live".

On emerging from his hiding-place Claudius, who is shrewd enough not to accept the lunacy at its face value, says thoughtfully "Love! his affections do not that way tend", and decides that Hamlet shall be sent to England for a change of air, but he is just a day too late: Hamlet has already arranged the presentation of the Gonzago-play for that same evening.

Hamlet's other manifestations of lunacy to Polonius, Rosencrantz and Guildenstern, and Claudius, are also deliberate performances in which he exercises his astonishing quick-wittedness, examples of what he admits to his mother is "madness in craft", evidences of his resourcefulness, but in no other way indicative of his true nature, which appears briefly in the graveyard scene at the end of the play.

The soliloquies are dramatic, not lyric or descriptive passages; they have a theatrical purpose; they indicate the changes within Hamlet; they are vehicles for the actor, pauses for explanation which do not interrupt the action, a sort of occasional cadenza in the score of the play: the above being, respectively, self-reproach-rage-recovery, and morbid thoughts—recovery. They are not static indications of character; like musical passages, they have their own internal structure and movement.

---

5   See later, under "Ophelia".

Note:
In full, the time-scale emphasises the spacing of the soliloquies:

ACT I   Duration: 24 hours
I,i   The battlements in the small hours. The Ghost appears.
I,ii   The next morning: council meeting
           SOLILOQUY: "O that this too, too solid flesh would melt":
           "a little month"
I,iii   Polonius' house: departure of Laertes for Paris
I,iv   The battlements again, in the small hours of next morning.
           Hamlet speaks to the Ghost.
           SOLILOQUY: "O all you host of heaven"
           Hamlet's companions are sworn to secrecy.

           (Very long interval of about two and a half months)

ACT II   Duration: one day
II,I   Polonius despatches Reynaldo; Hamlet's silent farewell to Ophelia
II,ii   Arrival of R. and G.; the ambassadors return; Polonius expounds his theory of
           "love" to the King and Queen.
           The Players arrive; Hamlet and the First Player speak the "rugged Pyrrhus"
           speeches. "We'll ha't [the Gonzago-play] tomorrow night."
           SOLILOQUY: "O what a rogue and peasant slave am I."

ACT III   Duration: next morning to just after midnight
III,I   Rosencrantz and Guildenstern: "The Players have order / This night to play
           before him."
           The King and Polonius eavesdrop on Hamlet and Ophelia.
           The soliloquy "To be or not to be."
III,ii   The same evening: The Gonzago-play is presented.
           Ophelia " 'Tis twice two months" [since your father's death].
           The King leaves the play. Hamlet is to go to his mother's closet.
           SOLILOQUY: " 'Tis now the very witching time of night," i.e. it is midnight
           or a little later.
III.iii   Hamlet is to be sent to England. Claudius at prayer:
           SOLILOQUY: "Now might I do it pat."
III,iv   The Queen's closet: Hamlet slays Polonius, then turns Gertrude away from
           Claudius.

           (Very brief interval)

ACT IV   Duration: two to three hours up to the end of IV,iv
IV,I   The King hears of Polonius' death: "It had been so with us had we been there,"
           and "The sun no sooner shall the mountains touch, But we will ship him hence."
IV,ii   Hamlet plays hide and seek with R. and G.
IV,iii   Hamlet sent off to England; the secret commission revealed.
IV,iv   Shortly after dawn: Young Fortinbras' army marches by.

The soliloquy "How all occasions do inform against me."

(An interval of seven to ten days? Duration of the remaining three scenes of this act: two days)

IV,v	Madness of Ophelia. Laertes bursts into the Castle.
IV,vi	Letter arrives for Horatio: Hamlet back in Denmark.
IV,vii	Claudius and Laertes conspire. Letter from Hamlet to King. Ophelia drowned.

(Interval of a day or two)

ACT V	Duration: one day?
V,I	The graveyard: Hamlet shown as his original carefree self
	Ophelia's funeral
	King "An hour of quiet shortly shall we see."
V,ii	Hamlet's account of his sea voyage
	The fencing match

The only question arising from this time-scale is the placing of Hamlet's silent farewell to Ophelia. If his "prophetic soul" has told him that he must give up all his hopes in setting right the "out-of-joint" time, why does he not make his wordless farewell to Ophelia much earlier? Its lateness must suggest that he does not lapse into despair for some time. "To be or not to be", which is spoken shortly afterwards, is then further confirmation of his mood after two-and-a-half months of frustrated idleness.

12

THE MURDER OF GONZAGO
Who wrote the play?

"The scene represented by the Players is in wretched verse."
Anon *Some Remarks on the Character of Hamlet* (1736)

In II,ii, Rosencrantz and Guildenstern enter, whom Hamlet greets with surprise and pleasure:

Hamlet   My excellent good friends! How dost thou, Guildenstern? Ah, Rosencrantz? Good lads, how do ye both?

At first he abandons his antic manner, regarding them as friends whom he can trust; however, Rosencrantz speaks of Hamlet's supposed "ambition", a very superficial diagnosis of his trouble. Then they hesitate to admit that they were sent for. Thereafter he distrusts them, but he picks up "ambition" and later uses it as an excuse for his madness.

They tell him that the Players have arrived, and after a discussion of the state of the theatre in what seems to have been the young people's lingo of the day ("cry out on the top of question", "no money bid for argument"), the Players enter. Hamlet greets them too, as old—even intimate—friends, addressing the First Player as "thou". This perhaps answers the question: how is that they agree to play *The Murder of Gonzago*, with lines by Hamlet, without manifesting any curiosity as to the reason for his request? They are, it seems, as loyal and silent as Horatio. Evidently, Hamlet is loved and respected by all who know him.

It occurs to him that although he can never obtain positive proof of the Ghosts's accusation, he can test it by presenting a facsimile of the murder on the stage and observing the King's reactions. Does any extant play contain such a facsimile? No, but *The Murder of Gonzago* contains the following features:

- There is a poisoning. The victim is probably killed by eating a poisoned dish or drinking poisoned wine; still, it is a poisoning.
- The murderer is nephew to a Duke, not brother of a King; still, the relationship is close enough.
- The murderer afterwards woos and wins the victim's wife—perfect!

So, although the play is not ideally suited to Hamlet's purpose as it stands, it will be after Hamlet has adapted its opening scenes! He therefore takes the First Player aside:

Hamlet   Dost thou hear me, old friend; can you play "The Murder of Gonzago"?
First Pl.   Ay, my lord.
Hamlet   We'll ha't tomorrow night. You could, for a need, study a speech of some dozen or sixteen lines which I would set down and insert in't, could you not?

(II,ii,510–515)

The "dozen or sixteen", necessarily vague because at this point Hamlet does not know exactly how many lines he will write, turns out to be a considerable understatement, for he actually rewrites the whole of the play's opening; in fact the whole of the Gonzago-play which its audience sees.

There are four styles of writing in Hamlet:
1. Shakespeare's own poetic style, almost always in iambic pentameters;
2. various prose styles, in accord with the character of the speaker: for example, compare Osric with the two Clowns;
3. the "rugged Pyrrhus" speeches, an imitation of the highly-charged style affected by some playwrights of the day and Marlowe in particular;
4. the style of the Gonzago-play

Compared with any of the others, its style—if not actually crude—is amateurish and no better than Hamlet's little posy (poem) to Ophelia (II,ii,116–124). It is in jingling rhyming couplets, which are not so well suited to the natural style of acting that Hamlet demands from the Players as blank verse would have been—a mistake on his part.

Before Lucianus enters, there is no passage which reads like an interpolation in an original work. Until he enters, the style is uniformly pedestrian. His six lines are too short for "a dozen or sixteen", are crudely melodramatic, and well below the standard of the "rugged Pyrrhus" speeches, which are presumably representative of the Players' repertory.

As an example of play construction it is very amateurish indeed. The ideal opening of a play rivets the audience's attention immediately, though this opening cannot be called riveting:

Player King Full thirty times hath Phoebus' cart gone round
Neptune's salt wash and Tellus' orbed ground,
And thirty dozen moons with borrowed sheen
About the world have twelve times thirties been,
Since love our hearts, and Hymen did our hands,
Unite commutual in most sacred bands.

(III,ii,143–148)

After thirty lines of repetitive mutual protestations, the Player King delivers an equally repetitive, sententious speech lasting another thirty lines, by the end of which any normal audience would be growing impatient.

The process of exposition has been not so much neglected as almost completely omitted. The Player King and Queen do not say that they are a King and a Queen or where they rule. In the original *Murder of Gonzago*, they are a duke and his duchess. Presumably to ensure that the performance meets his requirements, Hamlet has asked them to wear crowns.

After the Player King has rather suddenly composed himself to sleep, a character enters whose identity and relationship to the first two are unknown to the play's audience. Hamlet has to explain to Ophelia who he is, and who then pours poison into the Player King's ear, for a purpose which would also remain unknown to the audience if Hamlet did not explain it to Ophelia.

Hamlet has made his Player King either very old or very ill; otherwise there would be no reason for his long complaint of his wife's future fickleness. If he is as near his end as he says he is, why should this character trouble to murder him at all? A properly written play would explain the reason for such impatience.

All the sentiments expressed in this opening are Hamlet's own. The Player King's long speech is the expression of Hamlet's sadness that his heroic father has so soon been forgotten: "For, look you, how cheerfully my mother looks, and my father died within's two hours" and "Die two months ago and not forgotten yet?" (III,ii,118–123).

The Player Queen says:

Pl. Q.   The instances that second marriage move
    Are base respects of thrift and not of love.

(III,ii,170–171)

It can hardly be coincidence that these lines echo Hamlet's earlier bitter comment to Horatio:

Hamlet   Thrift, thrift, Horatio!—the funeral baked meats
    Did coldly furnish forth the marriage tables.

(I,ii,179–180)

The Dumb-show echoes Hamlet's "Why, she would hang on him / As if increase of appetite had grown / By what it fed on":

> [Enter a KING and a QUEEN very lovingly; the QUEEN embracing him and he her. She kneels, and makes show of protestation unto him. He takes her up, and declines his head upon her neck...]

In Hamlet's first speech after the Ghost has left him, there is a significant but small break in the rhythm of the pentameters:

Hamlet   Remember thee!...
    ...Yea, from the table of my memory
    I'll wipe away all trivial fond records,
    All saws of books, all forms, all pressures past,
    That youth and observation copied there;
    And thy commandment all alone shall live
    Within the book and volume of my brain,
    Unmixed with baser matter. Yea, by heaven!

(I,v,95ff.)

He pauses because a horrifying thought has struck him. Was his mother privy to the murder? Did she not marry his uncle with suspicious speed? At least she has laid herself open to the accusation. He continues:

O most pernicious woman!

Then, realising that if she had been a party to the murder it would have been Claudius who set her on, he explodes in fury.

O villain, villain; smiling, damned villain!

Gertrude is altogether too happy with her new husband—why else would the Ghost have complained of the "luxury" in the Royal bed of Denmark?—And Hamlet decides, as he writes his play, that he must test his mother's conscience as well as the King's. He therefore gives the Player Queen lines which will twice test Gertrude:

Hamlet   In second husband let me be accurst!
    None wed the second but who killed the first!

Pl. Q.   A second time I kill my husband dead
    When second husband kisses me in bed...

(III,ii, 167–8 and 171–172)

He will be watching Gertrude and Claudius very closely as these lines are spoken, for they may both "blench". When it is over, he says exultantly:

Hamlet Would not this... get me a fellowship in a cry of players, sir?
Horatio   Half a share.
Hamlet A whole one, I.

(III,ii,259–264)

The owners or lessees of the theatre and the playwrights, managers and principal actors in a theatre company were called the Sharers because they shared the receipts, expenses, and profits. Hamlet's claim to a whole share can only mean that he himself wrote the play and directed the performance!

(ii) Hamlet on the art of acting

The stage direction at the beginning of III,ii reads *"[Enter Hamlet and two or three of the Players]"*, which is followed by three long speeches from Hamlet on acting.

These speeches read as if Shakespeare was taking the opportunity to air his own views on the subject. Although he was, they are not in the play for that reason alone.

Hamlet And let those that play your clowns speak no more than is set down for them. For there be of them that will themselves laugh to set on some quantity of barren spectators to laugh too; though in the meantime some necessary question of the play be then to be considered...

If the speeches merely represented Shakespeare's own views, they would be an interruption at this particular moment of exactly the kind which he found objectionable, and it is therefore necessary to determine how they are related to the dramatic situation at this point.

The Players, who enter, of whom three appear in the play, are those who will speak the all-important lines that Hamlet has written. And it is clear that Hamlet has just finished rehearsing them.

He has written their lines and handed them to the First Player for them all to study; then he has called them to rehearsal to ensure that they know their lines and to direct them in their movements for he will only have this one chance to test the King's conscience. It is utterly out of the question that the King will allow the play to be presented a second time. There is no other way of testing him.

And they must play it in as natural a manner as possible. Any rhetoric, histrionics, or other affectation will come between the King and what he is seeing; naturalness offers the best hope of inducing him to forget that he is watching actors and to lose himself in the performance to the point where he betrays himself:

Hamlet Be not too tame, neither, but let your own discretion be your tutor. Suit the action to the word, the word to the action; with this special observance, that you o'erstep not the modesty of nature. For anything so overdone is from the purpose of playing, whose end, both at the first and now, was and is, to hold as 'twere the mirror up to nature.

(III,ii,16–21)

Hamlet cannot confide the intention behind this advice to the Players. He can only give them what appears to be a long disquisition on the art of acting, but is actually a betrayal of his anxiety that they 'get it right on the night.' And the night which will end his two-and-a-half months' wait is now only a few moments away; the rehearsals must have taken most of the afternoon and evening.

What is now the time of day?

At the end of the performance, Hamlet, left alone, will begin his brief soliloquy with " 'Tis now the very witching time of night", i.e. it will then be midnight. Since the whole scene does not take an hour, the Gonzago-play does not begin till after eleven o'clock in the evening. As it is getting dark outside, the King will call "Give me some light!" when he walks out of the play.

And what time of year is it?

Summer.

Elsinore lies at the same latitude as Central Scotland, where, on clear summer evenings, there remains a band of light in the western sky at midnight. Thus Polonius and Hamlet can still make out the outline of the cloud which is "very like a whale".

In summer, dawn comes early at those latitudes. The events of the play are now approaching their climax; between the beginning of this scene and Hamlet's departure for England, when the sun will be just touching the mountains, the action occupies only a few hours and is virtually continuous.

(iii) The Triple Sequence.

Hamlet, then, has written his play with two purposes instead of one. The Ghost had said:

Ghost But, howsoever thou pursuest this act,
Taint not thy mind, nor let thy soul contrive
Against thy mother aught. Leave her to heaven,
And to those thorns that in her bosom lodge,
To prick and sting her.

(I,v,84–88)

On the face of things, Hamlet has retained his scepticism with respect to the Ghost's story, but his disgust with his mother's happiness in her new marriage, his dislike of the uncle who has become his stepfather and whom in his heart he believes to be his father's murderer, and his suspicion of his mother, have caused him either to forget the Ghost's solemn injunction or to ignore it. He has certainly decided to ensure that any "thorns" are sharp, and, as he well knows, such needling of Gertrude will needle Claudius also. He has therefore made the Player Queen protest her eternal fidelity at some length; yet in doing so has jeopardized his plan.

Possibly he could not have avoided all reference to the Royal marriage, but he has overdone the Player Queen's protestations to the point where they, as well as the murder scene, constitute a gross and treasonable slander on the Royal couple: further, since the nation is under threat from Young Fortinbras, a slander at absolutely the wrong moment.

What if the King recognises the slander, decides that he will sit through no more of it, and rises and leaves before the all-important poisoning scene is reached? Will his reason for leaving be a disturbed conscience or simply anger? What if he is innocent, sits through the poisoning scene, and then leaves because he is angry? He is unlikely to tolerate more of such a play.

Hamlet has three strings to his bow: the Dumbshow, the Prologue, and the play itself, which will give him and Horatio three chances to observe the King for signs of "blenching". Hamlet does not expect anything more than "blenching"; his quarry is shrewd and tough, and must be observed "even with the very comment of thy soul". The three-fold sequence will exert a steadily increasing pressure on his man, for if the King leaves after the Dumbshow he will have given himself away immediately. He cannot leave after the Prologue either; he will have to sit through all three, while it is borne in upon him ever more strongly that his murder has somehow become known.

Such is Hamlet's plan.

While he intends the depiction of the murder to be the climactic episode, he both forewarns the King and gives him excellent reasons for rising and leaving before it comes. Not that the King does; he waits in order to confirm his increasing suspicions of what is in his supposedly lunatic nephew's mind. He will be pricking up his ears as early as the play's twenty-sixth line: "None wed the second but who killed the first!"

Chairs have been placed in arcs facing the stage. The King and Queen enter and take their seats at its centre, the courtiers on either side and behind. The King asks, "How fares my cousin Hamlet?" Suspecting that Rosencrantz and Guildenstern will have suggested to the King that the cause of his madness might be frustrated ambition, Hamlet plays up to this with "I eat the air, promise-crammed."

The Queen calls: "Come hither, my dear Hamlet, and sit by me." This will not do. If Hamlet sits beside her, the King—who is on her other side—will not be visible to him; and even if he were, Hamlet could hardly stare at him throughout the performance from such a position. So, seeing Ophelia sitting near one end of the arc, he replies, "No, dear mother, here's 'metal' more attractive," and lies on the floor in front of her. Sometimes he looks back at her as he talks and sometimes not. Meanwhile, Horatio has quietly stationed himself at the opposite end of the arc.

The Dumbshow is performed. Do the King and queen watch it?

When the performance of the play is well advanced the King later asks, "Have you heard the argument? Is there no offence in't?" and Hamlet replies, "You shall see anon," and repeats the phrase after the poisoning scene. If the King had watched the Dumbshow, he would have known very well what offence there was in it.

Shakespeare is explicit at such moments. If Hamlet was not expecting the Dumbshow and feared that his trap might be sprung prematurely, he would say as much in an 'aside'. He remains silent throughout its performance, only speaking when Ophelia speaks.

Dumbshows are for spectators who are uneducated or unaccustomed to plays. The King and Queen are neither and do not need to watch it, during which the King spends the time discussing Hamlet's madness with her and Polonius.

Prologue[6] now enters, waits for Hamlet and Ophelia to stop talking, and then says three short lines before bowing himself off the stage. Hamlet is surprised and disconcerted: "Is this a prologue or the posy of a ring?"[7]

The play itself begins at last. Hamlet remains silent for a time; then, because of the failure of the first two stages of his scheme, decides to reinforce its effect by interpolating 'explanatory' comments to Ophelia loudly enough to be heard by the King and Queen. Nothing unusual about this; Elizabethan audiences were by no means as silent as modern

---

6   The stage direction in Q2 before III,ii reads "Enter Hamlet and three of the Players". Only three Players are needed for as much of the Gonzago-play as is acted; the Player King and Queen have the main parts; the third Player will be Prologue and Lucianus.

7   A short motto inside a ring-band

ones. And perhaps Hamlet realises that his play, being almost devoid of exposition, needs such explanations.

The Player King reveals that he is not far from his latter end; the Player Queen protests eternal fidelity to his memory and Hamlet notes that Gertrude is beginning to fidget a little, for he mutters "Wormwood, wormwood!"[8] The Player King delivers his interminable thirty lines on the inconstancy of our purposes and the waywardness of fortune, to which the Player Queen replies III,ii,204ff.:

Pl. Q. Nor earth to give me food, nor heaven light!
Sport and repose lock from me day and night!
To desperation turn my trust and hope!
An anchor's cheer in prison be my scope!
Each opposite that blanks the face of joy
Meet what I would have well, and it destroy!
Both here and hence pursue me lasting strife
If, once a widow, ever I be wife!
Hamlet [Loudly to Ophelia, but with his eyes on the Queen]
If she should break it now!
Pl. King 'Tis deeply sworn. Sweet, leave me here awhile;
My spirits grow dull, and fain I would beguile
The tedious day with sleep.
Pl. Q. Sleep rock thy brain;
And never come mischance between us twain! *[Exit.]*
Hamlet [Needling the Queen] Madam, how like you this play?
Queen [Hesitantly] The lady doth protest too much, methinks.
Hamlet O, but she'll keep her word.
King [Intervening; he does not like this conversation; he knows that "our o'erhasty marriage" makes Gertrude an easy target and that she cannot defend herself against her son.]
Have you heard the argument? Is there no offence in't?
Hamlet No, no; they do but jest, poison in jest; no offence i'th' world.

This is the first mention of poison, introduced by Hamlet as a psychological pinprick after the failure of the Dumbshow and Prologue. Does the King blench? It seems not, for he continues:

King What do you call the play?
Hamlet "The Mousetrap."...
[This remark is offensive enough, Gertrude being an extremely submissive woman, and the more so because it comes from her own son, but Hamlet continues in the same vein of concealed sarcasm:]
...Marry, how? Tropically. This play is the image of a murder done in Vienna; Gonzago is the duke's name; his wife, Baptista. You shall see anon; 'tis a knavish piece of work; but what o'that? Your majesty, and we that have free souls, it touches us not; let the galled jade wince, our withers are unwrung.
[Too long an explanation, this, for the King now begins to anticipate what is coming.]

---

8   A bitter-tasting herb, once widely used to expel internal worms!

A Player as Lucianus enters, and Hamlet explains to Ophelia that he is "nephew to the king," although he has just said that Gonzago is a duke: either a slip of the tongue or an apparent slip which is intended to needle the King, but in either case it further alerts him. And it seems that the Player has either forgotten or chosen to ignore Hamlet's injunction to "play it naturally", for Hamlet interrupts his talk with Ophelia to exclaim angrily:

Hamlet [to the Player] So you mis-take your husbands.—Begin, murderer; pox, leave thy damnable faces and begin! ...

[Despite the lapse of "murderer" again revealing his knowledge of the play, he continues:]

...Come, the croaking raven doth bellow for revenge!

(III,ii,239)

This is no doubt spoken with a wild leer, but, being a veiled threat, is equally a lapse; the King is now fully alert.

Lucianus has not forgotten Hamlet's instructions. Since the audience could not be left watching the Player King slumbering for as much as a minute, he would normally have entered very soon after the Player Queen's "Sleep rock thy brain". The talk between Hamlet, Gertrude and Claudius has delayed his entry. Playing before the Court, he would not dare to interrupt royalty, least of all his temporary patron Hamlet.

So he enters in the natural pause after "Our withers are unwrung", only to find that Hamlet has again begun chit-chatting with Ophelia. Now that he is on the stage, what is he to do? He cannot shout Hamlet down; he can only ad-lib with wordless histrionics until Hamlet vouchsafes him some silence:

Luc. Thoughts black, hands apt, drugs fit and time agreeing;
Confederate season, else no creature seeing;
Thou mixture rank, of midnight weeds collected,
With Hecate's ban thrice blasted, thrice infected,
Thy natural magic and dire property
On wholesome life usurp immediately.

[He pours the poison into the King's ear.]

Hamlet [Loudly to Ophelia, but watching the King] He poisons him in the garden for's estate. His name's Gonzago. The story is extant and written in choice Italian; you shall see anon how the murderer gets the love of Gonzago's wife.

For the King, this is the last straw. He rises and the Queen with him; he is so overcome that she anxiously asks, "How fares my lord?" Polonius calls out "Give o'er the play," and the King demands "Some light" as he leaves with the Queen on his arm; all take up the cry, "Lights, lights, lights!"

Hamlet is grimly jubilant:

Hamlet O good Horatio, I'll take the Ghost's word for a thousand pound. Didst perceive?
Horatio Very well, my lord.
Hamlet Upon the talk of the poisoning?
Horatio I did very well note him.

Upon what talk? The King had actually risen, not upon seeing Lucianus perform the murder, but after hearing Hamlet's loud explanation to Ophelia, which is heard by everyone and in effect accuses him before his whole court of having murdered his brother and won the love of his brother's wife. He cannot possibly watch any more of such a scurrilous thing; further, he will now have to come to a decision as to what to do with this lunatic Prince and it will have to be drastic.

And what have Hamlet and Horatio perceived? A change of expression on the King's face, certainly, and of what kind? Might it not be mainly, perhaps even wholly, rage at the slander and the implied accusation? How can they be sure that there was remorse or guilt in it? In a few moments Guildenstern will describe the King as being, very naturally, "marvellous distempered with choler," and the Queen as "in most great affliction of spirit".

To Hamlet, his play has achieved its purpose; in fact it has achieved too much.

13

THE MURDER OF GONZAGO (CONT'D)

Notes:

At this point I imagine the reader saying, "You have argued that one of Hamlet's reasons for playing the lunatic might be to protect his mother, although he lets fall no explicit hint to that effect. Well, perhaps it does not need proving that a young man would instinctively want to protect his mother. Yet in arguing that he writes the whole Gonzago-play, you are also saying that he decides to test his mother's conscience in public!" Such a comment would suggest confusion on my part, but it is Hamlet who is confused.

He knows how the Court will react to a play which slanders the reigning monarch; being a Prince, he could hardly fail to know.

Who wrote the play may have been realised, for his loud comments to Ophelia will have given him away and, if he did not write it, he chose it; he is known to be fond of the theatre. Since his lunacy has long been an acute problem, it will hardly have gone unnoticed that he rehearsed the Players. All the same, no one will take the implied accusation of murder seriously, coming as it does from a lunatic. No one in the Court suspects, now or later, that there ever was a Ghost.

On the other hand, the slanderous and treasonable satire, implying that Claudius has usurped the crown by murder, is taken very seriously indeed because the monarchy is elective: Claudius must protect his political position. Also, the country has been in danger from Young Fortinbras and is still in danger from the Polack, and is rearming itself under Claudius' direction, i.e. the stability of his position is as important to his country as to himself. In spite of his oath, the threat from Young Fortinbras remains, for it is always dangerous to allow a foreign army on to one's own soil, particularly of mercenaries, i.e. "lawless resolutes" who owe allegiance to no one except the leader who pays them. And what if Young Fortinbras, returning victorious past Elsinore, elects to ignore his oath, seize the opportunity, and grab Denmark for himself?

Polonius calls the play "a prank too broad to bear with," arranges to listen behind the arras in the Queen's closet, and urges her to be "round with him". Rosencrantz and Guildenstern express the court's shock in their speeches at the beginning of III,iii: the monarchy must not be attacked in this way.

Hence, although the test of the two consciences is apparently given in public, Hamlet knows that it will only be fully understood by him. The attention of the Court will be wholly on the play's implied slanders. Even Horatio may not understand the test of Gertrude's conscience. As pointed out earlier, Hamlet only tells Horatio "the circumstance of my father's death" (III,ii,73) and does not ask him to observe both Gertrude and Claudius. Doubtless Horatio, being a law-student, naturally suspects Gertrude's complicity in the murder; if he does, he keeps the thought to himself.

That his mother is very much in Hamlet's thoughts is shown by his first soliloquy and by his harangue to her in her closet. And he knows that she is a "weakest body". The name "The Mousetrap" which he gives to his play is usually taken as referring to his intention of catching the King's conscience, though it actually refers to Gertrude, "mouse" being a term of endearment to one's lady-love:

Hamlet [To Gertrude in her closet]
   Let the bloat King...call you his mouse.

(III,iv,183–184)

The ambassador scenes display Claudius as an authoritative and capable monarch; he is no mouse. "Mousetrap" is double-edged: it refers to Hamlet's intention of catching the Queen's conscience as well as the King's, and to the ease with which Claudius caught the "weakest" Gertrude so soon after her first husband's death.

Hamlet is indeed confused to the point where he forgets the Ghost's "Leave her to heaven." The decision to test both consciences turns out to be a mistake. Claudius is given too many hints as to what the play is leading up to, and at the end knows that Hamlet is his bitterest enemy, whether truly lunatic or not (and the King has his doubts). Hamlet should have written scenes which contained no reference to his mother's sudden switching of her affections from one husband to the next, and at the end of which the murder came suddenly upon an unprepared King. He should have refrained from needling either the King or the Queen with his comments to Ophelia; there would then have been no satire to shock the court; to no one but Hamlet, Horatio and Claudius, would the murder scene have been anything but another stage murder. Claudius would have had no obvious reason to take action against Hamlet. As it is, the Gonzago-play turns out to be a series of prods with a blunt stick instead of the single sharp prick which might have goaded Claudius' conscience into the trap set for it.

When Claudius prays in III,iii, he refers to the prizes he has won by his murder, "My crown, mine own ambition, and my queen," from which it might be inferred that they are equally important to him. He also admits his guilt but, before the soliloquy, the Elizabethan spectators would have realised that for more reasons than one, Claudius could no longer afford to leave Hamlet at large.

To what extent does Hamlet realise, or even care, that his play is a political attack on Claudius at a time when the nation is under threat from Young Fortinbras? Since he is a Prince, he must know very well that it is, and since he dislikes his stepfather he might be willing to attack him in any way. His only openly stated intention (to Horatio) is to prove Claudius' guilt or innocence—but he tests his mother as well. Is the political attack another unstated intention?

Being highly confused, he does not care, although he certainly should. What if Claudius is innocent and sits through the entire play; what will Hamlet's position then be? Nominally, he remains aware that Claudius may be innocent. He does not seem to care that if he is, the play will have grossly and gratuitously offended him, and will compel him to take strong action against his mad nephew. It will certainly be impossible for Hamlet to remain "our chiefest courtier". The lines "The time is out of joint.—O cursed spite / That ever I was born to set it right!" suggest that, being faced with the loss of all his hopes, Hamlet has become indifferent to what offence he may give.

In *What Happens In Hamlet,* Dover Wilson (1959) argues that Hamlet is not expecting the Dumbshow, is consternated when it threatens to spring his trap prematurely, and is relieved when the Prologue turns out to be a mere "posy".

I have taken the opposite view.

The Dumbshow begins:

   [Enter a KING and a QUEEN very lovingly; the Queen embracing him, and he her. She kneels, and makes show of protestation unto him. He takes her up, and

declines his head upon her neck; lays him down upon a bank of flowers; she, seeing him asleep, leaves him. Anon comes in a fellow, takes off his crown, kisses it, pours poison in the KING's ears, and exit...]

While the stage performance ends at this point, the description of the Dumbshow does not:

[...The QUEEN returns, finds the KING dead, and makes passionate action. The POISONER, with some two or three MUTES, comes in again, seeming to lament with her. The dead body is carried away. The POISONER woos the Queen with gifts; she seems loth and unwilling awhile, but in the end accepts his love.]

This second part evidently covers a continuation of the first act of *The Murder of Gonzago*, which confirms Hamlet's confusion. If, as was concluded earlier, Hamlet writes as much of the Gonzago-play as is acted; and if, as was also concluded, the Dumbshow is part of his plan, either such a continuation already exists in the original or, more probably, he also writes both the beginning and an unacted continuation of the play after the poisoning scene. Why else would Hamlet say "You shall see anon," after both the Dumb-show and the poisoning scene?

His emotions have swamped his judgment, for the continuation is a prolongation of the satire on his mother's "o'erhasty marriage". He is aware that Claudius may be innocent of the murder, in which case the Queen will also be innocent. Yet he has created a long satire which includes considerably more than his stated intention of testing Claudius' conscience: so much more, in fact, as to make it impossible for him to determine the precise nature of Claudius' reactions to it. Claudius, who will be concerned to protect the Queen as well as himself, will be justified in rising and leaving before the poisoning is reached, in which case Hamlet and Horatio will not be able to decide exactly why he has left the play; or, if he is innocent, he may sit unmoved through the poisoning scene. However, to judge by the second part of the Dumbshow, Hamlet is ensuring that if he does leave, the marriage will be further satirised and the Queen's conscience further needled.

Clearly, his mother's early second marriage is as much on Hamlet's mind as the murder of his father—perhaps more. It appears, in fact, to be the cause of his loss of judgment. Why, after Lucianus has poured the poison into the sleeper's ear, does Hamlet say, "You shall see anon how the murderer gets the love of Gonzago's wife," and not "gets the throne and the love of Gonzago's wife"; and at the end of the play, as he stabs Claudius, "Follow my mother", not "Follow my father and my mother"? Such was Shakespeare's care over detail that these would not have been small inconsistencies in his writing.

No doubt while Hamlet is also swayed by his "prophetic soul," it is his disgust with his mother's happiness in her all-too-early second marriage and his dislike of the uncle who has become his stepfather which have caused him to cease to care and to lose his judgment.

"To be or not to be" appears to have been more responsible than any other soliloquy for the notion that Hamlet is excessively given to reflection; yet it stems from an emotional cause, with depression so acute that his thoughts dwell on suicide. Now such depression is almost by definition abnormal in any person suffering from it (how many people debate the pros and cons of suicide as a habit?): why, then, should it ever have been considered normal in Hamlet?

The soliloquy is spoken some hours before the presentation of the Gonzago-play, when Hamlet has nothing to do but wait. What if the evening's performance convinces him that his mother is as guilty as his uncle? What is he to do in that case? Is it a matter for censure or even surprise that his thoughts dwell briefly on suicide?

At the end of IV,iii, Claudius reveals that his secret commission requires the "present death" of Hamlet on his arrival in England. How would Shakespeare's audiences react to this revelation?

Courts were extremely sensitive to criticism. In 1605 the comedy *Eastward Ho!* by Chapman, Jonson and Marston (1605) was put on by the Children of the Queen's Revels. It contained two mildly sarcastic comments on King James' Scottish followers for which, although very brief, the three playwrights were sentenced to prison.[9]

By comparison with *Eastward Ho!* the Gonzago-play is a knife-thrust into both Claudius and Gertrude, and a double knife-thrust into Claudius. It is both a political and a personal attack on him at a time when Denmark is in potential or actual danger from Young Fortinbras and the Polack. The situation needs firm guidance from the top, i.e. it is treasonable for more reasons than one.

While the groundlings among the audiences would probably have seen Claudius merely as the villain of the piece who has just confessed to his murder, those who remembered the Anti-slander Acts, and the dramatic import of the ambassador scenes, would not be very surprised by his decision to send Hamlet to England for, apparently, "thine especial safety". They would know that in putting on the Gonzago-play Hamlet was risking severe punishment, and that his accidental slaying of Polonius was an attempt at regicide and therefore high treason, meriting the most severe of penalties.

On hearing that Hamlet is to be secretly executed in England (secretly because he is a popular Prince), they would know that Claudius' decision stems partly from private impulses: self-defence and retaliation. He should be having Hamlet examined and confined as a lunatic and is therefore "buying out" the law. Hamlet has also given him considerable public justification for it by his slander and his attempt at regicide. He must correct his earlier leniency towards Hamlet, and correct it drastically.

In *What Happens in 'Hamlet'*, Dover Wilson argues that the King and Queen do not watch the Dumbshow because they are discussing the cause of Hamlet's madness.

In his *Shakespeare and the Popular Dramatic Tradition*, Samuel.L.Bethel (1948) disagrees:

> Let the actors be the most subtle and intelligent in the world, how, without the use of dialogue, and while the Dumbshow is actually focussing the main attention, may they indicate that they are discussing whether Hamlet's madness originated in frustrated love or frustrated ambition? I submit that the feat is impossible.

In fact, nothing could be easier than to mime the discussion. When Hamlet lies down before Ophelia, Polonius says to the King, "O ho! Do you mark that?" (which comment alone suggests that Dover Wilson is correct), and draws the King's attention by pointing to them. The King looks round, watches them for a moment or two, and then turns back to Polonius, who is now pointing to himself with a pleased expression as if to say, "Does it not look as if my theory of love is correct?" The King, who has already said, "Love! his affections do not

---

[9] The comments are given at the end of Chap.23: "A Comparison of the First and Second Quartos of 'Hamlet'".

that way tend", looks thoughtful, perhaps shakes his head; the Queen contributes a remark or two to their inaudible discussion. Since the cause of Hamlet's madness is of far greater interest to them than any play, they continue until Prologue appears and interrupts them with speech from the stage; so the Dumbshow passes without their seeing it. For this reason the King later asks Hamlet, "Have you seen the argument?" in which the emphasis will be on "you".

Dover Wilson argues that Hamlet does not want the Dumbshow from his comment on "inexplicable dumb-shows". Among dumb-shows I have read, those before the acts in Norton and Sackvilles' *Gorboduc* (1561) are symbolic displays, their symbolism being explained in their descriptions. The Dumbshow towards the end of *The Spanish Tragedy* is also symbolic. Whether Elizabethan audiences would have understood their symbolism is open to question as Hamlet might well describe them as "inexplicable". Those in John Marston's *Antonio's Revenge* (1600) are preliminary explanatory displays; those in *Pericles* are actually additional episodes in the action which are mimed instead of spoken. Thus the Gonzago-play's dumb-show, a straightforward miming of the plot, may have been exceptional among Elizabethan dumb-shows in not being "inexplicable", and probably so by Hamlet's, i.e. Shakespeare's, intention.[10]

Hamlet's many comments on the theatre and the art of acting serve to explain to the audience why Hamlet can carry off his simulation of lunacy so well, but they amount to much more than are dramatically necessary. Why is so much of the talk of the theatre inserted when it is irrelevant to the action and the situation, and uninformative as to 'character'? The account of the Children's Theatres could be dispensed with; it explains why the Players have taken to the road. They could equally well have been asked to play before the Court as a diversion for the mad Hamlet. His exhortation to the Players to "play it naturally" is longer and more detailed than is necessary, as is his speech preceding the first part of the "rugged Pyrrhus" extract. The First Player's continuation of the speech, over three times as long, contributes nothing to the progress of the action or the elucidation of the situation at that point. The First Player's virtuoso performance of it gives rise to the "Hecuba" soliloquy, and Hamlet's reasons for requesting it are again longer and more detailed than is necessary.

Examination of Hamlet's comments suggests that Shakespeare was voicing his own views on the types of play his competitors were writing, their verse style, the prevalent style of acting, and the audiences. He put them into the mouth of his much-admired hero, whose taste in such matters was, by implication, "judicious":

Hamlet I heard thee speak me a speech once—but it was never acted; or, if it was, not above once; for the play, I remember, pleased not the million; 'twas caviare to the general. But it was, as I received it—and others, whose judgements in such matters cried in the top of mine—an excellent play, well digested in the scenes, set down with as much modesty cunning. I remember, one said there were no sallets in the lines to make the matter savoury, nor no matter in the phrase which might indict the author of affection, but called it an honest method, as wholesome as sweet, and by very much more handsome than fine.

(II,ii,411–421)

Shakespeare was complaining of the inability of his audiences to appreciate his plays,

---

10   Perhaps dumb shows and prologues were more common preambles to plays than we now suppose, which the printed quartos and folios do not contain. These were aimed at literate theatregoers who would not need them.

which were better constructed, better "digested in the scenes", subtler and, in consequence, quieter "set down with as much modesty as cunning", and written in a style which was free of "sallets" and "affection", "as wholesome as sweet and by very much more handsome than fine": direct yet elegant; not affected or over-refined).[11] The style of acting suited to them required that the actor "acquire and beget a temperance that may give it "smoothness"; he must not "tear a passion to tatters" but should "hold the mirror up to nature". Unfortunately, the groundlings were "capable of nothing but inexplicable dumb-shows and noise", i.e. they were simple-minded, since they apparently needed dumb-shows to explain the action beforehand, and were too easily impressed by bombast from the stage.

Evidently, Shakespeare's plays "pleased not the million" and were "caviare to the general"; perhaps they were not being as well supported as he felt they ought to be. That the play from which the "rugged Pyrrhus" speeches were taken, and which Hamlet so much admired, "was never acted, or, if it was, not above once", suggests that Shakespeare's quieter but richer style was not producing as many repeat performances of his plays as he could wish.

The flowering of the Elizabethan drama had begun only about fifteen years earlier. It seems also likely that Marlowe's early plays had established in the groundlings a taste for his long ranting speech: *Tamburlaine* has several forty-line speeches; his longest goes on for sixty lines. So Shakespeare chose a passage from what was apparently a popular play, Marlowe's *The Tragedy of Dido* (c.1594), and paraphrased it in such a way as to bring out the pathos of the episode more eloquently than its author, and in a style which comes nearer to being dramatic than the epic or narrative style of the original. Being briefer, Shakespeare's version is at least less of an interruption to the action. His actor, who could put on "distraction in's aspect", make "all his visage wanned", speak with a broken voice, and bring tears to his eyes, obtained the required effect without imitating the town crier, sawing the air with his hand, or otherwise tearing the passion to very rags.

Charles Lamb in his essay *On the Tragedies of Shakespeare* (1811) commented that the attention of the spectators is necessarily on what they see and hear on the stage, and that the actor's stage presence may distract attention from what Lamb calls the intellectual power of such characters as Hamlet, Macbeth, and Lear; the words of an inferior playwright would then serve as well as Shakespeare's to produce the required dramatic effect. Shakespeare's characters were being overplayed: "The practice of stage representation reduces everything to a controversy of elocution". He was wondering whether Shakespeare's plays should be read rather than acted, although Shakespeare himself would hardly have agreed with the suggestion. He does not appear to have noticed that Shakespeare had already complained of the "controversy of elocution" in his comments in *Hamlet*.

The comments of Lamb and Shakespeare might have been expressed in another way.

The most impressive actors and actresses are those who can project presence, which requires the projection less of physical than of intellectual presence, physical stature being less important than the suggestion of the mind behind the speaker's face, an ability possessed by all the greatest actors. 'Mind' implies width and depth of comprehension and the habit of controlled, disciplined thinking, whereas a ranting delivery negates the impression of self-control and may distract the hearer. Conveying the impression of intellectual grasp behind the words, or of the words being the product of thought, requires a quality of stillness which

---

11　　In the last act, Osric's style in speech—and Hamlet's improvement on it—may illustrate what Shakespeare meant by "fine". See again the end of Chapter 6.

does not exclude, and may even emphasise, emotional or intellectual power in the speaker. An overacted, over-emotional delivery swamps the suggestion of controlled intellect that is necessary for presence.

This, we may take it, is what Shakespeare meant when he made Hamlet urge the Players to "use all gently", to "acquire and beget a temperance which may give [your passion] smoothness".

Some of the speeches in Marlowe's plays might well have been written to be 'ranted'. Shakespeare's version of the passage from *Dido Queen of Carthage* is more compressed then the original and the words say it all, i.e. they suffice in themselves both to describe the event and to convey the emotion in the speaker.

Incidentally, in *A Midsummer Night's Dream*, Shakespeare had registered his amusement at the efforts of some amateur theatrical groups. In *Hamlet*, did the Gonzago-play indicate his opinion of the kind of thing that amateur playwrights were likely to turn out or actually had?

And did Shakespeare's fellow playwrights take his hints? In his essay *The Relations of Hamlet to Contemporary Revenge Plays* (1902), Professor Thorndike states that between about 1599 and 1604 "tragedies dealing with ghosts and revenge were especially popular in the London theatres", the genre having its origin in Kyd's *The Spanish Tragedy* and the Ur–Hamlet[12]. Many of the plays, which were written by minor playwrights for the 'market', have been lost, but a comparison of some which have survived (such as Marston's *Antonio's Revenge* (1600), and Henry Chettle's *Hoffman* (1631), both of them merely revenge-rant-and-gore) with those written after *Hamlet* shows a distinct improvement in quality. The theatre's blossoming continued after its early spring of the 1590s, and the hints in *Hamlet* may well have been read, marked, and inwardly digested. Lamb, who claimed to be the first "to draw the Public's attention to the old English Dramatists" and who was particularly fond of Beaumont and Fletcher, published a volume of old plays; he was concerned to show "how much of Shakespeare shines in the great men his contemporaries." In fact, Shakespeare owed a great deal to his contemporaries in respect of plot elements which had become conventional, particularly in revenge-tragedies; however, his plays may have raised the tastes of his audiences.

Shakespeare also put in a plea for the status of his fellow theatricals, who were classed as "rogues and vagabonds" unless their company had a noble patron (II,ii,497–501):

> *Hamlet* Good my lord, will you see the Players well bestowed? Do you hear, let them be well used, for they are the abstract and brief chronicles of the time. After your death you had better have a bad epitaph than their ill report while you live.

He may even have tried to convey a hint to his spectators. As there are only three Players, the third Player will play Prologue and Lucianus, and in both entries he must wait until Hamlet has ended his chats with Ophelia. The chats are not only inessential to the action at these moments, they interrupt, especially when Lucianus enters to commit his murder—a moment whose dramatic effect would be ruined by such distractions. Perhaps, significantly, Hamlet's own chit-chat ruins it. Why were they inserted? Did Shakespeare direct the Player to indicate his annoyance, perhaps by frowning at Hamlet, in order to suggest to his own spectators that they should not chatter at climactic moments?

---

12 The name given to an earlier play by an unknown author and mentioned in 1589

14

AFTER THE GONZAGO-PLAY

(i)

The climactic problem of the play

Before the end of the Gonzago-play, Hamlet cannot be accused of procrastination, for he may not take the Ghost at its word. It is his actions in the closet scene (III,iv) and afterwards that lay him open to the accusation; indeed, after that scene he seems not so much to delay as to abandon his drive to revenge.

When he comes upon the King at prayer, the King will be in his own closet, as he would hardly kneel to say his evening prayers in any of the Castle's public rooms. Since the King's and Queen's closets must be close together (they will be dressing rooms on either side of the Royal bedroom). After finding that he has killed the wrong man in the person of Polonius, Hamlet has only a short distance to go in order to find the right one; but he does not go. He has just announced his readiness to "drink hot blood" (III,ii,364) and given proof of it by rashly slaying Polonius; then the readiness apparently vanishes. Why?

He offers no resistance to being escorted to England; on his departure he insults Claudius openly:

King Thy loving father, Hamlet.
Hamlet My mother. Father and mother is man and wife; man and wife is one flesh; and so, my mother.

(IV,iii,49–51)

Why does he now betray his contempt for Claudius? He has not done so before; does he feel that he has nothing more to lose?

On his return from the sea voyage he writes letters to Horatio, his mother and the King:

King [Reads] "*High and mighty—you shall know I am set naked on your kingdom. Tomorrow shall I beg leave to see your kingly eyes when I shall, first asking your pardon thereunto, recount the occasion of my sudden and more strange return.*"

(IV,vii,43–46)

Why does he announce his return from such a sea voyage to his bitterest enemy? The letter might be a veiled threat, but if it is, why should he announce his return at all? And why, after such a leave-taking as his, is the letter now so respectful in tone?

As usual, an answer may be found in the words of the play. It is in terms of Hamlet's outlook as law-student, which constantly appears; also of his religious outlook.

After the King and Queen have left the hall, Rosencrantz and Guildenstern enter with the message from the Queen. Guildenstern finds it difficult to remain polite:

Guilden. Good my lord, put your discourse into some frame, and start not so wildly from the affair...Nay, good my lord, this courtesy is not of the right breed.

(III,ii,289–295)

Rosencrantz appeals to him:
Rosen. My lord, you once did love me...Good my lord, what is the cause of your

distemper? You surely bar the door upon your own liberty if you deny your griefs to your friend.

(III,ii,312–316)

"Liberty" hints at the possibility, of which both will be aware, that Hamlet may find himself confined as a lunatic.

Polonius enters to repeat the Queen's message. He humours Hamlet because he has accepted that Hamlet is mad, though Hamlet is aware that his two friends are not convinced of it.

When, on his way to his mother's closet, he comes upon the King at prayer, he decides to postpone his revenge for a reason which would give his spectators a thrill of horror: this is the moment when he imperils his immortal soul:

Hamlet   And am I, then, revenged,
    To take him in the purging of his soul,
    When he is fit and seasoned for his passage?
    No.
    Up, sword, and know thou a more horrid hent,
    When he is drunk asleep, or in his rage,
    At gaming, swearing, or about some act
    That has no relish of salvation in't,
    Then trip him, that his heels may kick at heaven,
    And that his soul may be as damned and black
    As hell, whereto it goes.

(III,iii,84–95)

This is the kind of revenge which no human has the right or authority to inflict upon another, as Hamlet well knows, and he has allowed hatred of his uncle to overpower the restraint he has so far displayed.

In Gertrude's closet, Polonius "sconces" himself behind the arras. When Hamlet enters and the altercation between him and the Queen develops, there is a shout for help from the hidden listener. Who else would it be but the King, about to join the Queen in bed and no doubt looking forward to doing so? Is it not the perfect "sinful" moment Hamlet has been hoping for? At once he shouts "A rat!" and drives his sword through the arras:

Queen   O what a rash and bloody deed is this!
Hamlet   A bloody deed!—Almost as bad, good mother
    As kill a king and marry with his brother.
Queen   As kill a king!

(III,iv,28–31)

He has said, "I will speak daggers to her, but use none." The accusation he suddenly throws at her is a repetition of the test of her complicity which he built into his Gonzago-play; her astonished reply tells him that she is innocent. He has by no means finished.

Then he lifts the arras and finds that he has killed not Claudius but Polonius.

The sight stops him in his tracks. He had intended to commit a deadly sin in the full knowledge of its nature, but has been prevented from doing so at the cost of a crime—the slaying of an innocent man:

Hamlet   `   For this same lord,
    I do repent; but heaven has pleased it so,

> To punish this with me, and me with this,
> That I must be their scourge and minister.
>
> (III,iv,173–176)

He regards his killing of Polonius as punishment for his presumption in planning an extreme revenge in defiance of the precept "Vengeance is mine, saith the Lord," and feels that he can no longer proceed against Claudius. Indeed, until his mother's death and his own impending death at the end of the fencing match tell him that Claudius has planned and executed yet another crime, he makes no attempt to do so.

What is left for him to do?

When he comes into Gertrude's closet, he is unaware that someone is listening behind the arras; his intention is to rebuke her for her disloyalty to his dead father:

> *Hamlet* You go not till I set you up a glass
>   Where you may see the inmost part of you.
>
> (III,iv,20–21)

On seeing the dead Polonius, he feels that he must abandon all thought of action against Claudius' life. He can still turn Gertrude's affections away from Claudius; and he does so at some length. His harangue becomes ever more furious until he once more reveals that she has married her first husband's murderer, although she is so overcome that the allusions do not appear to register with her:

> *Hamlet*   A murderer and a villain,
>   A slave that is not twentieth part the tithe
>   Of your precedent lord; a vice of kings;
>   A cutpurse of the empire, and the rule
>   That from a shelf the precious diadem stole
>   And put it in his pocket!
> *Queen* No more!
> *Hamlet* A king of shreds and patches—*[Enter Ghost.]*
>
> (III,iv,97–103)

The Ghost enters in time to prevent him from revealing too much to his mother: to convince Gertrude, who cannot see it, that her son is now having hallucinations; and to rebuke Hamlet for his "almost blunted purpose". To what is it referring: the long wait of two-and-a-half months, or Hamlet's excessive preoccupation with his mother's second marriage, or the apparent loss of his drive to revenge after the discovery of Polonius' body? Did it not say "Leave her to heaven"? Is she not a "weakest body"? Is it urging Hamlet to continue with his plans against Claudius after he has slain an innocent man?

After it has left, Hamlet continues more soberly. He reveals that he is "but mad in craft", urges secrecy on her, and ends:

> *Hamlet* I must to England; you know that?
> *Queen*   Alack,
>   I had forgot; 'tis so concluded on.
> *Hamlet* There's letters sealed. And my two schoolfellows—
>   Whom I will trust as I will adders fanged—
>   They bear the mandate; they must sweep my way,
>   And marshal me to knavery. Let it work;

> For 'tis the sport to have the engineer
> Hoist with his own petard.
>
> (III,iv,201–208)

While the Queen may know of the sealed letters, though their content remains secret, how has Hamlet come to know of them? The play does not say; however, we learn that Claudius' secret commission has been prepared. We are given a hint of what is in store for Rosencrantz and Guildenstern.

Although Hamlet says "I do repent", he is not penitent enough. He begins by hiding Polonius' body in order to give further proof of his lunatical irresponsibility. On his departure for England he cannot resist giving Claudius a parting slap in the face: "And so, my mother." Worst of all, he sends Rosencrantz and Guildenstern to instant execution—"Not shriving time allowed" (V,ii,47)—almost as extreme a fate as the one planned for Claudius, a fate which would appall his spectators as much as his "Up, sword, and know thou a more horrid hent" since criminals awaiting execution were not denied the solaces of religion. He sends them to their deaths as surrogates for his uncle and he must know that they were merely acting as obedient servants of the Crown; he says, "Why, man, they are not near my conscience" (V,ii,58).

On his return from the sea voyage he says to Horatio:

> *Hamlet* Does it not, think'st thee, stand me now upon—
> He that hath killed my king and whored my mother;
> Popp'd in between th'election and my hopes;
> Thrown out his angle for my proper life,
> And with such cozenage—is't not perfect conscience
> To quit him with this arm? And is't not to be damned
> To let this canker of our nature come
> To further evil?
>
> (V,ii,63–70)

'Conscience' again!—And twice within a few lines, although he has only mentioned it once before in "To be or not to be", and then as something which he should not allow to inhibit his will to act. If he really intends to kill Claudius, why should he now appeal to Horatio? Is he not attempting to revive his determination to kill Claudius by blustering, as a person may who has a bad conscience? His law-student's conscience should certainly be troubling him and he makes no mention of any actual plan against Claudius; he remains inactive.

His real nature, which is "Most noble, generous, and free from all contriving" (IV,vii,135) reappears when he "defies augury" (V,ii,202) and accepts the fencing match without "perusing" the foils. Does he do so in order to appease a bad conscience?

Claudius sends Hamlet to England to be executed, conspires against him on his return, and eventually dies without confessing to his wrongdoing, although his fellow conspirator Laertes confesses. He thus dies in an even more unhallowed moment than drinking or swearing, or in the incestuous pleasure of his bed. Hamlet does after all secure the kind of revenge he had hoped for, although it costs him his own life. His death is his expiation for his previous errors.

Would not his spectators see the hand of Heaven in this?

(ii)

In his essay, *Hamlet as Minister and Scourge* (1955), Fredson Bowers establishes the position of the climax of the play and the meanings of "scourge" and "minister":

> The climax is that scene in a play in which an action occurs which tips the scales for or against the fate of the protagonist in terms of the future action. The arguments for the prayer scene as the climax are superficial, for they turn only on the point that Hamlet suffers death in the catastrophe because he spared Claudius in this scene. Two considerations are always present in a tragedy. First, the climax must directly produce a train of action that leads to the catastrophe. Second, if we may briefly define tragedy as a series of morally determinate actions, the climactic scene must involve a morally determined action which justifies the tragic catastrophe to come. If we survey the prayer scene according to these two considerations, we may see that neither applies. Plotwise, no train of action results from the sparing of Claudius...On the contrary, as a direct result of the killing of Polonius the plot picks up Laertes as his revenger...By a direct and continuous line of action the catastrophe goes back to the killing of Polonius. What the action of the play would have been like if Laertes had not had the occasion to revenge the death of his father we cannot tell. This in itself is enough to remove the prayer scene from consideration as the climax from the point of view of the plot. As for the second requirement—the morally determinate action—if Hamlet's sparing of Claudius is to be a tragic error of such magnitude as to make his subsequent death an act of justice, we must take it that he should have killed Claudius at prayer. This would require the audience to believe that Hamlet's decision was wrong in the light of his belief that Claudius was in a state of grace. It is difficult to see how such a theory could be defended...The general Christian framework of Elizabethan tragic ethics demands that the slaying of Polonius be more than an unlucky accident. So far as I can see, the only way to give it a moral determinism is to argue, as I do, that it was a real error for Hamlet to attempt his private revenge at this time when Heaven had put him in a position of a minister for whom public justice would be arranged at Heaven's own pleasure. The tragic error consists in the fact that Hamlet's emotional drive is too strong to permit him to wait upon what appears to him to be Heaven's extraordinary delay...

Of "scourge" and "minister" he says:

> God's vengeance might strike a criminal by causing a sudden and abnormal sickness, by sinking him in a squall at sea, by hitting him over the head with a falling timber, by leading him accidentally into a deep quicksand or unseen pool. The Elizabethans, if there was any suspected reason, were inclined to see God's hand in most such accidents. But sometimes Heaven punished crime by means of human agents, and it was standard belief that for this purpose God chose for his instruments those who were already so steeped in crime as to be past salvation. This was not only a principle of economy, but a means of freeing God from the impossible assumption that He would deliberately corrupt innocence. When a human agent was selected to be the instrument of God's vengeance, and the act of vengeance on the guilty necessitated the performance by the agent of a crime, like murder, only a man already damned for his sins was selected, and he was called a scourge.

Any man who knew himself to be a scourge knew both his function and his fate: his powers were not his own...This idea is clearly stated at the end of Fletcher's *The Maid's Tragedy*:

> ...on lustful kings:
> Unlook'd-for sudden deaths from God are sent;
> But cursed is he that is their instrument...

A minister of God, in contrast to a scourge, is an agent who directly performs some good. In this sense, heavenly spirits are ministers of grace, as Hamlet calls them. The good performed by a human minister, however, may be some positive good in neutral or in good circumstances, or it may be some good which acts as a direct retribution to evil by overthrowing it and setting up a positive good in its place. The distinction between minister and scourge, thus, lies in two respects. First, a retributive minister may visit God's wrath on sin but only as the necessary final act to the overthrow of evil, whereas a scourge visits wrath alone, the delayed good to rest in another's hands...In the second respect, as a contrast to the evil and damned scourge, if a minister's duty is to exact God's punishment or retribution as an act of good, his hands will not be stained with crime. If in some sense he is the cause of the criminal's death, the means provided him by Heaven will lie in some act of public justice, or of vengeance, rather than in criminal private revenge.

Hamlet (says Bowers) "conceives an anomalous position for himself": is he to be the private-revenger scourge or the public-revenger minister? He sees himself primarily appointed as "an agent of God to set right the disjointed times, and may reasonably assume from the circumstances of the ghostly visitation that he is a minister."

However, as minister he should wait on Heaven's will. When the opportunity for private revenge comes in the prayer scene, it is "so far removed from divinely appointed public vengeance that Heaven would never have provided it for its minister, a sign that the time is not yet. He passes on, racking himself with bloodthirsty promises."

The killing of Polonius tells him that "he has irretrievably stained his hands with innocent blood by his usurping action, and foreseeing Heaven withheld his proper victim as its punishment". He realises that he must now wait till Heaven provides the opportunity for vengeance. His self-justifying "Does it not, think'st thee" speech to Horatio (V,ii,63–70) is a sign of new confidence. He has no definite plan of action, but "There's a special providence in the fall of a sparrow," and "The readiness is all." His death is the expiation of his error, and removes the blood-guilt from his killing of Claudius.

While I am enormously indebted to Bowers for emphasising the importance of the slaying of Polonius as the climax of the play, and of "scourge and minister", my interpretation of the phrase is somewhat different from his, and I find that he misses the logical inference to be drawn from his argument.

He goes astray when he says that the Ghost comes from Purgatory, and that its story "is not alone a personal call but in effect the transmission of a divine command." In fact, the tone of its command is very personal indeed and not at all that of a divine command: the Ghost seems to be suffering from physical jealousy! No Elizabethan spectator would assume that the Ghost was an agent sent by Heaven and therefore to be trusted. It may say it comes from Purgatory, but is it speaking the truth? Beginning with "Be thou a spirit of health or goblin damned" (I,iv,40), Hamlet repeatedly expresses his distrust. Orthodoxy requires him to be totally sceptical as to its origins and intentions. He is aware that it may be a "damned ghost"; therefore he "delays" for two-and-a-half months before putting on the Gonzago-play. (In this connection Bowers contradicts himself, for he says that Shakespeare never explicitly motivates this delay, although he has previously mentioned the doubts that arise in Hamlet's mind as to whether the Ghost is a divine emissary or a demoniacal entity.)

He also under-emphasises the importance of the "Now might I do it" speech, for Hamlet's "passing on, racking himself with bloodthirsty promises" is the moment when he falls into mortal sin. There is fact some moral determinism in the prayer scene, arising from Hamlet's sparing of Claudius for the wrong reason. It leads to the climax of the plot—the slaying of Polonius—which in turn brings in Laertes as the avenger, whereas the prayer scene brings in no avenger other than Heaven's wrath, which might be mitigated if Hamlet were sufficiently repentant after slaying Polonius.

Bowers points out an extremely important facet of Elizabethan law: that if anyone intending to commit a murder accidentally killed someone else, he was deemed a murderer because of his intent to murder; but, having failed (like all other critics) to realise that Hamlet is a law student, he does not also point out that the sight of Polonius' body will bring Hamlet to a halt because he will at once know that he has become a murderer instead of an avenger, and will be shocked by this thought.

By my interpretation, Hamlet decides to play the lunatic for the reasons already stated: he needs undisturbed leisure during which he may devise a means of testing the Ghost's story, and if he finds that he must kill Claudius, he must do so in the character of a lunatic. If he cites the Ghost's story as his motive, he will not be believed and will at once be deemed a regicide. He will then be regarded as a scourge; he will be confined, perhaps permanently, perhaps not, but he will certainly be regarded as a scourge for the rest of his life. At the same time, since he is bringing Claudius to justice, public justice being unobtainable, he will really be a minister; this will be small consolation for the loss of all his prospects in life: "O cursed spite / That ever I was born to set it right."

This thought causes him to fall into despair. He spares Claudius at his prayers for an altogether too presumptuous reason; he is usurping the function of Saint Peter! Wild with despair at the situation in which his fate has placed him and equally with rage against his uncle, he becomes indifferent to what sins he commits. He has decided that as a "scourge" he need no longer care for the welfare of his immortal soul.

He kills the owner of the voice behind the arras in the belief that he is obtaining the kind of revenge he had intended; then the sight of Polonius' body tells him that his presumption has made him a murderer. His "To punish me with this, and this with me" means: "Polonius' death punishes me for my presumption and him for meddling in a matter which was above his station."

He sees that he should have waited on Heaven's will, decides that from then on he must do so, and does, but at the same time is so confused that, sunk in despair, he fails to be repentant and commits further sins.

No good Christian should allow himself to fall into such despair. He was not responsible for the position in which the Ghost placed him, but always remained responsible for the welfare of his soul. His death at the end of the play would be seen by his spectators as the expiation, not merely for the death of Polonius, but for all the sins he commits from the prayer scene onwards. As for the logical inference: if Hamlet cannot take the Ghost at its word, and if after killing Polonius he must wait on Heaven's will, which are reasons that would weigh with an Elizabethan audience, he cannot be accused of proneness to "delay".

(iii)

In his book *Elizabethan Revenge Tragedy* (1940), Bowers gives an account of private revenge, both in real life and when used as a theme by the contemporary dramatists.

For many centuries private revenge was the only means of obtaining redress for a wrong, there being no system of state justice. Not until the first half of the fourteenth century did private revenge begin to be considered an offence against the state, as Bacon remarked in his essay *Of Revenge*, "It putteth the law out of office." Even when by Elizabethan times private revenge had become an offense, they remained common. For example duelling was rife and became more so after the arrival of the many Scots who followed King James to London after his accession to the English throne in 1603. Knife fights, such as the one in which Marlowe was killed, must also have been common. Bowers writes:

> In spite of the fact that justice was the sole prerogative of the state, with any encroachment of its newly-won privilege liable to severe punishment, the spirit of revenge had scarcely declined in Elizabethan times; its form was merely different...
>
> Chief Justice Coke, the ultimate authority for Elizabethan law, defines murder as the act of a man of sound memory and of the age of discretion who unlawfully kills another within the realm with malice aforethought, either expressed by the party or implied by the law, so that the person wounded or hurt dies within a year and a day. "Malice prepensed" is, when one compasseth to kill, wound, or beat another and doth it sedatio animo. This is said in law to be malice aforethought, prepensed, malitia praecogitata. This malice is so odious in law, as though it be intended against one, it shall be extended towards another. Si quis unum percusserit, cum alium percutere vellet, in felonia tenetur." Legally, therefore, Claudius in *Hamlet* is guilty of first-degree murder, and not of manslaughter, when Gertrude dies of the poisoned wine he has intended for Hamlet.

As he is at once aware, Hamlet becomes a first-degree murderer when he slays Polonius instead of Claudius.

Private revenge was denounced by the clerics and moralists as well as the legalists. The chief argument against revenge may be quoted from Thomas Becon (1560), although it was the staple of every other moralist: "To desire to be revenged, when all vengeance pertaineth to God, as he saith, 'Vengeance is mine, and I will reward'—this to do is forbidden." There was no gainsaying this direct command: "God would never have assumed the power of revenge as a parcell of his own prerogative in case his purpos had bene to leave all men to the revenge of their owne particularities."

With the word of God so expressly forbidding private revenge, it was only natural to believe damnation awaited those who disobeyed. Cleaver (1612) declares that the revenger "strips himselfe of Gods protection, he can neither pray for a blessing, nor have a blessing; because he is out of Gods defence, neither do his angels watch over him that is out of his ways." Bishop Hall (1612) predicts for the avenger a double death, of body and of soul.

There was thus a clash in the Elizabethan mind between the precepts of the legalists, moralists, and religious writers, and the knowledge that only too often private revenge was the sole means to the redressing of an injury. The solution adopted by the dramatists was:

where private revenge was the only means to justice, the avenger must obtain his revenge by methods which were not criminal or dishonourable; otherwise he too would become a villain who must in the end forfeit his own life. He must not become morally corrupt under the stress of frustration caused by the impossibility of obtaining public justice or the refusal of it; the crime against him or his family must not beget crime in him. Ideally, he would wait on Providence to provide justice.

Thus the nightmarish, evil-fairy-tale situations, stabbings and poisonings of the revenge tragedies, although they were calculated to appeal to the tastes of the audiences of the time, had at least nominally a moral purpose: all their villains and villainesses, such as those in Middleton's *Women Beware Women* (1657), come to bad ends:

> The dramatists may not preach, as Massinger does in *The Fatal Dowry*, but the interest with which they analyse their heroes—normal persons caught up by demands often too strong for their powers and forced into a course of action which warps and twists their characters and may lead even to the disintegration of insanity—indicates clearly that the playwrights were at least endeavouring to construct high tragedy. That their understandable love of the sensational occasionally led them astray and that they chose a particularly crude and melodramatic form for their attempt, are mere superficialities that have sometimes misled critics. The age of Elizabeth was not the age of Pericles, and each period and race must fashion from the materials at hand.

While this is a little flattering to the dramatists, who were turning out plays for the "market", their villains do meet with their due fates.

Three plays are relevant to the present purpose, the first being the early revenge tragedy, Thomas Kyd's *The Spanish Tragedy* (c.1587). We examine it in accordance with the method previously described: dramatic situation, plot, dramatic point and character, if applicable.

After the Second World War, the position of the Black in American society became an important social and political issue. Hollywood naturally made use of it in its films. In one of them, *Guess Who's Coming to Dinner*, a young woman working away from home becomes engaged to a brilliant young doctor. When she returns home and arranges for him to call and meet her parents, he proves to be black. So far, so good, but the scriptwriters intensified the situation: first, they made the girl's father a judge, a man who should be free from racial prejudice; second, they made the girl his only child; and thirdly, they made him a man unlikely to have more children in late middle age, i.e. a father to whom his only daughter would be very dear.

This dramatic situation was far from new, for Thomas Kyd had devised it three and a half centuries earlier in *The Spanish Tragedy*.

A glance at Kyd's list of dramatis personae tells us that Hieronimo is a Marshal of Spain, and at once we need to know what was meant by Marshal of Spain and why the dramatist made this position. On reading the play we learn that Hieronimo is a High Judge or High Magistrate; it is he before whom Pedringano is brought after murdering Serberine and who condemns him to death. He has even won a reputation as pleader for justice on behalf of all who need it, whether rich or poor, i.e. he is a man for whom private revenge should be utterly out of the question! Further, his son Horatio, who is murdered, is his only child, and he is an old man who mentions his "withered feet" whose son should have been the comfort and support of his old age. That he is a Marshal of Spain is thus crucial to the understanding of the play.

Kyd appears to be inconsistent in that he makes Hieronimo begin to demand justice and revenge in the same breath as soon as he discovers his son's murdered body; however, the situation is a little unusual. Normally, a young man will court a young woman where she is living. In fact Horatio has been meeting Bel-Imperia in the garden of her father's house but Kyd makes Bel-Imperia suggest that they meet at Hieronimo's house, so that Hieronimo discovers that his son has been hanged and stabbed in his own garden: a detail which further illustrates the principle that a good playwright will intensify his dramatic situation as much as he can.

For the present purpose, the important element in the play is its depiction of the four stages in the avenger's moral-psychological progress from "honourable" to "dishonourable" avenger. Hamlet passes through similar stages, his situation being more extreme than Hieronimo's in that actual evidence that his father was murdered is impossible to obtain.

The first is extreme grief over the death of a loved one; the second, rage that he was so foully murdered; the third, increasing frustration when public justice is delayed or proves impossible to obtain. Bowers talks of the delays as if they were introduced merely to string out the play. That is, if the avenger obtained his revenge quickly, the play would obviously come to an early end, while their purpose is to induce the frustration which eventually brings on the fourth stage: the bereaved person's decision to seek private revenge by dishonourable or criminal means. Kyd intensified these effects in his hero by making him a man who has devoted his whole life to law and justice but is eventually driven to abandon his dedication. While Kyd may have envisaged this psychological progression himself, I consider it more likely that he had seen some old person, perhaps even a judge, suffer a wrong and pass through the same stages. Hieronimo becomes distracted by grief and rage to the point of apparent "madness"; yet his madness is really a kind of disorientation, i.e. when, after the shock of his son's murder, his attempts to approach the King for justice are baulked, he finds that the guiding beacon of his life, his dedication to the law, has been extinguished. He no longer knows which way to turn.

Hieronimo's increasing frustration is expressed in a series of speeches delivered at intervals:

Hieronimo O sacred heaven! if this unhallowed deed
    If this inhuman and barbarous attempt,
    If this incomparable murder thus
    Of [son of] mine, but now no more my son,
    Shall unrevealed and unrevenged pass,
    How shall we term your dealings to be just,
    If you unjustly deal with those that in your justice trust?

(III,ii,5–11)

Hieronimo Thus must we toil in other men's extremes,
    That know not how to remedy our own...
    ...This toils my body, this consumeth age,
    That only I to all men just must be,*
    And neither gods nor men be just to me.

(III,vi,1–10)

*"That only I to all men just must be" is a key line.

He next complains that he is being prevented from approaching the King, his frustration being the greater because he has obtained evidence from letters which prove that his son's murderers were Lorenzo and Balthazar:

Hieronimo Yet still tormented is my tortured soul
   With broken sighs and restless passions
   That winged mount; and, hovering in the air,
   Beat at the windows of the brightest heavens,
   Soliciting for justice and revenge;
   But they are placed in those empyreal heights
   Where, countermured with walls of diamond,
   I find the place impregnable; and they
   Resist my woes, and give my words no way.

(III,vii,10–18)

In II, xii when at last he obtains access to the King, he is now so distraught—at one point he "diggeth with his dagger"—that the King judges him to be deranged.

In III, xiii he enters with a book in his hand, Seneca's *Tragedies*. He first quotes Deuteronomy 32,35: "To Me belongeth vengeance and recompense." Then he opens his book and reads lines, apparently at random; as he does so, his thinking changes until he decides that he will resort to subterfuge and crime:

Hieronimo And, to conclude, I will revenge his death!
   But how? not as the vulgar wits of men,
   With open but inevitable ills,
   As by a secret, yet a certain mean,
   Which under kindship will be cloaked best...
   ...Thus therefore will I rest me in unrest,
   Dissembling quiet in unquietness.

(III,xiii,20–30)

In III,xiii, although three citizens and an old man enter in the hope of obtaining justice through him, he "tears their papers", for he now regards his life's dedication to the law as having been futile.

The events of the last scene can only be understood in the light of "Marshal of Spain".

In his youth, he says, Hieronimo has written a tragedy (which conveniently contains stabbings), and in IV,i he persuades Lorenzo and Balthasar to present it before the court. They will take two of the parts, he and Bel-Imperia the other two. With splendid irony he says:

Hieronimo O that will I, my lords; make no doubt of it:
   I'll play the murderer, I warrant you,
   For I already have conceited that.

(IV,i,128–130)

The play is put on. After Hieronimo as the Bashaw (Pasha) has stabbed Lorenzo, and Bel-Imperia has stabbed Balthazar and then herself, he reveals to the court in a long speech that he was avenging his son's murder, then attempts to hang himself. Whereupon the courtiers, whom he has apparently locked into the gallery (IV,iii,12–13), break out and hold him. In his frenzy Hieronimo has forgotten to mention the evidence of the letters, the baulking of his attempts to approach the King for justice, and even his wife's suicide. When the King demands to know the reason for this bloody deed, he bites out his own tongue to prevent himself from speaking under torture. This would be splendid stuff for the Elizabethan spectators, but it has its dramatic point: Hieronimo is so disgusted with his descent from judge and protector of the law to common criminal that he will not speak of it.

The Duke of Castile now points out that Hieronimo can still write, and presumably drags him to a table where he forces him to sit. He "makes signs for a knife to mend his pen," then tries to stab himself with it; the Duke sees his intention and grabs his arm. They wrestle, and Hieronimo stabs the Duke in order to be free to stab himself.[13]

The death of the Duke seems at first sight to be merely more gory drama for the spectators, but it too has dramatic point: Hieronimo is no longer the kind of man that he was at the beginning of the play, for otherwise he would never have dreamed of stabbing an innocent man.

As a further example *The Revenger's Tragedy* (1605 or 1606, ascribed to Tourneur) illustrates the same theme, the revenger deliberately descending into criminality and acknowledging at the end that he must suffer the appropriate penalty.

Vindice enters, apostrophising the skull of his dead beloved, who had been poisoned by the lustful old Duke when she refused to submit to his advances. We later learn that his father had suffered at the hands of the old Duke and that he has been waiting for nine years for his revenge, i.e. that he is now very frustrated indeed and ready immediately to become a "villain".

His brother Hippolito enters and tells him that Lussurioso, the equally lustful son of the old Duke, is looking for someone to assist him in his amours—the whole court is corrupt. Vindice instantly accepts the opportunity:

Hippolito But the whole aim and scope of his intent
   Ended in this: conjuring me in private
   To seek some strange-digested fellow forth,
   Of ill-contented nature, either disgraced
   In former times, or by new grooms displaced,
   Since his stepmother's nuptials, such a blood,
   A man that were for evil only good;
   To give you the true word, some base-coined pander...
Vindice ...And therefore I'll put on that knave for once,
   And be a right man then, a man a'th'time,
   For to be honest is not to be i'th'world.
   Brother, I'll be that strange-composed fellow.

(I,i,74–96)

Offering himself to Lussurioso disguised as "Piato", he very soon finds that he will have to revenge himself on Lussurioso as well. He succeeds in poisoning the old Duke by a trick; at the end he and his friends make use of a masque to kill Lussurioso and his corrupt friends. Then Lussurioso's stepbrothers kill one another in dispute over who shall succeed to the dukedom. The whole court has now been cleared of corruption, and the new duke Antonio, whose wife poisoned herself after being ravished by the old Duke, has also been avenged. When Vindice reveals that he and his brother have accomplished the double revenge, Antonio is outraged:

Antonio You two?

---

13   The text goes: "KING: Look to my brother! save Hieronimo!", then the stage-direction *[He with a knife stabs the DUKE and himself.]*

Vindice   None else, i'faith, my lord, 'twas well managed.
Antonio   Lay hands upon those villains.
Vindice   How? on us?
Antonio   Bear 'em to speedy execution.
Vindice   Heart, was't not for your good, my lord?
Antonio   My good!
   Away with 'em; such an old man as he,
   You that would murder him would murder me.
Vindice   Is't come about?
Hippolito   S'foot, brother, you begun.
Vindice   May not we set [die] as well as the Duke's son?
   Thou hast no conscience; are we not revenged?
   Is there one enemy left alive amongst those?
   'Tis time to die, when we are ourselves our foes.
   When murders shut deeds close, this curse does seal 'em,
   If none disclose 'em they themselves reveal 'em!
   This murder might have slept in tongueless brass,
   But for ourselves, and the world died an ass;
   Now I remember too, here was Piato
   Brought forth a knavish sentence once—no doubt
   [Said he] but time
   Will make the murderer bring forth himself.
   'Tis well he died, he was a witch.
   And now, my lord, since we are in for ever,
   This work was ours which else might have been slipp'd,
   And if we list, we might have nobles clipp'd
   And go for less than beggars, but we hate
   To bleed so cowardly; we have enough;
   I'faith, we're well, our mother turned, our sister true,
   We die after a nest of dukes. Adieu.

(V,iii,101–128)

Both the brothers have become hardened and indifferent, and accept their impending executions. Vindice, who said "I'll put on that knave for once", admits that it is unacceptable to become a murderer just for once and expect to escape justice.

15
AFTER THE GONZAGO-PLAY (CONT'D)
(iv)

In *The Atheist's Tragedy or The Honest Man's Revenge* by Cyril Tourneur (1611), the avenger does not become a 'villain'.

The Atheist is D'Amville, who believes that man is free to follow 'Nature': "All other creatures in the natural world pursue their ends without remorse; why should Man allow himself to be burdened with a conscience?" As well as the natural world, 'Nature' to the Elizabethans meant man's own self-interested and corruptible nature, which, if not controlled by the Christian conscience, would cause community life to degenerate into the mere struggle for survival of animals in the wild.

In the opening scene, D'Amville expresses his views to his villainous servant Borachio:

D'Amville   Borachio, thou art read
   In Nature and her large philosophy.
   Observ'st thou not the very selfsame course
   Of revolution, both in man and beast?
Borachio   The same, for birth, growth, state, decay, and death;
   Only, a man's beholding to his nature
   For the better composition of the two.
D'Amville   But where that favour of his Nature is
   Not full and free, you see a man becomes
   A fool, as little-knowing as a beast.
Borachio   That shows there's nothing in a man above
   His nature; if there were, considering 'tis
   His being's excellency, 'twould not yield
   To nature's weakness.

(I,i,5–16)

Similarly, Edmund in *King Lear* begins his villainous course by deciding to follow "Nature":

Edmund   Thou, nature, art my goddess; to thy law
   My services are bound.

(*King Lear* I,ii,1–2)

D'Amville intends to win wealth and establish a posterity for himself by whatever means present themselves. He murders his brother Montferrers for his estate while Montferrers' son Charlemont is away at the wars, having first persuaded the young and spirited Charlemont to go to the wars against his father's wishes.

While on duty at night, Charlemont becomes uncontrollably sleepy and dreams that his father's ghost appears to him:

Montferrers   Return to France, for thy old father's dead,
   And thou by murther disinherited.
   Attend with patience the success of things;

But leave revenge unto the King of Kings.

(II,vi,19–22)

Meanwhile d'Amville has spread a report that Charlemont, the true heir to the estate, is dead. On his return, Charlemont is challenged by D'Amville's younger son Sebastian. They fight, and Charlemont is about to kill Sebastian when his father's ghost intervenes:
[SEBASTIAN is down.]
   Charlemont   Have at thee!
[Enter the ghost of MONTFERRARS.]
      Revenge, to thee I'll dedicate this work.
   Montferrers   Hold, Charlemont!
     Let Him avenge my murder and thy wrongs,
     To Whom the justice of revenge belongs.
   Charlemont   You torture me between the passion of
     My blood, and the religion of my soul.
[SEBASTIAN rises.]
   Sebastian   A good honest fellow.

(III,ii,29–36)

When d'Amville has Charlemont imprisoned for wounding Sebastian, Charlemont is rewarded when the grateful Sebastian releases him. D'Amville then bribes Borachio to murder Charlemont. While "dogging" Charlemont at night, Borachio tries to shoot him but the pistol misfires, and Charlemont kills Borachio. He is then extraordinarily "patient"; he insists on being arrested and tried for murder, offers no defence, and even prepares himself for execution. D'Amville, whose schemes have all come to nothing, snatches the executioner's axe with the intention of striking the fatal blow himself. As he raises it, he "strikes out his own brains". Before he dies he says:
   D'Amville   There was the strength of natural understanding.
     But nature is a fool. There is a power
     Above her that hath overthrown the pride
     Of all my projects and posterity...

(V,ii,254–257)

   Charlemont   Only to Heaven I attribute the work
     Whose gracious motives made me still forbear
     To be mine own revenger. Now I see
     That patience is the honest man's revenge.

(V,ii,272–275)

Charlemont's "patience" is rewarded when he marries his lady-love and comes into no fewer than three estates: his father's, his uncle's, and his wife's.

Atheism was anathema to the Elizabethans and to many generations before and after. Today, atheism merely means the refusal to accept the existence of a deity; an atheist may disbelieve in the deity while accepting the existence of a body of moral laws which all should obey. To the Elizabethans, such a doctrine was totally inadmissible.

For many centuries, when both the law and the means of enforcing it were grossly inadequate and the only education for many of the population was what they received in church, the belief in God and the conscience were the only factors preventing society from sinking into lawlessness. "The Lord not only exists; it was He who laid down the precepts by which we must regulate our conduct, and gave us consciences to ensure that we follow them. Anyone who denies His existence is also denying the need to obey the dictates of the Christian conscience."

To all those generations there were three obediences: to the Christian religion and its dictates as promulgated by the Church; to the king, who ruled by divine right; and to such law as there was: in practice they were regarded as one and the same obedience. In 1401 a statute against Lollardry was passed because the Lollards—early rebels against the dominion of the Church—were "...making and writing books, wickedly instructing and informing the people, exciting and stirring them to sedition and insurrection, and making great strife and division among the people." The statute was repeated in 1414, the Lollards' activities being "to the Intent to adnull, destroy and subvert the Christian faith, and the Law of God and the Holy Church within this same Realm of England, and also to destroy the same our Sovereign Lord the King and all other manner of Estates of the same Realm, as well Spiritual as Temporal, and all manner of Policy, and finally the Laws of the Land." Evidently, heresy and sedition were regarded as the same thing.

In 1534 the Act of Supremacy vested authority on all ecclesiastical matters in the Crown; in the following year Henry assumed, by Letters Patent, the title "on earth supreme head of the Church of England". Anyone denying the truth of the teachings of the Church was simultaneously denying the monarch's authority. His authority as Head of the Church of England counted as much as his temporal authority.

The fate of Kyd exemplifies the Elizabethan hatred of atheism. On the 18th May 1593, the Privy Council issued a warrant for the arrest of Marlowe, Kyd having been arrested on the 12th, on the grounds that they were suspected of holding "libellous" or seditious opinions. "Libel"—a written defamation of the Christian religion—"sedition" and "atheism" were evidently synonymous. "Atheistical" papers were found in Kyd's possession; in vain did he plead that they were Marlowe's and that they must have become "shufled" among his papers without his knowledge when he and Marlowe had been "...wrytinge in one chamber twoe yeares since." His patron turned him away; without a patron he was a vagabond, and it seems certain that no one would give him work, for he died in poverty and disgrace a year and a half later. His death was a major loss to the Elizabethan stage.

Among the statements in these papers are:
- That the first beginning of Religioun was only to keep men in awe.
- That Christ was a bastard and his mother dishonest.
- That Crist deserved better to dy than Barabbas and that the Jewes made a good Choise, though Barabbas were a thief and a murtherer.
- That the woman of Samaria & her sister were whores & that Christ knew them dishonestly.
- That St. John the Evangelist was bedfellow to Christ and leaned alwaies in his bosome, that he vsed him as the sinners of Sodoma.
- That they that love not tobacco and boies were fooles.
- That the Angell Gabriell was baud to the Holy Ghost, because he brought the salutation to Mary.

These writings were delivered to the Privy Council by one Richard Baines, whose note ends:

> These thinges, with many other shall by good & honest witnes be approved to be his opinions and Comon speeches and that this Marlow doth not only hould them himself, but almost into every Company he Cometh he perswades men to

Atheism willing them not to be afeard of bugbeares and hobgoblins, and vtterly scorning both god and his ministers as J Richard Baines will justify and approue both by mine oth and the testimony of many honest men, and almost al men with whome he hath Conversed any time will testify the same, and as J think all men in Cristianity ought to indevor that the mouth of so dangerous a member may be stopped...

If a young person early becomes a rebel with perhaps having reason to rebel against pressures on him, he may go on rebelling, perhaps to the end of his life. This appears to have been the case with Marlowe, for it is easy to see from the tone of the above statements, which, had they been the product of coolly reasoned thought, would have been expressed more moderately, that he was being offensive for the sake of being offensive.

It was originally intended that he should enter the Church, but such an occupation requires a vocation, and Marlowe's real inclinations lay elsewhere. His tutors must have continued too long in urging him to dedicate himself to a vocation for which he had no bent. Eventually he rebelled not only against them but against everything they stood for. He must have known that the Church was one of the few civilising influences of the time. The first statement quoted above, "That the first beginning of Religioun was only to keep men in awe" shows that he knew. He seems to have been wild by nature; if he took to "boies" it may have been the expression of both his wildness and his rebellion. Probably the combination of early rebellion and wildness caused him to lose his sense of proportion to the point where he had not recovered it at the time of his death.

An alternative explanation is possible that Marlowe, who is known to have been an intelligence agent, was pretending to be an atheist as a form of disguise, i.e. in the hope of being taken to be a malcontent whom agents from other countries might approach and so give themselves away. It is also evident from the tone of the statements and from Richard Baines' note that he was unacceptably offensive in speech and in his writings. It was enough to condemn Kyd that he had been the occasional associate of such an outspoken atheist; everyone would refuse to give him work in order to avoid incurring the suspicion of being sympathetic to his supposed views.

What is the relevance of *The Atheist's Tragedy* and of Kyd's fate to *Hamlet*?

After Hamlet has slain Polonius, he accepts that he must be punished as a murderer and that he should wait on Providence, but repents hardly at all. He is not patient enough: he makes use of the innocent Polonius' body to confirm his lunacy; insults the King on his departure (a considerable offence against the respect due to a monarch, even from the monarch's own nephew); vows that his thoughts henceforth will "be bloody or be nothing worth"; sends Rosencrantz and Guildenstern to undeserved deaths; and says "They are not near my conscience." When he finally asks Horatio "Is't not perfect conscience / To quit him with this arm?" he is approaching a dangerous verge: he is speaking of "perfect conscience" after apparently throwing his own conscience away.

(v)

By way of illustrating the use of the previously mentioned revenge-tragedy elements and of elucidating Shakespeare's intention, we consider possible alternatives to his plot.

1) In III,iii Hamlet steals in upon the King at his prayers viz.:

Hamlet   Do not shout for help. If you do, I shall run you through. I know that you murdered my father; his ghost told me how you murdered him. You may be sceptical, but why else would I have had your murder depicted to your face half an hour ago?

You must admit that I know.

Abhorrent as the executioner's duty is, I may now have to become one. The world will think that a lunatic has killed you; for my mother's sake I can never say why I killed you; the world must believe that my becoming a lunatic and killing you is simply a misfortune that has befallen her. I shall have to live on as a confirmed homicidal maniac in confinement, my only consolation being that I did my duty to my murdered father.

You may elect to spare me the executioner's task and end your life yourself. I shall then be able to recover from the apparent lunacy which has puzzled you and everyone else, and then, God willing, the Hamlet family will not come to an end, as it will if I must kill you.

Those are your options. Prepare yourself.

The dramatic possibilities of this situation are manifold. What if Claudius now pleads for himself, or even tries to justify his murder? As will be seen later, we need to know much more about the Hamlet family than the play tells us, and perhaps with such a plot we would learn it.

It is what Hamlet should say.

After feigning lunacy and putting on the Gonzago-play, both justifiable stratagems, he has been completely open with Claudius. He has not imperilled his soul, nor has he compounded his error by slaying Polonius; he has not allowed the long period of frustration to unbalance his judgment; he has even given his enemy the opportunity to prepare himself for his end. Whatever the outcome, he cannot lose his audience's sympathy.

A continuation must be devised: Claudius might plead for himself, then shout for his guards and defend himself until they have overpowered Hamlet, who is then escorted to England, etc. However, Shakespeare evidently decided that a young man of Hamlet's age and temperament would not be as completely self-controlled as the above Hamlet.

2) In the Queen's closet, Hamlet, on finding that he has killed the wrong man in the person of Polonius, immediately takes the few steps into the King's closet and kills the right one. What is now his standing in the eyes of the audience? Sympathy is forfeited. He has first imperilled his soul by sparing Claudius for the wrong reason, killed Polonius and become a murderer, and then, undeterred by the knowledge that he is a murderer, killed again and damned himself for all time.

He may now kill himself, or give himself up and be confined for life (and with little hope of any after-life other than in Hell); or, although Claudius is dead, he may still be escorted to England; or he may escape, and further adventures must be devised for him.

If he remains alive, the plot becomes for the audience merely a matter of waiting for the inevitable retribution, which will naturally come via Laertes as the avenger of his father. Laertes cannot be an "honourable" avenger, for he would then supplant the hero: a last-minute change in the object of the audience's sympathy which would destroy the play's unity of dramatic interest. He must be a "dishonourable" avenger, as, being a poisoner, he is in the play as it stands, and the audience will then be treated to the spectacle of two "villains" killing one another.

In terms of the morality of the revenge-tragedies, this plot is almost as satisfactory as the existing one, for it displays two young men falling victim to emotional stress and becoming "dishonourable", each in his own way, but it divides and weakens the play's dramatic impact. In Shakespeare's plot, sympathy for the hero is never quite lost, and the catastrophe is postponed to the end so that suspense is more effectively maintained.

Hamlet is thrown into an appalling situation:

a) Since the story of the murder comes from a ghost, there is immediate doubt as to whether a revenge situation exists. Hamlet can only rely on his "prophetic soul".
b) Since the murder can never be openly proved, there is no possibility of public justice, and Hamlet may have to become a regicide.
c) There is no physical barrier to revenge. If Hamlet can steal upon the King at his prayers, he can do so at any time.
d) There is no other impediment. Since only Hamlet and Horatio know that there may have been a murder, no one has any reason to spy on Hamlet, intrigue against him or otherwise impede him.

Hence Hamlet is totally alone with his problem. He cannot confide the Ghost's story to anyone other than Horatio who has also seen the Ghost, without which experience he too would be sceptical. Although in his heart Hamlet believes the Ghost, he is very scrupulous in deciding that he must first prove its story. The only barrier to immediate revenge lies in his conscience; his delay is to his credit.

The emotional stress of his enforced idleness gives rise to frustration in an active and fearless spirit to a degree which threatens to undermine his restraint, as appears from his first use of the word "conscience" in "Conscience does make cowards of us all."

In this context the word has been interpreted as meaning reflection or self-examination, but there is a better case for the usual meaning. Since examination of one's conscience is self-examination, the distinction between the two meanings would be very small in an age which was at once highly religious and somewhat lawless, the Christian conscience being one of the few contemporary restraints on lawless behaviour and all too often ineffective.

Hamlet is saying: "I have been as careful as my conscience dictated, but after two-and-a-half months of waiting I feel as if I have been a coward." Only a few hours previously during the evening of Day One, he has castigated himself quite violently for cowardice in his Hecuba soliloquy.

These two self-accusations, and in particular the rage accompanying the second, are signs that frustration is about to get the better of his conscience, that he is about to lose the "patience" he has so far displayed. The audience is prepared for his "Now could I drink hot blood," his sparing of Claudius at the priedieu and his slaying of Polonius.

After finding that he has become a murderer he halts, and it is again to his credit that he does so though he relapses immediately; in spite of his "For this same lord, I do repent," he does not display repentance.

Why does he relapse? Could the cause be the Ghost's second appearance to him? It certainly prevents him from revealing too much to his mother, though its intention is also to "whet thy almost blunted purpose". Does it spur his resolution at the wrong moment? Hamlet now appears to regard it as "honest", but should he?

The third self-accusation of cowardice in "How all occasions do inform against me" (IV,iv,32–66) is almost an explicit statement that he has now abandoned conscience:

Hamlet   Now, whether it be
  Bestial oblivion, or some craven scruple
  Of thinking too precisely on th'event—
  A thought which, quartered, hath but one part wisdom

>   And ever three parts coward—I do not know
>   Why yet I live to say, "This thing's to do"...
>   ...How stand I then,
>   That have a father killed, a mother stained,
>   Excitements of my reason and my blood,
>   And let all sleep?

Knowing perfectly well why the thing is still to do, he is trying to talk himself back into the mood for action. It was his conscience which drove him to seek the most positive proof he could obtain of his uncle's crime, and which later told him that the slaying of Polonius had made him a murderer, but it has now become "craven scruple / Of thinking too precisely on th'event":

> *Hamlet*   ... O, from this time forth,
>   My thoughts be bloody, or be nothing worth.
>
>   (IV,iv,39–66)

And his audience must now expect further bloody deeds.

Although some sympathy is restored when he briefly appears as his normal self in the graveyard, he soon horrifies his audience by revealing that after receiving a hint from Providence ("Sir, there was in my heart a kind of fighting / That would not let me sleep"—V,ii,4–5) that he should read the secret commission, he has made use of it by sending two servants of the Crown to unmerited deaths.

As always, Horatio's comments are those of a law student. Knowing that such a commission must bear the stamp of royal authority, he at once asks "How was this sealed?", and Hamlet must explain that he has his own seal. Hamlet's reply to his "So Guildenstern and Rosencrantz go to it" is a blustering attempt at self-justification. Again he speaks of his conscience:

> *Hamlet* Why, man, they did make love to this employment;
>   They are not near my conscience; their defeat
>   Does by their own insinuation grow.
>   'Tis dangerous when the baser nature comes
>   Between the pass and fell incensed points
>   Of mighty opposites.
>
>   (V,ii,57–62)

While it may be dangerous for the baser nature, are the mighty opposites permitted to forget their consciences merely because they are mighty?

> *Hamlet* Does it not, think'st thee, stand me now upon—
>   He that hath killed my king and whored my mother,
>   Popped in between th'election and my hopes,
>   Thrown out his angle for my proper life,
>   And with such cozenage—is't not perfect conscience
>   To quit him with this arm? And is't not be damned
>   To let this canker of our nature come
>   To further evil?
>
>   (V,ii,63–70)

Hamlet has been on dangerous ground for some time. He is not far from "atheism"; he has remained impenitent after killing Polonius, and in addition has effectively murdered his two former friends; and now he is apparently deciding for himself what is or is not conscience and what it is to be damned: totally impermissible.

However, he has not quite stepped over the dividing line, for the blustering tone of the first speech suggests that under it a remnant of his true conscience is still troubling him, while the second is not the statement of a definite resolve such as Hieronimo's "Not...with open, but inevitable ills" or Vindice's "Brother, I'll put on that knave for once"; it is a question, an appeal to Horatio for moral support.

In spite of the revelation of Claudius' villainy, Horatio does not give it. His thoughtful "So Guildenstern and Rosencrantz go to it" suggests that he doubts both the legality and the justice of Hamlet's action, his "Is't possible?" and "Why, what a king is this!" express his law-student's outrage that Claudius, who as king should set an example by obeying the law, should have attempted to evade it in that way. His remark, "It must be shortly known to him from England / What is the issue of the business there" is a warning which brings his friend down to earth. And Hamlet appears to take a hint from his friend's lack of enthusiasm, for after two more lines he drops the subject of revenge, recalling that he must make what apology he can to Laertes.

Some sympathy is restored when his true nature reappears at the end. Having accepted that he must wait on Heaven's will ("There's a special providence in the fall of a sparrow."), he enters the fencing match in spite of his forebodings ("Thou wouldst not think how ill all's here about my heart" (V,ii,194–195). As Claudius predicts to Laertes, he is "Most generous and free from all contriving" (IV,vii,135) and even refrains from "perusing" the foils.

When he excuses himself to Laertes with "His madness is poor Hamlet's enemy," he lies because he must for the sake of his mother: how can he explain his loss of self-control in his mother's closet? At least his "evil", the slaying of Polonius, was not coldly "purposed", whereas Laertes, demanding satisfaction in the way of "honour", is about to fight with a foil poisoned by himself.

Hamlet then dies, not in fair fight, but unfairly at the hands of a brace of poisoners and conspirators, and the audience leaves the theatre feeling, not satisfaction that a "dishonourable" hero has met a deserved end, but regret at the loss of such a young man:

Horatio   Good night, sweet prince;
And flights of angels sing thee to thy rest.

(V,ii,341–342)

(vi)

Few critics have ever admitted that *Hamlet* the play is the primary problem and that Hamlet the character is only secondary. And Hamlet the character has had an especial temptation for that most dangerous type of critic, the critic with a mind which is naturally of the creative order, but which through some weakness in creative power exercises itself in criticism instead.

T.S. Eliot, essay *Hamlet and his Problems* (1919)

I am in complete agreement with the first sentence, in which Eliot says, in effect, that more attention should have been paid to the construction of the play and to the dramatist's intention and less to character; and with the implication of the second, that 'creative' criticism is all too often only loosely related—if at all—to its subject-matter.

He goes on to quote Mr. J.M. Robertson, who contends that *Hamlet* is a "stratification", that it represents the efforts of a series of men, each making what he could out of the work of his predecessors. The play is about the effect of a mother's guilt upon her son, and Shakespeare was unable to impose this motive successfully on the "intractable" material of the old play. Eliot continues by saying that there is an emotion in Hamlet which is "inexpressible, because it is in excess of the facts as they appear". It should have an "objective correlative", i.e. a circumstance or an event which is recognisable as causing it; but Eliot cannot find one. This lack blunts the revenge motif by making Hamlet delay. His madness is a form of emotional relief; he is "baffled by the absence of objective equivalent to his feelings." So the play is an "artistic failure".

This opinion is surprising in a critic who was himself a playwright.

Do not the majority of playwrights start with some idea of the dramatic point they intend to make? Plays, it has been said, are not so much written as rewritten, and perhaps because of this the most satisfactory plays prove to have a definite beginning, a definite middle, and a definite end, from which it follows that the playwright should either have some idea of where his play is 'going' when he begins to write it or develop a definite 'line' as he writes. And it also follows that he would be unwise to embody material which he could not handle, so as to emphasise his dramatic purpose.

"Stratification" and "intractable" are not well-chosen words. The playwrights of the day were scriptwriters turning out plays for their theatre companies, and occasionally collaborating with one another. As there was no law of copyright, everybody lifted ideas for plots or episodes from wherever he could find them. Shakespeare, for example, is thought to have reworked the *Ur-Hamlet*[14], though I find that he was certainly indebted to *The Spanish Tragedy*. His reworking, if that is what it was, was done in his own manner and for his own consistent and dramatic purpose.

Eliot is implying that the effect of a mother's guilt upon her son was a psychological element which Shakespeare could not handle in combination with the others, though the play is actually about that and some other motifs, all successfully blended into the revenge-tragedy framework. Further, *Hamlet* is one of a series of Shakespearean tragedies containing rarely equalled psychological insights. To say that Shakespeare could not handle his chosen material is to underestimate both his insights into human nature and his skill as play-constructor.

Also, neither Eliot nor John M. Robertson define the precise nature of Gertrude's guilt.

Hamlet's emotionality is by no means "inexpressible because it is in excess of the facts as they appear", one of its objective correlatives having already been shown to be the clash between his suspicion of his mother as a possible accessory to the murder and his knowledge that she is a "mouse" or "weakest body" who needs protection.

It remains to show that there is another such cause, which is clearly indicated in the play, and that it too intensifies rather than weakens his drive to revenge.

---

14   A lost version of *Hamlet* of unknown authorship, mentioned as early as 1589 ('ur' is German for 'primordial')

PART IIB
THE TWO FAMILIES IN HAMLET

16

POLONIUS AND HIS CHILDREN
&
ROSENCRANTZ AND GUILDENSTERN

> Polonius, according to Shakespeare, is a Man of a most excellent Understanding and great Knowledge of the World, whose Ridicule arises not from any radical Folly in the old Gentleman's Composition but a certain Affectation of Formality and Method, mix'd with a smattering of the Wit of that Age (which consisted in playing upon words), which being grown up with him is incorporated (if I may venture the Expression) with all his Words and Actions.
>
> William Popple in *The Prompter*, no. 57, (May 1735)

It is difficult to assign a precise age to Polonius because the expectation of life in Shakespeare's time was much lower than it has since become. Today, we might put him at sixty-five to seventy, on the verge of retirement, slower in mind than he was, but still the valued and trusted servant of the Royal family, far from senile, and still capable of years of faithful service. Hamlet calls him a "great baby", but, considering his situation, Hamlet may be regarded as prejudiced. He is by nature not as quick-witted as Hamlet, nor as shrewd as Claudius, and although he is ageing—perhaps, as Dr Johnson said, "dotage is encroaching upon wisdom"—he is not aged. Nor is he slow-witted; rather he is thorough-going and careful; since he is Lord Chamberlain he will have had some legal training in his youth, as his phrase "prenominate crimes" suggests.

In terms of Shakespeare's time, sixty-five to seventy is too old by at least ten years; in any case, Laertes is perhaps twenty, and Polonius would hardly have waited till he was around forty before marrying. So we must put him at less than sixty. Not that his precise age matters much; the point is that the impression of near-senility which he gives in some of his speeches is misleading. In any case, I find from observation that older people tend to be less garrulous than some younger minds who have not yet learned to think and speak to the point. In I,iii, everything that Polonius says, and in particular his parting advice to Laertes, is completely to the point. If, then, he appears to dither all round the point in the Renaldo scene II,i, and in II,ii, in which he propounds his explanation of Hamlet's madness, we must ask "How is it that all these speeches can come from the same man? What is going on in Polonius' mind in these scenes?"

Polonius' wife must have been dead these many years. Perhaps she died when Ophelia was born, for even her memory is never mentioned in the play. Possibly Polonius has brought up his family singlehanded. Further, the absence of a mother has made the family a tightly-knit group, although the two children, as might be expected when their father is so much older than they and so often occupied with his duties as Lord Chamberlain, are closer to one another than to him. In I,iii, when Laertes takes his leave for Paris, the situation would be very different if there were still a Lady Polonius. It is Laertes who warns Ophelia that she must not trust Hamlet's "tenders", and Polonius seems to have learned of them only recently, for he becomes very angry: "You'll tender me a fool!" If Lady Polonius had still been alive, she would have learned all about the "tenders" as soon as they began arriving, and would have prevented her young daughter from giving her heart away too early.

Polonius is a very anxious father to his children, as his parting advice to Laertes and his rebuke to Ophelia show; however, we learn from the Renaldo scene (II,i) that he is not so unrealistic as to imagine that his youthful son will actually follow his father's good advice!

II,i, in which he briefs Reynaldo before sending him to Paris with money for Laertes, illustrates one of the pitfalls of an education in Latin sentence construction (II,I,37ff.):

Polonius   Marry, sir, here's my drift:
[He immediately introduces a parenthetical clause to explain his "drift", at which he has already hinted.]

    And, I believe, it is a fetch of warrant
    You laying these slight sullies on my son
    As 'twere a thing a little soiled i'th'working:
    Mark you.

[Renaldo is already marking him, but he continues with what is either an ablative absolute, "Your party having been engaged in conversation" or a present-participle descriptive clause: "Your party conversing with you", and follows it with another unnecessary descriptive clause. Polonius continues:]

    Your party in converse, him you would sound,
[Now another clause of the same type, its subject "he" coming later:]
    ...Having ever seen in the prenominate crimes
    The youth you breathe of guilty,
[At last, the subject and the verb]
                  ...be assured
    He closes with you in this consequence:
    'Good sir', or so...
[Again in parenthesis, he adds some unnecessary alternatives, with fatal effect:]
                 ... or 'friend', or 'gentleman',
    According to the phrase or the addition
    Of man and country—
Renaldo   Very good, my lord.
Polonius [His mind suddenly a blank]
    And then, sir, does he this—he does—what was I about to say? By the mass, I was about to say something—where did I leave?

This is the most complex sentence Polonius utters. All dramatic episodes, however slight, must appeal to the audience in some specific way, and this episode may have been intended to amuse those of Shakespeare's spectators who had learned Latin and fallen into the same trap themselves.

As we might expect from Shakespeare, the episode is not only comic but psychologically accurate. The psychologists tell us that whenever we 'forget' anything, it is for a reason: either something in us wants to forget it, or some urgent problem at the back of our minds has driven it out. Polonius considerably over-explains himself to Renaldo, then 'forgets' how his sentence was going to end because of his deep concern for his absent son, who only obtained his "slow leave" to return to Paris after "laboursome petition" (I,ii,58–59). His parting advice to Laertes in I,iii is the first expression of the concern.

In II,ii he over-explains himself to the King and Queen because he is again anxious, and this time for a quite different reason. He is the head of one family speaking to the joint heads of another, on a matter which is always of acute interest to both families in such a situation, namely the love of the son of one family for the daughter of the other, a matter always to be approached with tact, and particularly so in this case because, in an age when most marriages (in the wealthier families, at least) were arranged, their love had not previously been known to either family. Moreover, the young man comes of royal descent, whereas the young girl does not; worst of all, the love of the said young man for the said young girl has apparently driven him mad!

So Polonius approaches the subject very gingerly because he is both pleased with himself over his discovery and embarrassed by the situation. Though the Queen becomes annoyed, Claudius, knowing his man, simply waits (II,ii,86–96 and 131–142):

Polonius My liege, and madam: to expostulate
What majesty should be, what duty is,
Why day is day, night night, and time is time,
Were nothing but to waste day, night, and time.
Therefore, since brevity is the soul of wit,
And tediousness the limbs and outward flourishes,
I will be brief: your noble son is mad.
Mad call I it; for, to define true madness,
What is't to be nothing else but mad?
But let that go.
Queen [Tartly]   More matter, with less art...
[He feels bound to emphasise that he had not encouraged Ophelia.]
Polonius   But what might you think,
When I had seen this hot love on the wing—
As I perceived it, I must tell you that,
Before my daughter told me...

          ...No, I went round to work,
And my young mistress thus I did bespeak:
'Lord Hamlet is a prince out of thy star;
This must not be.'

[As Lord Chamberlain he is highly respected (II,ii,129–130):]
Polonius What do you think of me?
King As of a man faithful and honourable.

If Polonius were the corrupt ally of Claudius who many critics suppose him to be, he would not ask that question, nor would the King give that answer.

Even though Hamlet makes fun of him for his own purposes, he will not allow anyone else to do so:

Hamlet [To the First Player]
Follow that lord, and look you mock him not.

(II,ii,517)

He is a cheerful man, ageing but not too old to continue in his position, conscientious, and intensely preoccupied with his two children. To the Elizabethan spectators seeing the play for the first time, and unlike us, having no prior knowledge of its events, his death would come as a shock. Hardly less of a shock would be Hamlet's treatment of his body, evidencing as it does their hero's deterioration.

* * *

> The forward virgins are of the opinion that the best time for marriage is fourteen—if thirteen be not better—and they have for the most part the example of their mothers.
>
> *A Discourse of Marriage and Wiving*, Anon (1615)

How old is Ophelia? She hasn't had a particularly good press: Ruskin calls her "the one weak woman in all Shakespeare's plays", and even says that the bitter catastrophe follows because of her failure to guide him when he most needs her; J.M. Robertson—"inadequacy incarnate"; Masefield—"a doll without intellect", and it is futile to assess her character without first estimating her age.

She loses her mind because her father is suddenly killed when her brother is far away; she is alone and unprotected. She appears to be suffering from something akin to 'abandonment fear' which may overcome smaller children if their mothers leave them, if only for a short time: because her lover has apparently gone insane and rejected her; and because it was her lover who killed her father, which implies that even if he recovers his sanity she can never marry him. After giving her heart to Hamlet she would be unlikely to fall in love with anyone else.

The songs she sings, and her little distribution of wild flowers, suggest that her affliction has taken the form of an escape into childhood. Even in her madness she never mentions her mother, which suggests that she has no recollection of her. When a mind suddenly collapses like this, it is usually the effect of cumulative stress over a long period, and her breakdown may be due in part to a solitary, motherless childhood. The final blow comes at a time in her life when she needs the support and advice of a mother as never before. Although she should receive some from Gertrude, she appears to receive none.

If she had been Laertes' twin, i.e. about nineteen or twenty, she would be prostrated by the simultaneous loss of her father and lover, but would be too far past childhood to regress into it. She must be younger.

Why is it necessary for both her brother and her father to tell her (I,iii) that she must not trust Hamlet's "tenders"? Although Polonius has long been Lord Chamberlain to the Royal court, she has not yet learned that Hamlet, being a Prince, may not choose his wife himself. If she were eighteen she would have learned that a prince may not "carve for himself"; if sixteen, she would probably know. Indeed she must be younger.

Hamlet's exchanges with her immediately before and during the Gonzago-play (III,ii.105ff.) provide hints as to her age:

Hamlet Lady, shall I lie in your lap?
Ophelia No, my lord.
Hamlet I mean, my head upon your lap?
Ophelia Ay, my lord.
Hamlet Do you think I meant country matters?
Ophelia I think nothing, my lord.
Hamlet That's a fair thought to lie between maids' legs.
Ophelia What is, my lord?

Hamlet Nothing,
Ophelia You are merry, my lord.
Hamlet is teasing a young girl in a vein consistent with his lunacy. His company is far from unacceptable to her although he is at least talking sense at the moment, her "Ay, my lord" is a joking reply in the same spirit.

The Dumb-show is presented:
Ophelia What means this, my lord?
Hamlet Marry, this is 'miching mallecho'; it means mischief.
Ophelia Belike this show imports the argument of the play.
[Enter Prologue.]
Hamlet We shall know by this fellow. The players cannot keep counsel; they'll tell all.
Ophelia Will he tell us what this show meant?
Hamlet Ay, or any show that you'll show him. Be not you ashamed to show, he'll not shame to tell you what it means.
Ophelia You are naught, you are naught. I'll mark the play.

Ophelia's questions are those of a naïve and eager child who asks because she needs to know the answers. Since prologues and "dumbshows" were not uncommon features of plays (Hamlet speaks of "inexplicable dumbshows" and *King Henry V* has prologues to every act), her questions suggest that she has never seen a play before or has seen very few.

An aspect of Elizabethan life which must be grasped if the two female characters in *Hamlet* are to be understood (what follows may apply to Gertrude also) is that many girls were married at what we—at least, we in the West—now regard as an extremely early age. For many centuries the minimum ages for marriage remained in accordance with Roman law at fourteen for males and twelve for females. In Britain, not till 1929 did the Age of Marriage Act raise the minimum age to sixteen for both sexes.

Among the low-income families, the bridegroom was usually in his late twenties; he was expected to have created or be able to create an establishment in which he could support his wife and family. The bride was usually two to four years younger. Among the higher-income families, especially those wealthy enough that their children would not have to earn their own living, the ages of both sexes at marriage were often much lower.

Many girls must have been looking forward to and preparing themselves for marriage for some time before they reached puberty. Among the low-income families, the choice of spouse might be left to the children, but among the wealthier, marriages were arranged by parents and among the nobility, for dynastic reasons. Girls enjoyed virtually no freedom in the choice of a husband. An indulgent father might allow his daughter to marry the young man of her choice, provided that he considered him suitable; the suitor had, in particular, to have an estate which would enable him to provide for his wife and family to an acceptable standard. On the other hand, he might order her to marry a husband of his choosing. Sons might also be ordered to marry wives not of their choosing or risk disinheritance.

The theme was much used by the dramatists of the period as, for example, by Kyd in *The Spanish Tragedy*, Dekker in *The Shoemaker's Holiday*, Tourneur in *The Atheist's Tragedy*, and Shakespeare in *Romeo and Juliet*. The point of these to the contemporary audiences was that the lovers elope and marry without their parents' knowledge or consent; also in *All's Well That Ends Well*, in which the King, who has become Bertram's guardian, orders him to marry Helena; also by Sheridan in *The Rivals* (1775).

The atmosphere of married life must have been very different from what it is today. Girls were taught to be very respectful towards their husbands, such training being necessary if a girl was to be married in her early teens to an older husband who would have to be his wife's mentor and protector. Mistress Paston, who lived in the previous century, always began her letters to her husband with "Right worshipful (or Right reverend) husband, I commend me to you". Ophelia never fails to address both Polonius and Hamlet as "My lord"; when she contradicts Hamlet in reply to his "I never gave you aught" in III,i,97 she is more respectful than usual: "My honoured lord, you know right well you did." Similarly, when at the end of the play Gertrude disobeys Claudius' "Gertrude, do not drink", she replies: "I will, my lord; I pray you, pardon me."

Chaucer's Wife of Bath was married to the first of her five husbands at twelve, and the Nurse in *Romeo and Juliet* appears also to have been married at twelve (*Rom.* I,iii,3). Catherine de Vivonne, who as the Marquise de Rambouillet became the hostess of the previously mentioned salon in Paris in the mid-seventeenth century, was also married at twelve. In the diary of a Wiltshire apothecary who lived in the late seventeenth century, it is recorded that when he decided to marry at the age of thirty-four he chose a wife of twelve. In the essay by Richard Steele (1672–1728), "Mr. Bickerstaffe Visits a Friend", we learn that the friend and his lady were married at fifteen. At the end of his essay "On Asking Advice in Affairs of Love", Steele's contemporary Addison quotes a letter from a young girl, "B.D.", who has fallen in love with a young man who is "good-natured, ingenious, modest, civil, tall, well-bred, and handsome", but has no estate. "I have a good portion which they cannot hinder me of, and shall be fourteen on the 29th day of August next, and am therefore willing to settle in the world as soon as I can."[15]

In Jane Austen's *Pride and Prejudice* (1813) Lydia Bennett runs away to London with Mr. Wickham when she is sixteen. The problem is not that she is so young but that Mr. Wickham, who is spendthrift and shiftless, may not marry her; however, her uncle Mr. Gardner follows them to London to ensure that he does. Mrs. Bennett is then delighted that at last one of her five unmarried daughters (the others are all older than Lydia) has found a husband. Scarlett O'Hara, the heroine of *Gone with the Wind* (Margaret Mitchell, 1936), and sixteen when the novel opens, is afraid that if she doesn't find herself a husband soon, she will be regarded as an old maid. Her mother is then thirty-two.

Some royal brides were married very young. Margaret of Anjou (1430–1482) was married to Henry VI three months before her fourteenth birthday; Louise of Savoy (1476–1531), mother of Francis I of France, at twelve; Margaret (1489–1531), queen to James IV of Scotland, three months before her fourteenth birthday; Catherine of Aragon (1485–1536), wife to Henry VIII's elder brother Arthur and later Henry's wife, a month before her sixteenth birthday; Mary, Queen of Scots (1542–1587), at fifteen-and-a-half; Catherine de Medici (1519–1589), queen to Henry II of France, at fourteen; Anne of Denmark (1574–1619), queen to James VI of Scotland, at fourteen-and-a-half; Henrietta Maria (1609–1669), queen to Charles I, at fifteen-and-a-half; Marie Antoinette of France (1755–1793), at fourteen-and-a-half.

According to her Nurse, Juliet is "not fourteen" (*Rom.* I,iii,12–17). Lady Capulet became

---

15   An act of 1472 stipulated that women heiresses, if thirteen at the time of death of their parents, should have "livery of lands" at fourteen. Evidently this act was still in force in the early 18th century.

her mother at an even earlier age (*Rom.* I,iii,74–75); we naturally think of the Capulets as middle-aged parents, but Lady Capulet cannot be older than twenty-seven! Marina is fourteen (*Pericles* V,ii,8); Miranda is not yet fifteen (*The Tempest* I,ii,41 and 53). Ophelia cannot be older than these.

In Shakespeare's time, universities did not observe terms and vacations. As students usually stayed until they had completed their studies, Hamlet will have been away at Wittenberg for some years, having left Elsinore before Ophelia reached puberty. When he returns he finds that Ophelia has blossomed into a beautiful young woman of thirteen or fourteen!

The scenes in which she appears can only be interpreted in the light of her extreme youth. It explains Laertes' long exhortation to her in I,iii, and Polonius' shortness with her. It leads to the correct interpretation of Hamlet's "Where's your father?" in III,i: he suddenly realises that she would not have come into the Castle by herself. He lies down beside her before the presentation of the Gonzago-play so as to have an excuse for the "explanations" which will ostensibly help her to understand it but are actually directed at the King and Queen.

She sings songs to herself in her "madness" (IV,v,23ff.) to keep herself company, as a child may when playing alone:

Ophelia   *How should I your true love know*
                From another one?
            By his cockle hat and staff,
                And his sandal shoon...

            He is dead and gone, lady,
                He is dead and gone.
            At his head a grass-green turf,
                At his feet a stone...

[She seems to be thinking sometimes of her father, who is dead, sometimes of Hamlet, who is dead to her:]

            ...Tomorrow is Saint Valentine's Day,
                All in the morning betime,
            And I a maid at your window,
                To be your Valentine.
            Then up he rose and donned his clothes,
                And dupped the chamber door,
            Let in the maid that out a maid
                Never departed more.

[And later she sings:]

            His beard was as white as snow,
                All flaxen was his poll.
            He is gone, he is gone,
                And we cast away moan,
            God ha' mercy on his soul

She has never visited Hamlet's bed, but had been looking forward to the time when she would be able to do so.

Motherless, and having only a brother who is older than herself and a father who is very much older, she is a lonely figure, a lonely child. Hamlet, who in another respect is a lonely figure as he, too, is an only child, is attracted to her for that reason. He loves her with that fiercest of all young men's loves, the protective love for a young girl, to which she responds because she needs his protection.

The "tenders" from such a brilliant and handsome young man who is a Prince have had the effect they were bound to have on such a young girl whose mother is not alive to advise and guide her. Laertes' advice, "Fear it, Ophelia, fear it, my dear sister, / And keep you in the rear of his affection", and her father's admonition "Do not believe his vows, for they are brokers", come too late; she replies, "I shall obey, my lord", but her hopes have already blossomed, her heart is already committed:

Ophelia And I, of ladies most deject and wretched,
 That sucked the honey of his musicked vows...

(III,i,154–155)

The shattering of hopes that have been raised at too tender an age is too much for her. She is one of the saddest figures in tragedy, a young girl who has nothing to offer but love and the need for love, and becomes the victim of a situation over which she could never have had any control.

Note 1: In Shakespeare's time, women's roles were played by boys, presumably until their voices broke in early adolescence. Only in 1662 did actresses begin to play such roles. The Ophelia-Laertes conversation in I,iii would have been inserted in order to emphasise Ophelia's youth as early as possible in the play, for without it her age would have been uncertain for too long.

Note 2: Even before the Victorians made it a suitable accomplishment for young ladies of the middle classes, sending messages to a loved one by means of selected posies of flowers was an art cultivated by country folk for hundreds of years.

The most famous of all flower letters is of course the one which Ophelia left for Hamlet. This posthumous posy was in effect a suicide note. Ophelia, it will be remembered, was carrying a garland of "crow-flowers, daisies, nettles, and long purples". This unlikely-sounding posy had been composed because of the message the different elements in it conveyed.

The fact that Ophelia was about to hang her garland on a willow tree gives it an added significance. "The sole use of the willow," wrote the Victorian expert on Shakespeare's flowers, the Rev. Henry Ellacombe, "was to weave garlands for jilted lovers, male and female." The contents of the posy reinforce this theme of abandonment... See also an article by Carson Ritchie, "The Secret Language of Flowers", in *The Countryman* (Feb/Mar 1992). Gertrude describes the garland:

Queen There is a willow grows aslant a brook,
 That shows his hoar leaves in the glassy stream;
 Here with fantastic garlands did she come
 Of crow-flowers, nettles, daisies, and long purples
 That liberal shepherds give a grosser name,
 But our cold maids do dead men's fingers call them.

(IV,vii,167–172)

The crow-flowers may have been buttercups, which are poisonous; the nettles may have been the dead-nettle; the daisies represent the blighting of young love.

In her madness, Ophelia would not consciously intend suicide, but would no longer wish to live after the slaying of her father by her lover, so she climbs somewhat dangerously on to an overhanging willow branch in order to hang her little garland of wild flowers ("coronet weeds") on it, and when she slips into the brook makes no effort to save herself.

The message of the flowers is understood. At the beginning of V,i, the young Sexton's Assistant argues hotly that Ophelia has only received Christian burial because she is a gentlewoman, and the Sexton does not contradict him; later in the scene the First Priest confirms that she has only been granted it after "great command".

Note 3: I feel sure that the hypothesis of a lonely childhood is correct, although it implies a considerable oddity in the dramatic situation. Polonius has his own house (Hamlet: "[Let him] play the fool nowhere but in's own house"—III,i,132–133), and we know that he has at least one male servant, Reynaldo; would there be no female servants in his establishment who could comfort the lonely young Ophelia after his death? If, after losing his wife, Polonius elected not to marry again, would he not employ a duenna to help bring up his young daughter? Such duennas were customary in wealthy families: they are occasionally seen in other plays, such as John Ford's *'Tis Pity She's A Whore* (1629) and Sheridan's *The Duenna* (1775).

The facts remain that Ophelia's mother is never mentioned in the play; it is apparently Laertes who learns of Hamlet's "tenders" and warns Ophelia against them. Unless stage directions were omitted from Quartos 1 and 2, and Folio 1, Ophelia enters unattended in her mad scenes: as she leaves in IV,v,71 the King says "Follow her close; give her good watch, I pray you", implying that no one is caring for her.

Shakespeare evidently intended to re-emphasise Ophelia's youth, inexperience and loneliness, at the price of a considerable improbability in Polonius' domestic arrangements.

Note 4: The parallel between Hamlet and Corneille's *Le Cid* (1636), in which the hero kills the heroine's father at the beginning of the play, was noted by George Stubbes in 1736:

> It does not appear whether Ophelia's madness was chiefly for her father's death or for the loss of Hamlet. It is not often that young women run mad for the loss of their fathers. It is more natural to suppose that, like Chimene in *Le Cid*, her great sorrow proceeded from her father's being killed by the man she lov'd, and thereby making it indecent for her ever to marry him.

Many boys went up to a university at an earlier age than today, but Laertes can hardly be younger than eighteen, and is possibly a few years older, otherwise he would not be a match for Hamlet or nearly so in swordsmanship. At the beginning of the play he is returning to France (I,ii,51); like Hamlet, he will already have spent some time at his university, and will have returned to Denmark for the funeral of the old King and the coronation of the new.

He is described by Hamlet as "very noble" (V,i,205), which in those days meant "versed in courtly behaviour" and "trained in the arts of fighting and always ready to fight, regardless of the odds" (a gentleman could not refuse a duel). He is certainly lively and fearless. He also possesses the "gift of words", and indeed over-uses it. It serves him well when he rouses the rabble of Danes who break into the Castle, but his ranting in Ophelia's grave might well enrage Hamlet.

How are we intended to think of him? We revert for a moment to the construction of this revenge-tragedy. As mentioned in "After the Gonzago-play", he must be the bringer of retribution to Hamlet for the slaying of Polonius, but must not be an honourable avenger; otherwise he would divert sympathy and interest from Hamlet, the central figure of the play, at a late stage in its events.

Suppose that Claudius has both the poisons and persuades Laertes to poison his foil: Laertes might then be regarded as another young man who loses his judgment under heavy emotional stress and allows himself to become Claudius' tool, and might then be thought to deserve a little sympathy on account of his youth. We find that he has already bought poison for his foil in Paris, and it is this prior purchase which makes him a dishonourable avenger. He would certainly be dishonourable to spectators who lived in an age when sword fights were frequent. Whether such a poison was known and used is immaterial! Mysterious poisons are common in the plays of the time.

If there is a weakness in the construction of the play, it is the fate of Ophelia. Would there really be nobody in her father's house to comfort and console the poor child in her loneliness? At the beginning of IV,v Horatio announces that "She is importunate, indeed distract", and later leaves in obedience to the King's "Follow her close; give her good watch, I pray you" as if he had been appointed to look after her, but she nevertheless drowns. It is not even strictly necessary that she should die; her death rounds off the tragedy yet are not her madness and loneliness enough in themselves to make her a pathetic victim of the tragedy?

However, why does not Laertes first demand justice from the King, then comfort and console his young sister himself? Or better still, comfort Ophelia and then demand justice? Does he rouse the rabble of Danes before going to his father's house? Is he merely a loud-mouthed young braggart whose mind runs mainly on honour and revenge: "By heaven, thy madness shall be paid by weight / Till our scale turn the beam"? His picture is incomplete and inconsistent; his failure to care for Ophelia is in contradiction to the concern he displays in his parting advice to her in I,iii. Evidently he was not intended to be more than the dishonourable bringer of retribution, although his youth and the fact that his death completes the annihilation of his family, merit some sympathy.

Something of Shakespeare's intention with respect to Claudius is also indicated. If he possessed and suggested the use of both poisons, he would be the total villain and Laertes an easily misled young man. Yet Shakespeare evidently did not intend Claudius to be seen as the sole villain, for after he has suggested that one foil be unbated, it is Laertes who first mentions poison (IV,vii,140–148), the mention inspiring Claudius to poison the wine, i.e. Laertes shares Claudius' villainy in their conspiracy. His inciting of the Danes to rebellion is rightly described by Claudius as treason (IV,v,121). It would certainly be seen as treason by Shakespeare's spectators, particularly after the rebellion of the Earl of Essex early in 1601; the rebellion may in fact have inspired Shakespeare to write Laertes' insurrection into the play. Although Laertes could demand justice from the King without any rabble-rousing, he rouses the mob before attempting to speak to Claudius or even comfort his sister. This, his use of poison, and his bombast, confirm that he is not an honourable character.

Rosencrantz and Guildenstern are two lively and well-bred young men who were Hamlet's schoolfellows:

> *Hamlet* But let me conjure you, by the rights of our fellowship, by the consonancy of our youth, by the obligation of our ever-preserved love, and by what more dear a better proposer couldcharge you withal, be even and direct with me, whether you were sent for, or no.
>
> (II,ii,278–282)

He welcomes them as his very close friends—a fact which should dispel the notion that they are venial spies in Claudius' pay. Would Hamlet really speak in the above terms if they were such types? They have little opportunity to 'sound' Hamlet, for they arrive in Elsinore at the same time as the Players, the Gonzago-play is put on the following night, and Hamlet is sent to England the next morning. Hamlet begins to distrust them immediately after their arrival because they hesitate to admit that they were sent for, but they hesitate because his "too much changed" appearance deludes them as much as it has deluded everyone else.

They are loyal subjects of the King, and understand very well the damage which the Gonzago-play may do to the monarchy:

Guildenstern   Most holy and religious fear it is
    To keep those many many bodies safe
    That live and feed upon your majesty...
Rosencrantz   ...The cease of majesty
    Dies not alone, but, like a gulf, doth draw
    What's near with i... Ne'er alone
    Did the king sigh, but with a general groan.

(III,iii,8ff.)

So they escort Hamlet to England in obedience to the King's orders and with the conviction that what they are doing is necessary. Since the King only reveals the secret commission in a soliloquy, they are ignorant of its content.

It is now possible to evaluate the dramatic situation up to their departure.

Claudius does not fear Hamlet as a rival or as a dispossessed heir, and is genuinely eager to see his nephew cured of his affliction.

Gertrude is equally eager to see her son cured.

Polonius does his best to help. He has been shown to be a figure of gentle comedy; could he be a figure of gentle comedy and the venial ally of Claudius, as he is thought to be, at one and the same time?

Rosencrantz and Guildenstern also do their best to help in the short time they have.

Thus, although Hamlet is generally thought to be surrounded by spies and enemies who are all seeking to probe him, he is actually surrounded by friends who all love him and want to help him, but whose love he must repulse because he alone must avenge his father.

17
THE HAMLET FAMILY: GERTRUDE

Gertrude has made her principal contribution to the situation before the play begins, and thereafter makes virtually none to its events. Since she is the wife of one principal character and the mother of the other, she is a figure of much greater importance than her inaction might suggest. As the central figure of the Claudius-Gertrude-Hamlet triad, she occupies so much of the two men's thoughts that a full character-study of her is necessary.

(i)

In her first appearance (I,ii) she says nothing either during the briefing of the ambassadors or while Claudius is granting Laertes' request. She and Claudius then jointly urge Hamlet to abandon his mourning, the appeal being evidently the result of a bedroom discussion between them. Which of them first thought of making the appeal? Since Gertrude is the first to make it, and later offers her opinion that the cause of Hamlet's madness is "His father's death and our o'erhasty marriage", it may well have been she; on the other hand, Claudius' appeal is longer and more pressing.

Her invitation to her son to "Cast thy nighted colour off, / And let thine eye look like a friend on Denmark" not only shows that she has quickly found happiness with her new husband but also implies a drastic lack of perception on her part. Why cannot she leave her son alone for a while? Why must she compel him to explain what his "inky cloak" makes obvious, that he has "that within which passeth show"?

An episode in II,ii,40ff. suggests that she takes no interest in state affairs:

[Enter Polonius.]
Polonius Th'ambassadors from Norway, my good lord,
   Are joyfully returned.
King Thou still hast been the father of good news.
Polonius Have I, my lord? Assure you, my good liege,
   I hold my duty as I hold my soul,
   Both to my God and to my gracious king.
   And I do think—or else this brain of mine
   Hunts not the trail of policy so sure
   As it hath used to do—that I have found
   The very cause of Hamlet's lunacy.
King O speak of that; that do I long to hear!
Polonius Give first admittance to th'ambassadors;
   My news shall be the fruit to that great feast.
King Thyself do grace to them and let them in.

[Exit Polonius.]

   He tells me, my dear Gertrude, he hath found
   The head and source of all your son's distemper.
Queen I doubt it is no other but the main,
   His father's death and our o'erhasty marriage.

Why should the King have to repeat to Gertrude what Polonius has just said? Does she turn aside when Polonius enters and begin chatting with her ladies?

The extent to which she leaves everything to Claudius appears in a remarkable little episode in III,I,28ff.:

King	Sweet Gertrude, leave us too;

    For we have closely sent for Hamlet hither,
    That he, as 'twere by accident, may here
    Affront Ophelia.
    Her father and myself—lawful espials—
    Will so bestow ourselves that, being unseen,
    We may of their encounter frankly judge,
    And gather by him, as he is behaved,
    If't be th'affliction of his love or no
    That thus he suffers for.

Queen   I shall obey you.

A mother whose son has supposedly been driven mad by his love for a girl should be acutely interested in overhearing any conversation between them and ought to insist on overhearing it—is she not an even more lawful espial than Claudius?—but Gertrude leaves. Elizabethan drama being as short of stage directions as it is, we do not know whether she says "I shall obey you" with equanimity or disappointment—but she leaves.[16]

Is it she or Claudius who thinks of sending for Rosencrantz and Guildenstern? The idea will be the result of another bedroom discussion, and it might well be Gertrude: while she may be uninterested in state affairs, she does love her son.

She can put on the dignity of a queen, as when she promises a royal reward to Rosencrantz and Guildenstern on their arrival (II,ii,19–26); in private she displays none.

During the Gonzago-play she says little, being too embarrassed. Afterwards, Claudius tells her that Hamlet will be sent to England—" 'Tis so concluded on"—(III,iv,202). She has not asked what will be done with him there, not that Claudius would tell her!

In her closet she begins her attempt to be "round" with Hamlet in the worst possible way: "Hamlet, thou hast thy father much offended." He instantly loses his temper, and within a few seconds has vented it on Polonius. Was not the Gonzago-play as offensive to her as to Claudius? Why is she not round with him on her own behalf? And why does she speak of Claudius as Hamlet's father when Hamlet has clearly not responded to Claudius' appeal?

Evidently her "o'erhasty marriage" is on her conscience. Hamlet easily persuades her that it was self-indulgence. Further, her guilty conscience might be what prevents her from grasping the significance of Hamlet's references to Claudius as a murderer and, when he reveals that he is "but mad in craft", also from asking "Mad in craft to what end?" Admittedly, he has just slain Polonius and spoken to a Ghost which she could not see, and his appearance remains as lunatic as ever. Yet his last speeches are sober and moving, and we may well feel that she should be more alert. We must accept that she is far less shrewd than Claudius and less alert than a wife and mother should be.

Later, in IV,ii, she attempts to excuse her son for the death of Polonius—"He weeps for what is done"—but Claudius replies impatiently, "O Gertrude, come away!", and she does not ask what he has decided to do with the mad Hamlet.

After Hamlet's departure for England she appears to realise as never before how

---

16   The pirated Q1 has "Que. With all my hart", which suggests that she leaves quite cheerfully. See Chap. 26, "A Comparison of Q1 and Q2".

dependent she is on the men in her life. In IV,v,117ff. Laertes and his rabble invade the Castle:

King   What is the cause, Laertes,
    That thy rebellion looks so giant-like?
    Let him go, Gertrude; do not fear our person.
    There's such divinity doth hedge a king
    That treason can but peep at what it would,
    Acts little of his will.—Tell me, Laertes,
    Why art thou so incensed?—Let him go, Gertrude.
    Speak, man.

Although Hamlet's harangue in her closet has left her soul "sick", she has run forward to grasp Laertes' sword-arm, in fear for her husband's life.

Towards the end of the graveyard scene (V,i) Hamlet grapples with Laertes:

Hamlet Why, I will fight with him upon this theme
    Until my eyelids will no longer wag.
Queen O my son, what theme?
Hamlet I loved Ophelia. Forty thousand brothers
    Could not with all their quantity of love
    Make up my sum. *[To Laertes]* What wilt thou do for her?
King O he is mad, Laertes.
Queen For love of God, forbear him.

If these two fight in their present mood, one of them will kill the other. Gertrude is terrified at the thought of a duel between her son and Laertes, who has been polishing his swordsmanship in Paris.

(ii)

My first picture of Gertrude was of a girl who was once and perhaps still is very beautiful, had captured or allowed herself to be captured by the most heroic husband in the land, and thereafter had let everything come to her as her due; it soon became clear that this picture would have to be drastically modified. At the beginning of the play she certainly appears to be complacent, though she is not so much complacent as compliant, even submissive. Why does Hamlet call her a "mouse"—by implication from "The Mousetrap"? While beautiful women can usually look after their interests very well, Gertrude is so easily overcome by Hamlet in her closet that she appears to be incapable of doing so. She might reply that what middle-aged people choose to do in respect of a second marriage is their concern and no one else's, especially when their children are grown-up, but it does not occur to her to tell him so. Indeed, he succeeds in persuading her that her second marriage was pure self-indulgence, and leaves her so soul-sick that she can spare no thought for the mad Ophelia.

A second thought was: had she been married very young, had she been a child-bride, as Ophelia might have been; did she become habitually dependent on her husband, and has she remained so ever since?

Hamlet   ... Why, she would hang on him
    As if increase of appetite had grown
    By what it fed on.

(I,ii,143–145)

Whereas Hamlet is thinking of "appetite" and the "heyday in the blood", Gertrude may have hung on her first husband because she needed a husband on whom she could hang, just as she now depends completely on Claudius. She seems incapable of being a true helpmeet to a monarch, and to be less worldly-wise and mature than her own son.

It seems likely that Gertrude has a strong physical need for a husband as much as moral and intellectual need. The fact that the Elder Hamlet had reached the age when he habitually took an afternoon nap suggests that he had been much older than Gertrude and that Claudius had been his younger brother. Gertrude might not have been unhappy to take a second husband who was nearer to herself in age than her first husband had been. If a hint may be taken from the apparently advanced age of the Player King, the Elder Hamlet might have been quite old at the time of his death. Why else would the Ghost complain of the "luxury" in the Royal bed of Denmark? Its complaint does not put any new thought into Hamlet's mind, for, from the heartsick tone of his first soliloquy, Gertrude is letting her new happiness show all too clearly to everyone; she cannot have learned much tact.

Ghost Ay, that incestuous, that adulterate beast,
With witchcraft of his wit, with traitorous gifts—
O wicked wit and gifts, that have the power
So to seduce—won to his shameful lust
The will of my most virtuous-seeming queen!
O Hamlet, what a falling-off was there!
From me, whose love was of that dignity
That it went hand in hand even with the vow
I made to her in marriage, and to decline
Upon a wretch whose natural gifts were poor
To those of mine!

(I,v,42–52)

A display of two kinds of jealousy, this: of the "luxury", and of Claudius' gifts, which are by no means as poor as all that. Has he not been elected king? And why does the Ghost speak of having loved her with "dignity"? Dignity is not usually a component of love; one either loves a person without qualification, or not, or at least with few reservations. "Dignity" suggests that it had been an arranged marriage, which it almost certainly was, and that the Elder Hamlet's attitude to his wife had been somewhat condescending.[17] From the Ghost's and Hamlet's references to his "crimes" (I,v,12 and 76; III,iii,81), the Elder Hamlet may not have been an especially amiable person! How happy had Gertrude really been with him? Had she led a somewhat suppressed life with him, and does she welcome the kinder Claudius?

There seems to be a childlike or even childish element in her. She has been easily won by Claudius, she thinks that Hamlet can easily join them in her new happiness, she leaves all decisions to Claudius, she is easily silenced by Hamlet in her closet, his rebukes then occupy her mind to the exclusion of almost all else, and she is ignored by Claudius when he decides what he will do with her son after the Gonzago-play. Although she is the cause of Hamlet's shock at the beginning of the play, it takes her by surprise. If she is not the central pillar of her family which as wife and mother she ought to be, is it because she is self-centred, or light-minded and indifferent, or simply incapable of filling such a role? Is she a culpable

---

17   "Love" to the Elizabethans meant sexual love, also friendship, also esteem, e.g. "I loved you ever" (Hamlet to Laertes in the graveyard), and "I do receive your offered love like love" (Laertes to Hamlet before the fencing-match). The Ghost's love and dignity may imply too detached an attitude for a young wife.

person in the tragedy, or a pathetic figure?

If she is so inadequate as Queen, why is Claudius so attached to her? He addresses her as "my dear Gertrude" (II,ii,54), "sweet Gertrude" (III,i,28), "sweet Queen" (IV,vii,163); to Laertes he says:

King ...and for myself,
  My virtue or my plague, be it either which,
  She's so conjunctive to my life and soul
  That, as the star moves not but in his sphere,
  I could not but by her.

(IV,vii,12–16)

Does this mean that Claudius discusses everything with her in private, and relies on her as an adviser? Such a supposition does not fit her behaviour; or does this attachment imply more about Claudius than her?

(iii)

Enumerating my objections to Bradley's opinion of Gertrude helped to clarify my picture of her:

> She did not merely marry a second time with indecent haste; she was false to her husband while he lived...On the other hand, she was not privy to the murder of her husband...She had a soft animal nature, and was very dull and very shallow. She loved to be happy, like a sheep in the sun; and to do her justice, it pleased her to see others happy, like more sheep in the sun... Though she knew that [Hamlet] considered her marriage "o'erhasty", she was untroubled by any shame at the feelings which had led to it.

Shakespearean Tragedy Lecture IV (Part V)

My objections:

This description of a "dull" woman does not tally with that of a wife who "hung" on her first husband "As if increase of appetite had grown / By what it fed on," and in whose blood the "heyday" is not yet tame.

She followed her first husband to the grave "Like Niobe, all tears". She may have been simulating grief, as an adulterous widow might, but Hamlet does not appear to think so, and the Ghost's complaint is of the "luxury" in her second marriage, not of falsity before it.

The reference to the "o'erhasty" marriage comes from her, and does indicate shame on her part. Why else would she be so conscience-stricken after the closet scene?

A dull, sensual, animal of a woman would be quite out of place between the shrewd, authoritative Claudius and the brilliant Hamlet. In spite of her submissiveness, there must be some liveliness in Gertrude. All three members of the triad should attract the interest of audiences in their several ways, and since audiences include female spectators as well as males, Shakespeare must have intended to arouse pity and fear (if he thought in those terms) in both sexes and Bradley's "sheep" would be most unlikely to do so.

Incidentally I cannot think of any female character in Shakespeare who could be so described. Would it be wise of any playwright to put so uninteresting a character on his stage? What kind of wife and mother would be likely to arouse interest, perhaps sympathy, in the ladies? Bradley's Gertrude hardly meets that requirement.

(iv)

Most women fear becoming widows: they obviously fear the loss not only of the wage-earner but also of the husband who enabled them to have a family, provided them with comfort and security, and shared their responsibilities. They do not want a life of loneliness, and they know that it can be harder for a widow to find a second husband than for a widower to find a second wife.

How old is Gertrude?

According to the Player King, he and his Queen have been married thirty years, and Hamlet must be assumed to be referring to his own parents. If Gertrude had been another of those royal brides who were married very young, between twelve and fifteen or sixteen, and had given birth to Hamlet a few years later, and if Hamlet is now about twenty-six, she would now be a few years over forty. If the Elder Hamlet had married her when he was twenty-five, he would have been about fifty-five at the time of his death. I suspect that Claudius was his younger brother and is now approaching fifty, and that Gertrude is a few years younger than he.

How did a girl's life proceed in those days? As she grew up, she was invariably closely shepherded by her parents; today, she may embark on a career and become independent. However, if she wants a husband and family, this period of independence is usually not very long, and these days some career women are now leaving motherhood till quite late. In Shakespeare's day, when there were few careers for women outside marriage, she moved directly from the protection of her family to that of a husband who had often been found for her by her parents. Always accustomed to the atmosphere of a family and to the presence of a man in the house as helpmeet and protector, the sudden death of her husband would leave her feeling lost, lonely, and vulnerable.

Hence Gertrude, shattered by the sudden death of her first husband, has allowed herself to listen to Claudius' advances, and has accepted him after a month of widowhood.

When the play opens, she is evidently happy with her new husband, to a degree which shocks Hamlet and which she herself had possibly not expected.

Does she ever really understand that she has married her first husband's murderer? Since Hamlet virtually throws the information at her with his Gonzago-play and his furious ranting in her closet, it might be thought that she should understand; does the information really register? She knows nothing of the Ghost's story; since her son is mad, why should she believe him? He then shames her, and leaves her in dreadful confusion: she is afraid that she will lose her son's love if she does not separate herself from Claudius, but, as her running forward to protect Claudius against Laertes shows, she cannot bear the thought of losing a second husband. These two fears appear to drive out all other thoughts, for at no time after the closet scene does she refer to Hamlet's accusation again. Her running forward to grasp Laertes' sword arm in IV,v suggests either that the information has not registered or that something deep within her, the fear of losing a second husband, is not allowing it to register. At the end of the play, when she is happy to see her son recovered from his lunacy, the thought has disappeared. So we may assume that it never penetrated.

(v)

Shakespeare must have conceived Gertrude in detail before he began to 'write' her, and although her inaction and submissiveness make her picture somewhat indistinct, they are actually her distinguishing characteristics. Whereas a less sympathetic view of her is certainly possible, in the end it is necessary to decide between two alternatives: did

Shakespeare intend his Gertrude to arouse sympathy in the breasts of his female spectators, or to offer them a reprehensible or at least uninteresting female character? Was the Hamlet family originally as happy and united as the Polonius family, or was it rotten at the core because of an indifferent, self-centred, perhaps unfaithful and deceitful wife?

I lean towards the sympathetic view: I prefer to think that the family was happy and united before the murder (a view confirmed by Hamlet's first soliloquy); that the wife had been married when very young and to a husband not chosen by herself; that she had been a loving wife and mother if rather submissive, and had become dependent on a husband and protector to the point where she had never really become mature: she had never been compelled to become emotionally and intellectually independent. Why else would Hamlet complain that she would hang on his father? When does she ever display the capacity for deceit and hypocrisy that an unfaithful wife must possess if she is to cuckold her husband and even be an accessory to his murder? Why does the Ghost twice say "Leave her to heaven" and later call her a "weakest body"? Although she may be thoughtless and shallow, she is nothing worse: she loves her son, and is certainly capable of feeling shame.

Is she to be censured for her weakness and inaction?

I find that there is little point in censuring her. She is as she is, she was not born to be a strong figure, and by my interpretation of Shakespeare's intention it is necessary to the tragedy that she should be as she is, i.e. a constant preoccupation in the minds of both Hamlet and Claudius. She is largely what the circumstances of her life have made her. If the reader is inclined to think poorly of her, he is in effect complaining that she wasn't born as someone else, with a more forceful personality, perhaps in a different age when women had more opportunities—and so into a different life.

Hamlet is an Elizabethan play; Gertrude is an Elizabethan wife. The characters in a play must always be comprehensible to the theatregoers of its own time, and in an age when girls could be married in early adolescence, when women had few if any opportunities outside marriage, and when disease, in particular the frequent outbreaks of the plague, must have widowed many women prematurely, Gertrude would have been readily recognisable to the audiences of her own day.

Women's tragedies have been said to be quieter than those of men, but tragedies none the less. Gertrude is not a great tragic figure because she is not of heroic stature, and at times she suffers acutely as she is the opposite of strong. She should be seen as a pathetic rather than a culpable contributor to her own tragedy: not very perceptive, somewhat childlike, totally without malice and not a "most pernicious woman", as Hamlet calls her. She is immature for her age, neither as worldly-wise nor as self-possessed as a woman of her age usually is, possibly incapable of becoming worldly-wise or self-possessed, and occupying so much of the thoughts of Claudius and Hamlet because both men know that she needs protection. Trapped by Claudius' murder, she should be regarded as another of its innocent victims.

Gertrude's end is characteristic of her. By nature not quick to take hints, she is so happy to see her son safely returned from the sea voyage, recovered from his lunacy and, from his "Good madam!", also reconciled to her, that she disregards Claudius' urgent whisper:

Queen The Queen carouses to thy fortune, Hamlet.
Hamlet Good madam!
King Gertrude, do not drink!
Queen I will, my lord; I pray you, pardon me.

(V,ii,271–274)

18

HAMLET THE YOUNG MAN

(i)

The conventional view that Hamlet hesitates or delays because of his over-reflective make-up or other weakness of 'character' (possibly of a psychopathological nature) flies in the face of all the evidence. Whenever he needs to size up a situation, come to a decision, and act, Hamlet does so with enviable quickness; indeed, he is over-hasty when he slays Polonius. Stoll rightly asks, "If Hamlet is so inadequate, why does nobody in the play drop any hint to that effect?" The play tells us how we are meant to think of him:

Ophelia The courtier's, scholar's, soldier's eye, tongue, sword,
  Th'expectancy and rose of the fair state,
  The glass of fashion and the mould of form,
  Th'observed of all observers...

(III,i,150–153)

Fortin. For he was likely, had he been put on,
  To have proved most royally.

(V,ii,379–380)

I do not believe that Shakespeare would have constructed a revenge tragedy with a defective hero or, if he did, that he would have failed to make the nature of the character defect clear to his audience.

Much of Hamlet's emotion is the inevitable consequence of the situation in which he is placed by his fate; he cannot take the Ghost at its word, verifying its story seems impossible. If he must kill his uncle his prospects in life will have vanished.

According to the conventional view, the Gonzago-play causes Claudius to betray himself. I find that Hamlet betrays himself to Claudius more completely than the older and more experienced Claudius betrays himself to Hamlet. There is even doubt as to whether Claudius betrays himself at all.

I therefore infer that the causes of the emotions which bring about this fatal self-betrayal are factors which intensify rather than weaken Hamlet's reaction to the Ghost's story.

Remembering one essential feature of play construction, we note that Claudius' appeal to Hamlet and Hamlet's first soliloquy are spoken at the beginning of the play before Hamlet learns of the Ghost, i.e. that they are parts of the exposition. They are important explanatory passages intended for the information of the spectators which they are meant to remember as pointers to their hero's subsequent behaviour. One of the causes of Hamlet's emotion in his soliloquy "O that this too, too solid flesh would melt" is his disgust with his mother's evident happiness in her very recent second marriage, which is stated clearly enough, while the other is not directly expressed. His unfavourable comparison of the new husband with the old is, as much as anything else, the expression of his revulsion at Claudius' attempts to persuade him to accept him as a new father.

Since the adverse reaction of stepchildren to the step-situation appears to have been less studied than some other aspects of child behaviour, and since such adverse reaction in adult stepchildren appears by comparison to have been little studied, some little time will be spent on it; however, it must not be assumed that it is the only or the most important cause of Hamlet's emotionality. In due course it will be set in its place among the other causes.

(ii)

When a bereaved or divorced parent marries again, the children find that they have become stepchildren. Some stepchildren accept their new situation readily, and such as do seem to be in the minority. Some accept it but with difficulty. Some cannot stand it; for them, becoming a stepchild appears to inflict acute emotional shock.

Whether it is possible to predict what the child's reaction to becoming a stepchild will be, I am unable to say. The most important factors are the child's individual temperament, in particular his emotional independence of or dependence on the lost parent, and perhaps the degree of compatibility with the step-parent. Somewhat surprisingly, age and marital status do not seem to be factors. When he reaches (say) forty, the step-child should have acquired his own experience of married life and should have given some thought to what his own spouse would do if he himself died. Yet it does not follow that he will revise or rationalise his attitude to his stepparent. Whether the stepchild will not or cannot rationalise his attitude to his stepparent I am again unable to say, though I favour the latter alternative.

The following are examples of reactions observed in stepchildren ranging from pre-adolescence to retirement age.

A man lost his wife when he was just over sixty, his three children being then married and living in their own homes, the eldest having her own family. Before she died, his wife had told him: "You cannot live alone in the house, and at your age it would be pointless to wait the customary two years. Find another wife as soon as you can." She had been careful to tell her children and close relatives of what she had said. He took her at her word and married again within the year. The second wife was well-educated, pleasant, and tactful, but his two eldest children could never bring themselves to be more than formally polite to her, although, as everyone outside his own family could see, she was obviously making their father very content. After about eight years he died suddenly, leaving his second wife alone in the house. She lived another fifteen years; after her death, his eldest daughter who lived only a few miles away and was then past retirement age (she had even lost her own husband), admitted with regret and weeping as she spoke, that "We didn't visit her often enough."

A man who lost his wife when he was sixty, married again after the customary two years. The new wife's daughters were pleased that their mother had married again, but the man's youngest son—then twenty-four and a late arrival in his father's life—and his next older sister would not visit their father for several years afterwards.

A man lost his wife when they had two pre-adolescent children, married again and had three children by his second wife. His two elder children were never happy in their new situation and held themselves apart from the younger children, the family being always, so to speak, divided down the middle.

A man who had lost his wife married a divorcee who had two sons of about thirteen and fifteen. The younger boy took happily to the new life, in which he remained till he was about twenty. The older boy became morose and withdrawn, rarely speaking at meals, and going about by himself. After about two years he left to rejoin his father, later seeming unable to settle to any occupation. By contrast his younger brother, who took a succession of jobs elsewhere, always 'came home' to the village where his stepfather lived.

A young woman married and had two sons, then lost her husband. Marrying again, she lost this second husband after a few years. She did not look for a third as she had been left well provided for and did not need a husband to support her. She did not marry again because she had seen the effect on her sons of becoming stepchildren, and was unwilling to inflict the experience on them a second time. At a great age she died, having remained unmarried for the last forty-five years of her life: a considerable act of self-sacrifice.

I have seen the following phenomenon more than once. The stepchild is sitting at table where the conversation is general. When he speaks, he will turn his head towards the stepparent to include him or her in the conversation, but will only do so very briefly. As he does so his eyelids will droop and he will momentarily close his eyes.

I have seen a girl of about eighteen who had just become a stepdaughter going about with an air of rigid, formal 'correctness' at all times; in another family, a stepson of about the same age always wearing a fixed smile of goodwill when in the house. Such loss of spontaneity, a significant sign in adolescents, is unnatural in children when they are in their own homes.

In none of the above instances could the stepparent or the stepchild be described as difficult to get on with. Indeed, the reverse was always the case. Nor could the stepchildren's attitude be explained by anything which might be called a rational reason.

One possible reason may stem from the stepchild's childhood.

The principle of bringing up an infant has been stated to be that of 'continuous concern'. By instinct new-born infants only know two things: that at times they become hungry, since hunger in an infant—being an actual pain—causes them to howl loudly; and that they are totally helpless and vulnerable. When awake they must always be held close to their mothers' bosoms to assure them that they are continuously protected. This feeling of protection must continue for some years, until the child has become accustomed to its mother's absence and later to its father's absence also; otherwise it may suffer from abandonment fear, which can be acute. So the adult stepchild rejects the stepparent because of an early childhood memory: "When I was small, I would nestle up to my Mum or Dad, but not to any adult whom I didn't know well. Am I now expected to nestle up to a stranger? This house is no longer 'home' for me."

The acute reaction to the step-condition does not seem to have been given a name, so I shall call it 'stepchild's shock'. Sometimes temporarily and sometimes for a long period, acute emotional shock destroys the sufferer's natural ability to enjoy life spontaneously, and it is hard to imagine a better description of the condition than Hamlet's:

Hamlet I have of late—but wherefore I know not—lost all my mirth, forgone all custom of exercises; and, indeed, it goes so heavily with my disposition that this goodly frame, the earth, seems to me a sterile promontory; this most excellent canopy the air, look you, this brave o'erhanging firmament, this majestical roof fretted with golden fire—why, it appears no other thing to me than a foul and pestilent congregation of vapours. What a piece of work is man! How noble in reason! How infinite in faculty! In form and moving how express and admirable! In action how like an angel! In apprehension how like a god! The beauty of the world! The paragon of animals! And yet, to me, what is this quintessence of dust? Man delights not me, no, nor woman neither...

(II,ii,289–302)

His condition has been aggravated but has not been caused by the Ghost's story, for he has expressed it in more agonized form in his first soliloquy, which he starts before he is told of the Ghost:

Hamlet   O, that this too, too solid flesh would melt,
    Thaw, and resolve itself into a dew!
    Or that the Everlasting had not fixed
    His canon 'gainst self-slaughter! O God, God!
    How weary, stale flat, and unprofitable
    Seem to me all the uses of this world!
    Fie on't, O fie! 'Tis an unweeded garden
    That grows to seed; things rank and gross in nature
    Possess it merely—

(I, ii, 129–137)

...And so on, the interjections and broken sentences emphasising his difficulty in expressing himself adequately. His grief over his father's death, the replacement of his father by a new personality, and his mother's apparent forgetting of his father combine to throw him off balance. He has become insecure; he only wishes to be allowed to return to Wittenberg where he will feel, if not more at home, at least no longer in an atmosphere which has become alien to him.

A number of factors in his situation make his shock particularly severe.

He is an only child, and had therefore received the undivided attention of both parents since birth—not that he was spoilt by too much attention.

His parents had been an exceptionally united couple. It seems that the family had always been small, containing only three members. A larger number of children would have diluted the situation, but Hamlet is trapped within a very small family circle.

He makes very few references to his father; however, his words "He was a man, take him for all in all; / I shall not look upon his like again" suggest that as a boy he had hero-worshipped his great father. Although his references to Claudius during the play are contemptuous, he did not necessarily dislike him before his father's death. After hearing the Ghost's story Hamlet says, "My tables—meet it is I set it down / That one may smile, and smile, and be a villain." Clearly, Claudius has charm; equally clearly, the thought that he might also be a villain has only now occurred to Hamlet. Since Claudius would be overshadowed in Hamlet's mind by his heroic brother, Hamlet may well have given him no more thought than his charm might attract. After his father's death it would be impossible for him to accept Claudius as a new role-model or to accept anyone else, since he is no longer a child, and Claudius' approaches might well embarrass, then revolt him.

His mother is unexpectedly happy in her new marriage. Hamlet's complaint of her disloyalty to his dead father may well include an element of complaint of her disloyalty to him—naturally, since he admired his father. Yet I do not regard any such feeling of disloyalty to him as implying that he is excessively attached to or dependent on his mother. I assume that Hamlet has been away at Wittenberg for most, if not all, of the last few years (in Shakespeare's time, universities did not observe vacations), and that the experience has taught him independence of home to some degree. Nevertheless, what must have been the close mutual attachment of his early years prevents him from understanding how she could take to a second husband so soon after the first, and so completely.

His attitude to his mother appears to be ambivalent. Because he is a law student he at once suspects her complicity in the murder, and decides that he must establish her guilt or innocence. Since she is his mother, this is a frightful task! He knows that she is somewhat childlike and if she is innocent must be protected against the suspicion of others.

Unfortunately, Claudius' appeals to accept him as a new father have been much too pressing, and she offends him deeply by joining Claudius in this appeal: possibly another reason why he ignores the Ghost's injunction to spare her and builds his test of her complicity into the Gonzago-play.

These emotional pressures, and his helplessness in the situation, produce the burst of blind rage in his Hecuba soliloquy: "Am I a coward?" He recovers and reminds himself that he must be on his guard against his "weakness and melancholy", but they are too much for him; he gives way to his rage when he steals upon Claudius at prayer, and again in the closet scene when his mother opens her attempt to be "round" with him in the worst possible way: "Hamlet, thou hast thy father much offended," causing him to drive his sword through the arras without first looking behind it.

At the end of the scene, in which his harangue and his attempt to turn his mother away from his father's murderer have been the more intense, because he has also been venting his feelings against his uncle-stepfather, he is much relaxed. He vents them further with his parting "And so, my mother" to Claudius, which is his retort to Claudius' speaking to him in I,ii as if he were a petulant child, as a mother might. He completes his emotional catharsis by sending Rosencrantz and Guildenstern to their deaths as agents of his uncle.

At the end of the play, his rage has gone. While his own hatred has cooled, he does not understand how deeply he has offended Claudius.

(iii)

There is a process which scientists call imprinting. A new-born baby's first impressions are of its mother: her warmth, her bosom, the sound of her voice, the feel of her hands as she handles him and pets him, even of her heartbeat, and these first impressions register very deeply. Probably no other later impressions register as deeply. Although I have heard a scientist say, "The baby becomes imprinted on its mother," the meaning appears to have been inverted. To some extent, any imprinting will be a two-way process; since a new-born baby's mind is a blank sheet in respect of sense-impressions, the imprinting will be mainly on the baby.

This process takes place in other animals besides humans. If a puppy is given to a boy to bring up, it becomes its master's slave for life. Mary's little lamb would certainly go wherever she went if she had brought it up herself!

Initially, the baby is only aware of its mother as the source of the love, warmth and protection which it needs; only later does it become aware of its father as another source. Together, the parents then form what may be regarded as a psychic sheath or psychic placenta which surrounds the infant and provides it with the necessary sustenance of love, protection, and encouragement.

With the exception of identical twins, all humans are unique individuals; father, mother and child have their own individualities, with each playing a part in determining the nature of the psychic placenta. Further children may also make their contribution. Hence every family is a unique organism and do not all families have their own atmosphere?

Between parents and their own children there is a bond which amounts to more than physical resemblance; it is a psychic bond which has been called the tie of blood and which cannot be broken, even when family relationships have become soured. This bond does not exist between parents and adopted children or stepchildren, although something akin to it may come into being if the adopted child or stepchild is very young, when the ties of affection and gratitude may eventually become strong. Yet it is unlikely to become quite the same as the genetic bond of common blood. If the child becomes a stepchild after reaching adolescence or later, the stepparent must be very careful in case a part of the original 'psychic sheath' to which the child had become conditioned, is absent. He may, for example, give his own child an infuriated 'bawling-out'; the same 'bawling out' to a stepchild and particularly an older stepchild may destroy the possibility of a satisfactory relationship between them.

To the children, a family has an 'always' atmosphere. Their parents had 'always' been their parents, and had 'always' been married; the psychic placenta had 'always' been what it is. A strong, solid bond forms between the child and its parents, and it may imagine that the bond between its parents is equally solid. It cannot be, because the parents belonged to and were brought up in different families, but the child may be unable to understand that a bereaved or divorced parent can form a close bond with a new partner.

If there is a divorce or bereavement, the loss of a parent causes some of the psychic sheath to be torn away, leaving the child feeling vulnerable and insecure. To borrow a term from plastic surgery, if a step-parent arrives, he may offer 'replacement tissue'. Suppose, however, that the replacement tissue is not compatible with that of the sheath to which the child has become conditioned, and is rejected by his psyche: he will have an adjustment problem which he may or may not be able to overcome. As mentioned earlier, some stepchildren have continued to reject the tissue offered by a step-parent to the end of the stepparent's life, for no reason apparent to anyone outside the family. My own observation suggests that it is not so much a question of whether the child will or will not accept the proffered tissue, as of whether he is able to accept it. It might be supposed that an adult stepchild would eventually accept that a bereaved parent cannot be expected to live alone for the rest of his or her life. Again from observation, such rational acceptance of the situation does not necessarily occur even in mature adults—such may be the depth of the child's early impressions of, and attachment to, its lost parent.

The effect of the new bond between the natural parent and the stepparent is to change the nature of the sheath. Usually it will not be completely changed, because one parent's personality remains as part of it; but what if the original parent takes so completely to the stepparent that the atmosphere of the home also changes completely? This change happens within the Hamlet family when Gertrude immediately takes to and begins to "hang" on her new husband as she had "hung" on the old. Hamlet returns from Wittenberg and is thrown off balance when he finds that within "a little month" the Castle has ceased to be the parental home of his childhood. Small wonder that his sole wish is to return to his university, where, if not at home, he will at least be in a familiar atmosphere!

His uncomprehending stepparent not only forbids him to return but even presses himself on Hamlet as a new father, which approach his mother supports. If they had refrained and simply left him to accustom himself to the new atmosphere, he might eventually have accepted it, but they give him far too little time and he cannot escape his stepfather's over-eager approaches. Claudius' rebuke to Hamlet for not coming out of mourning, couched as if to a boy, is a totally out-of-place 'bawling-out'.

19
HAMLET THE YOUNG MAN (CONT'D)

When a family loses a parent and the remaining parent remarries, the child-become-stepchild may have the same difficulties in adjusting whether the loss is by bereavement or divorce.[18]

He may feel grief at the loss, depression caused by his alien and often inescapable situation, and rage which he may direct against himself; he may even self-flagellate, there being no other target. He may come to feel that human relationships are basically unstable to the point where later in life he does not attempt to form a stable relationship. He needs sufficient time in which to come to terms with his grief and, if he can, to accustom himself to the new family atmosphere.

His difficulties increase if the new stepparent offers himself even a little too strongly as a replacement parent.

He may consider or even attempt suicide.

Though not a child, Hamlet displays all these reactions. He feels grief at the loss of his father and is given too little time to accustom himself to the loss; he suffers acute revulsion at Claudius' pressing appeals to accept him as a new father after a mere two months, in particular because his mother begins them; he begins to see human relationships as unstable ("Frailty, thy name is woman" and "Get thee to a nunnery"); he self-flagellates with "Am I a coward? Who calls me villain?" and vents his rage both at the wrong moment and on Polonius—the wrong man. In addition, he vents it later on his two friends. He describes his depression at length to Rosencrantz and Guildenstern. As for the thought of suicide, it soon enters his mind ("Or that the Everlasting had not fixed / His canon 'gainst self-slaughter"—I,ii,131–2).

In his "Literature and Psychology", Frank L. Lucas considers Hamlet to be an obsessional neurotic who is "in the stage of paralysis", ascribes his condition to being "unduly tied to his mother", and quotes various cases from Wilhelm Stekel[19] in support of his thesis. This is the most extreme view I have come across, for which I find no justification in the play; he has been away at Wittenberg long enough to have emerged from dependence on either parent, and he is compelled to give much thought to his childlike mother.

In the closet scene, which might suggest an Oedipal problem, he is trying to turn her affections away from his uncle for a very good reason: she has unwittingly married her first husband's murderer. His predominant emotion is rage against his uncle; he is not trying to turn her affections towards himself.

One of his lines, "The rank sweat of an enseamed bed", might suggest the Oedipal problem, but another interpretation is possible. At puberty the sex urge comes over us, and from then on it occupies much of our waking and sleeping thoughts. And there is something we do not learn till later which we only discover from experience: that we may perspire freely when making love vigorously in a warm bed. Evidently Hamlet knows. Where will he have made the discovery? Obviously at Wittenberg, where a young man such as he would have little difficulty in finding a partner. If he has had the experience of making love with a woman

---

18   See *Psychotherapy with Children of Divorce* by Dr. Richard A. Gardner, M.D. (Jason Aaronson, N.Y., 1976).

19   Sigmund Freud's distinguished pupil

who was not his mother, any Oedipal problem—if he ever had one—should be over.[20]

Second or later marriages by bereaved spouses were probably much commoner in Shakespeare's time than today: it will be recalled that Chaucer's Wife of Bath had five husbands. The average expectation of life was far shorter than today; during the Middle Ages, possibly 35 years, provided you survived infancy, childhood and wars, after which one could expect another fifteen or twenty years; general expectancy was not much longer by 1600. The need for both private and public hygiene was not realised; as there was no piped water, human excrement was dumped in the channel or gutter running down the centre of each street; nor was the need for a balanced diet known. Diseases and their treatment were not understood and many of the ills of life were attributed to either the Lord's will or the machinations of the Devil or his helpers the witches—because there were no better explanations. Frequent outbreaks of the plague carried off large numbers of the population.

It is likely that entire families sometimes united, i.e. a husband who had children and had lost his wife would need another to look after them, and a wife who had children and had lost her husband would need another to support her, and they might unite from necessity.

So I surmise that Shakespeare chose to depict Hamlet's adverse reaction to his mother's second marriage because it was a topical family problem and one which many of his spectators would recognise. Since the characters and motives of the personages on stage must be recognisable to the spectators, it is unlikely that Shakespeare chose to depict an aspect of human psychology which would only be recognisable to few, or not recognisable by any; likely, in fact, that many of them recognised, perhaps from personal experience, the common step-child problem which in Hamlet has so far escaped recognition.

Other playwrights were aware of this:

Hippolito But the whole aim and scope of his intent
Ended in this: conjuring me in private
To seek some strange-digested fellow forth,
Of ill-contented nature, either disgrac'd
In former times, or by new grooms displac'd,
Since his stepmother's nuptials, such a blood,
A man that were for evil only good.

Cyril Tourneur (now attributed to Thomas Middleton), (1606)
The Revenger's Tragedy, (I,i,74–81)

Flamineo 'Faith, for some hours salt water will run most plentifully in every office o'th'court; but, believe me, most do but weep over their stepmother's graves.
Francisc How mean you?
Flamineo Why, they dissemble, as some men do that live within compass o'th'verge [the King's Court].

Webster *The White Devil* (V,iii,48–52)

Webster's lines are merely a passing conversational remark, but in Tourneur's play there are three stepsons of the old Duke who has married a second time, all of whom are malcontents They plot to murder their older stepbrother who is the old Duke's son and heir, become

---

20 As Dr. Gardner remarks, explanations in term of the Unconscious such as the Oedipus complex (which one professor ascribes to Hamlet), have the advantage that they cannot be proved or disproved! And how many theatregoers had heard of Freud's 'Unconscious' in Shakespeare's time? Many would not even have heard of Oedipus.

'villains' and perish. In neither case would the lines have been inserted unless the playwrights knew that some at least of their spectators would understand the allusions.

A related case is Edmund in *King Lear*, the illegitimate son who elects to follow 'Nature' and also becomes a villain. As the play's first few lines imply, his father's amused references to his mother and the circumstances of his birth have never allowed him to feel that he is his father's son as much as Edgar.

A principal character in John Galsworthy's third play *Joy* (1903) is an adolescent girl of that name whose parents have separated, and whose mother has taken a lover, Lever. He is quiet and courteous, but from her harangues to her mother she cannot bear his presence.

Two well-known writers who became stepchildren are Edgar Allan Poe (1809–1849) and Charles Baudelaire (1821–1867).

After Poe's mother died when he was not quite three, Mrs. Allan—a well-to-do childless lady—adopted him. Although she gave him motherly care and love, she was not seconded by her husband. Poe also came to love the mother of a school friend, who soon afterwards died. When he was twenty and Mrs. Allan died, he found another mother in an aunt. He was sent to a private school, then to the University of Virginia. Prevented from returning after his first year, he ran away and enlisted, spending three years as a soldier. The figures of the women he had loved and who had died appear so often in his stories and poems that they might well support F.L.Lucas's diagnosis of a "neurotic caught in the web of childhood" and excessively devoted to the mother-figures of his early years. Since he had become a stepchild before he was three and disliked his stepfather (strictly, 'adopted child' and 'adoptive father',) he had no acceptable male-parental model. He wrote macabre stories, became addicted to alcohol, which he never succeeded in giving up, and died at forty.

Baudelaire became a stepchild at seven, when his mother, who had been widowed for nearly two years, married the future General Aupick. He, too, disliked his stepfather, possibly because he resented the turning of her attentions from him to her husband after two happy years with her. At a dinner-party, he threatened to strangle his stepfather after the latter had rebuked him for an improper remark. When he came of age in 1843 and left home, he began to squander his patrimony, which had to be placed in trust. Even so, he got into debt. Although he did not marry, he lived for a while with a black actress; the poems in *Les Fleurs du Mal* were all on morbid subjects. During the revolution of 1848 he was heard to threaten to shoot his stepfather; he became the admirer and translator of Poe as "the master of the horrible", the "prince of mystery", and died at forty-six of the combined effects of alcohol and syphilis.

F.L.Lucas ascribes the behaviour of Hamlet, Poe, Baudelaire, and three other unnamed children to excessive attachment to their mothers, and in all cases a stepfather or lover had appeared.

The effect on children of divorce or parental separation can be very deep. During World War II the Nazis induced about thirty British prisoners-of-war to defect and join the British Free Corps on the promise of a life of luxury, although the Corps was not given any military duties, no doubt because there were too few of them. In her book, *The Meaning of Treason*, an account of the treason trials in London after WW II, Rebecca West remarks that most of those who defected came from broken homes. It seems that the consequent distrust of human relationships and the belief that they are basically unstable can lead the child to abandon belief not only in family loyalties but in all loyalties, including the love of country which is normally in all of us.

Today many young women are starting what they think of as single-parent families although, in this observer's opinion, there can be no such thing. Children need two parents; a woman can no more bring up or be a role-model to a boy, than a man can bring up a girl. Many of them live with one boy-friend after another, the length of the average relationship being about eighteen months. Their children thus have inflicted on them a series of stepfathers, usually negligent because uninterested and sometimes worse than merely negligent. There have been instances of cruelty to children by boyfriends; and the effect will be to produce an increasing number of young people who will never be able to live normal, stable lives. Having known nothing of family loyalties in their early years, they will understand nothing of others.

The point is relevant to Hamlet in that he stages the Gonzago-play, a slander on the King (who is an elected king whose position is not as safe as that of a hereditary king), at a time when his country is in danger of invasion and needs secure guidance from the top. At this point he cares not about the political situation.

Recent research in Britain has shown that if a marriage breaks up, the children fare best if they are left with their mother, and also if she does not take a second husband or partner. If she does and has the usual marital relations with him, even small children, who cannot yet understand the nature and purpose of sex relations, may acutely resent them. This finding may apply to Poe and Baudelaire, and to Galsworthy's Joy; does it also apply to Hamlet?

Both his first soliloquy and his long and intense closet harangue to his mother suggest that it does apply, but he is well out of childhood and adolescence, and its intensity is due to several causes:

a) He must at all costs turn his mother away from his father's murderer. "Avenge my murder", said the Ghost, "and put an end to the lust and luxury in the Royal bed of Denmark."

b) He remains enraged by her earlier appeal to accept Claudius as a new father. She has reminded him of it with "Hamlet, thou hast thy father much offended."

c) After finding that he has killed Polonius, he may have decided that she accepted allowing Polonius to eavesdrop on what he had intended to be a highly private conversation, and is further enraged. The play is not clear as to whether she has or he is enraged, but the notion is plausible.

d) At the time it was the strongly-held view that sexual desire has (or should have) died out by middle age,[21] and he, his mother and the Ghost appear to share this view, for he says "At your age / The heyday in the blood is tame" with the intention of shaming her, and she is shamed.

His first soliloquy might be taken as confirming that the above finding applies to him; however, if we go by its words, his disgust is occasioned by the "little month" and his dislike of Claudius. The question comes down to "How mature is Hamlet? Would he have accepted her happy relations with Claudius if she had remained a widow for a longer period, and if they had given him time to get over his grief before pressing him to accept Claudius as a new father? His "The rank sweat of an enseamed bed" and "What should such fellows as I do, crawling between heaven and earth?" suggest that he is well aware of his own sexuality; still, it remains difficult to decide, for he is an only child and may still feel some resentment at his mother's apparently total transfer of her attention from him to her new husband.

These references must not be taken as implying that Hamlet was in need of psychotherapy

---

21   See essay "The morality of Hamlet" by Patrick Cruttwell in *Shakespeare: Hamlet*, (Casebook Series, p.191).

before the play opens; I take the cheerful and relaxed Hamlet of the graveyard to be his normal self of the years before the opening of the play.

As always the question is: what was Shakespeare's intention? I find that he intended to create not a hero who was inadequate or even sick in mind, but a well-balanced young man who was far from immature for his age, whom he then placed in an impossibly stressful situation, and whose emotional problems would stem from causes familiar to many in his audiences.

(v)

It is now possible to list all the factors in the situation in which Shakespeare placed his hero.

Hamlet is not allowed a healthy mourning experience after his father's death. His mother has married again after a month.

Capable of loyalty himself, he is disgusted by her disloyalty to his dead father. She and Claudius even expect him to join them in their new happiness and to forget the father of his childhood.

Claudius has immediately begun to press himself on Hamlet as a new father, even speaking to him as if he were much younger than he is. His approaches revolt Hamlet.

The atmosphere of the Castle has completely changed; he is a stranger in what was the home of his childhood. He cannot voice his resentment or his grief nor can he escape to Wittenberg. Since Claudius is king, he must remain obedient and respectful: he is completely in the King's power.

The Ghost then reveals that it was murdered and demands revenge; Hamlet immediately realises that its story will be almost impossible to prove. Something impels him to believe it, but as an Elizabethan he must distrust the Ghost, and as law-student must not act without proof. He cannot even prove that there was a murder.

He sees that if he kills Claudius he will be a regicide and will have forfeited all his hopes, including the prospect of marrying Ophelia, whom he loves with a young man's intensely protective love. But uncertainty as to his future has compelled him to break with her, which is the deepest of disappointments for him.

Again as law-student, he suspects his mother of complicity in the murder because of the brevity of her mourning, and is faced with the possibility that she shares Claudius' guilt.

He is aware that he should not allow his dislike of his stepfather and his suspicion of his mother to bias him. At the same time, his knowledge that she is a "mouse" and would have been led on by Claudius gives him a dreadful problem. If she is guilty, what is he to do?

It should now be clear that the monarchy of Shakespeare's Denmark must be elective, i.e. that Shakespeare chose Denmark as the venue for his play because its monarchy was elective, that Claudius must not be a usurper, and that Hamlet must not have hereditary rights, for if Hamlet were the rightful heir, the emotional elements in his situation would be almost irrelevant, and Hamlet as the dispossessed heir would have ample reason for action against Claudius independently of any other factors. Although it is not easy to imagine a *Hamlet* without the Ghost, it too could be dispensed with.

Shakespeare chose an elective monarchy in order to ensure that the situation was totally hostile to his hero. It is as if a half a dozen sharp swords were all pointing at him and allowing him no escape route. His law-studentship is one of these: as in Hieronimo in *The Spanish Tragedy*, the lawyer's outlook sharpens the confrontation between the emotions which impel him towards revenge and the intellect which demands a detached approach to his problem.

There is no mental instability or other character defect in Hamlet; he must be seen as a perfectly normal young man who is placed under acute stress. Any additional tendency to true madness, present in him before the play begins, would grossly weaken Shakespeare's carefully arranged situation and convert the play into a kind of medical documentary. The emotional stresses alone must cause him to lose his judgment.

In Eliot's phrase, the above list contains all the necessary objective correlatives, the identifiable causes of Hamlet's emotionality which cause him to lose his detachment. Had he maintained it, the plot would have proceeded as in the first alternative in "After the Gonzago-play", but it would have made a far less interesting play.

(vi)

Considering the pressures on him, how would Hamlet have fared without Horatio? Did Shakespeare the child psychologist realise that a young man of Hamlet's age would only withstand his situation without support if he were superhuman rather than human? Why else did he make his hero reflect at length on suicide?

Evidently he decided that Hamlet needed a friend, and a friend rather than a brother or other relative: a close friend, but not a member of the Hamlet family. Such a personage would almost certainly have introduced emotional or other complications and distracted the audience's interest from Hamlet, where Horatio the friend is silent and unquestioningly loyal, yet detached.

A character study of him reveals inconsistencies. In I,ii Hamlet greets him: "Horatio—or I do forget myself!" and Horatio replies, "I came to see your father's funeral". Why was Hamlet not aware of his friend's presence till after his mother's wedding, a month later? How is it that Horatio only saw the Elder Hamlet once (I,i,41ff.) though is well known to the sentries on the battlements? Or that he does not know of the Danes' inclination to drink too heavily, heard in a passage which appears to have been inserted to explain why Claudius is "the bloat king"? These inconsistencies are trivialities; they affect neither the action nor Horatio's role in it.

Horatio's first contribution is in connection with the Ghost: he is the scholar whom the sentries ask to speak to it because they themselves are afraid to. When he does, he makes clear from the terms he uses that he is a law student; also that, being a law scholar, he is familiar with the Witchcraft Acts! He says little except in the first act, but what he does say is always in the character of law student.

His law-student's scepticism manifests itself in his first appearance. The Ghost, he says, is merely fantasy: "Tush, tush, 'twill not appear". When it does appear, he is harrowed with "fear and wonder", and admits: "Before my God, I might not this believe / Without the sensible and true avouch / Of mine own eyes." It eventually reappears, the purpose of its second appearance being apparently to convince him of its reality, but he is already convinced.

In I,ii, he describes the vision to Hamlet: "My lord, I think I saw him yester night." Hamlet, another law student, accepts his account as factually reliable where he might not have accepted the sentries' report.

When Hamlet asks him to observe the King's reactions during the Gonzago-play, for which he is the ideal type of witness, he replies:

Horatio   Well, my lord,
    If he steal aught the while this play is playing
    And 'scape detection, I will pay the theft.

(III,ii,83–85)

Again, this is a law student's comment.

When Hamlet tells him how he substituted his own secret commission for the King's during the sea voyage, his instant question is "How was this sealed?", i.e. with what seal did Hamlet give his commission the necessary Royal authority? His unemotional comments then help to restore his friend's sense of proportion.

Whether he is one of the referees in the fencing match is not clear. If he is, he does not notice that one of the foils is unbated[22].

How much do these inconsistencies matter?

Horatio could apparently be omitted from the plot without much effect, yet something would be lost if this were so. Is not Iras, the girl of few words in *Antony and Cleopatra*, little more than a background character, yet does she not prove to be very much alive, and would not the play be the poorer without her?

Occasionally, two boys or girls become close friends—inseparables. There seems to be no reason why they should but they do; the friendship just happens. They may have interests in common, or be engaged in a common activity which may be no more than being in the same class at school. They may not see one another anywhere but in school, or wherever else they may be thrown together. At some level their minds click: each knows that he can talk companionably to the other. At that level they accept one another completely. When they engage in activities together, self-interest disappears.

Today, it might be assumed that such a friendship might lead to a homosexual relationship, but there is always an element of self-gratification in sex, and both individuals know instinctively that any self-interested element would be incompatible with their friendship. The range of interests they have in common may be narrow; it may simply arise from, and be shaped by, a situation which constantly throws them together, but within it each accepts the other, neither makes demands on the other, and each knows that the other will not make demands on him. In after life such friendships are often remembered with gratitude because they contained no element of self-interest. Whether they occur is usually a matter of chance. Many people are not lucky enough to form them; some natures cannot form them or even believe that they could exist, either from egotism or perhaps because they have had to learn to defend themselves against their brothers and sisters and remain unaware of such a possibility.

There is a special factor in the relationship of Hamlet and Horatio: Hamlet is an only child, and Horatio is a loner.

Children who have brothers or sisters early develop a relationship with one another which is quite independent of their relationship with their parents, i.e. they learn quite soon in their lives what it is to be a member of a peer group with the other members of which they are in contact for a large part of each day. Since they are in one peer group at home and another at school, they are rarely out of the company of a variety of other minds and other personalities at their own level.

The only child misses much of this experience. He may be a member of a particular peer group at school, but loses such company when he returns home. The sibling at home is always accepting the support of his brothers or sisters or defending himself against them, whereas the only child is deprived of these experiences. He may not easily learn the protective camouflage which enables him to fit into a peer group. He may be regarded as self-centred, but is actually self-contained from necessity. Like everyone else, he needs friends

---

22   Made temporarily safe with a 'nob' on the end

and may take more readily to other loners than to other types of personality.

There are a number of such characters in Shakespeare. Some appear to be loners although it is not clear whether they have brothers or sisters or not; others are only children. Romeo, Juliet, Desdemona, Bertram, Helena, Florizel, Coriolanus, Ferdinand and Miranda are all only children, and it is to be noted that the first and last pairs are instantly attracted to one another. Othello, a loner nearly all his life, and Desdemona, an only child, are also attracted to one another.

Shakespeare evidently understood the psychology of the only child, since he understood everyone else! He did not make Hamlet an only child by accident. He intended to emphasise the absolute loneliness of his hero when faced with his problem, the soliloquies being the evidence of this intention, and it should be clear that if Hamlet had been given brothers or sisters, the character of Hamlet himself, the events of the plot, and the whole atmosphere of the play would have been quite different from what they are.

So Hamlet the only child and Horatio the loner have taken to one another. Horatio is much more than a confidant, a dramatic convenience. Hamlet expresses his gratitude to him in a speech which contributes nothing to the action of the play but is long enough to suggest that it carries more significance than appears on the surface:

Hamlet Horatio, thou art e'en as just a man
    As e'er my conversation coped withal.
Horatio O my dear lord—
Hamlet   Nay, do not think I flatter;
    For what advancement may I think from thee,
    That no revenue hast but thy good spirits
    To feed and clothe thee? Why should the poor be flattered?
    No, let the candied tongue lick absurd pomp,
    And crook the pregnant hinges of the knee
    Where thrift may follow fawning. Dost thou hear?
    Since my dear soul was mistress of her choice,
    And could of men distinguish, her election
    Hath sealed thee for herself. For thou hast been
    As one, in suffering all, that suffers nothing;
    A man that fortune's buffets and rewards
    Hast ta'en with equal thanks. And blest are those
    Whose blood and judgement are so well commingled
    That they are not a pipe for fortune's finger
    To sound what stop she please. Give me that man
    That is not passion's slave, and I will wear him
    In my heart's core, ay, in my heart of heart,
    As I do thee...

Friends do not lay out their friendship for examination, and Hamlet now becomes embarrassed by his display of emotion.

                  ...Something too much of this.

(III,ii,50–70)

This speech could only have been given to Hamlet to draw our attention to Horatio and to indicate that he plays a more important part in the situation than his few appearances suggest. Hamlet and Horatio became friends at Wittenberg, where they were fellow students in the law school. On visiting Elsinore, seeing the Ghost, and hearing something of the Ghost's story, Horatio—although not obliged to—has stayed on to give his friend what support he can.

In III,ii,42ff. after Hamlet has ended his lecture to the Players on the art of acting, Polonius, Rosencrantz and Guildenstern enter, and Hamlet says to Polonius:

Hamlet   How now, my lord! Will the King hear this piece of work?
Polonius   And the Queen too, and that presently.
Hamlet   Bid the Players make haste.   *[Exit Polonius.]*
    Will you two help to hasten them?
R. and G.   We will, my lord.
                                                                        [Exeunt Rosencrantz and Guildenstern.]
Hamlet   What ho, Horatio!
[Enter Horatio.]
Horatio   Here, sweet lord, at your service.

Evidently, after sending away the other three because he wishes to speak to Horatio alone, Hamlet knows that Horatio will be within call. He immediately enters, i.e. he appears to have been in attendance on Hamlet, lending his silent support to his friend, near him if not always with him, during much if not all of the long period of idleness and waiting.

We may infer that much of his contribution has been behind the scenes: during the long simulation of lunacy Hamlet has been able from time to time to relax with him. Hamlet chooses the moment immediately before the Gonzago-play to thank his friend because its performance will tell him what his fate will be, and he may not have another opportunity to thank him and also for helping to keep himself sane!

Although Hamlet does not succeed in keeping himself sane, Horatio may be classed with the characters in the comic relief scenes who introduce the zero-level of emotion. Quiller-Couch calls him a "point and standard of sanity...to which all enormities and passionate errors may be referred; to which the agitated mind of the spectator settles back as upon its centre of gravity, its point of repose." If Shakespeare intended him to be seen as such, he is indeed more than a minor character.

(vi)

Is the "incestuous" nature of Claudius' marriage to a deceased brother's wife of any importance in the action of the play?

In *What Happens in Hamlet*, Dover Wilson considers it "so important that it is scarcely possible to make too much of it," that it inflicts "a moral shock so overwhelming that it shatters all zest for life and all belief in it", that it is in fact the fundamental cause of Hamlet's manifestations of emotionality. This might have been the case if Hamlet were exceptionally devout, but he shows no sign of being so. Even if he were, the moral shock—by no means the same thing as an emotional shock—would be unlikely to shatter all his zest for life.

There are only five references to it in the play: two by the Ghost in the same speech (I,v,42 and 83), and three by Hamlet (I,ii,157; III,iii,90 and V,ii,64). No other characters refer to it. Particularly significant is the closet scene, in which Hamlet's verbal belabouring of his mother contains no mention of incest. Shakespeare appears to have introduced the references merely because many of his spectators would have expected him to do so, and compared with the other motivations he gave Hamlet, it is quite insignificant.

Any greater number of references might have been tactless or worse. The play is assigned to 1601 or 1602, a time when Elizabeth was still reigning. Would the Queen have cared to be reminded that her own father's marital progress had been somewhat unsavoury by the standards of the time? Henry VIII's first marriage had been to Catherine of Aragon, the widow of his deceased brother Arthur, for which a Papal dispensation had been obtained. From six pregnancies, i.e. two princes and three of four princesses stillborn or died in early childhood, the only survivor was the first child Mary. Catherine's failure to provide a male heir was ascribed by many of Henry's subjects to the curse on "incestuous" marriages. Desiring a male heir, Henry attempted to declare the marriage invalid, and married Anne Boleyn, who gave birth to Elizabeth, but the Pope refused to confirm the validity of this second marriage. Eventually, an English court under Thomas Cranmer confirmed the union; even so, Elizabeth's legitimacy was later questioned, for which reason her legitimacy and title to the throne were confirmed by an Act of Parliament very soon after her accession.

Claudius' reference to "your better wisdoms" in his first speech suggests that he is thanking his lords-spiritual for providing the dispensation for his marriage to Gertrude, and that Shakespeare was reassuring some of his spectators.

Did Shakespeare consider the possibility of making Claudius a more distant relative or even a non-relative of the Hamlet family in order to avoid the need to refer to incest? He probably did, but chose the brother-relationship because he saw possibilities which would not have arisen from anything more distant.

Claudius and Hamlet, being uncle and nephew, are closely connected by that mysterious link called the 'tie of blood', a link which everyone with any experience of family life understands intuitively but finds difficult to explain. It is simply 'there'; it goes far beyond the physical resemblances produced by a common genetic origin; it entails affinities which reside in the gut regions of our psyches, defy analysis because they are below the level of words, and constitute a kind of psychic rope which can never be severed. In this connection, the scholarly or literary approach to character fails because it is normally a detached approach, and the critic may assume that any personage being studied may view his own situation with similar detachment. But Claudius, Gertrude and Hamlet, being (so to speak) intertwined, cannot see one another with detachment. The critical mistake has in fact been to devote attention almost exclusively to Hamlet, and little to the other two, when he is one of a small, closely-knit family whose members are indeed members one of another.

This affinity normally produces strong attachments within families. While these attachments are developing it is also necessary for the members of a family to establish and protect their own selves; there must be a balance between the need to offer and receive love and the need to protect oneself. While the family affinity naturally favours the giving and receiving of love, it also renders the individual more vulnerable to hurt from other close members of the family than from anyone else. Offence from someone outside the family can usually be easily brushed off, but offence from a member of one's own family can penetrate much more deeply and be much more lasting in effect.

What to the children of a family is the 'always' atmosphere has already been mentioned. Their parents have 'always' been their parents; if brothers or sisters are born at reasonably close intervals, they are soon felt as having 'always' been there. So Claudius, who has 'always' been Hamlet's uncle, feels entitled to push his paternal intimacy and authority on Hamlet as his 'son', does so, and gives him far deeper offence than if he had been a more remote relative or a non-relative. Had he been the first of these, he might have tried such an approach, but would surely have been less pressing; if the second, he would hardly have attempted it at all. And the offence becomes a major cause of Hamlet's loss of detachment.

After hearing the Ghost's story, Hamlet exclaims, "O most pernicious woman!" Yet this pernicious woman is still his mother; he is still a part of her and she a part of him, and it is as inevitable that he should write his Gonzago-play as he does, and speak to her in her closet as he does, as that he should want to avenge his father.

After the Gonzago-play, his dislike of his uncle turns to furious hatred, yet he spares his uncle at his prayers in the hope that in a more suitable moment he may consign his uncle's soul to the flames of Hell for all time. This postponement of his revenge came to be regarded as evidence of his hesitant nature; but might he not hesitate before killing the uncle who had 'always' been his uncle? Could this be another element in the totally hostile situation in which Shakespeare placed him? The play contains no hint that he hesitates, but could he be silently suppressing the thought?

As he watches Fortinbras' army marching by, he exclaims, "I do not know / Why yet I live to say, 'This thing's to do.'" Is this merely conventional self-reproach, or does he really not know?

Claudius too suffers from the effects of family "affinity". His desire to proffer love to his nephew is entirely natural. At the priedieu, when he realises that it has been rejected, he cannot drag his feelings up to the light and examine them. Then Hamlet's parting insult "And so, my mother" penetrates so deeply that his proffered love turns to hatred so extreme that only Hamlet's death will quench it.

(vii)

How should Hamlet be acted? The first and most important aspect of Hamlet is that he is a Prince, a member of the ruling family and living in the Royal palace, the "most immediate" to the throne, his uncle's "chiefest courtier", as well versed in courtly behaviour as a Prince should be, and, from Ophelia's and Fortinbras' descriptions of him, possessing all the qualities which give him presence and authority and earn loyalty.

His courtesy appears in a little episode of I,ii immediately after his first soliloquy:
Hamlet   But break, my heart, for I must hold my tongue!
   [Enter Horatio, Marcellus, and Bernado.]
Horatio   Hail to your lordship!
Hamlet   *[Still lost in thought, but replying with automatic courtesy]* I am glad to see
   you well.
[Suddenly seeing who it is, and apologizing for his absentmindedness; emphasising "self" as indication of the closeness of their friendship.]
   ...Horatio!—or I do forget my self!
Horatio   The same, my lord, and your poor servant ever.
Hamlet   Sir, my good friend; I'll change that name with you.
   And what make you from Wittenberg, Horatio?—
[Remembering to acknowledge the other two:]
                            Marcellus!
Marcellus   *[Bowing]* My good lord—
Hamlet   I am very glad to see you.
   [To Bernardo] Good even, sir. *[Bernardo bows.]*

Only if Hamlet is first shown as the courteous Prince does the contrast between his normal behaviour and his simulated lunacy become as theatrically effective as Shakespeare intended it to be.

He only allows his emotionality to appear in his private moments, as when he is soliloquizing, or with his mother in her closet, or to a limited extent with Horatio. In his soliloquies a principal emotion is anger at his own supposed cowardice. He is neither a dreamer nor an uninhibited adolescent.

At the beginning of the play, he is the Prince to all around him; at the end of it, when he has apparently recovered from his lunacy, he is the Prince again; between these times when he is playing the lunatic, he is still recognised as the Prince, for no one ever fails to address him as "my lord".

If he is not played as a Prince in a Renaissance court, the play loses much of its point. Admittedly, while it is a family tragedy, the family is a Royal family whose members are permanently in the public eye and are expected to conduct themselves accordingly. In Shakespeare's time a Prince was a figure to be looked up to (some twentieth-century versions of the play's principal character would be incomprehensible to the audiences for whom it was written). Hamlet's fall is the more pathetic because it is from a much greater height than that of a member of an ordinary family.

20

CLAUDIUS

> A felt propriety and truth from causes unseen, I take to be the highest point of Poetic composition. If the characters of Shakespeare are thus whole, and as it were original, while those of almost all other writers are mere imitations, it may be fit to consider them rather as Historic than Dramatic beings; and, when occasion requires, to account for their conduct from the WHOLE of character, from general principles, from latent motives, and from policies not avowed.
>
> Maurice Morgann An Essay on the Dramatic Character of Sir John Falstaff (1777)

> "Well, of course, if you can't love him, you'll never be any good in him, will you?"
>
> Tyrone Guthrie to Laurence Olivier playing Sergius in Shaw's Arms and the Man in 1944; in Olivier's On Acting

Bradley describes Claudius as "a man of mean appearance, a mildewed ear, a toad, a bat". If he is right, Claudius is a most untypical Elizabethan king. In Shakespeare's time, kings claimed divine right as the source of their authority, wielded much more direct power than today, and were by far the most important figures in their kingdoms. Shakespeare began his writing career with "histories" because he could people his stage with kings, queens, and other high-born personages who would be god-like figures to most of his spectators. Since Claudius is a King, he must be regarded as the dominant figure in any scene in which he appears a much more important figure even than Hamlet, who is only a Prince. And he is the head of his family as well as of the state.

Of all the character studies which had to be written for this account of the play, this for Claudius proved to be the most difficult. He has been regarded as merely a conventional villain, but since he is Hamlet's antagonist, such diminution of him diminishes the entire play. He must be envisaged as a warm, living character and on the stage must be seen to be so, as well individualized as Hamlet. However, not wishing to divert too much attention from the play's hero, Shakespeare gave him too few words to say—too few, that is, to permit of an analysis which is independent of surmise. Much surmising has been necessary in arriving at a plausible picture of him; Shakespeare would not have begun to "write" him without having first formed his own complete picture of him, including the "latent motives" and "policies not avowed" arising from his previous life.

At least, Claudius' motives at crucial moments can be deduced with reasonable certainty from the facts of his situation. A pity he was not given more soliloquies, although they would have lengthened a play which is already very long. And perhaps Shakespeare refrained from giving him more soliloquies for another reason: he was concerned to express undertones.

(i)

Claudius' opening speech is to his lords. He tells them what they already know (although we the audience do not), that he has "taken Gertrude to wife"; a little later we learn from

Hamlet's soliloquy that he married her "a little month" after the Elder Hamlet's death. His speech is beautifully expressed; the Ghost's reference to his "wicked wit and gifts, that have the power / so to seduce", and Hamlet's "smiling, damned villain", suggest that Claudius has charm as well as kingly authority.

After he has briefed and despatched his ambassadors, the formal business of the meeting is completed, and it breaks up; the lords move away to converse in groups or depart, and Polonius and his son approach to make their request. Claudius' manner to Laertes is extremely genial:

King And now, Laertes, what's the news with you?
You told us of some suit; what is't, Laertes?
You cannot speak of reason to the Dane
And lose your voice. What wouldst thou beg, Laertes,
That shall not be my offer, not thy asking?

(I,ii,42–46)

Dare we suspect, from the pleasure he takes in granting the request, that he envies Polonius his "very noble" son?

Their petition granted, Polonius and Laertes bow and retire, leaving the three members of the Hamlet family alone in the centre of the stage. Claudius and Gertrude would hardly broach an intimate family matter in the presence of non-members of the family; in particular, Claudius would not be so tactless as to rebuke Hamlet the Prince in the terms he uses—he calls Hamlet obstinate, impious, unmanly, impatient, simple-minded, and peevish—in the presence of another young man such as Laertes. His speech is therefore not a public oration.

He begins a little ominously with "But now," (not "And now", as to Laertes) "my cousin Hamlet and my son", an opening which could hardly have been better calculated to raise Hamlet's hackles. Hamlet's punning reply, "Not so, my lord: I am too much i'th'sun", indicates that Claudius has already made approaches to Hamlet and that they have not been welcome; "peevish" suggests that they have acutely irritated Hamlet. But Claudius refuses to be put off by Hamlet's coldness. He is now on the throne, he is happy with his queen; if his brilliant young nephew would abandon his mourning and accept him as a new father, his happiness would be complete.

The Queen begins with her "Let thine eye look like a friend on Denmark"; then, after preparing the ground with his rebuke, Claudius continues with an eloquent and persuasive appeal:

King   We pray you, throw to earth
This unprevailing woe, and think of us
As of a father. For let the worlds take note,
You are the most immediate to our throne,
And with no less nobility of love
Than that which dearest father bears his son
Do I impart toward you.
[He pauses to emphasise what he has said and then continues:]
                            For your intent
In going back to school in Wittenberg,
It is most retrograde to our desire,
And we beseech you, bend you to remain

Here in the cheer and comfort of our eye,
[He comes to the climax of a carefully prepared speech:]
Our chiefest courtier, cousin, and our son.

(I,ii,106–117)

For the second time he emphasises "cousin" and "son". He urgently means all that he says; not only does he wish to keep Hamlet at Elsinore as an ornament to his court, he would like to take him up as his own son and groom him for the monarchy, so ensuring that it remains in the family.

Court etiquette now requires Hamlet to answer immediately and to express acquiescence, a request from the King having the force of a command. This appeal to forget his father after a mere two months (and begun by his mother) so sickens and dumbfounds him that he cannot speak! Seeing him silent, the Queen repeats the appeal with "Stay with us, go not to Wittenberg". Now forced to answer, he replies coldly, and to her instead of to the King: "I shall in all my best obey you, Madam."

Hamlet's 'accord' is neither unforced nor gentle. He must stay at Elsinore because he has no choice in the matter, and he snubs the King by replying to his mother, at which Claudius affects to welcome his acquiescence with a "rouse" and the firing of cannon, offending Hamlet yet further.

He is much too eager. No son could take to a new father so soon after the death of the old. Claudius might be feeling that if Hamlet accepts him as a new father he will to some extent be atoning for the murder of the old, but the real cause of his eagerness is that he is a childless man who now realises that he would have liked a son to whom he could pass on some of the wisdom he has acquired during his own life. He has discovered the satisfactions of marriage, and would like to become the head of a united family.

His eagerness betrays itself again in a little episode in II,ii:

Pol Th'ambassadors from Norway, my good lord,
   Are joyfully returned.
King Thou still hast been the father of good news.
Pol. Have, I my lord? Assure you, my good liege,
   I hold my duty, as I hold my soul,
   Both to my God and to my gracious king.
   And I do think—or else this brain of mine
   Hunts not the trail of policy so sure
   As it hath used to do—that I have found
   The very cause of Hamlet's lunacy.
King O tell me that; that do I long to hear!
Pol. Give first admittance to th'ambassadors;
   My news shall be the fruit to that great feast.

(II,ii,40–52)

So eager is Claudius to hear Polonius' discovery that he forgets that the ambassadors are waiting and that state business must come first!

His interest in Hamlet's madness is genuine and not in the least that of a guilty murderer who fears discovery and is spying on his stepson, or of a usurper who fears the real heir. In the latter case, as emphasised earlier, he would welcome Hamlet's lunacy. He is shrewd enough to suspect that Hamlet's madness is caused by something "more than his father's death" (II,ii,8), and that the cause is not love (III,i,161). However, at no time does he suspect the true cause, for—apart from Hamlet, Horatio and the sentries, whom Hamlet swears to secrecy—neither he nor anyone else ever hears of the Ghost. Even at the end of the play, he does not really understand why Hamlet kills him. Though the Gonzago-play depicts his murder to his face, there is no reason why he should take the depiction seriously. It certainly reawakens his conscience, while the chief effect of the Gonzago-play is to open a window into Hamlet's mind for him. And what he sees shatters a dear hope.

(ii)

As we have seen, Claudius strides out of the Gonzago-play in a fury. Difficulties now arise: he has already decided that Hamlet shall be sent to England for a change of air. At what moment after the Gonzago-play does he decide that Hamlet shall be executed when he arrives there?

The King mentions the secret commission three times: to Rosencrantz and Guildenstern at the beginning of III,iii; to Gertrude after the death of Polonius (IV,i,29–30); and after Hamlet's departure at the end of IV,iii. Not till the last moment does he reveal that the commission "imports...the present death of Hamlet" (a last-minute revelation to the audience which was evidently intended by Shakespeare as a dramatic stroke).

After the wanton slaying of Polonius there would be good reason for having Hamlet executed, especially since the King himself had been the intended victim ("It had been so with us, had we been there"—IV,i,13). There is no mention of any alteration to the commission. Hamlet mentions it in Gertrude's closet: "There's letters sealed" (III,iv,203), though how he has come to know of it we are not told. Since at this last point, late in the closet scene, the King has not yet heard of the death of Polonius and does not yet know that Hamlet is after his life, and since we do not hear of any alteration in the commission, it appears that he has decided on Hamlet's execution immediately after leaving the Gonzago-play. It must be the whole import of the Gonzago-play, not merely the murder scene which awakens his conscience—otherwise he can ignore it—which causes him to decide to rid himself of Hamlet.

But has he really finally decided? The uncertainty arises from the nature of his soliloquy at the priedieu:

  King O my offence is rank, it smells to heaven;
    It hath the primal, eldest curse upon't—
    A brother's murder!—Pray can I not,
    Though inclination be as sharp as will.

(III,iii,36–39)

The remaining thirty-three lines of the soliloquy are merely an enlargement on this theme, such that Claudius' conscience is so tortured that he cannot pray. He mentions none of the other problems confronting him.

The soliloquy is usually regarded as merely an admission that Claudius did commit the murder, and, since the secret commission is already written, that his conscience will become even more tortured after the execution of a nephew. If it is no more than that, why does it go on for thirty-seven lines, when a dozen would be enough for a confession, and when in any case he has already given the audience a hint of his guilt with "How smart a lash that speech doth give my conscience" (III,i,50)? Why does he reflect that he is "buying out the law", i.e. that he has decided to evade the law, something which would not trouble him if he were truly hardened. Why does he almost immediately add "Try what repentance can"? He must be very confused, or how could he commit the near-equivalent of a second murder and then repent? Has he really made up his mind, or is he still tortured by doubts?

And why is the soliloquy so inexplicit? The soliloquy and 'aside' of Elizabethan drama were intended to reveal the speaker's inmost thoughts to the audience only, as do Hamlet's. This speech is merely the repetition of one thought, that his murder and the prizes it has brought him prevent him from praying.

So far, it is easy to infer from the play that Claudius has more than a single problem on his mind. And it may be suspected that the inexplicitness of the soliloquy is psychologically accurate, i.e. that if Claudius does not discuss his problems with himself, it is because he cannot force himself to do so. By my interpretation, his mind is in turmoil because some of his problems lie too deep for conscious discussion.

The depiction of his murder has re-awakened his conscience but, since he knows his murder was beyond detection, it has raised no other problem. His inability to pray will not be a recently arisen problem either, for he is almost certainly repeating to himself some of what he has been saying in his prayers every evening since the murder. The depiction has merely shocked the court by its implied slander. Since Claudius knows that his crime can never be proved against him, he is not panicked into believing that it has somehow been discovered; he regards Lucianus' stage murder as strangely coincidental but no more than that. He is as shrewd and tough as a king needs to be; he would not be so moved as to betray his guilt when he has been living with his bad conscience ever since the murder.

As a satire on the Royal marriage and a slander of the King, the Gonzago play is an attack on Claudius' political position, which is more than annoying in a country where the monarchy is elective and the populace as lively as Laertes' uprising shows it to be, and where Prince Hamlet is popular; and worse than offensive because of Young Fortinbras and the Polack. He must think first of safeguarding Denmark. Yet it is little more than that. Though not as popular as Hamlet, Claudius is respected by everyone. All he needs to do is to have the mad Hamlet confined. Why, then, is he so "distempered with choler" when he leaves the play that he soon resolves on Hamlet's execution?

From Hamlet's known interest in the theatre, he cannot have failed to realise, both from the knowledge of the play which Hamlet reveals during its performance and from his veiled threats, that Hamlet himself was the author. It suggests that Hamlet is scheming to dislodge him, and it is not the only such suggestion: he remembers Hamlet's "I eat the air, promise-crammed" before the start of the play and his "While the grass grows", which is spoken to Rosencrantz and Guildenstern on their arrival which they will have been reported to him.

He is troubled by more than one aspect of the Gonzago-play. The satire on the Queen tells him that Hamlet will wreck his new domestic happiness if he can, while the fact that Hamlet has presented such a play makes only too clear that the paternal love he has so eagerly been proffering to Hamlet is being thrown back in his face. Who wants to see such proffered love rejected, let alone rejected in such a manner? He had hoped to groom Hamlet as his successor on the throne and not as his supplanter, nor as the wrecker of his marriage. His hope of being the head of a united family has gone.

Some thoughts which must be in Claudius' mind are notably absent from the soliloquy. As is universally supposed, if he has realised that Hamlet is out to avenge his father's murder, his first care should be to protect his own life, but the soliloquy contains no hint of this thought. Although he should be unwilling to add the death of a nephew to that of a brother, this thought too is never explicitly expressed. Only after he hears of Polonius' death does he realise that Hamlet was out to kill him, from which it might be supposed that only then would he finally decide that Hamlet must be executed. Why, then, does he write his secret commission so soon?

He is tortured by the thought that two of his dearest hopes must be given up. That Claudius has found happiness with Gertrude is made clear in the play and in particular by Hamlet's closet harangue to his mother; they might be a honeymoon couple! We may even suspect that Claudius has not been married before; that he is suffering from child-hunger is equally clear. Why, then, are these thoughts absent from the soliloquy? It is the loss of these hopes which make his soliloquy so inexplicit, because they lie too deep for discussion.

There is an even more notable absence. Claudius cannot be totally flooded by remorse, for his bad conscience has not prevented him from performing his kingly duties extremely well or at times expressing his thoughts. The grace and eloquence of his opening speeches, in particular his appeal to Hamlet, show him to be anything but inarticulate. He does not as yet know that Hamlet is after his life, but the Gonzago-play has told him that Hamlet is his enemy. Why, then, does his soliloquy contain no mention of Hamlet's name? Evidently, Claudius cannot express what he feels.

On separate occasions I have seen a childless couple and an unmarried uncle looking with longing at their small nephews and nieces. Even if they were suffering from child-hunger, would they have said so? Child-hunger is simply 'there'.[23] While couples may speak of their hope of a child to their relatives or close friends, there is no one to whom Claudius could or would speak of it as a personal need. He can only try to persuade Hamlet to accept him as a second father.

Which is more important to Claudius, his attachment to Gertrude or his hope of becoming Hamlet's second father?

Clearly, he is not so attached to Gertrude as his speech to Laertes at the beginning of IV,vii suggests, for he is obviously ignoring the effect that the news of her son's execution would have on her. She is very submissive and incurious. Will he be able to satisfy her with some sort of lie? What if she learns the truth, as she sooner or later may?

One reason why he does not consider her is that he must protect his position on the throne before anything else, for the sake of Denmark as well as himself; and Hamlet has both slandered him in public and thrown his proffered love back at him. His thoughts are less on Gertrude than on Hamlet, who has shown himself to be his enemy both as king and as would-be father. If he has Hamlet confined, the Queen will visit her son, who will continue to undermine his marriage. If he is eventually released, as is possible, he may also continue to attack Claudius as King. Yet even this possibility is not enough to account for his decision to have Hamlet executed, for in the event of further attacks Claudius could have him confined again, perhaps permanently, or at least till Hamlet came to his senses. If he ever did, he could hardly become the "chiefest courtier" again.

Though unwittingly, Hamlet has found his weak spots, for his mind is on his father's murder and his mother's possible complicity; he cares nothing for Claudius' feelings. Claudius is shrewd but vulnerable; the Gonzago-play has thrown him into shock and left him quite unable to think clearly. He can only pray for divine guidance which is not granted. Hence his soliloquy turns out to be a long "symphony on one note", the undertones which,

---

23   One of the most intense moments in the lives of many, if not most of us, is the begetting and conceiving of a child that both parties want, and the most intense expression of our emotions is found in poetry. Yet I have not yet come across a poem on this moment. Why not? Is it beyond even poetry?

from the evidence in the play, must be inaudibly present in his mind. He is not suffering so much from remorse as from rage, resentment and disappointment. And he is not the kind of man who will swallow his resentment tamely.

Perhaps a comparison with Macbeth makes Claudius' position clear. Macbeth leaves the banqueting hall to discuss inwardly his motives in planning the murder of Duncan, and reaches the point where he is about to ask himself, "Can I withstand having such a murder on my conscience?" Claudius, who must be regarded as being at least as intelligent as Macbeth—if not more—is unable to advance further than the beginning of his attempt at discussion. "A brother's murder" being on his conscience, he is proposing to add Hamlet's execution as another burden; he does not say so explicitly. Why does he not, if he has a "heart with strings of steel"? It can only be that for some reason he cannot.

As confused as Hamlet, Claudius should choose the lesser of two evils: to have Hamlet confined and hope for the best, although his conscience is fighting a losing battle with Hamlet's destruction of his hopes. When he kneels to pray he is really trying to shuffle his way out of a situation which, if he could bring it to the surface of his mind, he might be able to resolve. "But 'tis not so above; / There is no shuffling"; Divine assistance is refused him.

King Bow, stubborn knees; and heart with strings of steel,
   Be soft as sinews of the new-born babe!

(III,iii,70–71)

He is still uncertain, but when he hears of Polonius' death, his doubts vanish.

After hiding Polonius' body, Hamlet is eventually brought before him. The King speaks down to him, as to a confirmed lunatic (IV,iii,17ff.):

[Enter Hamlet and Guildenstern.]
King Now, Hamlet, where's Polonius?
Hamlet [Still talking in his "antic" manner]
   Not where he eats, but where he is eaten. A certain convocation of politic worms are e'en at him. Your worm is your only emperor for diet. We fat all creatures else to fat us, and we fat ourselves for maggots. Your fat king and your lean beggar is but variable service—two dishes but to one table; that's the end.
King Alas, alas!
[The King seems to have concluded that Hamlet is beyond hope. What would he do if Hamlet dropped his pose and professed contrition? But Hamlet does not relent; he continues with his pose in order to needle Claudius:]
Hamlet A man may fish with the worm that hath eat of a king, and eat of the fish that hath fed of that worm.
King *[Becoming impatient and suspicious]*
   What dost thou mean by this?
Hamlet Nothing but to show you how a king may go a progress through the guts of a beggar.
King [Forcibly] Where is Polonius?
Hamlet In heaven; send thither to see. If your messenger find him not there, seek him i'th'other place yourself. But indeed, if you find him not within this month, you shall nose him as you go up the stairs into the lobby.
King [To some attendants] Go seek him there.
Hamlet He will stay till you come.

King [Speaking simply and clearly as to a confirmed lunatic:]
    Hamlet, this deed, for thine especial safety—
    Which we do tender, as we dearly grieve
    For that which thou hast done—must send thee hence
    With fiery quickness. Therefore prepare thyself;
    The bark is ready, and the wind at help,
    Th'associates tend, and everything is bent
    For England.
Hamlet [As if surprised] For England!
King   Ay, Hamlet.
Hamlet   Good.
King So is it, if thou knew'st our purposes.
Hamlet I see a cherub that sees them. But come, for England!
[As he turns to go] Farewell, dear mother.
King [Unsuspecting] Thy loving father, Hamlet.
Hamlet [Solemnly correcting him] My mother. Father and mother is man and wife;
    man and wife is one flesh; and so, my mother. *[To Rosencrantz and Guildenstern]*
    Come, for England! *[Exit.]*

This piece of insolence suggests to Claudius that his approaches to Hamlet could never have succeeded because Hamlet had always held him in contempt as a man. When crossed, some people become so tense that for a moment they can hardly breathe, and Claudius is one of these; his fury can be heard in his short, gasping sentences:

King Follow him at foot!—Tempt him with speed aboard!—
    Delay it not!—I'll have him hence tonight!—
    Away!—for everything is sealed and done
    Which else leans on th'affair.—Pray you, make haste!
                                       [Exeunt Rosencrantz and Guildenstern.]
[He pauses to recover his breath and then continues with colder venom:]
    And, England, if my love thou hold'st at aught—
    As my great power thereof may give thee sense,
    Since yet thy cicatrice looks raw and red
    After the Danish sword—thou may'st not coldly set
    Our sovereign process, which imports at full
    By letters conjuring to that effect,
    The present death of Hamlet. Do it, England;
    For like the hectic in my blood he rages,
    And thou must cure me. Till I know 'tis done,
    Howe'er my haps, my joys were ne'er begun.

From now on, Claudius' hatred of Hamlet will never abate. Hamlet will return from the sea voyage having apparently lost his lunacy and even recovered his respect for the King, but nothing less will satisfy Claudius than Hamlet's death.

Sometimes, when proffered love or friendship is rejected, it may suddenly turn into dislike or even active enmity. Claudius' proffered love, rejected by Hamlet with scorn, has now become its antithesis.

From the eloquence of Claudius' appeal to Hamlet to accept him as a new father, the length of his tortured soliloquy, and the venom of his final hatred, the suspicion must arise that Claudius had begun hoping that he would be able to induce Hamlet to join him in a family ruler-ship of Denmark; and that this hope had arisen not immediately after his marriage to Gertrude but before he planned his murder. Could not the depth of his hatred be explained as the effect of the humiliating rejection, not of a recently arisen hope, but of one which he had been cherishing for some time?

(iii)

Poisoning has been said to be the most cold-blooded form of murder. Yet Claudius is enjoying married life with Gertrude; he eagerly offers his love to Hamlet; when he strides out of the Gonzago-play he is "marvellous distempered with choler", and we have just seen him thrown into a fury again by Hamlet's parting insult: evidences as to his temperament which do not suggest that he is a cold-blooded type of man. And his piety at the priedieu and his attempt to pray—clearly genuine—show that he is by no means cold, evil, or calculating. Why, then, did he murder his brother?

The basic human needs, apart from food, warmth and shelter, are for status and love or concern. Everyone needs to receive status, to feel that he is seen as somebody by others and is respected by them, and to accord status in return; everyone needs to give love and to receive it, to feel concerned for someone else and to feel that someone is concerned for oneself.

For most of us, the family is the natural group within which we give and receive status and concern, although we also need to accord status to, and receive it from, people outside the family. The total egotist demands, even exacts, status and concern from all from whom he can exact them, and will only accord them in return if he thinks it will pay him to do so. Claudius is not one such, for he is genuinely attached, even grateful, to Gertrude in his new married happiness, eager to be accepted as Hamlet's new father, and therefore eager to see Hamlet cured of his madness. His eagerness suggests that he had been deprived of these necessities in his earlier life, i.e. while greed may appear to have been the motive behind the murder of his brother, the real cause may have been need.

The Elizabethans set great store by physical beauty which, considering the conditions of the day, must have been both rare and short-lived in those fortunate enough to have been born beautiful—a fact emphasised in their lyric poetry. It is clear that Claudius has none; on the contrary, his appearance is distinctly unprepossessing. Hamlet calls him a "paddock" or toad, a "moor" to the Elder Hamlet's "mountain", a "satyr" to the Elder Hamlet's "Hyperion". So Claudius is short, even squat, in a nation of tall men, and fat "the bloat king". He is also ugly, for Hamlet speaks to Rosencrantz and Guildenstern of "those who would make mows at him while my father lived". If people made faces at him as he passed, he must be almost grotesque in appearance.

Was he the Elder Hamlet's older or younger brother? Almost certainly the latter, for, as previously mentioned, the Elder Hamlet had reached the age when he habitually took an afternoon nap. 'Kid' brothers sometimes suffer by merely being kid brothers, especially if they are overshadowed by a handsomer, more heroic elder brother, and Claudius may well have been regarded as the little runt of a kid brother. If he rebelled against being treated with condescension or contempt, he would come to be regarded as the nasty little runt of a kid brother, and he would rebel the more because, as the Ghost admits, he had "wit and gifts", and would be frustrated if they were denied scope.

In his soliloquy at the priedieu he mentions only "a brother's murder", never "a dear brother's murder" or even "my brother's murder", almost as if it were a crime in the abstract; from which we may infer that little love had been lost between the two brothers. Probably a strong, even bitter, rivalry had developed between them.

In one family of two brothers, the elder by two years was shorter than average, his brother distinctly taller than average. The shorter brother suffered badly, and for a time became something of a rebel because he was so much patronised by his taller brother. The situation appears to have been similar in the Hamlet family, except that Claudius would be patronised the more because he was both shorter and younger.

The Elder Hamlet was tall and Hamlet will also be tall. Has Claudius been starved of status because of his shortness (short people tend to be overlooked), and does he hope to appease a long-standing hunger in himself by winning Hamlet's regard? Does he also hope that some of Hamlet's popularity will rub off on to him? If such hopes were present in his mind, he would be quite unable to speak of them to himself in his soliloquy.

Had Claudius been married at any time before the play opens? The Ghost calls him an "adulterate beast", but not "adulterous beast", and I do not think that the phrase refers to any adultery with Gertrude before the murder. It may refer to Claudius' "adulterate loyalty"[24], or to the marriage, which in the eyes of the Ghost and Hamlet is "incestuous", i.e. invalid and therefore adulterous, though not in the eyes of anyone else in the play. In fact Claudius will have obtained the necessary dispensation: when, in his opening speech to his lords I,ii,15ff., he refers to "your better wisdoms, which have freely gone / With this affair along", he will be glancing in acknowledgement towards his archbishops. It is carrying surmise rather far to suggest that he had been unable to find a wife because of his ugly looks or had refrained from marrying, perhaps as an expression of rebellion, and had cut a swathe through whatever women were available. Nevertheless, his happiness with Gertrude and his over-eager offer of paternal love to Hamlet require an explanation. How is his shrewdness as King to be reconciled with his total lack of insight into Hamlet's feelings after his father's death? He cannot have had any experience of family life; he must be childless.

There is no suggestion in the play that Claudius is or ever was an unpleasant, self-centred, or villainous type of man; on the contrary, he is on excellent terms with Polonius, Cornelius, Voltimand, Rosencrantz and Guildenstern. As well as natural authority, Claudius has charm—"wit and gifts", "the power so to seduce"—which he may have been compelled to develop as an antidote to his unprepossessing appearance, or in the hope of being noticed in spite of his shortness. He uses it without success in his appeal to Hamlet, who, refusing to abandon his mourning for his father, is the sole discordant element in his life.

I have come to believe that Claudius intended the murder to open more than one door for him. Did he marry Gertrude because he realised that he needed a permanent companion in his life (or, perhaps, simply because a king needs a queen), find happiness with her, then suddenly realise that he would have liked a child of his own; or had he come to admire his brilliant young nephew, and did he plan his murder in the hope of winning three prizes, "my crown (mine own ambition)", "my queen", and Hamlet's respect and love?

He could not have been totally deprived of status in the political sphere, for he had enough political acumen to time his murder while Hamlet was away at Wittenberg, win the election, and prove himself a capable king who is respected by all around him.

Status and concern were lacking in his personal life; what eventually brings him to

---

24 Not "adulterous"; see Chap. 27, *Further Notes on Hamlet*.

disaster is his extreme but natural reaction to Hamlet's refusal to accept his love or to accord him status.

(iv)

The probable sequence of events can now be summarised: probable because it has been necessary to rely so much on inference and the interpretation of undertones though I feel that Shakespeare visualized Claudius completely before he began to "write" him, in particular the past life which, as is the case with all of us, made him what he is.

Possessing high intelligence as well as charm, Claudius calculated everything beforehand; patronised by and hating his brother, he eventually decided to retaliate by taking for himself everything his brother possessed: his life, his throne, his wife and his son. After the election he would quickly woo Gertrude, and then win Hamlet's filial love and support.

Perhaps he disagreed with his warrior-brother's policies as king, for his handling of Young Fortinbras shows that he prefers diplomacy to the cruelties of war.

His calculation proved correct with respect to the loving and submissive Gertrude, but not to Hamlet. Although he knew that a Hamlet loyal to him would be an enormously valuable asset as "our chiefest courtier", his hope of winning Hamlet's love was not a politician's cold calculation; he had always admired his brilliant nephew, knew that he himself would have liked to have such a son, and was looking forward to Hamlet's acceptance of him as a new father. Hamlet's love might have meant more to him than Gertrude's. Such is his married happiness with her that he may well have discovered it for the first time in his life, but he would also know that she could never be a true helpmeet to him. Hamlet, as companion and "chiefest courtier" to him, would be the ideal masculine mind.

At the beginning of the play we see his eloquent appeal to Hamlet. From Hamlet's "Too much i' the 'sun' ", it is not the first but is perhaps the longest and still failing to produce a response. Then Hamlet begins to go out of his mind for no reason that anyone can discover; in vain do Polonius, Rosencrantz, Guildenstern, and Claudius himself try to probe it, Claudius being the most eager.

The Gonzago-play is put on, and suddenly everything that Claudius has won is under threat and from the nephew whom he least wants to see as his enemy. It is so obviously calculated an attack that Claudius, bitterly disappointed in his hopes and driven to defend himself, decides to rid himself of Hamlet, lunatic or not, and he has his suspicions in spite of Hamlet's convincing impersonation of lunacy.

So stunned is he by the crushing of his hopes that he cannot think clearly. He attempts to pray for Divine guidance, but cannot express his thoughts; he 'chokes' at the priedieu; he cannot even bring himself to speak of Hamlet, although Hamlet is the cause of his problems.

Since he is displayed as a capable King, he must also be regarded as a conscientious King who rules with the welfare of his country at heart. Must he not do so to justify both his own election and his hope that Hamlet will be elected after him? But the Gonzago-play tells him that he could never have won Hamlet's love and support: if Hamlet is executed, his death coupled with the murder of his father will overwhelmingly burden his conscience; the Hamlet family will end with his own death as there are no other possible direct successors; and Hamlet's slander of the monarchy will have compelled him to forfeit his married happiness to the welfare of Denmark which, by the above interpretation, is the first time he has known such happiness.

Small wonder that his words fly up and his thoughts remain below, and it is not easy to decide which of his thoughts will weigh most heavily upon him.

His doubts are resolved by the slaying of Polonius, and his decision is further confirmed by Hamlet's parting "And so, my mother", which leaves him incapable of further balanced judgment with regard to his nephew.

His problems have no satisfactory solution, a situation in which any decision raises difficulties. His first mistake, stemming from his "choler" after the Gonzago-play, is the secret commission, although having Hamlet confined (as suggested by Polonius in III,i,185) would be both less extreme and ultimately the lesser evil. He then makes a weak attempt to cover up the death of Polonius by having him interred "hugger-mugger", forgetting that such an interment will be an affront to Laertes. Neither he nor Gertrude can spare any thought for the poor mad Ophelia, considering that Polonius' long service to the Royal family has put them under an obligation to care for her.

When Laertes bursts into the Castle, he makes what excuses he can, his professed attachment to Gertrude being little more than an excuse. His other excuse that Hamlet is loved by the "general gender" is partly true; behind it lies his own hope of winning Hamlet's love and support.

Taken by surprise by Hamlet's return, he enters into a conspiracy with Laertes. Hamlet has apparently come to his senses, perhaps regaining his respect for Claudius as king and giving Claudius the opportunity to reconsider his attitude to him. After Hamlet's parting insult nothing less than Hamlet's death will satisfy him.

So far, Claudius has shown himself to be anything but conspiratorially minded. In his soliloquy he speaks of "my murder", not of "our murder"; he has consulted the "better wisdoms" of his lords before marrying Gertrude; after the death of Polonius he says, "Come, Gertrude, let's call up our wisest friends", and to Laertes he makes the offer: "Make choice of whom your wisest friends you will, / And they shall hear and judge 'twixt you and me"; but now, obsessed by his hatred of Hamlet, he enters into his foolish conspiracy with Laertes.

Who and what is Osric? He is a young man; as he carries Laertes' challenge to Hamlet, he must be a friend of Laertes. He is one of the referees in the fencing match and must therefore have examined the foils beforehand; it is he who gives Laertes the unbated, poisoned foil in exchange for the one Laertes first tries.

This conspiracy is proof both of Claudius' lack of conspiratorial experience and of the failure of his judgment under deep emotional stress. Does he not know that a conspirator always puts himself in the hands of his fellow conspirators? If Hamlet dies of a touch from the poisoned foil, will it really be possible to gloss over the cause of his death? Laertes will remain silent for his own reasons though he will always have a hold on Claudius. How can the King be sure of Osric, whom Hamlet describes as a "chough" or chatterer, and whose speech proves it?

If the scheme succeeds, how will he dispose of the wine which has the "union" in it?

In the event, the fencing match does not go as expected, the innocent Gertrude, whose company had meant so much to him, drinks of the poisoned wine, and he must watch her die before he himself dies.

Shakespeare twice makes Claudius confess to the murder, and I sometimes wish that he hadn't. What a play it would then have been—the greatest "whodunit" of all time! There would have endless debate as to whether Claudius committed the murder or not, but at least he might have received the attention he deserves. He is no mere two-dimensional villain: he is a living human being with his own needs, hopes and fears; he has his pathetic aspects; he is no more the all-black silhouette of a villain than Hamlet is the dreamy hero. He is almost a major tragic figure in his own right, and if his soliloquy at the priedieu had been a more forthcoming discussion of his problems as King, husband and stepfather, he might have been seen thus. However, Shakespeare evidently intended to divert no more than the minimum of attention from his central figure of Hamlet.

PART IIC
HAMLET
CONSTRUCTION
CRITICAL HISTORY

21
WHAT KIND OF PLAY IS HAMLET?
(i)

Hamlet may be regarded as containing two plays side by side. They may be called the 'outer' play and the 'inner' play.

The 'outer' play was for the younger spectators, a melodrama for those who wanted suspense, violence, and excitement, a combination of revenge tragedy and detective mystery, a kind of 'whodunit', or rather a 'did-he-do-it-and-was-she-in-it-too' in which for a while the answers are not clear.

The 'whodunit' of today is usually set in an ambience which is modern, i.e. perfectly familiar to the modern reader or theatregoer, and in many respects *Hamlet* was topical to its audiences:

- It was set in the familiar type of Renaissance court in a country not remote from England, with the usual assembly of Royal and high-born personages and even its own Swiss Guards ("Where are my Switzers"—IV,v,93).
- Its opening situation would not be far-fetched to audiences who believed in the objective reality of ghosts.
- The atmosphere in a country under threat of invasion would be no novelty to them either, for none of them could have forgotten the Armadas.
- They would at once recognise the Gonzago-play as a slander on the monarch deserving severe punishment, and the slaying of Polonius as an attempt at regicide.
- Since Hamlet's sixteenthth-century garment the doublet is mentioned, performances were in dress modern to them.
- Many would be aware of elective monarchies, in particular that of Denmark.
- Since girls could be married when very young, they would recognise Ophelia as young and Gertrude as a wife who had become dependent on her older husband, probably because she too had been married when young.
- Some would be aware of the Danes' drinking habits.
- Hamlet's talk of "perfect conscience" to Horatio would be seen as un-Christian.

Blended into this framework is the 'inner' play, which is a slightly loose term, since it has no plot of its own. At the same time, both plays come to the same catastrophe and for much the same reason: a study of the relationships within two small, closely-knit families, one of which is in a healthy emotional state, while the other is not. It was for the older, more perceptive spectators, in particular those who had had certain experiences of family life.

The blending raises the question: what kind of tragedy was the play intended to be?

The Greek tragedies, based on episodes from their legends, were tragedies of situation and tacit criticisms of the religion of which their legends formed a part. Why should individuals who have committed no crime find themselves placed by Fate in a situation which requires them to be punished?

As an example: after Polynices is slain in combat, the ruler of Thebes orders that his body shall be left exposed to rot, but Polynices' sister Antigone decides that it must be given the customary rites of burial—and is then punished by being entombed alive in a deep dungeon, where she hangs herself.

As another: when Oedipus is born to the king and queen of Thebes, an oracle predicts that he will kill his own father; he is then given to a shepherd who is to expose him and leave him to die. But the shepherd gives him to the king and queen of Corinth who adopt him as their own son. When an oracle predicts that he will kill his own father and marry his own mother, he attempts to evade this fate by leaving for Boeotia, where he kills the Sphinx which has been persecuting the Boeotians. He becomes the king of the country by marrying its widowed queen; however, when he learns that he has indeed killed his own father and married his own mother, though unwittingly, he is so horrified that he blinds himself.

The aforementioned *Horace* by Corneille is another such tragedy, for it is the humane and perceptive Curiace who, quite undeserving of his situation, perishes in the combat.

Hamlet is yet another, for the Ghost's story pitchforks its hero into a situation which he has neither desired nor deserved, and whose outcome for him, as he instantly sees, may be either execution as regicide or confinement for life as a lunatic. The rapidity of his decision to play the lunatic gives the lie to his "hesitancy".

It is a tragedy of situation in another respect, for when Hamlet finds that he has become a stepchild to an over-eager stepfather, it is also a position which he has neither desired nor deserved.

As in the Greek tragedies, the personal idiosyncrasies of the hero are virtually irrelevant, and the soliloquies, which have given rise to so much speculation as to Hamlet's 'character', are dramatic necessities whose purpose is to inform the audience of the progression in his moods, the only character trait of importance being his unswerving determination to avenge his father.

'Character' plays a part in the 'inner' play, which is a question not of conscious motivation or of responses stemming from individual temperament or outlook, but of the profound, instinctive family urges which are in the vast majority of us and may be below expression in words.

The two 'plays' must be considered separately, for if the family elements were omitted or given less emphasis, the 'outer' play would still stand as an eventful and exciting revenge tragedy. It is the underlying rather than the overt or conscious motivations in the personages of this Elizabethan revenge-tragedy which constitute its timeless and universal aspects.

After the contrast between the two families is established in the first act, the two 'plays' come to different climaxes. That of the 'outer' play is Hamlet's rash slaying of Polonius, which halts him in his drive to revenge, and leads to the retribution of the last act, while that of the 'inner' play is Hamlet's parting insult to Claudius, which also leads to the final catastrophe. The polite tone of his letter to the King on his return from the sea voyage might suggest that his resentment of Claudius has abated, but even if it has, and if there were no conspiracy against him and no fencing match, their family relations would never again be more than superficially polite.

(ii)

At the risk of wearying the reader, I give my character-summaries in order to compare them with other interpretations:

Hamlet
1) Courageous; instantly overcomes his fear of the Ghost.
2) Highly intelligent and quick-witted: immediately sees the necessity for the "antic disposition".
3) Capable of wit as he repeatedly shows.
4) Capable of dedication and loyalty to his dead father and to such friends as Horatio; has earned admiration and loyalty in return.

5) As law-student: cautious, seeks proof.
6) As well acquainted with himself as could be expected in a young man of his age.
7) Consequently, the kind of Prince who "was likely, had he been put on, / To have proved most royal".

In general, a little too young and lively in mind and body to be able to restrain himself as completely as his situation demands.

Claudius
1) As King, capable, authoritative, shrewd; from his murder, ambitious, though mere greed for position was almost certainly not his true motive; not a tyrant; not a usurper; capable of being ruthless, but not conscienceless. Has political acumen, since he chose his moment to snatch the throne.
2) As husband, attached to his new wife though she necessarily takes second place to his throne.
3) As stepfather, hungry for a child of his own, but lacking in experience of family life.
4) Although older and supposedly more mature than Hamlet, not more able to withstand emotional pressures; his judgment fails as badly as Hamlet's after the Gonzago-play.

As happens with Macbeth, his murder eventually brings him as many problems as it solves. Unfortunately, we are given too little concrete information about his life before the murder.

Gertrude
1) Deeply attached to her brilliant son.
2) Now attached to Claudius, for his early rescue of her from widowhood, and perhaps because he is a younger husband than her first.
3) Immature for her age: not interested in state affairs; tactless enough to betray her new happiness too clearly; incapable of resisting her son in her closet; probably never wanted to be anything but a wife and mother. Was almost certainly married very young; felt lost and lonely after the Elder Hamlet's death, and welcomed a new protector.
4) Not devious by nature or capable of pretence—not hypocritical enough to be unfaithful to a husband or connive at his murder; thoughtless and tactless, perhaps childish but no worse.

Both men know that she needs a protector, although Hamlet decides that he must test her conscience and Claudius ignores her when writing his secret commission.

Polonius
1) A loving and anxious father to his children whom he has been bringing up single-handed.
2) For many years the trusted and faithful servant of the Royal family; respected by Hamlet ("Look you mock him not").
3) Ageing but not senile.
4) Fond of his own wit but not as shrewd as Claudius or as quick-witted as Hamlet.
1) Not a "spy"; not venial; like everyone else, does his best to help the mad Hamlet. Intended to appear gently comic; his death then the more pathetic.

Laertes
1) Perhaps nineteen or twenty. Lively, brave: "very noble".
2) Tends to dramatise himself; can rabble-rouse.
3) Young enough to be easily led by Claudius. His buying of poison in Paris possibly a youthful-foolish action.
4) Otherwise little characterised. In no way the equal of Hamlet; never intended to be a dramatic foil to him (if we must speak of dramatic foils, it is the two families which are dramatic foils to one another). Introduced at the beginning of the play because as the bringer of retribution he must come from somewhere in the dramatic situation, i.e. he should not suddenly appear at the end of the play. His purchase of poison makes him a villain.

Ophelia
1) Very young if she does not know that a Prince may not "carve for himself", and has to ask Hamlet the meaning of the Dumb-show and Prologue to the Gonzago-play.
2) An obedient daughter to her father, as girls had to be; showing the first signs of adolescent independence in accepting Hamlet's "tenders" without telling her father of them.
3) Has almost certainly had a motherless childhood.
4) Has given her heart to Hamlet at too early an age.
5) Her lonely childhood a principal factor, coupled with Hamlet's slaying of her father, in bringing about her breakdown.
6) Hamlet loves her with an intensely protective love; he is heartbroken when he is compelled to break off their friendship. A truly pathetic victim of Claudius' murder.

Horatio
A law student; reserved, deliberate, thoughtful; the ideal witness to the Gonzago-play. Loyal and silent; a necessary support to Hamlet as his faithful confidant.

Rosencrantz and Guildenstern
Lively and well-bred young men. Rosencrantz' suggestion of ambition is not altogether tactful but indicates their previous intimacy with Hamlet. Loyal servants of the Crown who try to help Hamlet in the short time they have; their fate is entirely undeserved.

We now consider some alternative interpretations:

Hamlet: either melancholic and over-reflective or over-excitable and somewhat unstable; in either case a weak hero.
Claudius: a mean, contemptible figure, an "Italianate poisoner", a "King Paddock" who "rushes shrieking from the hall" (Dover Wilson).
Gertrude: a slow, dull, sensual animal of a woman (Bradley).
Polonius: both senile and corrupt.
Ophelia: a "doll without intellect" who fails to give Hamlet the support he needs.
Laertes: a complete contrast to Hamlet: brave and ready to act instantly (and by implication a major figure in the tragedy, almost its hero).
Rosencrantz and Guildenstern: spies, spongers on the King.
Horatio: a nonentity, unnecessary to the play.

What was Shakespeare's dramatic intention? Which of these two sets of characters produces the subtler and more appealing play? Did Shakespeare really intend to stage such a collection of crudities as the second set?

(iii)

The 'outer' play contains nearly all the elements which would thrill an Elizabethan audience:
- a Ghost, which they would find both terrifying and fascinating;
- a mystery: did he do it?
- a handsome, brave, brilliant hero, with a faithful, silent friend;
- a beautiful, pathetic heroine; a Queen who perhaps is still beautiful;
- a squat and ugly (but shrewd) antagonist to the hero;
- an ageing, gently comic Lord Chamberlain;
- a brilliantly improvised impersonation of lunacy by the hero;
- a play within the play;
- a secret plan against the hero's life;
- a small rebellion against the villain by a wronged young man. (Did Shakespeare have a stagehand behind the scenes chopping wood to represent doors being "broke"?)
- the beautiful young heroine going genuinely mad;
- a conspiracy against the hero;
- some ironic wit in a graveyard (of all places!)
- a fencing match with one foil poisoned.

About the only item missing from this list is a battle! Still, an army marches by in the fourth act. And if the reader wonders why I have enumerated these elements at such length, it is to emphasise my astonishment that so many critics of the play should have failed to realise that a dreamy or hesitant hero simply would not have matched such a framework or satisfied its audiences.

It is known that the Elizabethan theatre companies spent large sums on dress, splendid costumes being necessary for court scenes, of which *Hamlet* contains a number. As well as being action-packed, therefore, the play contained a large element of spectacle.

Hamlet even contains thriller elements which are in use to this day, the 'third-time-lucky' sequences.

Around 1930 I saw a film called "The Bishop Murder Case" (Dir. Nick Grinde); it is a tribute to the effectiveness of the triple-sequence device that I now remember nothing of this film except that its bishop was a black bishop from a chess set and that it contained the following episode: at dead of night a man is sitting on a low wall, waiting for an accomplice. As he sits, two black-gloved hands rise behind, ready to grab him. When he nervously looks round, they vanish. They rise again; he shifts his position a little and they vanish once more. A third time they rise and this time he does not move. They grab him by the neck and drag him down into the blackness behind the wall.

In the 1962 film of the D-Day landings in Normandy *The Longest Day* (Prod. Darryl F. Zanuck), a battalion of U.S. Rangers lands at the foot of cliffs which they are to scale in order to destroy gun emplacements at the top. A grapnel with rope attached is fired up, though it only catches in a few strands of barbed wire, and is easily broken loose. Although it is fired up again and drops where the wire is thicker, someone below puts his weight on it, which breaks it loose again. When it is fired up a third time, the rope catches on a dense tangle of wire and holds.

This dramatic device contributes nothing to the characterisation or the action, yet is most effective in bringing audiences to the edges of their seats.

Such a triple-sequence can be read into the presentation of the Gonzago-play. The Dumb-show is put on. Hamlet observes the King and Queen closely, who do not trouble to watch it.

Prologue appears, but instead of a full prologue says only three lines before retiring—another arrow has missed.

At last the play itself is presented, with success!

In spy thrillers, it is almost a standard device that the hero should pretend to be something or someone he is not. Two or three times (not too often!) he arouses suspicion but escapes discovery, until at last he is 'rumbled'. Hamlet contains three self-betrayals by its hero as he plays the lunatic.

In II,ii, the Players arrive; Hamlet not only greets them as old friends but remembers and delivers the "rugged Pyrrhus" speech so well as to earn Polonius' hearty commendation. Now Polonius has done some acting himself in his younger days; does he begin to suspect that Hamlet's "antic" behaviour might not be all it seems? No, he is not as wily as he once was, and in any case he thinks that the cause of Hamlet's trouble is love.

In III,i, Hamlet, suspecting hidden listeners behind the arras, begins to rant at Ophelia, but overdoes matters for he lets slip, "Those that are married already, all but one, shall live." "Oh", say the audience, "he shouldn't have said that; won't the King be suspicious?" He is, though he doesn't know quite what to suspect: "Love!—his affections do not that way tend", and he decides that Hamlet "shall with speed to England", but is just a day too late. (Dramatic irony here, since he is genuinely interested in seeing his nephew cured of his madness.)

Comes the Gonzago-play—and Claudius learns all that is in Hamlet's mind.

Eavesdropping by a character who is pretending to be someone he isn't is also a standard element in thrillers, and in Shakespeare's own productions of *Hamlet,* I suspect that the hero eavesdropped on the villain as much as the villain eavesdropped on the hero! Such stage directions as there are in Elizabethan drama are all too brief, and two important episodes can only be explained by adding stage directions describing Hamlet's movements.

In II,ii, just after Polonius has diagnosed the cause of Hamlet's madness as frustrated love, the King and Queen leave, Hamlet enters reading, and Polonius "boards" him. Is it coincidence that early in their conversation Hamlet asks, "Have you a daughter?" If an appropriate stage direction is inserted at the appropriate spot, it becomes no coincidence, and some comedy is added at the expense of Polonius.

Cornelius and Voltimand enter with their news from Norway. Immediately after they leave, Hamlet enters reading his book, sees the King, Queen and Polonius in conference, slips behind the arras to listen, hears Polonius expound his love-theory, and then realises that he has been given a useful peg on which to hang his madness.

When does he slip out? From the standpoint of spectator-thrill in the nunnery scene, I think that he decides to leave just before Polonius says, "At such a time I'll loose my daughter to him; / Be you and I behind the arras then," and so is not forewarned against Polonius' little scheme.

Polonius has just explained the cause of Hamlet's madness at such length and with such pleasure in his discovery as to make the Queen impatient, and has ended his explanation with:

Polonius [Weightily]
    Hath there been such a time—I'd fain know that—

>   That I have positively said 'tis so
>   When it proved otherwise.
> *King*   Not that I know.
> *Polonius* [*Pointing to his head and shoulders*]
>   Take this from this, if this be otherwise;
>   If circumstances lead me, I will find
>   Where truth is hid, though it were hid indeed
>   Within the centre.
>
>   (II,ii,153–160)

When Hamlet re-enters, he is reading or apparently reading his book. He decides to use his 'peg', but does not overdo things: after Polonius' long divagations around the subject of Hamlet's madness, only a light touch from Hamlet is needed to make him look foolish. To Polonius, after identifying him as a "fishmonger", he merely says, "Have you a daughter? ...Conception is a blessing, but not as your daughter may conceive." And Polonius mutters: "Still harping on my daughter...He is far gone, far gone."

In III,i, after Ophelia has been placed as the bait, Hamlet wanders in with nothing to do but think his own thoughts while waiting for the evening's performance of the Gonzago-play. Eventually he sees Ophelia, and at first speaks to her in a vein which is intended to convey "You must regard me as dead to you." Then he realises that she would not have come into the Castle by herself, asks "Where's your father?", becomes sure that someone is listening, and begins to rant at her in the manner which he thinks the listeners want to hear.

The spectators thus see their hero walk into a trap and talk his way out of it.

At the end of the closet scene (III,iv), Hamlet says to his mother: "I must to England; you know that?" She knows, for she replies, "Alack, I had forgot," and he continues, "There's letters sealed." How has he come to know of them? His knowledge of them can only be explained by another eavesdropping episode in III,iii.

The King enters with Rosencrantz and Guildenstern. Immediately afterwards Hamlet tiptoes to the door with hand on sword. Realising that his two friends will prevent him from killing the King, he waits and hears the King say, "I your commission will forthwith despatch, / And he to England shall along with you."

When he hears his friends say, "We will haste us", he at once disappears and hides, because they are coming out through the same door. He must remain hidden, for Polonius is coming in to speak to the King. He remains hidden until Polonius leaves, and so does not hear Polonius say: "My lord, he's going to his mother's closet; / behind the arras I'll convey myself."

He remains hidden for some little time after Polonius leaves, and then once more steals in, now with half-drawn sword. When he finds the King praying, he decides to postpone his revenge.

At the beginning of III,iv, the spectators see Polonius "sconce" himself behind the arras. This time their hero does not suspect that someone is listening. And they see him kill the wrong man.

(iv)

Can any other motifs be read into Hamlet? Are not a revenge tragedy and a study of two families enough for one play?

While both 'plays' come to the same termination, the 'inner' play is open-ended. Quite what would happen within the two families if their members were not all dead at the end of the play it is impossible to say, but I feel that Shakespeare would have preferred us to reflect on such a question rather than some of the ethical, philosophical, or even sociological motifs which have been read into the play.

As an example, Caroline Spurgeon finds that *Hamlet* is principally about the corrupt state of Denmark:

> In *Hamlet*, naturally, we find ourselves in an entirely different atmosphere. If we look closely we see that this is partly due to the number of different images of sickness, disease or blemish of the body, in the play (see Chart VII), and we discover that the idea of an ulcer or tumour, as descriptive of the unwholesome condition of Denmark morally, is, on the whole, the dominating one...
>
> To Shakespeare's pictorial imagination, therefore, the problem in *Hamlet* is not predominantly that of will and reason, of a mind too philosophic or a nature temperamentally unfitted to act quickly; he sees it pictorially not as the problem of an individual at all, but as something greater and more mysterious, as a condition for which the individual himself is apparently not responsible, any more than the sick man is to blame for the infection which strikes and devours him, but which, nevertheless, in its course and development, impartially and relentlessly, annihilates him and others, innocent and guilty alike. That is the tragedy of *Hamlet*, as it is perhaps the chief tragic mystery of life.
>
> *Shakespeare's Imagery*, pp.316–319 (1939)

So Shakespeare wrote *Hamlet* mainly because he had a pictorial imagination? And it is really a sociological document about the condition of Denmark? And we, Hamlet's fellow Danes, are all guilty?

What the play actually tells us about Denmark does not in the least suggest disease or corruption. Marcellus only says that "something" is rotten in the state of Denmark.

It has just won itself an empire by conquest. England, its "tributary", is still "raw and red / After the Danish sword."

The heroic Elder Hamlet is dead, and the new King, Claudius, is capable, authoritative, and loyally served.

Under Claudius, Denmark is busily increasing its armaments.

Laertes' insurrection shows that there is a lively democratic element in the population. Though he calls it distracted, Claudius respects the multitude.

If the First and Second Clowns are any guide, its "manuals" are sharp-witted and independently-minded!

Throughout history, these have been signs of national vigour rather than decay and decadence. About the only habit for which the Danes might be criticized is that they drink too much, though they can presumably afford to do so.[25] Any sickness in Denmark is strictly confined to the Castle, and even there, only the Hamlet family is sick. Which is the better way of emphasising the sickness of the Hamlet family: placing it in a uniformly sick, corrupt nation, or contrasting it with the healthy normality around it?

Did Shakespeare intend any kind of moral problem to be read into Hamlet?

The question "Is Hamlet a good man or a bad man?" which is the not very meaningful title of a critical essay does not arise. Such a question might arise and would be answered

---

25   For yet another reading of "Doth all the noble substance of a doubt", see Note 2 in Chap.27, *Further Notes on Hamlet*.

in the play, if he were compelled to choose between two courses of action and debate his choices with himself, the choice of private revenge being criminal—which he is not. A duty is laid on him; his loyalty to his father impels him to accept it instantly; if he can prove his uncle's guilt he will carry it out. At no time does he consider himself to have the option of not carrying it out, nor would his spectators consider him to have that option.

Self-awareness is an important aspect of moral character; is Hamlet self-aware? His "I am myself indifferent honest" suggests that he is; if he really is the Prince who is "th'expectancy and rose of the fair state", he must be. He certainly sees what faces him after hearing the Ghost's story. His self-awareness deteriorates under the stress of his appalling situation, but while deterioration under stress may have tragic consequences, it does not necessarily indicate a defect of character. Acute stress offers an explanation, even an excuse, for the loss of detached judgment in a young man. Brilliant though he is, Hamlet is not superhuman.

The question might arise with respect to Claudius because he is older and is faced with a moral choice after the Gonzago-play: should he secure his position by ridding himself of Hamlet (and by-passing the law of lunacy), or leave him alive and accept the resulting problems? In the hands of the French tragedians, and perhaps of John Dryden if he had seen the possibilities in Claudius, the soliloquy at the priedieu would have been an explicit discussion of his dilemma. By my interpretation, however, it is not such a discussion for profound psychological reasons and Shakespeare evidently did not intend too much attention to be diverted from his central character.

The impossibility of bringing the miscreant to public justice was a condition of the plot without which a revenge tragedy would have had little point in the eyes of Elizabethan audiences. Few of Shakespeare's spectators would have considered Hamlet as having the option of not carrying out his duty to his dead father; nevertheless, some of them would have left the theatre reflecting on the contemporary attitude to private revenge.

In his *The Spanish Tragedy,* Kyd had intensified the dramatic situation by making his hero a judge who normally would not dream of taking private revenge and therefore proceeds with caution. Briefly he is contrasted with the Viceroy of Portugal, who does not, then making him succumb to frustration. Shakespeare followed Kyd's lead in choosing a law student as a hero who is conscientious in seeking proof, and in making him suffer from frustration, although for a different and dramatically more effective reason: Hieronimo obtains proof of his son's murder, and while public justice should be obtainable for him, such proof is impossible for Hamlet. He therefore does not quote "Vengeance is mine, saith the Lord" or discuss the morality of private revenge, as does Hieronimo, for Hamlet must take either private revenge, if given proof, or none.

Shakespeare introduced what I have called the religious vein: the avenger endangering his soul. He clearly was aware of contemporary thoughts on the subjecy, as later formalised in Bacon's essay *On Revenge* in which he objected to private revenge primarily on legal grounds: it "putteth the law out of office." However, the essay ends with "Nay, rather, vindicative persons live the life of witches, who, as they are mischievous, so end they infortunate." Shakespeare may have decided to expand this theme in his own way.

There might have been a character problem if Hamlet weighed the duty of avenging his father against its consequences on himself, though he never does. If he discussed the morality of private revenge or of regicide, he would be considering a moral problem, which would be a reason for hesitating; he does not. His first problem is how to obtain satisfactory proof of his uncle's guilt or innocence, which naturally drives out all other thoughts. His delay, stemming from his conscience, is to his credit. If he were as hesitant, reflective, philosophical—or whatever else—as he is supposed to be, would he not naturally soliloquise at some point in the play on the morality of private revenge, such a consideration being an excellent reason for hesitating? It plays no part in his thinking.

At the same time, in Hamlet the Elizabethan spectators would see a character problem of a specifically Elizabethan kind.

Two questions would occur to them as they listened to the Ghost's story: young as he is, will Hamlet be man enough to abandon all his hopes in life and dedicate himself to proving the Ghost's story and if necessary avenging his father, regardless of the cost to himself? The answer, of course, is an immediate Yes.

Secondly, is he mature enough? Will he, when testing the Ghost's story, be sufficiently on his guard against his dislike of his stepfather to retain his detachment? While Hamlet himself suggests that he is, the answer proves to be No.

We recall that in those days there was no clear dividing line between religion and superstition, that the age was intensely religious, and as we now see it, intensely superstitious.

In *Macbeth*, the witches' tempting of Macbeth leads to the deaths of Duncan, his grooms, Banquo, Lady Macduff and her children, an unknown number of other innocent victims, and indirectly to Lady Macbeth, and Macbeth.

In *Hamlet*, the Ghost's story leads to the deaths of Polonius, Rosencrantz, Guildenstern, Ophelia, Gertrude, Laertes, Claudius—all of them, with the exception of Claudius and the possible exception of Laertes, innocent of crime—and finally of Hamlet himself.

Claudius' confession to the murder shows that the Ghost was speaking the truth, but to the Elizabethan spectator this would be no proof that it was non-malevolent. Do not the witches speak only the truth to Macbeth? And does not the Ghost's story, also true, lead to the extinction of two families?

How many of Shakespeare's spectators would see Hamlet's failure to control his own emotions as causing him to fall victim as much to the Ghost as to Claudius? Since the Ghost does indeed speak the truth and has good reason to demand revenge, this can hardly be called a rational thought, but seeing significance in almost anything, the superstitious mind is not rational. Hamlet does fail to control his own emotions: his disgust with and suspicion of his mother causes him to betray himself in the Gonzago-play, his hatred of his uncle to waste an opportunity for revenge, and then to kill the wrong man. From that point, death follows death; the last, inevitably to the Elizabethan spectator, being Hamlet's own. It was only to be expected from a ghost's tale.

Is Hamlet not a 'real' character; is he to be regarded as merely a stage personage, overidealised for dramatic effect, as some critics have maintained?

No. If he were, we would feel that he is overdone. For four centuries he has fascinated us all because his qualities are recognisable to us. We do not feel it improbable that he should have them. Granted that such a combination of qualities as he possesses is rare, people certainly exist who have them: high intelligence, zest for life, fearlessness, and the gift of inspiring loyalty. Such people are most likely to emerge during a war, and all too often they do not survive it. To anyone who has met or known of such types, Hamlet is not an overidealized hero.

We were never intended to watch a dreamy non-hero muttering his way through soliloquy after soliloquy. We were meant to leave the Globe feeling great regret for the loss of such a young man as Hamlet, the ladies among us to be weeping for Ophelia and Gertrude, and parents of families to be feeling very thoughtful.

22

A SHORT HISTORY
OF
THE CHARACTER PROBLEM IN HAMLET

"In fact, had there been no critics, I believe there would have been no difficulties."
F.L.Lucas, *Literature and Psychology*, ch.1 (1951)

How did all the critical "fog and smoke", as Quiller-Couch called it, come to envelop Hamlet?

Examination of the critical comments on the play suggests that it began to arise about a century after Shakespeare's death, and that its cause was the gradual forgetting of a number of things.

I surmise that until the Puritans closed the theatres in 1642, the plot of *Hamlet* remained fully understood by all.

In the *Amleth* story, the hero discovers and kills one of the usurper's confederates spying on him, though there is no suggestion that he regrets the killing or that he allows it to delay him in his progress to revenge. The *Ur-Hamlet* which is presumed to have been written by Kyd is lost. How he used this element in the story is not known, though he would have used it because it would make an exciting episode on the stage.

Shakespeare, I surmise, decided to introduce an unexpected twist into his plot by making his hero kill not an enemy but a would-be helper—an innocent man—and by making his hero pause because he realises that he is now a murderer. (In *The Spanish Tragedy*, Kyd made his hero kill an innocent man, but not till the end of the play). The episode became the climax of the play, obviously to increase the suspense in his spectators, i.e. what will our hero do next?

By reinforcing the 'outer' play with the 'inner' play he even introduced additional reasons for the rage which causes his hero first to imperil his soul and then to act too rashly.

In these respects the plot of Hamlet was almost certainly unique, and more original and exciting than that of any other revenge tragedy. Now I cannot imagine Shakespeare introducing such a twist into his play without making the reasons for his hero's apparent delay perfectly comprehensible to his audiences, nor can I imagine his spectators failing to understand them. Plays, I am prepared to repeat ad nauseam, are written to make money from contemporary audiences, who must understand them. So I surmise that these reasons remained understood for many years after Shakespeare's death.

The age remained superstitious and the seventeenth century was the age of witch-hunts. According to Dr. Johnson, "Witches were every day discovered, and multiplied so fast in some places that Bishop Hall mentions a village in Lancashire where their number was greater than that of the houses." The physician Sir Thomas Browne (1605–1682) wrote in his *Religio Medici*: "I have ever believed, and do now know, that there are witches: they that are in doubt of these...are obliquely and upon consequence a sort, not of infidels, but of atheists." John Bunyan (1628–1688) also believed in witches. The New Englander, Cotton Mather (1663–1728), wrote books on witchcraft and demoniacal possession which are considered to have been partly responsible for the Salem witch-hunts of 1692. He was also a Fellow of the Royal Society, who advocated inoculation against smallpox.

Thus the Elder Hamlet's Ghost would remain as impressive as ever.

Then various 'forgetting' processes began. While Hamlet continued to be played, where most of the plays by contemporary minor playwrights were not, I again surmise it was gradually forgotten that its plot was unique.

However, for other reasons no character problem was read into the play until the beginning of the eighteenth century.

After Charles II returned from France in 1660 and the theatres reopened, the criticism of Shakespeare centred on the question: was he to be censured for his failure to observe any such 'Rules' as those adopted by the French playwrights and critics, or did his undoubted genius justify his lapses from 'correctness'? Opinions varied, although no one appears to have reflected that while the French audiences were the most civilized the world had seen and could appreciate plays which were all talk and no action, the Elizabethan audiences had demanded entertainment in the form of spectacle, variety of character and dialogue, intrigue, violence, and blood. They had been totally uninterested in unity of time, place and action, dignified language, or any other aspect of "correct" play-writing. One question was: were his plays moral enough, was "poetick justice" observed (that a play should point a moral being one of the French 'Rules'). Another: were his lapses from good taste in his dialogue, his occasional obscurity of language, and other faults, outweighed by the naturalness of his characters? Even though he had his defenders as well as his critics, criticism was always in terms of a set of rigid principles. Little attention was given to the possibility of profound psychological truths in his portraits of the individuals in his plays. Character criticism, i.e. the examination of the psychology of individuals, and in particular of Hamlet, only began after about 1710.

In any case, Betterton, who appears to have been one of the greatest Shakespearean actors, was playing Hamlet.

Thomas Betterton (c.1635–1710), beginning his acting career in 1660, was still acting a year before his death. In 1668 Samuel Pepys recorded his opinion of him:

> To the Duke of York's playhouse...and saw Hamlet... and mightily pleased with it, but, above all, with Betterton, the best part, I believe, that man ever acted.

In his *Roscius Anglicanus or An Historical Review of the Stage* (1708), the prompter John Downes made the following entry:

> *The Tragedy of Hamlet*; Hamlet being performed by Mr. Betterton, Sir William (having seen Mr. Taylor of the Blackfryars company act it, who being instructed by the author Mr. Shakespeur) taught Mr. Betterton in every particle of it.

"Sir William" was Sir William Davenant, poet, playwright and producer of the mid-century; "Mr. Taylor" was Joseph Taylor, an actor who did not join Shakespeare's company till three years after his death; however, the professions, which include the stage, form their own fraternities within which their members meet one another. As Shakespeare knew Jonson and the other playwrights with whom he collaborated, it is hardly likely that he knew only the actors of his own company; hence, since Taylor, who died in 1652, would have been a young actor looking for work during Shakespeare's last years in London, he would have been careful to meet the leading playwright of the time and to learn from his own lips how his parts should be played.

In the preface to his edition of Shakespeare (1709), Nicholas Rowe said:

> I cannot leave *Hamlet* without taking notice of the Advantage with which we have seen this Masterpiece of Shakespeare distinguish itself upon the Stage by Mr. Betterton's fine Performance of that Part. A Man who, tho' he had no other good Qualities, as he has a great many, must have made his way into the Esteem of all Men of Letters by this only excellency. No Man is better acquainted with Shakespeare's Manner of Expression, and indeed he has study'd him so well and is so much a Master of him that whatever Part of him he performs he does it as if it had been written on purpose for him, and that the Author had exactly conceiv'd it as he plays him.

Since Colley Cibber virtually repeated the last comment in 1740, Downes' note may be taken as correct.

Charles Lamb remembered Betterton's reputation a century later:

> The character of Hamlet is perhaps that by which, since the days of Betterton, a succession of popular performers have had the greatest ambition to distinguish themselves.
>
> *On the Tragedies of Shakspeare, Considered with Reference to their Fitness for Performance* (1811)

When Betterton played Hamlet for the last time in 1709, a year before his death, Steele reported him in *The Tatler* as follows:

> Had you been to Night at the Playhouse, you had seen the Force of Action in Perfection. Your admir'd Mr. Betterton behaved himself so well, that, though now about Seventy, he acted Youth, and by the prevalent Power of proper Manner, Gesture and Voice, appear'd throughout the whole Drama a Youth of great Expectation, Vivacity, and Enterprise.

"The last words", comments Dover Wilson, "give a hint of his reading of the part—not as a languid ineffectual dreamer."

Evidently Betterton was playing Hamlet 'straight'. Since the part is at its most appealing when played straight, why have its actors not always played it straight? So, in effect, said Aaron Hill in 1735, when Betterton's successors were beginning to play Hamlet as a melancholy and irresolute young man. Hill was complaining that no actor represented both the gay and the serious aspects of Hamlet, Wilks being too light and Booth too solemn:

> This play has always pleased, still pleases, and will forever continue to please while apprehension and humanity have power in English hearts.

To what excess, then, would it not move were Hamlet's character as strongly represented as written?

After Betterton's death his successors developed their own interpretations, and other forgetting processes now had their effect.

The Age of Reason was beginning, when fervent religious belief and equally fervent superstition were yielding in many minds to theism, deism, scepticism, even atheism. The importance of the Ghost and of the religious motif in the play were no longer appreciated. Ghosts remained effective figures on the stage, as is shown by the comment of Addison quoted at the beginning of *The Ghost*. Addison not only remarked on the frequent use of ghosts to save a poor play, since sensational elements have always been used to save poor plays and scripts, and no doubt always will be. Strangely for a dramatic critic he even appears to have approved of the practice. Nevertheless, the Eye of Reason was beginning to see the Ghost less as a living, frightening figure than as an effective and skilfully used dramatic device:

> "The appearance of the Ghost in *Hamlet* is a masterpiece of its kind."
>
> Joseph Addison in *The Spectator* (April 20, 1711)

> ...I shall conclude what I have to say on this scene [the Ghost's first appearance] with observing that I do not know any tragedy, ancient or modern, in any nation, where the whole is made to turn so naturally and so justly upon such a supernatural appearance as this. Nor do I know of any piece whatever where a spectre is introduced with so much majesty, such an air of probability, and where such an apparition is managed with so much dignity and art.
>
> Rev. George Stubbes *Some remarks on the Tragedy of Hamlet* (1736)

Although Stubbes was aware that the action turns on the Ghost, his and Addison's comments have an air of dramatic connoisseurship which suggests that the Ghost was no longer being taken as seriously, at least by the critics, as by audiences in Shakespeare's day. Betterton had always been aware that Hamlet is deathly afraid of the Ghost, for it was recorded of him that when he first saw the Ghost he made his face, which was naturally ruddy and sanguine, turn "as pale as a neckcloth", and trembled all over.

The existence of elective monarchies had also been forgotten. That of the Holy Roman Empire was now only nominally elective, for the Hapsburgs had established a de facto title to its throne which in practice they inherited. 'Elector' remained the principal title of the members of the Electoral College, which remained in being until Napoleon dissolved it in 1806. George I was Elector of Hanover before he came to the British throne in 1714. The Polish monarchy remained elective until 1793, when the country was partitioned. The Danish monarchy had remained elective till 1660.

Thus there was little excuse for overlooking the absence of any mention by Hamlet of his rights as heir, his "Popped in between the election and my hopes", Rosencrantz's suggestion of "ambition", the Danes' "Choose we, Laertes shall be king", and Hamlet's giving his "dying voice" to Young Fortinbras, but they were overlooked, and Claudius came to be regarded as a usurper. In 1736 George Stubbes remarked that the Ghost required Hamlet to prevent Denmark from remaining "the scene of usurpation and incest", although a closer reading of the play would have told him that no one in it ever talks of usurpation.

Perhaps the two Jacobite attempts, by the Old Pretender in 1715 and then the Young Pretender in 1745, to assert the hereditary claims of the Stuart family to the English throne induced the critics to forget the existence of elective monarchies.

These 'forgettings' gave rise to what must have seemed the obvious question: if the Ghost can be taken at its word, and if Claudius is a usurper, why does Hamlet not kill his enemy immediately?

In 1736 an anonymous critic gave what must have seemed the obvious answer:

> To speak truth, our poet by keeping too close to the groundwork of his plot, has fallen into an absurdity, for there appears no reason at all in nature, why the young Prince did not put the usurper to death as soon as possible, especially as Hamlet is represented as a youth so brave, and so careless of his life.
> The case indeed is this: had Hamlet gone naturally to work, as we could suppose a Prince to do in parallel circumstances, there would have been an end of our play. The Poet was therefore obliged to delay his hero's revenge, but then he should have contrived some good reason for it.
>
> Some Remarks on *The Tragedy of Hamlet* (attr. George Stubbes)

This I regard as dramatic criticism at its lowest! Why did the author not reflect that if Hamlet had been deprived of his rights as an heir, he and others in the play would have said as much, and more than once? The cause of Hamlet's delay began to be looked for in his character.

> It has been remarked that there is a great want of resolution in Hamlet, for when he had so good an opportunity to kill his uncle and revenge his father, he shuffles it off with a paltry excuse, and is afraid to do what he so ardently longs for.
>
> William Guthrie *The Beauties of Shakespeare* (1752)

The significance of Hamlet's "paltry excuse", his "Now might I do it" speech, was no longer understood, although it shocked some minds:

> Hamlet's speech on seeing the King at prayers has always given me great offence. There is something so very bloody in it, so inhuman, so unworthy of a hero, that I wish our poet had omitted it. To desire to destroy a man's soul, to make him eternally miserable by cutting him off from all hopes of repentance; this surely, in a Christian prince, is such a piece of revenge as no tenderness to any parent can justify.
>
> George Stubbes *Some Remarks on the Tragedy of Hamlet* (1736)

> ...too horrible to be read or to be uttered.
>
> Dr. Johnson, footnote to his edition of *Hamlet* (1765)

Both critics missed the obvious argument: the more offensive or apparently inconsistent the speech, the greater the need to identify the dramatic reason for it.

In his *Miscellaneous Observations on the Tragedy of Macbeth* (1745), Dr. Johnson justified the use of the witches in his usual magisterial style. He begins:

> In order to make a true estimate of the abilities and merit of a writer, it is always necessary to examine the genius of his age, and the opinions of his contemporaries. A poet who should now make the whole action of his tragedy depend upon enchantment, and produce the chief events by the assistance of supernatural agents, would be censured as transgressing the bounds of probability. He would be banished from the theatre to the nursery, and condemned to write fairy tales instead of tragedies. But a survey of the notions that prevailed at the time when this play was written will prove that Shakespeare was in no danger of such censures, since

he only turned the system that was universally admitted to his advantage, and was far from overburdening the credulity of his audience.

He continues by mentioning the possible origins of the belief in enchantments, the witch trial at Warboys in Huntingdonshire, King James' *Daemonologie*, and the relevant sections of the Witchcraft Act of 1603. He ends:

> Thus, in the time of Shakespeare, was the doctrine of witchcraft at once established by law and by the fashion, and it became not only impolite but criminal to doubt it...
>
> Upon this general infatuation Shakespeare might be easily allowed to found a play, especially as he has followed with great exactness such histories as were then thought true; nor can it be doubted that the scenes of enchantment, however they may now be ridiculed, were both by himself and his audience thought awful and affecting.

When he came to edit *Hamlet* in 1765, he had apparently forgotten this essay, for he only mentioned the Ghost in a few brief remarks. If it had occurred to him that the use of the Ghost deserved the same justification as the use of the Witches in *Macbeth*, i.e. that orthodoxy required Hamlet to fear and distrust the Ghost and to be sceptical of its story, and that his distrust would justify his delay, he might have corrected the course which the criticism of the play had begun to follow. Unfortunately, it did not:

> Of the feigned madness of Hamlet there appears no adequate cause, for he does nothing which he might not have done with the reputation of sanity.

(End-note to his edition of Hamlet)

In 1763 the actor and critic Thomas Sheridan, grandfather of the playwright Richard Brinsley Sheridan, summed up the position (he is reported by Boswell):

> He made it clear to us that Hamlet, notwithstanding of his seeming incongruities, is a perfectly consistent character. Shakespeare drew him as the portrait of a young man of good heart and fine feelings who had led a studious and contemplative life and so become delicate and irresolute. He shows him in very unfortunate circumstances, the author of which he knows he ought to punish, but wants strength of mind to execute what he thinks right and wishes to do. In this dilemma he makes Hamlet feign himself mad, as in that way he might put his uncle to death with less fear of the consequences of such an attempt. We therefore see Hamlet sometimes like a man really mad and sometimes like a man reasonable enough, though much hurt in mind. His timidity being once admitted, all the strange fluctuations which we perceive in him may be easily traced to that source. We see when the Ghost appears (which his companions had beheld without extreme terror)—we see Hamlet in all the agony of consternation. Yet we hear him uttering extravagant sallies of rash intrepidity, by which he endeavours to stir up his languid mind to a manly boldness, but in vain. For he still continues backward to revenge, hesitates about believing the Ghost to be the real spirit of his father, so much that the Ghost chides him for being tardy. When he has a fair opportunity of killing his uncle, he neglects it and says he will not take him off while at his devotions, but will wait till he is in the midst of some atrocious crime, that he may put him to death with his guilt upon his head. Now this, if really from the heart, would make Hamlet the

most black, revengeful man. But it coincides better with his character to suppose him here endeavouring to make an excuse for his delay. We see too that after all he agrees to go to England and actually embarks.

No attempt was being made to place the play in its Elizabethan context, to establish the nature of the political situation, or to analyse the events of the plot. The play was no longer being closely read. Hamlet and his companions do not behold the Ghost without extreme terror, he does not agree to go to England, and when he spares his uncle at prayer he is very "black and revengeful" indeed.

> His remarks that the spirit he has seen may be a devil and that the devil may have power to assume a pleasing shape favour very strongly of a weak superstitious mind, and give us no idea of the prince's head, however favourably we judge of his heart.
>
> Francis Gentleman *The Dramatic Censor* (1770)

Hamlet's distrust of the Ghost, expressed six times, is that of the orthodox Elizabethan which would have been a matter for surprise if he had expressed any other attitude.

By the end of the century the notion that Hamlet is temperamentally irresolute had become established in a number of versions, though no critic reflected that since his version was not quite the same as any other, it might be the case that nobody really understood Hamlet. As examples: a melancholy disposition (Henry Mackenzie and others before him); a nature too pure and noble for the burden cast upon it (Goethe); weakness and "hypocrisy towards himself" (A.W. von Schlegel); "powers of action eaten up by thought" (William Hazlitt); "the prevalence of the abstract and generalizing habit over the practical" (Coleridge).

Sheridan's extract contains what may have been the first suggestion, "sometimes like a man really mad", that there might be a vein of true mental disturbance under Hamlet's assumed pose of lunacy. Others appear to have taken it up:

> The view of Hamlet's character exhibited in my last number, may, perhaps, serve to explain a difficulty which has always occurred both to the reader and to the spectator, on perceiving his madness, at one time, put on the appearance, not of fiction but of reality; a difficulty by which some have been induced to suppose the distraction of the Prince a strange unaccountable mixture, throughout, of real insanity and counterfeit disorder.
>
> Henry Mackenzie in *The Mirror* (22 April 1780)

The idea took firmer root in the next century, as the science of medical psychology began to emerge:

> In a word, Hamlet, to my mind, is essentially a psychological exercise and study. The hero, from whose acts and feelings everything in the drama takes its colour and pursues its course, is doubtless insane, as I shall prove hereafter. But the species of intellectual disturbance, the peculiar form of intellectual malady under which he suffers, is of the subtlest character...
>
> William Maginn *Shakespeare Papers* (1836)

Hamlet, that tragedy of madness, this Royal Bedlam, in which every character is either crazy or criminal, in which feigned madness is added to real madness...

Chateaubriand *Sketches of English Literature* (1837)

Hamlet's mental condition furnishes in abundance the characteristic symptoms in wonderful harmony and consistency...

> On the supposition of his real insanity we have a satisfactory explanation of the difficulties which have received such various solutions. The integrity of every chain of reason is marred by some intrusion of disease.

Dr. Roy *American Journal of Insanity* (April 1847)

> The leading opinions as to Hamlet's sanity are (1) that he is "neither mad nor pretends to be so"; (2) that he feigns madness; (3) that at times he is mad and at times feigns madness; and (4) that he is really mad. Furness asks the advocates of the theory of feigned insanity: "How they account for Hamlet being able, in the flash of time between the vanishing of the Ghost and the coming of Horatio and Marcellus, to form, horror-struck as he was, a plan for the whole conduct of his future life?" The advocates of the theory of real insanity, among whom are many distinguished mental pathologists, lay stress upon the facts (1) that madness is "compatible with some of the ripest and richest manifestations of intellect," (2) that Hamlet himself both affirms and denies his madness and (3) that at the last, in his generous apology, his solemn appeal to Laertes, V,ii,216–234, where it is surely unjust to pronounce him insincere, he alleges his mental disorder as fairly entitling him to the pardon he asks for the offence he has given.

Rev. H.N.Hudson *The New Hudson Shakespeare*, intro. (1881)

It may have been these mental pathologists who caused Oscar Wilde, himself a playwright, to threaten to write a work entitled *Are the Commentators on 'Hamlet' Really Mad or Only Pretending to Be?* Unfortunately, he did not trouble to write it.

In this century Dr. Ernest Jones, a Freudian, decided that Hamlet is suffering from an Oedipus complex, although in Shakespeare's time Freud would not even be heard of for more than three centuries. Few among Shakespeare's audiences would be familiar with the legend of Oedipus; F.L.Lucas, that he is inhibited because he is excessively attached to his mother.

If the reader of Shakespeare needs to have acquired some knowledge of human psychology, the psychologist reading him needs to know something of the theatre, in particular that *Hamlet* is a play, and that plays are primarily intended to be watched, not read, and by audiences who understand them. If the protagonist's motivations are unknown to him because they are rooted in his Unconscious, they are likely to remain unknown to the audience also!

If the central character of a play is suffering from some malady, physical or mental, diagnosed or not, which is at the root of his motivations, the result will be of the nature of a medical documentary; I distinguish between documentaries and plays. Ordinary audiences prefer their protagonists to be consciously, preferably articulately and as aware of their motives as their natures and situations permit. A truly disturbed Hamlet could only be appreciated by an audience of medical psychologists, supposing that they actually wanted to watch such a Hamlet on their evening out.

The ultimate argument is in terms of Shakespeare's intention, which is communicated by the spoken words of the play. What Hamlet has within is not past expression, as indeed Shakespeare did cause him to express it. I see no need to read into him more than Shakespeare caused him to express.

After Bradley had written what came to be regarded as the last word on character in his *Shakespearean Tragedy* of 1904, new and original approaches had to be found. The literal approach or examination of the spoken words of the play became thoroughly discredited after 1930, when Wilson Knight and L.C. Knights spoke of Shakespeare's dramatic intention and characterisation as "irrelevant".

Subsequent critical approaches have already been mentioned in the Preface. Among them is 'deconstructuralism', one of the trends (to quote my German supervisor again) towards "playing with concepts".

The deconstructuralist critic approaches his subject-matter (as do members of other schools) in terms of a quasi-philosophical or quasi-metaphysical system of abstractions which leaves him free to wander through whatever intellectual regions his extensive command of them may suggest, while the question of whether any of his concepts have real bearing on the author's intention in the play under discussion is irrelevant.

One such essay, entitled *Telmah* (*Hamlet* in reverse!), describes the curtain call as a "complex of revisionary ironies"; Claudius' opening speech as "his great revisionary proposal", "his reinterpretation of the past"; the Ghost's description of its murder as a "slow-motion action replay"; "The Mousetrap" as Hamlet's "most recursive moment"; his "Very like a whale" conversation with Polonius as "a famously deconstructive moment". Oddly, about two-thirds of it is devoted to Dover Wilson's early interest in Socialism.

In an end-note to another essay possibly by a 'linguist', I came across the following:

> The center could not be thought in the forms of a being-present...but a function, a sort of non-locus, in which an infinite number of sign-substitutions came into play. This moment was that in which language invaded the universal problematic; that in which, in the absence of a center of origin, everything became a system in which the central signified, the original or transcendental signified, is never absolutely present outside a system of differences.

While this critic appears to have learned a smattering of mathematical terms, it may be doubted whether this comment has any meaning either to mathematicians or to any others than his fellow deconstructuralists or linguists—whichever he is. What is the linguistic approach? Do none of us really understand what we are saying? If we do not, how are plays possible?

In late 1997 came a reaction in France against certain intellectuals whose jargon included scientific or mathematical terms, the meanings of which they did not understand.

Some critics and actors have always believed that Hamlet should be played 'straight'. Of the Hamlets I have seen, the least satisfactory was that of Olivier, who was merely dreamy: what appeal would a dreamy hero have had to Elizabethan audiences? The most pleasing—that of Sir John Gielgud, whom I saw in the part in Liverpool during World War II when I was one of the troops. He says:

> The play is so familiar that the temptation is to play up the 'show' scenes—the closet scene, the nunnery scene, the play scene, the graveyard scene—instead

of making it a play with progressions in which the audience does not know what is going to happen next. It was for this reason that I loved acting Hamlet to the troops during the war. Quite unfamiliar with the play, they followed it with breathless interest, wondering what would happen next.

J. Guildgud, J. Miller, J. Powell *An Actor and his Time* (1979)

His experience supports my contention that what fascinated the early *Hamlet* audiences for whom the play was written, (and although it has been read and played the world over since then, it was not written for any others), was mainly the exciting events of a varied and eventful plot. The play was intended to be a thriller first, a psychological study second.

In summary: the critics of *Hamlet* have been guilty of several failures. They did not establish the play's topical Elizabethan background, and they did not ask themselves whether a dreamy hero would really have suited the tastes of Elizabethan audiences. They did not begin by analysing the dramatic situation and the plot before examining character which, in addition, they failed to define; they paid no attention to Hamlet's oft-expressed doubts of the Ghost's intentions; they assumed Claudius to be a usurper, although even Hamlet and the Ghost never mention usurpation; they did not reflect that the outbursts of strong emotion in his soliloquies might not be characteristic of the normal Hamlet.

Since more has been written on *Hamlet* than on any other comparable creation, the result of these failures has almost certainly been the longest and greatest critical aberration in all literature.

23

COMPARISON OF THE FIRST AND SECOND QUARTOS OF HAMLET

The First Quarto (Q1) is less than two-thirds as long as the Second (Q2). In its admittedly corrupt state, does it represent a first version of the play which was later extended by Shakespeare and printed as the Second Quarto, or is it a pirated and unreliable version?

It was initially suggested that it was a first draft by Shakespeare; then that the play was pirated by a short-hand writer who sat in the gallery and copied what he heard as fast as he could; and then that an actor in the play wrote out as much as he could remember and sold his version to a printer. A scene-by-scene and line-by-line comparison shows that the last hypothesis is correct. He was not one of the principal actors who were Sharers in the theatre company and would not have betrayed their own playwright; he was a minor actor who doubled as Marcellus, Voltimand, Prologue, and Lucianus, and probably appeared as a non-speaking extra in some other scenes. Marcellus has already been named as one part he played, but he doubled in those four parts, and it is possible to deduce how he was occupied when he was not speaking lines. The First Quarto also gives a few important hints as to the acting. It might be charitably supposed that after acting in the play the actor became ill and unable to work, wrote out a version in his chamber, and offered it to a printer because he needed money.

Certain spelling errors, such as "invelmorable" for "invulnerable" (I,i,108), "impudent" for "impotent" (I,ii,29), "courage" for "comrade" (I,iii,31), "dreames" for "drains" (I,iv,8), "ceremonies" for "cerements" (I,iv,26), and others, suggest that the printer was occasionally unable to read his handwriting but, being in haste to publish the version, did not trouble to verify the spelling with him. His major errors, i.e. the wrong placing of scenes or passages; the omission of scenes; the considerable truncation of the later scenes and the errors in them, suggest that he began to write his version of the play or was bribed by the printer to do so some time after he had last acted in it, when his recollection was beginning to falter.

Some passages are identical in the First Quarto, the Second Quarto, and the First Folio, except for odd words, and their style is Shakespeare's own. Others contain many of Shakespeare's lines and phrases, but long speeches are abbreviated, many lines appear to be improvised, and the style in these is grossly inferior to anything Shakespeare ever wrote, so much so that the "first draft" suggestion is a commentary on the absence of stylistic sense of the critics who decided that Q1 might be one. In 1592 and 1593 Shakespeare had already proved that he could write perfect poetry as naturally as he breathed by writing *Venus and Adonis* and *The Rape of Lucrece*, which together contain over four hundred verses, every one of them flawless. Eight years or so later, would he really have written any of the inferior blank verse in Q1, even as a first draft?

Mainly in the later part of the play, other passages are improvisations, again in a much inferior style. There are also errors in the plot. And it is unlikely that a playwright of Shakespeare's reputation would have tolerated such spelling errors in a printed version. The differences of style alone suffice to show that Q1 could never have been Shakespeare's own version, and also that a shorthand writer could not have been employed in the pirating.

As has also been suggested, it is unlikely that more than one actor did the pirating. If, say, three had cooperated, more of the minor parts—of which there are not many—would have been correctly rendered, and three combined memories would have produced a more generally correct version.

When an actor learns his lines he must also learn his cues along with the last lines of all the speeches preceding his own. All speeches, whether long or short, may contain pauses for dramatic effect; hence the actor must learn their last lines if he is not to begin speaking during such pauses. He will also learn or at least remember one or two of the lines to be spoken immediately after his own by the actor whom he himself is cuing. The evidence is beyond coincidence: in the scenes in which the actor had a speaking part he remembered his own cues and lines, also a line or two after his own, almost to the word, also much of the other characters' dialogue. When on the stage in a non-speaking part or waiting off-stage for his entry, he heard and remembered much of the content of the dialogue but was usually compelled to paraphrase or shorten it. When not waiting just off-stage and unable to hear the dialogue, he only remembered the gist of scenes, and then not very well. If he played Marcellus, Voltimand, Prologue, and Lucianus, and entered as an extra in Hamlet's departure for England, he would have to be present up to the latter point during all rehearsals as well as performances. If he then had no entry for a while, as probably in the fourth act, he would not be present during either, and would hear and remember little or none of the actual dialogue.

Examination of the play's early scenes shows that Marcellus' cues and lines are reproduced with almost perfect accuracy; one or two lines after his, with good accuracy. A typical passage near the beginning of I,i goes:

Mar. Break off your talk, see where it comes againe.
2. In the same figure like the King that's dead.
Mar. Thou art a scholler, speake to it Horatio.
2. Lookes it not like the King?
Hor. Most like, it horrors me [sic] with fear and wonder.
2. It would be spoke to.
Mar. Question it, Horatio.
Hor. What art thou, that thus usurps the state, in
   Which the Maiestie of buried Denmarke did sometimes
   Walke? By heaven I charge thee speake.
Mar. It is offended. *exit Ghost.*
2. See, it stalkes away.
Hor. Stay, speake, speake, by heaven I charge thee speake.
Mar. 'Tis gone and makes no answer.
2. How now Horatio, you tremble and looke pale.
   Is not this something more than fantasie?
   What thinke you on't?
Hor. Afore my God, I might not this beleeue, without the sensible and true avouch of
   mine owne eyes.
Mar. Is it not like the King?
Hor. As thou art to thy selfe...

At the end of the scene, the speeches after Marcellus' "O we doe it wrong, being so maiesticall", in particular his own eight lines beginning "It faded on the crowing of the Cocke", are reproduced equally well.

The actor then changed rapidly (he would have to change his sentry's armour for the costume of an ambassador), and entered as Voltimand towards the end of the King's long opening speech in I,ii, of which he only heard and remembered the lines preceding his own single line:

King   ...and Wee heere dispatch
   Yong good Cornelia, and you Voltemar
   For bearers of these greetings to olde
   Norway, giuing to you no further personall power
   To businesse with the King,
   Then those related articles do shew:
   Farewell, and let your haste commend your dutie.
Gent.   In this and all things will wee shew our dutie.
King   Wee doubt nothing, hartily farewel.

(Q1: I,ii,3–11)

For this reason, the First Folio of 1623 has a stage direction indicating the entry of the ambassadors after two-thirds of the King's opening speech, although, being important members of his court, they would normally be present with his other lords from the beginning of this—his first council meeting:

King Importing the surrender of those lands
   Lost by his Father: with all Bonds of Law
   To our most valiant Brother. So much for him.
[Enter Voltemand and Cornelius.]
   Now for our selfe, and for this time of meeting
   Thus much the businesse is...

After leaving the stage he quickly replaced his armour and re-entered later in the scene as Marcellus; while waiting, he heard and was able to reproduce the gist of the conversation between the King, Queen, and Hamlet, and of Hamlet's "O that this too much grieved and sallied flesh" soliloquy. After his entry the scene is very well remembered, as are I,iv and I,v, the scenes of his final appearances as Marcellus. (If Shakespeare himself played the Ghost, as he is reputed to have, these scenes would be very well rehearsed! This may be another reason why the first act of Q1 is more accurate and complete than any other part of it.)

He heard the speeches of Leartes (so spelled), Ofelia and Corambis well enough to remember more than the gist of their conversation, since his version includes a number of Shakespeare's own lines and phrases (as, for example, in Corambis' parting advice to Leartes). He also remembered the content of II,i (the Reynaldo scene) with Ophelia's description of Hamlet's entry into her closet, but few of the actual lines.

He next appeared in II,ii as Voltimand, whose cue and 21-line report of the mission to Norway are word-perfect but for one trifling error: "that enterprise" for "this enterprise" in the nineteenth line.

His final speaking appearances in the first half of the play were as Prologue and Lucianus, whose lines and cues are almost perfectly recorded. Again he was initially waiting off-stage, and was able to remember much of the dialogue with good accuracy from II,ii (the arrival of Rosencrantz, Guildenstern and the Players) to the end of the presentation of the Gonzago-play. He would enter as one of the Players on their arrival, though he had no lines to speak as yet; hence he was able to recollect much of the dialogue, of the "rugged Pyrrhus" speeches, of Hamlet's advice to the Players, and of the events leading up to his entries.

He took part in the Dumb-show, which he eventually wrote in abbreviated form, and re-entered first as Prologue, then as Lucianus. At each entry, he found Hamlet chatting to Ophelia, had to wait for silence before speaking his lines, and so remembered most of their actual words and phrases, if not always in the right places: he placed Hamlet's "Let the devil wear black" speech after Lucianus' entry instead of before the Dumb-show. He then appears to have remained close to the stage for a while, although his recollection from the end of the Gonzago-play onward became less accurate, as it would if he only had to enter thereafter as a non-speaking extra.

His memory of the plot failed him at a number of points. He placed "To be or not to be" and the rest of the Nunnery scene immediately after Corambis' suggestion that he and the King should listen behind the arras with Ofelia as bait, i.e. at the beginning of Act II and before the arrival of the Players instead of after their arrival and at the beginning of Act III. He placed Corambis' suggestion to the Queen that she should summon Hamlet to her closet and that he should hide behind the arras before the Gonzago-play instead of after it, and he omitted IV,ii and IV,vi.

Occasionally he misplaced lines. In the closet scene he gave two lines to Hamlet which are spoken by the Ghost in I,v, and made Hamlet reveal explicitly that his father had been murdered:

Ham. Whose heart went hand in hand euen with that vow
   He made to you in marriage, and he is dead.
   Murdred, damnably murdred, this was your husband...

(Q1: III,iv,34–36)

In consequence, he seems to have thought that the information that she had married her first husband's murderer registers with Gertrude, for towards the end of the scene he made her say:

Queene Alas, it is the weaknesse of thy braine
   Which makes thy tongue to blazon thy hearts griefe:
   But as I haue a soule, I sweare by heaven,
   I never knew of this most horride murder:
   But Hamlet, this is only fantasie,
   And for my love forget these idle fits...
Queene Hamlet, I vow by that maiesty
   That knowes our thoughts, and lookes into our hearts,
   I will conceal, consent, and doe my best,
   What stratagem soe're thou shalt deuise.

(Q1: III,iv,89–95 and 104–108)

He may have entered as a soldier guarding Hamlet with "Rossencraft" and "Gilderstone" in IV,iii, when Hamlet departs for England. The King begins the soliloquy in which he reveals the content of the secret commission to England with "Gertred, leaue me", Gertrude's presence being an error arising from the actor's omitting IV,ii and combining IV,i and IV,iii. The soliloquy is then paraphrased.

The first part of Q1 up to any point between the end of the Gonzago-play and Hamlet's departure for England contains about two-thirds as many lines as the corresponding part of Q2, most of the deficit being in the abbreviated longer speeches, whereas the second part of Q1 contains fewer than half as many lines as the second part of Q2. Further, many of Shakespeare's own lines and phrases appear in the first part, while the second part contains far fewer. Probably the actor was quite often on or near the stage during the first half, but not on or near it for much of the second half, the fourth act after Hamlet's departure for England being largely the pirate's own improvisations. Hamlet's important soliloquy "How all occasions do inform against me" is omitted, as is his account of the sea voyage and his exchange of the commissions.

He remembered the songs that Ophelia sings in her mad scenes, which were probably well-known children's' songs.

He invented a scene between the Queen and Horatio in which Horatio instead of Hamlet describes the latter's exchange of the secret commissions and the fate of "Rossencraft" and "Gilderstone", and in which the Queen says:

Queene Then I perceive there's treason in his lookes
That seem'd to sugar o're his villanie:
But I will soothe and please him for a time,
For murderous mindes are alwayes jealou...

(Q1: IV,vi,10–13)

After this, while the Queen should be wary of the wine in the final scene, she is not, nor before that scene is she shown as soothing and pleasing Claudius. Neither Q1 nor Q2 contain any suggestion that she does; however, the actor may have remembered Gertrude's protecting Claudius by running forward and grasping Laertes' sword-arm in IV,v. Alternatively, he had previously acted in the *Ur-Hamlet*, and, since his recollection of this part of the play is very poor, he was confusing the plots of the two plays. Possibly the Queen's above-quoted second response to Hamlet's "As kill a king" in the closet scene was also wrongly remembered from *The Spanish Tragedy*, in which Bel-Imperia promises to help Hieronimo to his revenge.

He also made the King provide and suggest to Leartes the use of both the poisons in the fencing match.

The most accurately rendered portion of the play after Hamlet's departure for England is the fifth act, although the dialogue is not perfectly reproduced. The only minor speaking parts in V,i are those of the two Clowns and the First Priest, and since their dialogue is not accurately given (the First Priest's few lines are paraphrased), the actor did not play them; however, he would remember the content and much of the phraseology of the dialogue if, after waiting off-stage from the beginning of the scene during both rehearsals and performances, he entered as one of the lords in Ophelia's funeral cortege.

The last scene is much abbreviated and largely paraphrased. The stage direction at the end of the scene reads "*Enter Voltemar and the Ambassadors from England, enter Fortenbrasse with his traine*", which suggests that he entered in his original ambassador's costume; however, he was neither the English ambassador nor Fortenbrasse, as otherwise he would have remembered their lines as well as his previous parts.

In his edition of Kyd's works (1951) W.W. Greg surmises that Q1 was based on Kyd's lost *Ur-Hamlet*, finds parallels of word or phrase between Q1 and *The Spanish Tragedy*, and considers that "evidences of Kyd's hand, though partly overlaid, are, as I have tried to show, scattered sufficiently through the text to vindicate his share in the creation of the modern world's most wonderful tragedy." Such parallels would more probably have been due to the pirating actor's being familiar with the extremely popular *The Spanish Tragedy*, possibly because he had acted in it (he did include the echo of it which is quoted below), perhaps, as suggested above, because he had acted in the *Ur-Hamlet* also.

Where the lines are not Shakespeare's own, the general style is not that of any contemporary playwright but of a mind which could create somewhat pedestrian blank verse at need, i.e. when it was necessary to fill-in an imperfectly recollected scene. Kyd's style is inferior to Shakespeare's, and some of the lines in Q1 are inferior even to his.

In the absence of any knowledge of the *Ur-Hamlet*, it is impossible to determine how much Shakespeare owed to it. He was certainly indebted to *The Spanish Tragedy* for his hero's law-studentship, his psychological progress, and the play-within-the-play, acknowledging his indebtedness with an echo of it:[26]

Hieronimo And if the world like not this tragedy,
    Hard is the hap of old Hieronimo.

(*The Spanish Tragedy* IV,i,190–191)

Hamlet For if the king like not the comedy,
    Why, then, belike—he likes it not, perdy.

(*Hamlet* III,ii,276–277)

Q1 gives a little guidance as to how some lines were spoken, and to some stage business. In III,i, Claudius says "Sweet Gertrude, leave us too," and Gertrude replies "I shall obey you." Does she obey with disappointment or equanimity? Evidently she obeyed quite cheerfully under Shakespeare's direction, for in Q1 she replies "With all my hart." The request, incidentally, is given to Corambis instead of Claudius.

The closet scene begins:

Ham. Mother, mother, O are you here?
    How is't with you mother?
Queene How is't with you?
Ham. Ile tell you, but first weele make all safe.
Queene Hamlet, thou hast thy father much offended.
Ham. Mother, you have my father much offended.
Queene How now, boy?
Ham. How now, mother! come here, sit downe, for you shall heare me speake.
Queene What wilt thou doe? thou wilt not murder me: Helpe hoe.

"Weele make all safe" suggests that Hamlet first bolted the door to prevent interruption, then, when Gertrude tried to leave, dragged her back to her chair;[27] the passage quoted earlier, that she reacted with outrage to Hamlet's "As kill a king".

Hamlet's manner to Claudius in their exchanges during the Gonzago-play and before his departure for England must have verged on the insolent in a Prince speaking to a King, for in Q1 he sarcastically addresses Claudius as "Father" twice during the Gonzago-play and five times in the scene of his departure for England:

Ham. Y faith the Cameleons dish, not capon cramm'd, feede a the air. father: my

---

26   The echo is pointed out by Professor Thorndike in his essay *The Relations of Hamlet to Contemporary Revenge plays* (1902). Hieronimo's lines are spoken before the play-within-the-play, and Hamlet's after.

27   Pointed out in the Penguin edition of *Hamlet*

lorde, you played in the Vniuersitie...
Ham. The image of a murder done in Guyana, Albertus
Was the Dukes name, his wife Baptista,
Father it is a knavish peece a worke...

Ham. Father, your fatte King, and your leane Beggar
Are but variable services, two dishes to one messe:
Looke you, a man may fishe with that worme
That hath eaten of a King,
And a Beggar eate that fish,
Which that worme hath caught.
King What of this?
Ham. Nothing father, but to tell you how a King
May goe a progresse through the guttes of a Beggar.
King But sonne Hamlet, where is this body?
Ham. In heau'n, if you chance to misse him there,
Father, you had best looke in the other partes below...

Evidently, the actor playing Hamlet was directed to display Hamlet's revulsion at Claudius' step-fatherly approaches.

From the reasonably accurate rendering of the dialogue in the last-named scene, the actor probably entered as a soldier, one of the King's "Switzers" guarding Hamlet with Rosencrantz and Guildenstern.

Stage directions during the graveyard scene read *[Leartes leapes into the graue]* and *[Hamlet leapes in after him]*.

A little piece of ad-libbed stage 'business' is introduced into Hamlet's conversation with Osric which Q2 and F1 do not hint at. Whether suggested by an actor or by Shakespeare himself while directing, it was probably a comment on the courtiers of his time. There were no piped water supplies to houses, nor did they have bathrooms although there were 'hot-houses' where people could strip and bathe their bodies, nor was there dry cleaning for doublets or breeches become odorous—there were no toilet rolls! Perfume was much used to conceal odour from body or clothing by those who could afford it:

Gent. Now God saue thee, sweet prince Hamlet.
Ham. And you sir: foh, how the muske-cod smels!

Ham. Goe tell his maiestie I will attend him.
Gent. I shall deliuer your most sweet answer. exit
Ham. You may sir, none better, for y'are spiced,
Else he had a bad nose could not smell a foole.
Hor. He will disclose himselfe without inquirie.

(Q1: V,ii,3–4 and 29–33)

Evidently the conversation with Osric, which is quite long but considered as a plot-element, contributes much less to the advancement of the action than its length might imply. It was intended as a little extra comic relief between the swings of emotion in the graveyard scene and the play's final catastrophe, i.e. the above by-play might have been acceptable to Shakespeare in spite of the remarks he gave to Hamlet on what clowns should not do.

Some extra lines on unwanted interpolations by clowns were also included in Hamlet's lecture on the art of acting. Whether these had actually received Shakespeare's approval we cannot know. Since Hamlet, for his own reasons, intends his lecture to the Players to be taken very seriously, examples of ad-libbed clowning might be out of place at that moment, but less so in the conversation with Osric.

The passage describing the children's' theatres that possibly refers in the first place to the Children of St. Paul's, appeared as a few typically abbreviated and paraphrased lines in Q1:

Ham. How comes it they travel? Do they grow restie?
Gil. No my lord, their reputation holds as it was wont.
Ham. How then?
Gil. Yfaith my lord, noueltie carries it away,
For the principall public audience that
Came to them, are turned to priuate players,
And to the humour of children.

In Q2 it is almost equally short:

Ham. How chances it they travel? their residence both in reputation, and profit was better both wayes.
Ros. I thinke their inhibition, comes by the meanes of the late innouation.
Ham. Doe they hold the same estimation they did when I was in the Citty; are they so followed?
Ros. No indeede are they not.
Ham. It is not very strange, for my Vncle is King of Denmarke, and those that would make mowes at him while my father lived...

The mention of the Children's Theatres ("the humour of children") in Q1, the complete absence from Q2 of even so brief a mention, and its sudden change of subject from the Players to the King, suggest that the passage was excised before the printing of Q2, i.e. that it was spoken in the play's first performances, but omitted before Q2 was printed. In 1603, three or four months after James' accession, Henry Evans and Edward Kirkham obtained a Royal licence to "practize and exercise" the Children of the Chapel "in the quality of playinge", the Queen becoming their patron and the Children being thereafter known as The Children of the Queen's Revels. Presumably Shakespeare, whose company had been taken under the patronage of King James only a month or so earlier, and so could not afford to express condescending opinions of any children's company now that one was under the Queen's patronage, then decided to omit the comments from performances and from the official Q2 so as to avoid offending her.

Their eventual re-inclusion in F1, possibly earlier in performances after 1605, may be explained by the Children's production in that year of *Eastward Ho!*, a comedy by Marston, Chapman and Jonson containing two contemptuous remarks on the "thirty-pound knights" and "knights without feathers": young Scots who had followed James to London in the hope of preferment and obtained the right to the title 'Sir' on payment of a fee. The Court was extremely sensitive, and the comments, though amounting to no more than a sentence each, were enough to cause the three playwrights to be sentenced to prison and the Queen to withdraw her patronage and the title from the Children.[28] Shakespeare would then be free to restore his remarks on "little eyases".

The earlier suggestion (it is admittedly based on feel rather than evidence) that the actor began to write his pirated version some time after acting in *Hamlet* may be correct, i.e. he remembered some lines or phrases, and the names "Corambis" for "Polonius", "Montano" for "Renaldo", and "Albertus" for "Gonzago", from previous plays in which he had acted. From the echoes of Kyd which have been noted, *The Spanish Tragedy* may have been one of them.

Note:
The comments in *Eastward Ho!* i.e. sarcastic references to James' sales of peerages and knighthoods to his Scottish followers, and probably spoken with an assumed Scottish accent, were:

1 Gentleman I ken the man weel; he's one of my thirty pound knights.

(IV,i,167–168)

Golding What! A knight and his fellow thus accoutred? Where are their hats and feathers, their rapiers and their cloaks?
Constable They say knights are now to be known without feathers, like cockerels without spurs, sir.

(IV,ii,193–199)

---

28   The episode previously referred to in "The Murder of Gonzago" (cont'd)—See Note following.

24
FURTHER NOTES ON HAMLET

(1) Playing with Probability: Investigating the Applications of Probability Theory to the Duelling Odds of Hamlet and Laertes.

Elementary probability theory, which began to be investigated in the mid-seventeenth century by the French mathematicians at the request of their gamblers, proved useful in a number of connections. Its elementary theorems are based on the expected results from such gambling devices as dice, tossed coins or well-shuffled packs of cards.

If an event may take place so as to satisfy a previously stipulated condition, the probability that it will do so is given by the ratio of the number of outcomes in which it may satisfy the condition to the total number of possible outcomes. A tossed coin has two equiprobable faces; hence the probability of either result is ½. Similarly, the probability of any stipulated result from a die having six faces is 1/6.

The odds in favour of a particular result are the ratio of the number of favourable outcomes to the number of unfavourable outcomes. Since a die has six faces, the odds are 5/1 against selecting the correct face. If the probability that A will win in a contest against B is 6/10, i.e. that he will win six times in every ten, the odds are six to four on A.

If an event will certainly satisfy a condition, the probability that it will do so is unity. The probability that a coin will display one of its two faces is 1/2 + 1/2 = 1; that a die will display one of its six faces, 1/6 + 1/6 + 1/6 + 1/6 + 1/6 + 1/6 = 1.

This is the maximum value of a probability, from which it follows that all probabilities which are not certainties are fractions of unity.

If a number of independent events may take place so as to satisfy stipulated conditions ('independent' meaning that no event influences the outcome of any other), the probability that they will all do so is given by the product of their individual probabilities. If two coins are tossed, the probability of two heads is 1/2 x 1/2 = 1/4, a result easily verified by counting. A head from the first coin may be associated with a head or a tail from the second; so may a tail. Hence there are four possible outcomes, of which two heads are only one. If a coin is tossed and a die simultaneously thrown, the probability of a head and a six is 1/2 x 1/6 = 1/12. A head may be associated with any of six results from the die; so may a tail; hence there are twelve possible outcomes, of which a head and a six are only one. A well-known example is the accumulator bet on a sequence of horse races, the figure on which the bookmakers pay being obtained by multiplying, not the individual odds, but the individual probabilities derived from the odds.

As the number of independent events increases, the effect of multiplying their probabilities, each being a fraction, is to produce an ever smaller final probability.

Statistical methods can only be applied to a large number of samples. Where a single event contains a number of individual elements that give it its particular character—without any of which it would have been different from what it was—it is possible to apply the theorem of independent events? To estimate the probabilities of the individual features, multiply them; and lastly, if the final fraction is very low, ask: did these elements combine purely by accident? In real life it is often impossible to assign definite values to the probabilities that an event would contain all the features which it was seen to have. However, if an event contains a number of features which give it its peculiar, perhaps unique, flavour, and if any or all of them could easily have been different from what they were, the possibility must be considered that their simultaneity was not accidental[29]. Editors sometimes use this argument (knowingly or not) when they assign some anonymous work to a known author on the grounds of "internal evidence", i.e. resemblances of style, presentation, argument or subject-matter which they do not consider to be purely coincidental.

a) The Fencing Match.
> *Osric* The King, sir, hath wagered with him six Barbary horses, against the which he has imponed, as I take it, six French rapiers and poniards, with their assigns... The King, sir, hath laid that in a dozen passes between yourself and him, he shall not exceed you three hits...He hath laid on twelve for nine...
> (V,ii,140–142 and 156–158)

The "Problem of Points" was first propounded in 1654 to Pascal by a French gambler, the Chevalier de Mère, the contestants being assumed to be equal in skill. A solution in which the two players are assumed to be unequal in skill did not appear till 1714, when Montmort published his version. It is best illustrated by an example.

A and B agree to play a snooker match in which the winner will be the first to win nine frames. A is considered the better player of the two, the accepted odds on him against B being six to four. The frames take longer than expected, and the match must end when A has won five frames and B has won six. The purse, originally put up on a winner-take-all basis, must now be divided between them in accordance with their respective probabilities of winning; in what proportions should it be divided?

The probability that either man will win is given by the sum of the probabilities of all the ways in which he can win.

Since the match may go to eight-all, the winner then winning the last frame, the maximum number of frames is seventeen. Eleven frames have been played, leaving a maximum of six more.

A may win (a) the next three frames and the last; (b) any three of the next four frames and the last; (c) any three of the next five frames and the last.

B may win (a) the next two frames and the last; (b) any two of the next three frames and the last; (c) any two of the next four frames and the last; (d) any two of the next five frames and the last.

The accepted probability that A will win any frame is 0.6; that B will win it, 0.4. Taking as an example the case in which B wins two of the next five frames and the last, the probability that he will win two frames is $(0.4)^2$, that he will lose three frames $(0.6)^3$, and the number of ways in which he can win "any two from five" is the combination $C_{5\ 2} = 10$; that he will win the last frame, (0.4). The full expression for this case is:

$(0.4)^2 \times (0.6)^3 \times 10 \times (0.4) = (0.4)^3 \times (0.6)^3 \times 10 = 0.13824$.

Tabulating and summing all the ways for each player (a similar calculation for the fencing match is given in full below):
...Pr *[A wins]* = 0.54432..;   Pr*[B wins]* = 0.45568...
The sum of these probabilities, which cover all the possibilities, is 0.9999... = 1.

---

29   A saying reputed to be current in Chicago during the days of Prohibition and gang warfare was, "The first time, it's happenstance; the second time, it's coincidence; the third time, it's enemy action!"

In round figures, the purse is now divided into 22 parts, A receiving twelve and B ten.

It may seem unfair that B should have to take the smaller share when he is leading, but the calculation is in terms of the odds accepted before the match begins. If they change during the match, the calculation must be in terms of some later figure. If, for example, the odds have become evens before the match ends,

$Pr[A \text{ wins}] = 0.34375..; \quad Pr[B \text{ wins}] = 0.65625..,$

and B takes nearly two-thirds of the purse.

The King ostensibly arranges the fencing match both to satisfy Laertes and to entertain his court; it will be between two supremely skilled swordsmen, and long enough to test the stamina of both. He has heard reports of Laertes' prowess in Paris (IV,vii, 95–102), and thinks that he will prove the better "scrimer" of the two, but that in a match of twelve passes he will not score three more hits than Hamlet. If he only scores seven hits and Hamlet the other five, he loses, since he does not lead Hamlet by three hits; he must therefore score eight or more hits out of the twelve.

An alternative interpretation, that Laertes wins if he ever leads Hamlet by three hits, is not feasible. The match is to be of twelve passes, and Hamlet might fall behind by three or more hits at an early stage, and then reduce the deficit later, i.e. Laertes must lead by three hits when the match ends. Another alternative, that Laertes must have scored twelve hits when Hamlet has scored only nine, is also not feasible, for the match might then go to twenty-one passes, an excessive number for a bout in which both contestants will be playing all-out, and inconsistent with "a dozen passes".

In terms of odds, a figure must be assumed for the King's assessment of Laertes' superiority. Trial and error suggests six to four as the figure in his mind, i.e. the probability that Laertes wins any pass is 0.6; that Hamlet wins is 0.4. Their chances are then determined as in the snooker match, by calculating and summing the probabilities of all the ways in which each can win. Laertes can win with 8 hits in 8, 9, 10, 11, or 12 passes, Hamlet with 5 hits in 5, 6, 7, 8, 9, 10, 11, or 12 passes.

As in the snooker match, one of the hits must be the last hit in each sequence of passes. Consider Hamlet's winning 5 in 8 passes: the combination is "any four from seven" = 7.6.5.4/1.2.3.4 = 35, the full expression being $(.4)^4 \times (.6)^3 \times (.4) \times 35 = 0.077144$.

Tabulating and summing all the ways for each man:

Hamlet:
5 in 5   = $(.4)^5$ = 0.0102400...
5 in 6   = $(.4)^5 \times (.6) \times 5$ = 0.0307200...
5 in 7   = $(.4)^5 \times (.6)^2 \times 15$ = 0.0552960...
5 in 8   = $(.4)^5 \times (.6)^3 \times 35$ = 0.0774144...
5 in 9   = $(.4)^5 \times (.6)^4 \times 70$ = 0.0928972...
5 in 10 = $(.4)^5 \times (.6)^5 \times 126$ = 0.1003290...
5 in 11 = $(.4)^5 \times (.6)^6 \times 210$ = 0.1003290...
5 in 12 = $(.4)^5 \times (.6)^7 \times 330$ = 0.0945959...
                      Sum   = 0.5618215...

Laertes:
8 in 8   = $(.6)^8$ = 0.0167961...
8 in 9   = $(.6)^8 \times (.4) \times 8$ = 0.0537477...
8 in 10 = $(.6)^8 \times (.4)^2 \times 36$ = 0.0967458...
8 in 11 = $(.6)^8 \times (.4)^3 \times 120$ = 0.1289945...
8 in 12 = $(.6)^8 \times (.4)^4 \times 330$ = 0.1418939...
                      Sum   = 0.4381780...

Pr *[Hamlet wins]* = 0.5618215...; Pr *Laertes wins]* = 0.4381780...
(check: sum = 0.999999... = 1).

The odds on Hamlet are thus about 1.28 to 1, only a little short of 4 to 3 or "twelve for nine". Not surprisingly, he says, "I shall win at the odds". If the odds on Laertes are reduced only slightly, from six to four to seven to five, the odds on Hamlet rise to 1.55 to 1, or 3 to 2.

As it stands, the bet will not be acceptable to Laertes, but the King has redressed the balance with his wager of "twelve for nine", the value of his six Barbary horses against the six French rapiers and poniards which Laertes has "imponed". Laertes' French rapiers would be among the best available; yet rapier manufacture was widespread whereas Barbary horses or "Barbs", the fastest available at the time, would be the greater rarity in that they came only from Spain, to which the Moors had brought them.

Laertes has accepted the bet; he will have to fight hard to win, but he stands to win more than he stands to lose. Of course, he needs to score only one hit with the poisoned foil, but Hamlet is unaware of this, and the bet must appear attractive to him.

When the match begins, Hamlet wins the first two passes, leaving Laertes with the task of winning eight of the remaining ten passes; is this policy on Laertes' part, to induce Hamlet to relax by letting him win them? Although he says "My lord, I'll hit him now", the King replies glumly "I do not think't", i.e. contrary to his hopes, Hamlet has proved to be the superior swordsman, and Laertes has realised this. His "Have at you now!" is then a sudden attack which catches his opponent before he is ready, Hamlet having waited for the referee to start the pass.

No one in Shakespeare's time could have worked out such a calculation, the theory of probability being still undeveloped, but Shakespeare's three men weigh the situation by the feel of it, in a way which is typical of many gamblers.

After one of the passes, the contestants pause, and Osric says "Nothing, either way." So far, it has been assumed that drawn passes do not count towards the total of twelve, or that they cannot be drawn, i.e. that all passes must continue to a hit; does this pass count? If they can be drawn, the calculation becomes much more complex, for probabilities must be assumed for the three cases in which one man wins a pass, or the other man wins it, or it is drawn, and the probabilities of all the possible sequences summed; however, the assumed figures must still produce odds on Hamlet of roughly "twelve for nine", in accordance with the King's offer.

(b) *Hamlet*: apparent coincidences.

Nine parallels were noted between the description of spirits in King James' *Daemonologie* and the Ghost in *Hamlet*. Either Shakespeare followed the accepted doctrines when he created his Ghost, although the Ghosts in *The Spanish Tragedy* and *The Atheist's Tragedy* are not in the least like the Elder Hamlet's Ghost. This raises the questions of what the accepted doctrines were and which doctrines the dramatists followed; or he read the *Daemonologie* in anticipation of James' accession and created his Ghost accordingly. The question is resolved by further oddities: the fact that King James became Shakespeare's theatre company's patron very soon after his accession, the immediate new Witchcraft Act which prohibited commerce with spirits whether invoked or not and the later writing of *Macbeth*. Since Shakespeare was a man of business, it is unlikely that all these oddities were purely coincidental.

Three oddities were noted in the Gonzago-play: Hamlet's "O most pernicious woman" (in I,v) in conjunction with the two couplets given to the Player Queen, the echo of "thrift", and his claim to "a whole share" at the end. Examination of the Gonzago-play's construction and style then showed that it would hardly have been written by a professional playwright; of its content—that it must have been written by Hamlet himself. All the events in a play must be directly related to at least one of the personages in it, otherwise they have little or no point, and Hamlet is the only personage who could have any interest in the staging of such a play, in particular its test of Gertrude's conscience as well as the King's.

The passages on the theatre and on acting are also oddities. Why did Shakespeare introduce digressions which, in despite of Hamlet's advice to the Players, considerably interrupt the action and contribute nothing to the characterisation? He can only have intended to insert his own views on the plays, the acting, and the audiences of his time.

In the F1, the near perfection with which the cues and speeches of Marcellus, Voltimand, Prologue, and Lucianus are reproduced cannot be purely coincidental. The pirate's causing Hamlet to address Claudius sarcastically as "Father", and Gertrude's "With all my hart" are significant hints.

The parallels noted between *The Spanish Tragedy* and *Hamlet* are:
a) Hieronimo is a judge, Hamlet a law student; both require proof.
b) Both are enraged when a near and dear relative is murdered.
c) Public justice being unobtainable, both become frustrated.
d) Both display lunacy.
e) Both eventually fall victim to frustration and become criminals.[30] Kyd delayed the killing of the innocent Duke of Castile to the end of his play; Shakespeare made the killing of Polonius the climactic event of his tragedy; in each case, the killing indicated the change for the worse in the hero's mood.
f) Each obtains revenge by a play-within-the-play (written by himself).
g) Both enter reading a book. Shakespeare may have used this episode in *Hamlet* because it had become a conventional little element, and Ford used it in *Tis Pity She's a Whore*; in neither play is it crucial to the action as in Kyd's play.

Taken together these parallels, which are beyond coincidence, suggest that *The Spanish Tragedy* inspired Shakespeare as much as the lost *Ur-Hamlet*, if not more. It was a popular play; many of Shakespeare's spectators would have recognised the reasons for Hamlet's changes of mood as resembling Hieronimo's.

(2) Adultery
"Doth all the noble substance of a doubt/ To his own scandal."

(I,iv,37–38)

The O.E.D. gives as meanings for adultery: illicit sex relations, and figuratively, adulteration, or the condition of being adulterated. The example quoted is from Ben Jonson (1609):
> Such sweet neglect more taketh me
> Than all the adulteries of art.

(*Epicene* I,i)

It also gives "adoutry" as an obsolete spelling of adultery. The line may therefore have been intended to read "Doth all the noble substance oft adout." Most editors either accept

---

30   G.Bullough notes nineteen parallels between the two plays, ending by briefly mentioning frustration. He does not expand the notion to explain Hamlet's soliloquies.

Dowden's "often dout" or merely insert a footnote to the effect that the line is corrupt. The above version fits the sense, the scansion, and the sound.

Only the first four lines of this 26-line speech are given in Q1, which suggests that Shakespeare learned of the Earl of Rutland's report of the drinking habits of the Danes and added the remaining 22 lines before the printing of Q2, as a topical comment which would add to the play's contemporary atmosphere. Since they did not appear in *F1*, which retains only the first four lines, he may have deleted them because (as has been suggested) they offended Queen Anne, James' Danish consort, or because he or his successors decided that they were no longer of topical interest.

(3) Adulterate:
Ghost Ay, that incestuous, that adulterate beast,
With witchcraft of his wit, with traitorous gifts.........

(I,v,42–43)

Shakespeare occasionally used 'adulterate', occasionally adulterous, and while the latter meant (and means) *disloyal to the marriage vows*, adulterate had a wider meaning: capable of disloyalty or treachery in other respects.

Adriana I am possest with an adulterate blot;
My blood is mingled with the grime of lust;
For if we two be one, and thou play false,
I do digest the poison of thy flesh,
Being strumpeted by thy contagion.

(*The Comedy of Errors* II,ii,139–143)

From the first two lines, "adulterate" here appears to mean corrupt, while "being strumpeted" does not suggest that Adriana herself intends adultery.

Constance Of Nature's gifts thou mayst with lilies boast
And with the half-blown rose; but Fortune, O!
She is corrupted, changed, and won from thee;
Sh'adulterates hourly with thine uncle John.

(*King John* III,i,52–55)

Here "adulterates" means conspires treacherously, Fortune being "corrupted".

Q. Margaret Th'adulterate Hastings, Rivers, Vaughan, Grey.

(*King Richard III* IV,iv,69)

A footnote in the play's Arden edition defines adulterate as: "Adulterous. Margaret refers to the scandal with Mistress Shore". Sexual adultery is not a theme in this play, Mistress Shore being only mentioned briefly in connection with Hastings' appeal to her to plead on his behalf before the King (I,i,71 on), and again briefly later (III,i,185). The lords are executed, not for adultery, but for their opposition to Richard: "All you without desert have frowned on me" (II,i,68).

Thus the Ghost's "adulterate beast" should not be taken as indicating adultery by Claudius and Gertrude before the play opens. Its "my most virtuous-seeming queen" is a complaint of the speed with which she has transferred her affections to Claudius, not of adultery, which it never mentions, although if Gertrude had been adulterous with Claudius before the murder, it would surely do so. Any adultery by Gertrude before the murder would have been treason on her part: Anne Boleyn was executed by Henry VIII on a trumped-up charge of adultery; the play contains no hint to that effect. When Hamlet harangues his mother in her closet, he accuses her of giving way to the "heyday in the blood" with her new husband, but not of having given way to it with him before the murder. When the Ghost calls Claudius "incestuous", it is referring to the canonical incest of Claudius' marriage to a deceased brother's wife, as does Hamlet with his "He that hath killed my king and whored my mother", but incest is mentioned by no one other than the Ghost and Hamlet, i.e. it is not a major issue in the situation.

(4) *[Aside]* The time is out of joint.—O cursed spite
    That ever I was born to set it right!
    [Aloud] Nay, come, let's go together.

(I,v,189–191)

The first two lines express despair aroused by the Ghost's story, and must be an aside, for Hamlet has refused to reveal anything to his friends, and therefore would not voice such a thought aloud to them.
    Alternatively, the aside begins at "O cursed spite."

(5) *Ophelia*: That sucked the honey of his music vows.

(III,i,155)

The Second Quarto has "musickt vowes"; the First Folio, "musicke vowes", which appears to have been preferred by all editors. "Musickt" or "musick'd vows" makes the phrase a reference to the "posies"—"tenders" partly in verse—which Hamlet has sent to Ophelia and which she has unwillingly returned to him a few minutes earlier at her father's order.

(6) "Fool":
    Polonius Tender yourself more dearly,
        Or—not to crack the wind of the poor phrase,
        Running it thus—you'll tender me a fool.

(*Hamlet* I,iii,107–109)

Polonius here cracks an apt pun. In the *New Shakespeare* edition of *Hamlet*, Dover Wilson gives "? baby" and "dupe" as the meanings of fool. In the editions I have read, no other editor suggests this meaning, nor does my Glossary include "small child" as one. The O.E.D. derives it from the French "fou" (mad), and gives its basic meaning as someone ignorant, simple-minded, easily duped, or otherwise foolish in behaviour. A derived meaning—infant, suckling child, or small child—appears to have become established in Shakespeare's time:
    Nurse When it did taste the wormwood on the nipple
        Of my dug, and felt it bitter, pretty fool...

(*Rom.* I,iii,32–33)

    Iago To suckle fools and chronicle small beer.

(*Othello* II,i,160)

Who is suckled besides infants? The Nurse's episode took place when Juliet was two and, from "nipple", was still being wet-nursed by her.

At the end of III,ii, Hamlet says "They fool me to the top of my bent" (III,ii,356). "They" are not fooling him; on the contrary, he has been fooling them; hence the line should read "They 'fool' me to the top of my bent", i.e. "They are humouring me as if I were a baby." Cleopatra, weary of pandering to Antony's addiction to pleasure, says:

Cleo I'll seem the fool I am not; Antony
  Will be himself.

(*Antony and Cleopatra* I,i,42)

Fool: a puree of fruit or vegetables suitable for infants before their teeth have appeared must have been an extension of this meaning.

The Elizabethans appear to have derived much amusement from the antics of small boys and the babblings of babies. The Court Fool or Jester is expected to be witty, also to behave like a naughty small boy, and occasionally babble like an infant, e.g. the Clown in *Twelfth Night*, who is addressed by Sir Andrew as "fool" and whose "fooling" is praised by him:

Sir Andrew In sooth, thou wast in very gracious fooling last night, when thou
  spokest of Pigrogromitus, of the Vapians passing the equinoctial of Queubus.

(*Twelfth Night* II,iii,21–24)

He was allowed considerable freedom in speech and behaviour, and was even expected to take liberties, as in *King Lear* I,iv:

Lear Dost thou call me fool, boy?
Fool All thy other titles thou hast given away; that thou wast born with.

Lear would be unable to find a reply to this quip, since by the above meaning of "fool" he had certainly been born one!

(7) Clown:

This word is absent from my Glossary. The O.E.D gives: a countryman, rustic, or peasant; a mere rustic, a boor; an ignorant, rude, or uncouth person; a fool or jester. Judging by the Clowns in *Hamlet*, *Antony and Cleopatra*, and *The Winter's Tale*, it appears to have meant simply 'Male engaged in a manual occupation, perhaps husbandry; perhaps a country-dweller', the Elizabethan equivalent of 'churl' or 'peasant'. This meaning seems to have persisted, or at least to have been remembered, for a long time:

  The voice I hear this passing night was heard
  In ancient days by emperor and clown.

Keats *Ode to a Nightingale* (1819)

There seems to have been no word for the female equivalent. No doubt, despite that many clowns were rustic and limited in ideas, outlook and speech because of the circumstances of their lives, not all of them would have been. Shakespeare introduced clowns who were not, such as the afore-mentioned Clown in *Twelfth Night*, who seems to have received a good education, and the First Clown in *Hamlet*, in order to please and amuse his groundlings, some of whom would themselves have been 'clowns'.

(8) "And fall a-cursing like a very drab, / A stallion!"

(II,ii,561-2)

F1 has "scullion", and all editors (in the editions I have read) have preferred it to the "stallion" of Q2, but Dover Wilson points out that a meaning given in the New English

Dictionary is 'male prostitute', which appears preferable in the context of 'drab' and 'whore'. The O.E.D. (which replaced the N.E.D. in 1989) gives both 'a woman's paid paramour' and 'female prostitute'.

(9)   *Hamlet*   I have heard
That guilty creatures sitting at a play...

(II,ii,563–569)

This passage is usually thought to have been inspired by *A Warning for Fair Women*, a play acted by Shakespeare's company before the writing of *Hamlet*, in which a woman who sees the stage depiction of a husband's murder is moved to confess to murdering her own husband; however, the anonymous author (and perhaps Shakespeare himself) may have known of a much earlier source. Ibycus, a Greek lyric poet of the sixth century B.C., was attacked and murdered by robbers while on his way to Athens; as he lay dying, he called on a flight of cranes passing overhead to avenge him. Some time later, the murderers were watching a play:

> Were not the murderers of Ibycus caught in the same way? They were sitting in a theatre, and when cranes came in sight, they laughed and whispered to each other that the avengers of Ibycus were come. Persons sitting near overheard them, and since Ibycus had disappeared and for a long time had been sought, they caught at this remark and reported it to the magistrates. And thus the slayers were convicted and were led off to prison, not punished by the cranes, but compelled to confess the murder by the infirmity of their own tongues, as it were some Fury or spirit of vengeance.
>
> Plutarch, essay "On Talkativeness" in *Opera Moralia*

Thomas Kyd must also have known of the essay, for at the end of *The Spanish Tragedy*, Hieronimo bites out his tongue to prevent himself from speaking of his crime under torture. Says Plutarch in the same essay:

> Zeno the philosopher, in order that even against his will no secret should be betrayed by his body when under torture, bit his tongue through and spat it out at the despot.

25

AN ELIZABETHAN SPOOF: TROILUS AND CRESSIDA

It was first issued with the statement on the title page As it was first acted by the King's Maiesties servants at the Globe. This was, however, cancelled, a new title page inserted, and a prefatory letter added calling it "a new play, never stal'd with the Stage, never clapper-clawd with the palmes of the vulger", and declaring it "passing full of the palme comicall", and as worthy of study "as the best Commedy in Terence or Plautus". This suggests that Shakespeare wrote the play for some private occasion, but not, as some think, for performance at Court before Elizabeth, since the whole tone of the piece makes this impossible. At one of the Inns of Court, however, its scurrilities would be in keeping with their tradition of "lewd and lascivious plays" and wittily obscene speeches...if it was written for a group of worldly-wise young clerks, hardened, in theory at least, like the Wife of Bath's fifth husband with his delight in reading of the wiles of women, then the cynicism of the piece need not be taken at its face value, but rather as a device to startle these simple worldlings out of their complacency.

Peter Alexander *Shakespeare's Life and Art* (1939)

Professor Alexander's suggestion, who appears to have been the first to make it, must be correct, for the play is quite different in construction from all Shakespeare's other plays in that it has a beginning and a middle, contains two loosely connected actions, the Greek action and the Trojan action; but is open-ended, i.e. it comes to no definite or decisive resolution as do the other comedies and tragedies. And some of its personages display strange inconsistencies.

It was written not for ordinary audiences but for an educated audience who would be familiar with Homer's *Iliad*, the later *Troilus and Cressida* addition, and the works of Plato, and capable of appreciating the rich, Latinate style of much of its verse.

It was written for an all-male audience, almost certainly of young men. Pandarus is apparently a pander, and the song which the lovely Helen persuades him to sing in III,i is unusually 'blue'. Another example can be found in III,iii,114, when Ulysses tells a 'bathroom' joke:

    Ulysses   I do not strain at the position—
                    It is familiar...

This jest would raise a guffaw in the audience, for the Elizabethans knew nothing of the need for fresh fruit, vegetables and fibre in the diet, and ate far too much meat. When in 1648 the German chemist Glauber discovered the laxative properties of sodium sulphate and, a little later, Nehemiah Grew came upon those of magnesium sulphate (Epsom salts), they were hailed as benefactors of mankind, and Glauber's salt became known as 'sal mirabile'). And Shakespeare must have known that it would raise a laugh, for playwrights do not write accidental double-entendres into their dialogue!

As for the two female characters, both beautiful, both possessing their own brands of wit, the one eventually accepting living in sin (so to speak) with a lover, and the other already happily living in sin with hers, are they not the kind of young woman whom the average young male dreams of being marooned with on a desert island? What else is the dramatic point of the brief depiction of Helen in III,i?

The play was written for a legal audience, which it amused by satirising it to its own face. The Greek discussion opens with an extraordinarily long and courteous preamble from Agamemnon, no doubt in the manner of lawyers opening their cases in court; its subject is the lack of respect for 'degree'. Any actual gathering of senior army officers, who met to discuss failing morale or slack discipline among the troops, would come to the point very much more quickly! As for the Trojan debate, it does come to the point quickly, but again suggests a satire on the law. A judge may say, "I appreciate the arguments from the plaintiff, to the effect that (etc, etc), that (etc, etc), and that (etc, etc)—but in the end I must find for the defendant": exactly what Hector does. Sometimes a lawyer will use the pronoun 'I' when he is speaking 'in the person of' his client or illustrating some argument, which Troilus does when he says "I take today a wife." This too would raise a laugh from the audience, for it is just what Troilus does not intend!

It gave the legal audience some ethical questions to discuss. The Greek discussion in I,iii contains nothing controversial; its intention is to indicate to the audience the problem in the Greek army confronting Agamemnon and his officers, and to lead eventually to Ulysses' discussion with Achilles of the need to maintain one's reputation by being seen to maintain it. The Trojan debate gives rise to questions of which the principal points are the validity of Troilus' "Is aught but as 'tis valued?", and of Paris' "I would have the soil of [Helen's] fair rape / Wiped off in honourable keeping her". What is the validity of "honourable" in this context?

Did the legal audience discuss the morality of exchanging an innocent girl against her will in order to help the Trojan cause? (An American, whose name I unfortunately do not recall, said, "There are some things a man should not do, even to save his country").

Lawyers must assess their clients and witnesses carefully, and the play gave them some cases to consider. No other play contains so many indications of character followed by indications to the contrary. Some of the latter, such as Cressida's "Yet hold I off" at the end of I,ii, and Pandarus' monologue at the end of the play, were red herrings intended to throw the audience off the scent (a clue here is that they are in the more artificial rhyming couplets instead of the usual blank verse).

What kind of man is Nestor? He is the second after Menelaus to snatch a kiss from Cressida when she appears in the Greek camp; is he really as aged and venerable as his first appearance suggests?

What kind of man is Ajax? He is first described as "blockish", and soon after is seen as blockish and childishly susceptible to flattery, yet at the end of his fight with Hector in IV,v, he suddenly speaks as if he were the soul of courteous chivalry-cum-defiance.

There is a strong intelligence element in the play. Ulysses says:

Ulysses　They tax our policy and call it cowardice,
　　Count wisdom as no member of the war,
　　Forestall prescience, and esteem no act
　　But that of hand. The still and mental parts,
　　That do contrive how many hands shall strike
　　When fitness calls them on, and know by measure
　　Of their observant toil the enemy's weight—
　　Why, this hath not a finger's dignity.

(I,iii,197–204)

> *Ulysses* 'Tis known, Achilles, that you are in love
> With one of Priam's daughters.
> *Achilles* Ha, known?
> *Ulysses* Is that a wonder?
> All the commerce that you have had with Troy
> As perfectly is ours as yours, my lord.
>
> (III,iii,194–208)

What kind of man is Thersites? He rails continuously and with scurrilous eloquence at his fellow Greeks (and his scurrility would amuse the young lawyers), and is constantly hanging around and listening in the background (as in V,ii). His abuse is amusing to Achilles, who calls him "My cheese, my digestion", but is this the only reason why Achilles describes him as a "privileged man" (II,iii,55)? At the beginning of V,i, he brings a letter to Achilles from Queen Hecuba concerning Polixena; how has he received it from within Troy?

Pandarus is first seen noting who has returned from, or asking who is arming for, the day's battle. At the end of V,iii he brings a letter from Cressida to Troilus; how has he received it from within the Greek camp? Just what are the real occupations of these two? Could they be double agents who meet one another at night outside the walls of Troy to exchange intelligence and, as the play indicates, letters?

What kind of man is Calchas? He is a priest who has apparently deserted Troy because he does not believe that Troy can win the war, but is he really a traitor?

> *Calchas* You have a Trojan prisoner called Antenor,
> Yesterday took: Troy holds him very dear.
> Oft have you—often have you thanks therefor—
> Desir'd my Cressid in right great exchange,
> Whom Troy hath still denied; but this Antenor,
> I know, is such a wrest in their affairs
> That their negotiations all must slack,
> Wanting his manage; and they will almost
> Give us a prince of blood, a son of Priam,
> In change of him. Let him be sent, great princes,
> And he shall buy my daughter; and her presence
> Shall quite strike off all service I have done
> In most accepted pain.
>
> (III,iii,18–30)

Is Calchas really a traitor if he proposes the exchange of his own daughter (a form of daughter-sacrifice) for the Trojans' most able general?

And what of "Oft?" Have the Greeks repeatedly asked for Cressida? If they have, these requests must surely be well known on the Trojan side? Who in Troy knows of them—Pandarus, Troilus, Cressida herself?

Pandarus certainly knows. Is he really a pander? He is trying to bring his niece under the protection of a prince of the Royal family, whether married to him or not, in the hope of preventing her exchange, and at one point reveals that the situation has become urgent. He even hopes that she will soon find herself expecting a child: he appears to be unmarried, and Cressida appears to be his only relative, so a child will continue the family line (III,ii,101–102). Unfortunately, his hope is denied by the decision of the "general state" (general staff) of Troy that Cressida must be exchanged. He then weeps for his niece and the loss of his hopes.

Although the play is less explicit with respect to Troilus and Cressida, they also appear to know.

In V,iii,99ff. Pandarus is weeping for Cressida again, and trying to conceal his sobs by complaining of a tickling in his throat, which makes him cough, and a rheum which is bringing tears to his eyes:

Pandarus Here's a letter from yond poor girl.
Troilus Let me read.
Pandarus A whoreson tisick, a whoreson rascally tisick, so troubles me, and the foolish fortune of this girl, and what one thing, what another, that I shall leave you one o'th's days; and I have a rheum in mine eyes, too, and such an ache in my bones that unless a man were cursed I cannot tell what to think on't. What says she there?
Troilus Words, words, mere words, no matter from the heart;
Th'effect doth operate another way.
[Tears the letter]

What kind of young man is Troilus? He demands total loyalty, yet is not equally ready to give it by marrying Cressida; is he a mature adult, or an excessively idealistic, perhaps somewhat spoilt, young man? Cressida is the daughter of a priest, and priests were highly respected, so, although Troilus is a prince of the Royal family, he could marry her if he wished; why, then, does he profess eternal devotion without offering marriage? Could he be an eloquent Don Juan who is hoping to make another conquest?

And is Cressida really a flighty girl? She must know of the Greeks' requests for her, if only because Pandarus would hardly have failed to tell his own niece, and she is exchanged against her will; is she then to be blamed if she decides to make the best of her situation in whatever way she can?

In IV,v she arrives in the Greek camp, and after being grabbed and kissed five times, refuses further kisses, and is taken to her father's tent. In V,ii Diomed appears outside her tent in the darkness; when he calls for her, Calchas sends her out. What has he said to her in their tent? Why did he request the exchange in the first place?

What kind of picture of Cressida did Shakespeare intend his spectators to form? When he decided to dramatise a story, he built his plot in his own way, sometimes adhering to his sources, sometimes departing from them, and created his characters to suit his own dramatic purpose, so his Cressida is not necessarily anyone else's Cressida. She gives herself to her lover, but only after much hesitation; she is of the kind, as Pandarus says, who are slow to make up their minds but will "stick like burs". Then she finds herself cast into the Greek camp to become the plaything of a bunch of woman-hungry warriors, and is abandoned by her lover. Does not her fate suggest that she was intended to be seen as a pathetic, even tragic figure?

These are the principal questions which the play was intended to raise in the spectators' minds. A question that arises in my own is: how did the commentators on this supposedly bitter comedy overlook the utter improbability of the climax of the play, the wartime exchange of a captured enemy general who was the Trojans' most able general—for a girl?

When writing his version of the story, Dryden "undertook to remove that heap of Rubbish under which many excellent thoughts lay wholly bury'd", "new model'd the Plot", and turned the play into a tragedy, treating Cressida as a tragic figure. At the end, his Cressida, on being rebuked by Troilus for her faithlessness, stabs herself to give him "satisfaction". To justify his remodelling of the play as her tragedy, he inserted the conversation between her and her father in their tent (IV,ii) which Shakespeare left unreported:

> Calchas   O, what a blessing is a vertuous child!
>   Thou hast reclaimed my mind, and calmed my passions
>   Of anger and remorse: my love to Troy
>   Revives within me, and my lost Tyara
>   No more disturbs my mind.
> Cressida   A vertuous conquest.
> Calchas   I have a woman's longing to return,
>   But yet which way without your aid I know not.
> Cressida   Time must instruct us how.
> Calchas   You must dissemble love to Diomede still.
>   False Diomede, bred in Ulysses' School,
>   Can never be deceiv'd,
>   But by strong arts and blandishments of love:
>   Put 'em in practice all; seem lost and won,
>   And draw him on, and give him line again.
>   This Argus then may close his hundred eyes,
>   And leave our flight more easy.
> Cressida   How can I answer this to love and Troilus?
> Calchas   Why, 'tis for him you do it: promise largely;
>   That ring he saw you wear, he much suspects
>   Was given you by a lover; let him have it.
> Diomede
> *[Within]*
>   Hoa, Calchas, Calchas!
>   Hark! I hear his voice.
>   Pursue your project; doubt not the success.
>
>   John Dryden *Troilus and Cressida or Truth Found Too Late* (1679)

Whence did Dryden derive the inspiration for the above insertion? It must have been his own, for, while some commentators speak of the play's humorous moments, neither he nor any other realised that under the "rubbish", the play was intended to be a joke on the legal spectators.

26
ALL'S WELL THAT ENDS WELL

Giletta, a Phisitions daughter of Narbon, healed the French King of a Fistula, for reward wherof she demaunded Beltramo, Count of Rossiglione to husband. The Counte being married against his will, for despite fled to Florence, and loved another. Giletta, his wife by pollicie founde means to lye with her husband, in place of his lover, and was begotten with childe of two sonnes, which knowen to her husband, he received her againe, and afterwards he lived in great honour and felicitie.

Boccaccio [tr. William Painter] *Decameron* (1575)

Bertram has been mainly responsible for the notion that this play is a bitter comedy or problem play, but what kind of young man is he?

He is a very young man, hardly out of boyhood, as the play repeatedly emphasises: "unseason'd courtier" (I,i,67); "Youth, thou bear'st thy father's face" (I,ii,19); "my young lord" (III,ii,3); "rash and unbridled boy" (III,ii,26); "twenty such rude boys" (III,ii,81); "a foolish idle boy" (IV,iii, 211).

He refuses to marry Helena (II,iii,124) because she is no more than "a poor physician's daughter"; however, since he still refuses to marry her after the King has promised to ennoble and enrich her, this cannot be his real reason. He might be unwilling to accept having so personal a matter as the choice of a lifetime's mate dictated to him, even though the refusal proves costly to him, as it might in an age when fathers (or in this case the King who has become his guardian) chose spouses for their children, but this too is not his real reason.

When he leaves his mother's house for the court, he is looking forward to a period of freedom during which he can move about the world, learn more of it than he has been able to learn at home, and prove his abilities. While girls today often hope to marry and start their families in their early twenties, many young men prefer on reaching their majority, to enjoy an initial period of freedom and independence during which they can explore the world, prove their mettle, and establish a position in it, leaving marriage until later. Bertram hints as much in his first few lines:

Bertram And I in going, madam, weep o'er my father's death anew; but I must attend his majesty's command, to whom I am now in ward, evermore in subjection.

(I,i,3–5)

Evidently he dislikes the idea of being in ward to the King—why else would he say "evermore in subjection"? Is he anticipating that being in ward will prove disastrous to his hopes?

His dumb feeling of disaster proves to be justified, for he finds himself compelled to marry Helena and prematurely chained down:

Bertram Undone, and forfeited to cares for ever!

(II,iii,263)

(He later repeats "undone" in his letter to his mother: "She hath recovered the king and undone me" III,ii,20–26.) So he swears that he will never "bed" Helena and leaves for the wars:

Bertram   Wars is no strife
   To the dark house and the detested wife.

                                                    (II,iii,290–291)

As we eventually learn, he does not detest Helena because she is Helena, but because he had not wished to be married just yet. He is acutely disappointed at losing the period of freedom and exploration to which he had been looking forward after his upbringing in the relative isolation of Rossillion.

In III,iii we learn that he has been appointed commander of the Duke of Florence's horse. Although young he is both a leader of men and a valorous fighter; would he not have hoped to prove his abilities before being shackled (as he sees it) by marriage?

In the play's last scene he describes another reason why he had not wanted to be married just yet:

King   All is whole.
   Not one word more of the consumed time;
   Let's take the instant by the forward top;
   For we are old, and on our quick'st decrees
   Th'inaudible and noiseless foot of time
   Steals ere we can effect them. You remember
   The daughter of this lord?
Bertram Admiringly, my liege. At first, *[with Helena]*[31]
   I stuck my choice upon her, ere my heart
   Durst make too bold a herald of my tongue;
   Where, the impression of mine eye infixing,
   Contempt his scornful perspective did lend me,
   Which warp'd the line of every other favour,
   Scorn'd a fair colour or expressed it stol'n,
   Extended or contracted all proportions
   To a most hideous object. Thence it came
   That she whom all men praised, and whom myself
   Since I have lost, have lov'd, was in mine eye
   The dust that did offend it.
King   Well excused.
   That thou didst love her, strikes some scores away
   From the great compt...

                                                    (V,iii,37–57)

Bertram is another of Shakespeare's only children and I find that he understood their psychology as well as he understood everyone else's!

When he enters in I,i, since he, the Countess and Lafew are "all in black" (his father having only recently died), he clearly has not been deprived of a father during his formative years; the absence of brothers or sisters has been another kind of childhood deprivation. He is saying, "When Helena and I were together in my parents' house, I at first saw and learned to value all her qualities, but familiarity began to make them seem ordinary, to the point where I even began to find them too ordinary. I now realise what I have lost."

If Bertram had had any sisters, proximity to them would have taught him something

---

31   See Note at end of chapter.

of the other sex, and Helena's virtues might not have come to seem so ordinary to him. He had been hoping for a period of freedom during which he could both learn something of the world and (possibly) meet other girls, a perfectly natural hope.

The letter he sends to Helena after she has returned to his mother's house is a challenge whose consequences are quite unanticipated by him, which in fact proves to be a crucial event in the plot:

> When thou canst get the ring upon my finger, which never shall come off, and show me a child begotten of thy body that I am father to, then call me husband; but in such a "then" I write a "never".
>
> (III,ii,55–58)

However, at the end of the play, he is completely reconciled to Helena, for a reason which does not appear in the words of the play and must therefore depend on something seen on the stage rather than spoken.

In V,i, Helena, the Widow and Diana arrive at Marseilles, only to find that the King and his court have left for Rossillion where they must now travel. Although the scene seems unnecessary to the plot, it has its function: to suggest that some time elapses between Helena's arrival in Florence and her final meeting with the King. From what seems to be the only possible interpretation of the last scene, the time is of the order of several months though the play contains no clear indications of time-scale.

So, when Helena enters in the last scene, it is at once evident that she is expecting a child. And when she returns Bertram's ring, he realises that she had schemed to occupy his bed because she had wanted his child! "Will you be mine", she says, "now that you are doubly won?" i.e. "now that both I and the child within me are yours?" As in the original story, the sight reconciles him completely to her.

Is Bertram so very unusual? Is he not simply a somewhat 'green' young man who hopes to remedy his 'greenness'; is not his later behaviour the struggling of a boy who feels that he is not yet sufficiently adult and is enraged when he finds himself, as he sees it, prematurely trapped? Since at the end he speaks of his "high-repented blames" (V,iii,36–7), is he not then shame-faced? Does his conduct really raise any profound ethical problems? And at the end, does he not prove that he has the instincts of a husband and father after all? (Why does one editor describe him as "evil"?)

Though Parolles is regarded as the villain of the piece, he is not, for the intentions of a true villain are malicious. Examples of such villains in two other comedies are Don John and Borachio in *Much Ado*, and Sebastian and Antonio in *The Tempest*; however, Parolles is not malicious by nature. Although the scenes in which he appears have been described as a sub-plot, they do not deserve the name, for his dramatic function is simply to emphasise Bertram's extreme 'greenness' in accepting him as mentor.

In his younger days he had decided to become a soldier, yet now seems to have had his fill of war:

2nd   Lord O, 'tis brave wars!
Parol.   Most admirable! *[Aside]* I have seen those wars.

(II,i,25–26)

This remark must be an aside or a semi-aside, spoken aloud, and quietly and with inner reservations: Parolles does not remember his experiences of war with any pleasure as his later remark suggests:

> *Parolles* ...there do muster true gait, eat, speak and move, under the influence of the most receiv'd star; and though the devil lead the measure, such are to be followed.
>
> (II,i,52–55)

Parolles knows that in war the devil does indeed lead the measure. He perhaps decided to become a soldier because honour may be gained in war, then became a realist, and then passed through realism into cynicism: not an uncommon progression. His description of the "muster-file, rotten and sound" in IV,iii,164 is much like Falstaff's in *Henry IV Part I*.

From IV,i,69–73, he can even speak several languages, which is presumably the reason why he is called Parolles. His knowledgeable talk has impressed the young Bertram to the point where Bertram has completely accepted him as mentor and refuses hints that he might be mistaken:

> *Lafew* But I hope your lordship thinks not him a soldier.
> *Bertram* Yes, my lord, and of very valiant approof.
> *Lafew* You have it from his own deliverance.
> *Bertram* And by other warranted testimony.
> *Lafew* Then my dial goes not true, I took this lark for a bunting.
> *Bertram* I do assure you, my lord, he is very great in knowledge, and accordingly valiant.
>
> (II,v,1–8)

In III,vi the two French lords decide that Bertram must be disabused of his faith in Parolles, and in IV,iii they show him up as somewhat less of a warrior than his talk suggests. Bertram is both enlightened by the showing-up and matured by the realisation that everyone but himself had seen through Parolles. The episode is in fact the first stage in the maturing effects on Bertram of the play's final events.

As Parolles is not malicious, he is therefore not a villain, and he has had his bellyful of war. All he hopes for is to exist in some occupation above absolute poverty, in this case as the hanger-on of some nobleman, whom he must please. "The Count's a fool [child] and full of gold" (IV,iii,203); so, having impressed the youthful Bertram with his knowledgeable talk, he encourages him to go to the wars, then panders for him in his approaches to Diana. He is hardly more than another Bobadill or perhaps an educated Ancient Pistol in a higher social stratum; he adds some comedy of much the same kind.

Since the younger women in the play are all beautiful and virtuous and the older women dignified and virtuous, Helena should be regarded as its principal heroine: she becomes the leader of a feminine confederacy which recaptures the errant male and returns his feet to the path of virtue. Shaw described the Countess as "the most beautiful old woman's part ever written" although if Bertram is so young she will not yet be very old. Like so many wives of the time, she was probably married during her adolescence. Is not Helena, whose love for Bertram is totally selfless, the most appealing of heroines?

Helena has fallen completely in love with Bertram: from I,i,83–99 and she will probably never want anyone else (being highly intelligent and perceptive, she appears to have understood the underlying Bertram more clearly than some of his critics!). On hearing that he must go to the King's court, she at once fears the temptations to which such a very young man will be exposed (I,i,166–177). A plan soon occurs to her: she will follow him and offer to cure the King of his fistula with her father's potion, asking as reward a husband of her own choosing.

Just as Bertram's "evermore in subjection" suggests misgivings (and perhaps because she is an extremely modest young woman), she too is hesitant before making her choice:

Helena I am a simple maid, and therein wealthiest
That I protest I simply am a maid.
Please it your majesty, I have done already.
The blushes in my cheeks thus whisper me:
"We blush that thou should'st choose; but be refused,
Let the white death sit on thy cheek for ever,
We'll ne'er come there again"...
... *[To Bertram]* I dare not say I take you, but I give
Me and my service, ever while I live,
Into your guiding power...

(II,iii,66–72 and 102–105).

Bertram at once refuses her; while listening to the King's rebukes to him, she realises that she must on no account marry him if he is unwilling to accept her, for she loves him too much to want to force herself on him, and interrupts the King to withdraw her request:

Helena That you are well restored, my lord, I'm glad.
  Let the rest go.

(II,iii,147–148)

She is saying: "That my potion has cured you contents me entirely—please allow me to withdraw my request for Bertram's hand." Unfortunately, the King replies that his promise touches his honour and that they must be married, so she is as much forced into the marriage as Bertram.

She then decides to leave Rossillion, for her remaining there would prevent him from returning to his home: "My being here is all that holds thee hence" (III,ii,123), and explaining in her letter to the Countess that she will become "Saint Jacques' pilgrim". She now begins to display great feminine resourcefulness and determination, for her choice of the shrine in Florence, in the service of which city Bertram will be fighting, could hardly be accidental. Either there is such a shrine in or near Florence, perhaps for the purposes of the play—St. Jacques le Grand is mentioned in IV,iii,46—or there is not, in which case Helena has decided to camouflage her real intention, which is to follow Bertram to Florence in the hope of encountering and recovering him there. Perhaps the Bed-trick is already a possibility at the back of her mind, put into it by Bertram's challenging letter, although if it is, she will naturally keep the thought to herself).

III,v is a cleverly constructed scene, for Shakespeare uses it for several purposes. Elizabethan audiences were impressed and entertained by 'display' in one form or another: kings, queens and nobles were 'display'; stage battles were exciting 'display'; if there could be no battle, an army might be marched across the stage as in *Hamlet*.

In this scene, Shakespeare:
- inserts some military display;
- informs us of the activities of Parolles, who has been making approaches to Diana on Bertram's behalf;
- confirms that Bertram, young as he is, has won repute by "worthy service";
- enables Helena to meet the Widow and Diana, and the Widow unwittingly to suggest to Helena that there might be an opportunity for the Bed-trick:

Diana   Alas, poor lady!
   'Tis a hard bondage to become the wife
   Of a detesting lord.
Widow   I warrant, good creature, wheresoe'er she is,
   Her heart weighs sadly. This young maid might do her
   A shrewd turn if she pleased.
Helena   How do you mean?
   Maybe the amorous count solicits her
   In the unlawful purpose?
Widow   He does indeed...

                                                                                   (III,v,63–70)

Helena's reply to the Widow suggests that the Bed-trick has indeed been a possibility at the back of her mind and quite soon it will be at the forefront.

She is aware that her purpose is both moral and immoral:

Helena   Is wicked meaning in a lawful deed,
   And lawful meaning in a lawful act,
   Where both not sin, and yet a sinful fact.

                                                                                   (III,vii,45–47)

To her Elizabethan spectators, she would be preventing her husband from committing the sin of adultery.

She succeeds, then gives out that she is dead (IV,iii,45–51): news which contributes to the maturing of Bertram by causing him to realise what he has lost. When at the end he accepts that she is indeed expecting his child, he is completely reconciled both to being married and to being married to her. The King then completes the happy ending by promising a dowry to the maid Diana, who has been Helena's confederate in the recovering of Bertram, and, being the daughter of a poor widow, would be unable to attract a suitable husband without one.

Why was this play classed as a 'bitter comedy'? Essentially it is a fairy-tale—when was a fistula cured with a potion? It is a feminine success-story. Today it might serve as the basis for a story in a women's magazine: "Beautiful, Dedicated, Virtuous Wife Recovers Estranged Husband". Evidently, it was intended to appeal principally to the ladies among Shakespeare's spectators.

The plot is slight enough to need a good deal of padding-out.

In I,i Parolles enters and at once asks Helena "Are you meditating on virginity?", possibly trying her out for his own purposes; their "conceited" talk then goes on for some time, but without revealing more about either character or advancing the action (an unknown number of lines were omitted after line 161, presumably to shorten this conversation), and continues to the end of the scene. Parolles' showing-up at the end is longer than is necessary to the action; it is lengthened in order to introduce some black comedy.

Lavatch the Clown is only thinly connected with the plot, for he merely acts as occasional messenger; why are his conversations so long? Like Parolles, he is merely hoping to continue as hanger-on in a great house; being fertile in "conceited" talk, he has made himself accepted as a kind of Court Fool by his ability to talk amusingly:

Lafew   A shrewd knave—and an unhappy.

Countess So 'a is. My lord that's gone made himself much sport out of him: by his authority he remains here, which he thinks is a patent for his sauciness.

(IV,v,60–63)

He amuses the old nobleman Lafew enough to cause him to hand him his purse. Why does Lafew describe him as unhappy? Is it because he has brains and knows it, but has been unable to find any better use for them than to ingratiate himself as hanger-on by playing the Court Fool to a noble family?

He is comic relief; he offers a change of atmosphere, and brings the audience down to earth by contrasting the noble characters who have problems with the ordinary man who has no unusual worries.

Of Parolles, the editor of one edition of the play says somewhat obscurely, "The gallantry of war is stained by Parolles no less than the erection of virtue into nobility." While the King offers to ennoble and enrich Helena the poor physician's daughter, Parolles receives no such offer. From his hints, Parolles knows that war is by no means all gallantry; having done his share of fighting in the past, he has had his fill. Admittedly although he talks too much and too loudly, he is compelled to remain in his chosen occupation as soldier, justifying himself with martial talk. If we were sufficiently charitable to remember that Shakespeare saw all his characters from their own standpoint, we might diagnose him as suffering from something akin to battle fatigue.

Of the Clown, the same editor says, "The same effect is produced by Lavatch, for whom the wounds of honour and syphilitic chancres are indistinguishable." Could Lavatch be talking "dead-pan", i.e. is he really to be taken seriously in everything he says? Here we need to know how he was acted under Shakespeare's direction, which unfortunately we cannot know. Probably he was intended to appear dead-pan which is something that any comic actor must be able to do, and his humour would be recognised as such by his audience. If he hoped to be kept on in such a house as the Countess's, would he really boast of being a syphilitic? When he talks of marrying Isabel, is he not saying "Like everyone else, I find it better to marry than burn" as an excuse for amusing, if saucy, talk?

Incidentally, the same editor says, "There was little sense among Shakespeare's contemporaries that this [the Bed-trick] was a degrading and unsatisfactory way of getting a husband." However Helena uses it not to get a husband, for she has already been forcibly married but to win him back to her. If he is right, Bertram's letter would at once suggest the Bed-trick to at least some among the ladies in Shakespeare's audiences.

The arguments over the rings prolong the last scene with more comedy; they extend the dénouement with a little suspense before its happy resolution.

If the play had been intended as a dark comedy or tragi-comedy, its construction would have been tighter in order to intensify the plot; it would have had more dark moments; it would in particular have contained less of what can only be called padding. However, the central Bertram-Helena action is too slight for anything more than a short play, and its dark moments are not especially dark. Bertram's refusal of Helena introduces a tense situation, as does the slander on Hero in *Much Ado about Nothing. W*hat is comedy—or any true drama—without some tension? *Much Ado* has never been regarded as a dark comedy, even though it develops tragic potential when Beatrice attempts to avenge the slander on Hero by persuading Benedick to kill Claudio.

In tragedy there is (or should be) a feeling that events will move in accordance with the logic of character or situation to an inevitable end. Molière's comedies have been described as tragedies which end happily, because they too move towards tragedy in accordance with the logic of character, until an outsider, a 'deus ex machina', steps in to avert the catastrophe.

In *Much Ado About Nothing* and *The Tempest* there are villains whose scheming arouse tension in the audience ("Will their malice be forestalled?"), but in *All's Well That Ends Well* there are no villains. Parolles is merely a hanger-on who at the end has done no actual harm; the Clown's main function is to fill spaces in the action with the kind of spicy, conceited talk which would tickle the palates of Shakespeare's audiences. Soon after the beginning of *All's Well* there is an apparent disaster when Bertram rejects Helena. Though his action arouses tense interest, he is not a villain, while his intention is neither malicious nor criminal. Then, as we follow Helena's progress, we (the ladies in the audience) begin to feel that she may eventually win through, as indeed she does. Is there really a sense of coming tragedy in this play?—Of coming difficulty, certainly, but accompanied by the hope that all may yet end well.

Too many problems have been read into it, in spite of its fairy-tale plot. It was intended simply to be a comedy which would appeal to the ladies among its audiences and come to the same totally happy ending as Boccaccio's story.

Note:
>*King*   You remember
>The daughter of this lord?
>*Bertra*m   Admiringly, my liege. At first, [with Helena],
>I stuck my choice upon her...
>Thence it came,
>That she whom all men praised, and whom myself
>Since I have lost, have lov'd, was in mine eye
>The dust that did offend it.
>*King*   Well excused.
>That thou didst love her strikes some scores away
>From the great compt...
>
>(V,iii,42–57)

Bertram is so young that he is still in ward to the King; Helena has given out that she is dead, and the King, who is still his guardian and must now find him another wife, has been suggesting Lafew's daughter (later referred to as "the fair Maudlin"). The two bracketed words have been inserted because without them, the "her" in Bertram's second line would refer to Lafew's daughter, although he has not been brought up in the same house as she. His last lines show that he has been speaking of Helena; the King's reply—that he has understood Bertram to have spoken of Helena.

Even with the added words, the change of subject is unnaturally abrupt. It can only be explained by the assumption that lines are missing, perhaps (as at I,i,162) excised to shorten a discussion which does not contribute to the movement of the play, in this case of a young lady who is quite extraneous to the plot. They would be given to the King, the senior in this conversation. After a few more lines on "the fair Maudlin" he would ask Bertram why he had rejected Helena.

27
MEASURE FOR MEASURE

(i)

This play is a problem play not so much because of the ethical or religious issues it raises as of a construction so unsatisfactory that it is impossible to determine which of its themes Shakespeare intended to be the central theme or even, since its happy ending makes it nominally a comedy, whether he set out to write a tragedy and then changed his mind.

He appears to have decided to put together a plot on lines somewhat similar to those of *All's Well*, possibly because that play had been a success, but even more a fairy-tale plot. As before, it contains a heroine, Isabella; no one who could properly be called its hero. In *All's Well* the King is not the central character but the 'deus ex machina'; in *Measure for Measure* the most important character, the Duke, becomes the omnipotent, omnipresent, omniscient 'deus in machina' who moves about his city in disguise and manipulates his subjects. Disguises are always completely convincing in Elizabethan plays! No doubt such parts were played by principal actors accomplished enough to be able to assume a different demeanour, a different bodily carriage, a different vocal quality. This particular disguise is carried rather far; the Duke cannot be a fully accredited cleric, otherwise he could not propose marriage to Isabella at the end, yet he mentions having shriven Barnardine (IV,ii,205) and confessed Mariana (V,i,523).

In the last scene of *All's Well*, Diana's boggling replies over the rings make it a teasing ending, the audience being of course in the know, and *Measure for Measure* was to have the same kind of final scene.

He used a traditional element that he had already used in *All's Well*, the Bed-trick, and added two more, the Disguised Ruler and the Corrupt Magistrate, yet with important changes in the latter. In his sources, the heroines are normal young women, though Shakespeare changed his heroine into one who intends to dedicate herself to a religious life and to whom her chastity is doubly precious. He made Angelo an apparently ice-cold, iron-hard, incorruptible man of principle: a confrontation of "mighty opposites" in which a man's life is at stake, a situation having so much tragic as to have no comic potential. He even wrote some of his most intense poetry into it:

>   *Claudio*   Death is a fearful thing.
>   *Isabella*   And shamed life a hateful.
>   *Claudio*   Ay, but to die, and go we know not where;
>   To lie in cold obstruction, and to rot;
>   This sensible warm motion to become
>   A kneaded clod, and the delighted spirit
>   To bath in fiery floods, or to reside
>   In thrilling regions of thick-ribbed ice.........
>   (III,i,115–122)

Was such a passage ever in place in a comedy?

By way of comic relief, he early introduced some low-life characters: Lucio and Mistress Overdone, then Elbow the malapropising constable, Froth (who does not reappear), and Pompey the bawd. After the climax the atmosphere of the play had to be lightened if it was to end as a comedy; so the Duke suggests the Bed-trick to Isabella. Helena's conversations with the Widow and Diana are in verse, although Shakespeare perhaps felt that prose would be more appropriate to the Duke's confidential, conspiratorial proposal of such a scheme after such an opening.

Abhorson and Barnardine provide some black comedy in IV,ii, a scene which may have been inspired by II,vi of Kyd's *The Spanish Tragedy* in which Pedringano, who has been found guilty of murder and condemned to death but believes he will be rescued by his master, backchats cheerfully with the Hangman until, as the stage direction says, the latter suddenly 'turns him off'. However, although the Hangman and Pedringano have a direct connection with their plot, Abhorson and Barnardine have next to none with theirs.

Lucio plays an important part in the action: what exactly is his dramatic function; what kind of man is he, how are we meant to think of him?

In I,ii he learns from Claudio of the latter's arrest, agrees to inform Isabella, advises her to appeal to Angelo, accompanies her and gives her all the support and encouragement she needs. When he enters in IV,iii, he is "pale at mine heart" to see her so sad. He then describes the Duke as "the old fantastical duke of dark corners" and a "woodman" or chaser of women, and even claims that "I was once before him with getting a wench with child", accusations which the Duke naturally denies; yet Lucio is always so much more open and candid than the Duke, even when speaking of his own early libertinism, that we are left wondering "Which of them is should we believe?"

In the play's last scene Lucio's interjections get him whipped and married to his "punk", although this punishment seems unduly harsh after the help and encouragement he has given to Isabella in her frightful dilemma.

How was he acted? Was he depicted as being always a little the worse for drink? Perhaps... but why is he first shown as so lucid when giving his early advice and support to Isabella?

In his final scene he remains oddly certain in his accusations of the "Friar": more comic relief, but is it really in place in a scene at the end of which Angelo is condemned to death before being reprieved by Mariana's pleading?

As principal character, the Duke unbalances the play. He gives the impression of moving through it as a puppet-master whose string-pulling allows the other characters no truly independent existence; they come alive in their speeches, and are or will be manipulated by him. The ending, which occupies the whole of the fifth act, is an excessively teasing cliff-hanger for the audience, the Duke's machinations being too ingeniously dramatic. In fact, if the play's last two lines are to be taken literally, the teasing continues past the end of the play:

    Duke So bring us to our palace, where we'll show
           What's yet behind that's meet you all should know.

He informs Isabella beforehand that Claudio's head "is off and sent to Angelo":
    Duke   She's come to know
        If yet her brother's pardon be come hither;
        But I will keep her ignorant of her good
        To make her heavenly comforts of despair
        When it is least expected.
                                               (IV,iii,106–110)

So, unlike Helena and Diana, Isabella is never fully in the know until the "Friar" is revealed to be the Duke at the very end of the final scene.

When Mariana makes her appeal, stating that she has yielded her chastity to Angelo, he affects to receive it sceptically and asserts Angelo's innocence and integrity, to her outrage, and has her taken out under guard; Friar Peter supports him with "Most wrongfully accus'd your substitute" (but the Duke later calls him "thou foolish friar" in V,i,240).

After Mariana has told her story and been received with the same apparent disbelief, the Duke elects to depart, leaving Escalus in charge and offering no hope of justice to the two women. He soon returns in disguise as Friar with Isabella and the Provost. Lucio, who now seems to be suffering from partial amnesia, accuses the apparent Friar of being the "rascal" who slandered the Duke, Escalus orders the Friar to prison, he resists, and Lucio pulls off his hood. The Duke still assures Isabella that her brother is dead (V,i,386–397); how can this cruelty to her be "heavenly comforts"? Why torture her at such length with the belief that her brother has been executed? By what stretch of imagination can it be called comedy?

When Claudio eventually proves to be alive, the Duke proposes marriage to Isabella, which she does not decline. Has she really forgotten her dedication to religion so soon—or are we to take it, implausible as it seems—that her change of mind is the effect of the "heavenly comforts"? Shakespeare is usually explicit in indicating the reasons for such changes of heart but on this occasion he leaves her silent. Or has she yielded to the attraction of a highborn wealthy husband? Nowhere in the play is there any suggestion of true love between them.

Was Shakespeare satirizing such women as Isabella by suggesting that she first places an excessively high valuation on her chastity, then—so to speak—sees the light? This notion is improbable, partly because nothing in the play indicates it explicitly. Lucio's expressions of respect for her in I,iv do not suggest any satiric intention, partly because such satire would have offended many of his spectators. Yet Isabella's conversion is implausibly rapid. How was she played under Shakespeare's direction? Did her expression change to a pleased smile, indicating that she was flattered by an offer coming from the Duke himself? Were the play's last lines intended to suggest this?

Will the forgiving of his murder to Barnardine really cause him to become a reformed man? And although Mariana insists on it, will her marriage to the disgraced Angelo really be a happy ending for her? And if Angelo is spared the execution he deserves, why is Lucio not spared marriage to his "punk"?

Although there has been no suggestion that the play was a collaboration, some of the episodes and in particular the happy ending, are very crudely contrived comedy. For example, compare the much subtler depiction of Polonius' absent-mindedness or the two graveyard Clowns in *Hamlet*, that it might almost have been one in which Shakespeare supplied most of the lines for another playwright's plot (as may have been the case with that odd play *Pericles*). There is reason to doubt that the construction of *Measure for Measure,* in particular the ending, was entirely due to Shakespeare. Did he concoct his plot from suggestions from the members of his company, or manufacture roles (such as Varrius in IV,v) for them at their request? Was the play concocted by a committee, so to speak, instead of a single playwright's mind?

The richness of its language induces the reader to take *Measure for Measure* seriously. It is really not so much a dark comedy as failed, because excessively ingenious and strained, the quality of its style has diverted attention from its construction. Great plays are not necessarily great in style, and while great style may impress, even such style as Shakespeare's does not necessarily make a play great, the choosing or devising of a plot and the writing of its dialogue being interdependent yet distinct procedures. *Measure for Measure* is unusual for Shakespeare in that it lacks the unity and consistency of the dramatic purpose which all plays must have, especially if they are to produce the maximum effect on audiences. They must induce a feeling of inevitability as their endings approach. But *Measure for Measure* induces no such impression; Shakespeare even seems to have been careful to prevent it from arising in his audiences' minds.

What was Shakespeare's intention in devising such a plot?

For a few years before and after 1600, the Children's Theatres were competing so successfully with the adult companies that (as described in *Hamlet*) the latter had been compelled to travel to the provinces to find audiences. I surmise that Shakespeare wrote these two plays in the hope of maintaining attendances: the first a successful light comedy with a slightly spicy plot, then a spicy comedy to end all spicy comedies, having a much more tense central situation, a greater number of low-life characters, and a setting in a city which is apparently crowded with "houses of resort" and where at the same time the penalty for the "rebellion of a cod-piece" is execution (has it ever been so?). Obviously, a fairy-tale city!

And he overdid it. The play contains no character with whom we can sympathise, except Isabella in her acute dilemma. Her failure to refuse the Duke's offer of marriage at the end leaves us guessing as to her true character. So the play is a problem play because of the author's (or the committee's) failure to write it with a consistent and easily recognised dramatic purpose.

Was it Shakespeare himself who overdid it? The play was not printed till 1623, ten years after his retirement to Stratford. Did the text become modified and corrupted by Sharers in his theatre company who thought that they understood as much of the art of playwriting as its author? For example, Varrius, who enters towards the end (IV,v) then exits without ever speaking, suggests much chopping and changing. Was it originally a short play, and did they decide to lengthen it? I find it impossible to accept that Shakespeare would have tacked together such a string of implausibilities and spur-of-the-moment surprises and called the result a plot. If the supposition is correct, their ingenuity has made a satisfactory reconstruction impossible.

Whether it maintained attendances we do not know, but Shakespeare may have had a fit of conscience. It has been suggested that he wrote these plays and followed them with tragedies because his personal outlook had darkened, possibly because of some event in his private life. Alternatively, the Londoners were demanding tragedies, this type of play having the most sensational type of plot; there is always a demand for sensation. However, it is equally possible that he was becoming so disgusted with some aspects of the behaviour of his fellow Londoners that he decided that from then on he would write with a moral purpose. *Measure for Measure*, a play which is almost as much tragedy as comedy, would then mark the end of a stage in Shakespeare's development as dramatist and the beginning of another, the moment when he knew at last the kind of play that he really wanted to write, and the kind of theme he really wanted to write about.

Note

I once saw a play in the National Theatre, called *Abingdon Square* that had been written in a theatre workshop in New York directed by María Irene Fornés (1987). I did not find it an effective play, almost certainly because it had been written by a "'committee' instead of a single, innately-gifted playwright's mind—hence the suggestion, that Shakespeare's original text of *Measure for Measure* was meddled with after his retirement by self-appointed 'improvers' in his theatre company.

28
THE EMERGENCE OF THE THEME

(i)

Some critics have inferred that because Shakespeare changed from writing histories and comedies to "bitter comedies" and then to tragedies, his outlook had darkened, perhaps because of some setback in his private life:

> Shakespeare seems to be torn in this play *[Measure for Measure]* as nowhere else, save in *Troilus and Cressida*, and, to some extent, in *Hamlet*, between deeply stirred idealistic thought and reflection, and a tendency to cynical bitterness and grim realism which delights in a certain violence and even distortion of speech and figure, and sometimes of incident...
>
> C. Spurgeon *Shakespeare's Imagery* Ch. XIII p.289

In the hope of justifying some remarks in my preface, I quote an extract from a critic (name withheld from kindness!) who took this view to an extreme:

> The great plays that follow this one in psychological sequence, *Timon of Athens* and *King Lear*, are expressions of a further phase of the same sequence; disintegration is accomplished, "Nature's germens tumble all together, Even till destruction sicken" and the judgment surrenders. In the moment of surrender the mind perceives another dimension of reality, and this perception leads in the end to the positive, spiritual revaluation in the last plays. But *Troilus and Cressida* stands at a lower point of negation in this sequence than *Lear* or even *Timon*. For, while its material is still that of the actual world, the mood is that of a man who has come to the end of that world's resources; emotional, intellectual, and moral values resolve alike into futility; even the imagination, the high constructive power, looking ahead into a dark night of the soul, sees no further ideal form, no "unbodied figure of the thought" waiting upon creation. This last experience is an area of suffering peculiar to the artist's mind, but it can derive from an experience potentially common to all men, the vision of the disjunction and disintegration of civilization—the ideals it rests upon and the achievements it bequeaths—while these are still coextensive for him with the universe of thought. It is, in fact, in this very image that Shakespeare chooses to embody his experience in this play. What is recorded in *Troilus and Cressida* is thus the acutest point of suffering in this sequence, before the understanding has surrendered its moral, intellectual, or imaginative synthesis and accepted dis-integration; the fullest possible realisation of imminent dissolution before its accomplishment brings anaesthesia.

To quote my German supervisor again, this is indeed "playing with concepts!"

Objections immediately come to mind as the condition would surely include or be a form of writer's block. However, Shakespeare continued to write approximately one new play every six months, to collaborate with other playwrights, and to act in his and their plays, until he retired to Stratford. And as has previously been suggested, he appears to have formulated the Ghost in *Hamlet* to please King James, and was rewarded when James became patron of his company, i.e. although there may have been some unhappy event in his private life between perhaps 1600 and 1603, he remained very much the man of business. Could he really have done all this if he had reached disintegration and could see no further figure of the thought waiting on creation?

He would surely have lost his sense of humour but did not, as his passages of dead-pan humour show. 'Dead-pan' humour is perhaps the most amusing form of humour, provided that one is an onlooker and not the butt! As examples: in her first appearance Cressida deploys a form of it for some time:

Pandarus Look you there: there's no jesting, there's laying on, take't off who
 will, as they say; there be hacks.
Cressida ["Simple", wide-eyed] Be those with swords? (etc, etc)

(I,ii,199–201)

Helen can also be 'dead-pan'.

For most of this scene, the conversation has been in prose, but now its style changes to the more dignified blank verse:

Paris They're come from the field: let us to Priam's hall
 To greet the warriors. Sweet Helen, I must woo you
 To help unarm our Hector. His stubborn buckles,
 With these your white enchanting fingers touch'd,
 Shall more obey than to the edge of steel
 Or force of Greekish sinews: you shall do more
 Than all the island kings—disarm great Hector.
Helen [Drawing herself up to her full height, speaking with regal dignity, and even using the royal "we", to which in Troy she is not entitled:]
 'Twill make us proud to be his servant, Paris.
 Yea, what he shall receive of us in duty
 Gives us more palm in beauty than we have,
 Yea, overshines ourself.
Paris [Delighted] Sweet, above thought I love thee!

(III,i,144–155)

The Servant whom Pandarus encounters at the beginning of the scene is another skilled dead-pan humourist and since he is not seen again, he must have been inserted merely to display his gift:

Pandarus Friend, you, pray you, a word: do you not follow the young lord Paris?
Servant Ay sir, when he goes before me.
Pandarus You depend upon him, I mean.
Servant Sir, I do depend upon the Lord (etc).

(III,i.1–5)

With the possible exception of a few passages, such as the rarely equalled love poetry in the courtship of the two lovers, the play is dead-pan throughout. Shakespeare even made use of the thought of Plato, as serious a philosopher as ever was, in what is actually a parody of the legal profession. And there are other such passages in the later plays; for example, the brief conversation between Desdemona and the Servant at the beginning of III,iv in *Othello*.

Another objection arises from the fact that anyone who acquires a profession soon learns that his approach to whatever problems his occupation may bring him, must be professional, in the sense of detached and impersonal. The actor must be no less professional. As a hypothetical case, the actor may find on returning home after an evening's performance, that his daughter has set fire to the kitchen, or that his son has crashed the family car, or even that his wife has left him for another man, but he must still turn up at the theatre the following evening and put on the required performance precisely as before. The point was emphasised by the eighteenth century encyclopédiste Diderot in his "Paradoxe sur le Comédien."

Plays are always written in accordance with a particular set of dramatic conventions (a fact which makes the stage more artificial than real life); hence plays written by playwrights living in different countries or at different epochs require different acting methods. "The actor who can play a scene by Shakespeare knows nothing of the art of playing Racine", and both arts must be learned as techniques.

In the French 17th century plays, emphasis was on the general rather than the individual type of character: "L'Avare and Tartuffe were based on all the world's misers and hypocrites"; hence the actor must observe and imitate the general type when creating his role. If he is to deepen his interpretations, his study of human types must never cease: "The best actors are the most experienced."

Actors must not let their own individualities colour their interpretations, for if they did, no role could be played in the same way by different actors. Also, the actor "qui joue d'âme" cannot reach and maintain a uniformly high and professional standard of playing; his acting will be alternately "plat et sublime."

On the stage, the actor himself feels none of the emotions he is representing; he is inducing the appropriate response in the audience by a coldly calculated and thoroughly practised performance. Diderot says:

> "C'est l'extrême sensibilité[32] qui fait les acteurs médiocres; c'est la sensibilité médiocre qui fait la multitude des mauvais acteurs; et c'est le manque absolu de sensibilité qui prépare les acteurs sublimes."

In their private lives the greatest actors have displayed little or no "sensibilité".

He had once believed that "enthousiasme" and "sensibilité" were the marks of the greatest geniuses, but now takes the opposite stance, that they are absent from the make-up of the greatest imitative artists.

Diderot might have added: "When we hear a striking story for the first time, we are impressed; if it is an amusing story, we may roar with laughter; but what if we hear it from a succession of acquaintances? After the third or fourth telling, we have lost interest, we can no longer respond to it because it has become 'old stuff' to us." Similarly, after the actor has rehearsed and played his part a number of times, he has become unable to feel the emotions he is depicting. He is then able to review and improve his performance by further observation of people around him because he can approach it with detachment. As experience increases, he will eventually feel no emotions even when studying his part; he will consider only the necessary acting techniques. If he lacks "sensibilité" in his private life, it is because of his habitually detached attitude.

If the actor must be as professional as this, surely the playwright must be equally professional; particularly if, as did Shakespeare, he writes his own plays, collaborates with other playwrights, and acts in his and their plays? To repeat Rattigan on "sense of drama": it

---

32   "Sensibilité": not "sensibleness"; sensitivity, proneness to emotion, willingness to share the feelings of others.

is "a controlled schizophrenia which will allow a dramatist to act as audience to his own play while writing it"; i.e. while visualising what his characters should say and how they should say it, he simultaneously visualises the audience's response. Could Shakespeare have become the greatest playwright the world has seen if he had not been the completely detached professional? Like the actor when creating his role, he based his indications of character on observation of the human types around him, necessarily excluding all of himself except his astonishing capacity for empathy, and I do not accept that any aspect of the private Shakespeare can be deduced with any certainty from his plays.

Why, then, did Shakespeare turn to tragic themes for his later plays? I quote again the note from Aubrey's *Brief Lives*: "The more to be admired [because] he was not a company keeper, lived in Shoreditch, wouldn't be debauched, & if invited to writ; he was in paine."

"Wouldn't be debauched" suggests that Shakespeare himself lived a moral life in his later years at least, because he had come to disapprove of the sexual licence he saw around him.

I imagine him saying to himself, "A sound family life is essential to us all. From my observations of the human types around me, I note that if a man's family life is solidly founded, all—barring accident or the malice of enemies—should go well with his outside life, but if anything is amiss in his family life (and it can go amiss in a wide variety of ways), the effect on the whole of his existence is likely to be disastrous, whether the fault is his or not.

So: from now on I shall choose plots turning on a family theme, and if the situation contains tragic potentiality I shall no longer retrieve it with some such happy chance as the overhearing of the plot against Hero in *Much Ado*, or Helena's encounter with the Widow in *All's Well*, or the resemblance of Ragozine's head to Claudio's in *Measure for Measure*, and make a comedy of it; I shall let it develop in accordance with its own 'logic' to a tragic conclusion".

(ii)

The earlier tragedy *Romeo and Juliet* had a contemporary family theme: the elopement and marriage of two young people without their parents' knowledge or consent. His first 'tragedy of character' was *Richard II*, but it contains no hint of the family theme, which—considering only the tragedies—first appears in *Julius Caesar*.

In II,i, Portia complains that Brutus is not confiding in her:

Portia   Think you I am no stronger than my sex
    Being so fathered and so husbanded?
    Tell me your counsels, I will not disclose 'em.
    I have made strong proof of my constancy,
    Giving myself a voluntary wound
    Here in the thigh: can I bear that with patience,
    And not my husband's secrets?

(*J.C.*II,1,296–302)

"Why", my wife once asked, "does she wound herself in the thigh? Why not in the arm? Is Brutus so much of the Stoic that he has been denying himself the pleasures of the marital bed, and does she wound herself in the thigh so that she can expose it and arouse some desire in him?"

Brutus is the Stoic; has he pursued Stoicism to the point where he has been denying, both himself and her, the pleasures of marital relations? Perhaps he has only been doing so recently, for Portia has complained in her earlier lines that "You've ungently, Brutus, stole from my bed." She does speak of her "once commended beauty". Unfortunately, it is only possible to speculate on the course of their marriage.

When determining Shakespeare's dramatic purpose, a personage who exemplifies the need to study not only his adherences to, but also his departures from, his sources is Cassius, in that the historical Cassius was married to Brutus's sister Junia and had children, whereas his wife and children are not mentioned in the play. Shakespeare's Cassius appears to be a middle-aged bachelor.

How does the wealthy middle-aged bachelor spend his days; more particularly, how does he spend his evenings? The married man can go home to the bosom of his family, but the bachelor, having no family, must rely on finding company among a coterie of friends. Cassius is not of the Stoic temperament; he is the Epicurean who gives free rein to his emotions whom Plutarch describes as turning against Caesar not so much from republican principles as from malice; thus, when he hears the Soothsayer trying to make himself heard by Caesar and seizes the opportunity to approach Caesar but finds himself "cut" by him, pique at being denied recognition by the great man then turns him against Caesar.

In this play, then, Cassius is a middle-aged bachelor, Brutus's married life does not appear to be entirely normal, and Caesar and Calpurnia are longing for a child to their marriage:

Caesar Calpurnia,—

Calpurnia Here, my lord.

Caesar Stand you directly in Antonius' way
When he doth run his course. Antonius!

Antony Caesar, my lord?

Caesar Forget not in your speed, Antonius,
To touch Calpurnia, for our elders say
The barren, touched in this holy chase,
Shake off their sterile curse.

(*J.C.* I,ii,1–9)

The desire for a child appeared very briefly in *Troilus and Cressida*. Pandarus appears to be unmarried and to have no living relative other than Cressida, and is therefore hoping to bring her under the protection of a prince of the blood royal for more reasons than one. He is not quite what he appears to be:

Cressida Well, uncle, what folly I commit I dedicate to you.

Pandarus I thank you for that: if my lord get a boy of you, you'll give him me.

(III,ii,101–104)

Bertram's welcoming of a child provides the happy resolution at the end of *All's Well*.

Except for the last instance, an essential element in the play's completely happy ending, these features of the plays were peripheral to their main themes. In *Hamlet* the family element was much nearer the core, blended into the revenge tragedy rather than central to it. The theme of *All's Well that Ends Well,* a potentially unhappy because premature and forced marriage, was developed into a comedy that would appeal to the ladies: the theme of *Measure for Measure* was sexual indulgence outside marriage, without any effective emphasis on its potentially tragic effects, whether before or after marriage.

The family theme in one form or another then became the central motif in all the subsequent tragedies.

29

OTHELLO

"Ye shall know the truth, and the truth shall make you free.[33]
                                Gospel according to St. John, ch.8,v.32

"The foundation of morality is to have done, once for all, with lying."
                                T.H.Huxley *Science and Morals* (1886)

There are people whose slogan in life is to live openly. They refuse to attempt to deceive in speech or action or to be devious or furtive; they prefer to live lightheartedly or as lightheartedly as the circumstances of their lives permit. They refrain from burdening their minds with the recollections of things said or done which might later give rise to shame or remorse, nor do they arouse resentment against which they might have to defend themselves. Small children delight their parents because they are so spontaneous, their spontaneity arising from their innocence, and those who live openly are careful to preserve their innocence as completely as they can. Othello is about such people: why else would the words "honest" and "honesty" appear on almost every other page?

In his essay *'Honesty' in Othello* (1951) William Empson begins by mentioning their fifty-two uses in the play, points out that in Shakespeare's other plays the words are often used with a patronising, condescending and even sarcastic connotation as to a social inferior, and concludes that they are used in *Othello* in similar meanings. They sometimes are, but in *Othello* honesty means more: complete openness, an absolute, as a principle of personal conduct, referring in particular to two of the play's principals. It is one of the play's main motifs.

(i)

Desdemona lives openly:

> *Desdemona*   To my unfolding lend your prosperous ear,
>   And let me find a charter in your voice,
>   And if my simpleness...
>
>   (I,iii,244–6)

Since she is aware of her simpleness, she is speaking of her deliberate simpleness. She and Cordelia in *King Lear* might be sisters:

> *Desdemona*   My noble father,
>   I do perceive here a divided duty:
>   To you I am bound for life and education,
>   My life and education both do learn me
>   How to respect you, you are lord of all my duty.
>   I am hitherto your daughter: but here's my husband;
>   And so much duty as my mother show'd
>   To you, preferring you before her father,

---

33   For "the truth" read "truthfulness".

>   So much I challenge, that I may profess,
>   Due to the Moor my lord.
>
> (I,iii,180–189)

> *Cordelia*   Good my lord,
>   You have begot me, bred me, loved me,
>   I return those duties back as are right fit,
>   Obey you, love you, and most honour you.
>   Why have my sisters' husbands, if they say
>   They love you all? Haply when I shall wed,
>   That lord whose hand shall take my plight shall carry
>   Half my love with him, half my care and duty.
>   Sure I shall never marry like my sisters
>   To love my father all.
>
> (*King Lear* I,i,94–103)

Both have accepted what their obligations will be, first as daughter, then as wife, and are determined to meet them faithfully.

According to her father, Desdemona had always been a reserved young lady:

> *Brabantio* So opposite to marriage, that she shunn'd
>   The wealthy curled darlings of our nation...
>
> (I,ii,67–8)

>   A maiden never bold
>   Of Spirit so still and quiet, that her motion
>   Blushed at herself...
>
> (I,iii,94–96)

There is little reason for surprise that she should marry Othello, for he is evidently a highly able and intelligent man. In I,ii,21–22 he claims royal descent and is now Venice's general. She is first impressed by and then comes to admire not so much the face as the mind behind the face; she senses and sympathises with a need within it, and decides that she will satisfy both his need and hers for a companion in life:

> *Desdemona* That I did love the Moor, to live with him,
>   My downright violence and scorn of fortunes
>   May trumpet to the world; my heart's subdued
>   Even to the utmost pleasure of my lord;
>   I saw Othello's visage in his mind,
>   And to his honours and his valiant parts
>   Did I my soul and fortunes consecrate.
>
> (I,iii,248–254)

Being a person who lives openly, Desdemona recognises another in Othello, as he recognises her.

In I,iii they plead with the Elders of Venice to allow her to accompany him to Cyprus:

> *Desdemona* So that, dear lords, if I be left behind,
>   A moth of peace, and he go to the war,
>   The rites for which I love him are bereft me,
>   And I a heavy interim shall support
>   By his dear absence; let me go with him.

Othello Your voices, lords: beseech you, let her will
    Have a free way; I therefore beg it not
    To please the palate of my appetite,
    Nor to comply with heat, the young affects
    In my defunct, and proper satisfaction,
    But to be free and bounteous of her mind;

(I,iii,255–265)

In his last lines, described as "one of the most famous cruxes in Shakespeare", he is saying: "I do not ask that she accompany me because of youthful lust, now dead in me" (from III,iii,269–270 he is in late middle age: "declined into the vale of years"), "or to consummate our marriage" (their nuptial rites are not consummated till his arrival in Cyprus II,ii) "but that I may enjoy the truthfulness and candour which so please me". As the passage stands, there is a break in the sense, for only Desdemona can be "free and bounteous" of her own mind. Lines may have been omitted; alternatively, the line was misread by the compositor—as "in my defunct" must have been—the original version probably being:

Othello Nor to comply with heat, the young affects
    In me defunct, and proper satisfaction,
    But that she's free and bounteous of her mind.

(I,iii,263–265)

He expresses his delight when he disembarks in Cyprus:
Othello It gives me wonder great as my content
    To see you here before me. O my soul's joy,
    If after every tempest come such calmness,
    May the winds blow, till they have wakened death?
    And may the labouring bark climb hills of seas,
    Olympus-high, and duck again as low
    As hell's from heaven. If it were now to die,
    'Twere now to be most happy, for I fear
    My soul hath her content so absolute
    That not another comfort like to this
    Succeeds in unknown fate...
    ...I cannot speak enough of this content;
    It stops me here, it is too much of joy...
                ...O my sweet,
    I prattle out of fashion, and I dote
    In mine own comforts.

(II,i,183–207)

Desdemona proves to be open to the point of naïveté, for in III,iii she is much too insistent when she urges Othello to reappoint Cassio as his lieutenant. She is all love and sympathy but, being young and never having been a general herself or learned anything of military discipline, she has not realised that she should not attempt to influence her husband's decisions; at the same time her sympathetic nature has delighted Othello.

How old is she? In those days girls were often married much earlier in adolescence than today. Suitors might have come to seek her hand when she was fourteen, only to find her "opposite to marriage". At the same time she is old enough to have become confident, perhaps too confident, that she can influence her husband. So she may be eighteen to twenty.

Such pleasure as Othello's is extreme even in a husband newly married to a young, beautiful and virtuous wife. Why? We know that he was pushed out into the world to survive alone as a small child ("Since these arms of mine had seven years pith", I,iii,83), and might surmise that his later years have given him no early experience of life in a normal family of two parents and one or more brothers and sisters. From necessity he has become a loner, having first come to accept the bachelor-cum-soldier's way of life as satisfactory and fulfilling, and then begun to feel the need for a helpmeet and companion in life as most of us eventually do. Possibly he has experienced or observed disloyalty in the other sex; and from Iago's "old black ram" (I,i,88) he may not be unfamiliar with it. At any rate, he has waited until he was "declined into the vale of years" before deciding to marry:

> *Othello*   For know, Iago,
> But that I love the gentle Desdemona
> I would not my unhoused free condition
> Put into circumscription and confine
> For the sea's worth.
>
> (I,ii,24–28)

These lines might suggest that until now Othello has been entirely happy in his combination of soldier's and bachelor's life, though he may be interpreted as having refrained from marrying until he met a partner of the right kind for him.

Desdemona is another loner in that she is not only an only child but a motherless only child, as are Ophelia, Cordelia and Miranda; their mothers are never mentioned in their plays. Perhaps from lack of familiarity with the other sex she has been "opposed to marriage" when approached by the "wealthy curled darlings of our nation". So, when the two meet, each recognises a kindred spirit in the other.

(ii)

At the opposite pole are those who regard openness as childish, whose minds are ruled solely by self-interest, are quite ready to be evasive or deceptive, are adept at concealing their purposes, and for whom conscience has little meaning:

> *Iago*   O villainous! I ha' looked upon the world for four times seven years, and since I could distinguish between a benefit and an injury, I never found a man who knew how to love himself...why, the power, and corrigible authority of this, lies in our wills.
>
> (I,iii,311–326)

Anyone who elects to be devious must dissemble. Iago is a highly skilled actor who has long persuaded Othello of his openness and devotion to him; Othello repeatedly calls or refers to him as "honest Iago". He has convinced everyone around him, including Cassio and the Elders of Venice, that he is totally honest:

> *Iago*   ...three great ones of the city,
> In personal suit to make me his lieutenant
> Off-capped to him...
>
> (I,i,8–10)

Iago is too well aware that Othello lives openly:
> *Iago*   The Moor is of a free and open nature

That thinks men honest that but seem to be.

(I,iii,397–398)

The actor may occasionally find himself compelled to ad-lib; and Iago is quite confident of his ability to play by ear:

Iago If sanctimony, and a frail vow, be not too hard for my wits, and all the tribe of hell, thou shalt enjoy her...

(I,iii,355–359)

How old is Roderigo?

Iago Put money in thy purse, follow these wars; defeat thy favour with an usurp'd beard...
Thus do I ever make my fool [child] my purse,
For I mine own gained knowledge should profane
If I would time expend with such a snipe
But for my sport and profit.

(I,iii,340–2; 381–4)

From "usurp'd beard" he is an adolescent who has not yet acquired the experience he needs, for he "wastes himself out of means" (IV,ii,187) on the promise that he will enjoy Desdemona's love; moreover, he is hoping for her illicit love, and he even agrees to kill Cassio on Iago's behalf:

Roderigo I have no great devotion to the deed,
And yet he has given me satisfying reasons;
Yet 'tis but a man gone; forth, my sword, he dies.

(V,i,8–10)

Granted that he may be young enough to be easily gulled, is he still to be regarded as an innocent victim of Iago's machinations? He appears to have been intended as a warning to male adolescents who imagine that financial independence from possibly inherited wealth brings with it the ability to make judgments as competently as if they were ten to fifteen years older and truly independent adults.

Since Shakespeare's characters are so vivid because he could think himself into their skins and see them from their own standpoint, we must ask "Can anything be said in Iago's behalf? How does he see himself?"

Iago is not a sadist who takes pleasure in cruelty or malice for its own sake; however, he is calculating, acting only—as he says to Roderigo—by "permission of the will". He has already been enriching himself at the expense of the romantically-minded Roderigo and others before him. At the same time his "permission of the will" (I,iii,335) is "honest" advice offered paternally: "We must all learn to direct our lives with deliberation and self-control" though he well knows that the fuzzy-minded youth will not follow it. He is certainly not emotionless, for he has long been suffering from acute resentment and, more recently, from acute disappointment at being overlooked in the promotion stakes. His first attempt at revenge is the rousing of Brabantio to inform him of his daughter's elopement, for he knows that Brabantio will appeal to his fellow senators to have the marriage annulled and Othello at least expelled from Venice. When the scheme fails, he soon devises another.

He has created a 'perdurable' image of himself as honest and loyal, and has not been a mere sycophant, or Othello would surely have seen through him. He could only have created his "image" by actually being an efficient soldier and a dedicated comrade-in-arms. When

he says:
> *Iago*   You shall mark
> Many a duteous and knee-crooking knave
> That, doting on his own obsequious bondage,
> Wears out his time much like his master's ass,
> For nought but provender, and when he's old, cashiered.
> Whip me such honest knaves...
>
> (I,i,44-49)

He is making a valid point, for if anyone after giving long and faithful service receives no reward or even acknowledgement, he feels that he is not respected and must take what steps he can to restore his self-respect.[34] He will resent the promotion of the "arithmetician" Cassio, if only because the successful soldier must be able to deploy some cunning, of which Iago possesses far more than Cassio. However, he cannot have been well-educated, for, as Cassio says to his face (II,i,165), he is too much the plain soldier, the rough diamond and too little of the "scholar" to be suitable for such a position as deputy to a General of Venice. He does not see himself as clearly as he needs to.

The appellation "honest Iago", which he hears far too often from everyone above him in social rank ("good ancient" and "good Iago" from Cassio—II,i,97), is indeed patronising and has long aroused acute resentment in him although he could never afford to let it show. Since Desdemona, who as daughter of a senator is much above him in social rank, also uses it, he does not hesitate to make use of her in his revenge.

Iago was not born into a wealthy family; otherwise he would not need to persuade young "fools" to put money in their purses. He did not learn the politer social forms and conventions of the wealthy. He would not always have been a calculating schemer, for he only embarks on revenge when Cassio's promotion comes as a slap in the face. Allowing him some warmth and humanity fills out his picture; he should be regarded not as a devilishly ingenious villain but rather as a man motivated by quite normal human feelings and subject to recognisable human failings. He is the Ancient, the senior N.C.O. or Warrant Officer who has impressed his C.O. by his hyper-efficient loyal service, expects to be promoted to officer's rank, and hopes, though wrongly, that his service and experience will outweigh his lack of formal education.

(iii)

Is Othello a Moor or a Black? Consideration of his ethnic origin must first establish the meaning of Moor to the Elizabethans.

Sir John Hawkins (1532–1595) was also the first Englishman to engage in the slave trade, buying his slaves from West African ports, sailing directly across the Atlantic on the trade winds, and selling them to the Spanish settlers in the New World. None of them would actually be seen in England because of the pointless long northward detour. The Elizabethans in London would have heard of them, also of the Moorish pirates who infested the Mediterranean; they would also know, if only from "Barbary horses", that the Moors had once occupied Spain, but how many black faces did they actually see?

The dictionaries define the Barbary States as Morocco, Algiers, Tunis, and Tripoli, which

---

34   "To plume up my will" (I,iii,384) combines two meanings: a) of a bird, to preen its feathers and restore its appearance and comfort; b) to plume oneself on (take pride in) an achievement.

occupied the western half of the south Mediterranean coast, with the Berbers as a group of North African tribes living in Barbary and the Sahara. Under "Berbers" the *Britannica* gives: "In regard to the ethnic variations of the Berbers, on the monuments of Egypt their ancestors are pictured with the comparatively blond features which many of them still display. Though considerable individual differences of type may be found in every village, the Berbers are distinctively a 'white' race". Moors are described as "a long-headed, fine-featured people of medium height with oval faces, hooked noses, and slender supple limbs, inhabiting Mauritania and the Northern Sudan".

If today we hear the word 'blacks', our usual mental picture is of African, West Indian or American blacks. Othello and Aaron in *Titus Andronicus* are Moors who are given Negroid features. Did the Elizabethans consider all black-faced types as Moors because they had seen too few to note their facial differences? That they did is suggested by the emergence by the end of the sixteenth century of "blackamoor" as the general term for dark-skinned people. Possibly Shakespeare himself had seen too few dark faces, and in describing Aaron and Othello as Negro-Moors was relying on the common impression rather than actual observation.

Since Othello's career has led him into the service of a city-state of the North Mediterranean (he has spent "till nine moons wasted" (I,iii,84) in his rise to his present position), and since Iago calls him a "Barbary horse" (I,i,111), he will hail from a Barbary State on the South Mediterranean coast, and might be a Muslim. Or, as Iago hints (IV,ii,224) he might hail from Mauritania, which may explain his black skin and thick lips: since Mauritania lies much nearer Central Africa than the Barbary States, he may be of mixed Moorish-Negro blood.

As for his trust in Iago, it is too easy to say merely that he is too trusting without inquiring "Why is he so trusting?" It seems, in fact, that he trusts Iago to the point of naïveté, although as Commander-in-Chief of the Armed Forces of Venice he would hardly be as simple-minded as he appears. Iago has cultivated his intimacy in the hope of being promoted to the lieutenancy, and his comradeship in war may have helped Othello to feel that he is accepted by at least someone in a white society, in particular because Iago is widely accepted as "honest".

We might infer another reason why Othello should be so trusting. Compelled to survive alone from such an early age, he would soon realise that he would be given food and shelter more readily if he was always candid and truthful with anyone whom he might ask. Later in his career he would learn that if an officer is to win the confidence of his men, he must be open and candid, a point emphasised by another personage in the play:

Montano If partially affin'd, or leagu'd in office,
  Thou dost deliver more or less than truth,
  Thou art no soldier.

(II,iii,209–211)

He might have been inclined by temperament to be open, and would therefore be happiest in the company of other open types, though it is also possible that he spent his earliest years in a family atmosphere in which openness was the rule. He would then be delighted beyond measure when a girl who was not only beautiful and virtuous but as open as himself consented to marry him.

(iv)

As Othello is regarded as a tragedy of jealousy, what are the meanings of 'jealousy'? In the dictionaries, a first meaning is usually 'the feeling of resentment against a successful rival or at success'. This definition, almost synonymous with 'envy', makes Iago the jealous character in the play, since he certainly envies Cassio's promotion to the lieutenancy, and eventually revenges himself on Cassio as well as Othello. He professes to suspect that "twixt my sheets [Othello's] done my office" (I,iii,385–6) and even to "fear Cassio with my nightcap too", but these are the kind of excuse which some minds justify their malice to themselves, particularly those who read the worst motives into others' actions because they themselves are habitually devious. When Emilia tells Desdemona that she would think little of being unfaithful to her husband if her infidelity would advance his career, there is no suggestion in the play that she actually has been unfaithful to him.

Another meaning is 'troubled by fears or suspicions of rivalry, as in matters of love'; and Othello is persuaded by Iago that Desdemona is being unfaithful to him. Is his reaction merely jealousy in this sense?

Othello Avaunt, begone, thou hast set me on the rack.
　I swear, 'tis better to be much abused
　Than but to know't a little.
Iago　　　　　　　　　　　　　　How now, my lord?
Othello What sense had I of her stol'n hours of lust?
　I saw't not, thought it not, it harmed not me,
　I slept the next night well, was free and merry;
　I found not Cassio's kisses on her lips;
　He that is robbed, not wanting what is stol'n,
　Let him not know't, and he's not robbed at all.
Iago I am sorry to hear this.
Othello I had been happy if the general camp,
　Pioners, and all, had tasted her sweet body,
　So I had nothing known.
　　　　　　　　　　　　　　　　　　　　　　(III,iii,341–353)

If Othello can say this, he is not overcome by the obsessive, inflamed imagination and physical jealousy of Ford in *The Merry Wives of Windsor* and Leontes in *The Winter's Tale*, or the total misogyny of Posthumus in *Cymbeline*. He is suffering from something else.

Anyone who has been in the Armed Forces will know that whenever the soldier is given leave, he hopes to be able to go home, for home is the familiar place where he had received love, sustenance and encouragement from his earliest years, where he can relax and draw new strength and reassurance from his roots. Christmas, the traditional season for family gatherings, could be the least welcome time to be on leave by oneself and unable to go home i.e. to realise, if one did not already know it, that there is indeed no place like home.

When Othello first met Desdemona's father Brabantio, he was then invited to his house, where he described his adventures since his seventh year. Desdemona "did seriously incline" to hear his stories of disastrous chances, hairbreadth escapes and wondrous sights. First she pitied him and then, being a woman whose first task in life is to become the homemaker and central pillar of her family, she realised that he had had no home since he was seven, and decided that she would become that central pillar, i.e. create the anchorage which had been lacking in his life for so many years.

He trusts Iago because Iago has long been a faithful comrade-in-arms. He has not realised that there is a core of cunning in Iago, a core which is intolerably piqued by Othello's passing over him when he chooses Cassio as lieutenant and leaves Iago as his "ancient". When Iago convinces him that Desdemona is being unfaithful to him, and that the haven which had become his dearest hope is an empty shell, all his great achievements in war become equally empty for him:

Othello   O, now for ever
>Farewell the tranquil mind, farewell content,
>Farewell the plumed troop, and the big wars,
>That makes ambition virtue: O farewell,
>Farewell the neighing steed, and the shrill trump,
>The spirit-stirring drum, the ear-piercing fife,
>The royal banner, and all quality,
>Pride, pomp, and circumstance of glorious war!
>And, O ye mortal engines, whose wide throats
>The immortal Jove's great clamour counterfeit,
>Farewell: Othello's occupation's gone!
>
>(III,iii,353–363)

By "occupation" he means his preoccupation, the silent hope during his years of war and wandering, that he might at last find an anchorage in life with a wife of his own temperament and outlook. Those years are now "gone", wasted.

No less extreme than his earlier delight in his marriage is his devastation when his new happiness is undermined:

Othello If she be false, O, then Heaven mocks itself,
>I'll not believe it...
>...If thou dost slander her, and torture me,
>Never pray more, abandon all remorse,
>On horror's head horrors accumulate;
>Do deeds to make heaven weep, all earth amaz'd,
>For nothing canst thou to damnation add
>Greater than that.
>
>(III,iii,282–3 and 374–379)

At one point he even loses both mental and physical control:

Othello Lie with her, lie on her?—We say lie on her, when they belie her,—lie with her, zounds, that's fulsome! Handkerchief—confessions—handkerchief! To confess and be hanged for his labour. First to be hanged, and then to confess; I tremble at it, Nature would not invest herself in such shadowing passion without some instruction. It is not words that shake me thus. Pish! Noses, ears, and lips. Is't possible?—Confess?—Handkerchief? O devil! (He falls down)

(IV,i,35–43)

To Desdemona he says:

Othello   Had it pleased heaven
>To try me with affliction, had he rained
>All kinds of sores and shames on my bare head,
>Steep'd me in poverty, to the very lips,
>Given to captivity me and my very hopes,
>I should have found in some part of my soul
>A drop of patience; but, alas to make me

> A fixed figure, for the time of scorn
> To point his slow unmoving fingers at... oh, oh.
> Yet could I bear that too, well, very well:
> But there, where I have garnered up my heart,
> Where either I must live, or bear no life,
> The fountain, from the which my current runs,
> Or else dries up, to be discarded thence,
> Or keep it as a cistern, for foul toads
> To knot and gender in!
>
> (IV,ii,48–63)

Believing that she has inflicted on him a double destruction of the anchorage "Where either I must live, or bear no life", he resolves to kill her, then himself:

Othello Put out the light, and then put out the light...

—but significantly, not first his supposed cuckolder Cassio, as another husband might although he urges Iago to kill Cassio.

> *Othello* Within these three days, let me hear thee say
>   That Cassio's not alive.
> *Iago*   My friend is dead.
>   'Tis done at your request,
>   but let her live.
> *Othello*   Damn her, lewd minx: O damn her!
>   Come. Go with me apart, I will withdraw
>   To furnish me with some swift means of death
>   For the fair devil...
>
> (III,iii,479–485)

Othello is suffering from acute disillusionment and disappointment rather than physical jealousy; his rage is mainly directed against Desdemona, the betrayer of his hope.

Thus far, this interpretation of Othello is partly inferential, though without such conjecture it must be accepted either that his early delight and later devastation are the signs of an acute and long-unsatisfied need; that his marriage to Desdemona has satisfied that need to an extraordinary degree; or that a Generalissimo of Venice is prone to swings of emotion as uncontrollable as those of a child. Generals do not suffer from such swings because they must not, and Othello cannot normally be prone to them. His crowd scenes, first in Venice and then Cyprus, display him as possessing the natural presence and authority which must stem from complete self-command. In Venice he calms the situation with a touch of humour: "Keep up your bright swords, for the dew will rust 'em"—both a little joke and an order from a general. In Cyprus he at once assumes control by threatening to lose his temper: "Now by heaven / My blood begins my safer guides to rule": in effect, another order.

Why, then, does his early delight in Desdemona turn to such rage that he decides to kill her?

(v)

What will be Othello's emotions as he puts out his own light, when he realises that he has "murdered innocence", and that his own "innocence" has led him into doing what he has done?

Othello   An honourable murderer, if you will;
For nought did I in hate, but all in honour.

(V,ii,295–6)

Of course, it is not Othello but Iago who "murders innocence". Does he really understand that he is murdering something more than the happiness of a middle-aged husband in his marriage to a young, beautiful and virtuous wife? Othello describes him as "knows all qualities" (III,iii,263). How deep is his penetration of human motives? He will not accept that he himself is too much the plain soldier. He certainly displays complete understanding of both his General's "quality", to the point where Othello's faith in him has become absolute; and of Cassio's, for Cassio has also accepted him as totally honest and proves to be no wiser. Still, he calls Desdemona a "super-subtle Venetian" (I,iii,357) although she is the reverse of super-subtle. As for Emilia, his exchanges with her (II,i and V,II) do not suggest that he has ever seen her as a haven, and he fails to anticipate that, dedicated as she is to her mistress, she will reveal the true history of the handkerchief. If he knew that he was destroying what to him is a "haven", he would surely hint as much, but nowhere in the play does he do so.

(vi)

If all good plays should cause the audience to leave the theatre feeling thoughtful, they should embody or illustrate a message of some kind; what was Shakespeare's message in Othello? Iago is the principal character in the play who is given more lines than any other, is introduced at length in its first scene, and thereafter becomes the instigator and manipulator of its events; the play's main message might be simply that villains will eventually meet with "poetick justice". However, concluding that this alone would have been far too simple a message for Shakespeare the penetrating psychologist, I read another into it: that a good marriage should be seen as a haven by both parties, in the ideal case as a lifetime's haven, and that it is most likely to become so if both are completely open and truthful with one another. (When deciding to dramatise the story of Othello, did Shakespeare remember lines from his Sonnet 66 "simple truth miscalled simplicity" and Sonnet 116 "Let me not to the marriage of true minds / Admit impediments"?)[35].

Another interpretation might be: Shakespeare created two extremely open characters in order to satirise or at least point out the dangers of complete openness and candour; this is an unacceptable alternative. Shakespeare chose a plot pivoting on a marriage which is most unusual in that it is a not only a mixed-race marriage, but a mixed-age marriage, the husband being in late middle-age and the wife still young and also, as will be shown, a mixed-religion marriage. Further, before meeting her, he has apparently been content with his long bachelor's life and she, according to her father, has not been attracted to any previous suitors; both very soon see that although its circumstances are exceptional, it will be a "marriage of true minds", in which perhaps happiness in the marriage-bed will not be an especially important factor.

What exactly, then, was Shakespeare's tragic intention? Is it correct to think of it as a tragic lesson? At the end of *Hamlet* we the audience were intended to leave the theatre very regretful for the loss of an admirable young man; on leaving *Othello* were we again intended to be moved merely by the pathos of its ending? While tragic endings to plays are often the effect of character defects in the principals, is it fair to Othello or Desdemona to label the character defect which leads to their deaths as their 'openness'?

---

35   The Sonnets are thought to have been mainly written before Othello.

(vii)
Othello—Some Apparent Loose Ends

There are two brief scenes in which there is a little dead-pan humour and whose dramatic purpose is unclear: III,i, in which the Musicians enter (probably a conventional musical entr'acte such as the Witches' dance in Macbeth), and III,iv in which the Clown exasperates Desdemona. What was the purpose of the latter? It might have been an attempt to introduce the 'zero level' of emotion, as in the Graveyard scene in *Hamlet* and the entry of the Clown in *Antony and Cleopatra*, but is too short, and in any case would have been much more effective if introduced as an interruption nearer or during the final catastrophe.

Probably this was the purpose of the matter-of-fact conversation between Desdemona and Emilia in IV,iii, in which she asks Emilia whether she would be unfaithful to her husband if she could thereby advance her husband's career, a dumb premonition that she herself will be accused of infidelity. There are other premonitions in Shakespeare, such as those already mentioned in *Hamlet*. It is unlikely that Shakespeare would have introduced them if he had not accepted that they were true to life.

Again, what is the dramatic purpose of Cassio's mistress Bianca who, incidentally, seems to be a Cypriot rather than a Venetian? She is a pathetic figure, a woman who is alone in the world, has no fortune or dowry, and is compelled to exist as best she can. She makes clear that Cassio is by no means as deserving of sympathy as Desdemona supposes; otherwise she makes no contribution to the action. In IV,i Iago introduces her as a topic of conversation with Cassio while Othello listens outside. When he asks whether Cassio intends to marry her, Cassio roars with laughter. Would not this reveal enough of Cassio without the need to introduce Bianca herself? Was she intended to arouse sympathy for such women?

An apparent inconsistency in the time sequence of events is the long interval in the middle of the play when Othello and Desdemona sail to Cyprus. Since they sail separately—their nuptial rite not being consummated until he re-joins her in Cyprus—the sea voyage has no effect on the progress of their relationship.

More to the point is: why did Shakespeare change the location from Venice to Cyprus? The answer: to introduce the situation in which Cassio loses his lieutenancy.

On arriving in Cyprus, Othello proclaims that the whole island should join in his celebrations; since Cyprus lies much nearer Turkey than Venice and the Turk remains a threat, the island must remain under military guard, with Cassio as lieutenant in command of it. His becoming somewhat drunk on duty is then a serious breach of military discipline which justifies his dismissal.

Though this seems an unnecessary artificiality in the plot, it is not easy to see how else it could have been done. Shakespeare may have been using a topical situation since the Turk remained a threat in the eastern Mediterranean, even after the Christian naval victory of Lepanto in 1571.

In II,i there is a brief conversation between Iago and Desdemona in which she asks "What wouldst thou write of me, if thou shouldst praise me?", and he replies that "my invention / Comes from my brain as birdlime does from frieze", but then delivers an extempore succession of perfectly phrased rhyming couplets. Why was this passage inserted? To suggest that his resentment is justified because he is much more of a scholar than Othello and Cassio see him? Or to imply that he has overdone his performance as the "honest" and faithful Ancient? Or simply to impress audiences with some rhymed poetry, as the earlier passages in I,iii,202–219 may have been (and in other plays also)?

On first readings, the most prominent loose ends seem to be the play's apparent failure

to provide clear answers to three questions:
1) Exactly why has total openness apparently become such an acute need in Othello's life that his marriage must be one in which "Either I must live, or bear no life", and that his ready acceptance of Iago's insinuations make him appear surprisingly simple-minded for a general? Why is he so ready to accept them? Is he swayed by memories of his own previous sex life? Or is there a factor in the make-up of some husbands which makes them unusually susceptible to suspicion of their wives? (Was this the intended message of *The Merry Wives*, *Othello*, and *The Winter's Tale*?) Is Othello a 'noble savage' who has become a great fighter without progressing beyond the emotional age of a boy?
2) Whose tragedy is it—apparently Desdemona's more than his?
3) If the dramatist must have formulated his dramatic intention before beginning to write, what was Shakespeare's? The protagonists in the later tragedies of *Macbeth, Lear, Antony and Cleopatra,* and *Coriolanus*, deserve their fates, but can Othello and Desdemona really be labelled 'culpable'?

(viii)

In November 1600 John Pory published his translation of John Leo's "A Geographical Historie of Africa" which, said Geoffrey Bullough, "Shakespeare almost certainly consulted" (Bullough, 208). Pory's dedication referred to the Moorish ambassador's presence in London. Leo, a Moor brought up in Barbary, wrote at length about his countrymen:

> Most honest people they are, and destitute of all fraud and guile, very proud and high-minded, and wonderfully addicted vnto wrath...Their wits are but meane, and they are so credulous, that they will beleeve matters impossible, which are told them *[—like Othello?]* ...No nation in the world is so subject vnto iealousie, for they will rather leese [lose] their liues, then put up any disgrace in the behalfe of their women.

Contrary to popular belief, other black men had "crept into the realm" in sufficient numbers to be designated a problem: re. 1601 Negroes and Blackamoors.

> —Whereas the Queen's Majesty is discontented at the great number of 'negars and blackamoores' which are crept into the realm since the troubles between her Highness and the King of Spain, and are fostered here to the annoyance of her own people...In order to discharge them out of this country, her Majesty hath appointed Caspar Van Zeuden, merchant of Lubeck, for their transportation... This is to require you to assist him to collect such negroes and blackamoors for this purpose.
>
> Quoted in the intron. to the *Arden* third edition

If it is accepted that Shakespeare's audiences had become familiar with both the faces and the minds behind the faces of the Moors in London, these extracts go far towards answering the above questions, provide the key to the character of Othello, and justify insistence on honesty as a prime motif in the play.

In the Koran, truth has two meanings, the second derived from the first and merging into it: the truth of the Islamic religion as revealed through Mohammed and other prophets; and truthfulness in all one's dealings with one's fellow humans:

<u>Surah 2,42</u>: Confound not truth with falsehood, nor knowingly conceal the truth.

Surah 3,95 and 168: Say, Allah speaketh truth. Follow the religion of Abraham, the upright. Avert death from yourselves if ye are truthful.

Surah 4,135: Be ye staunch in justice, witnesses for Allah, even though it be against yourselves or your kindred.

> "My son! Honesty guards [both] the faith and the worldly affairs of man. Be honest so that you may be always free from want...I recommend two things to you: one of them is truthfulness and the other is honesty, for these two are the key to sustenance"
>
> Imam al Sadiq, prophet

These injunctions explain the apparent simple-mindedness of the Moors in London: having been brought up to speak only the truth and having lived only among others who spoke the truth, they would easily fall victim to self-styled humorists who amused themselves by testing their credulity with "matters impossible".

They also explain Othello's too-ready acceptance of Iago's slanders on Desdemona, since he must have been brought up as a Muslim during his first seven years, i.e. the child's formative years when early impressions may register so deeply as to become ineradicable. That total truthfulness has long been his guiding principle is suggested by an early phrase:

Iago   These are the raised father and his friends;
     You were best go in.
Othello   Not I, I must be found.
     My parts, my title, and my perfect soul
     Shall manifest me rightly.

(I,ii,30–32)

Of women the Koran says:

> Surah 4, 34 and 19: Men are in charge of women, because Allah hath made the one of them to excel the other and because they spend of their property (for the support of women). Consort with them in kindness.

Of "lewdness" in women, it says:

> Surah 4, 15: As for those of your women who are guilty of lewdness, call to witness four of you against them. And if they testify (to the truth of the allegation) then confine them to houses until death takes them.
> The adulterer and the adulteress, scourge ye each one of them with a hundred stripes...And those who accuse honourable women but bring not four witnesses, scourge them with eighty stripes and never (afterward) accept their testimony.
>
> Surah 24, 2,4,6,7: As for those who accuse their wives but have no witnesses except themselves; let the testimony of one of them be four [repeated] testimonies, (swearing) by Allah that he is one of those who speak the truth. And yet a fifth [time], invoking the curse of Allah on himself if he is of those who lie.

At the same time, the Koran nowhere stipulates death as the punishment for "lewdness"; why, then, does Othello decide on it?

The answer is suggested by his opening lines in the play's last scene:
Othello It is the cause, it is the cause, my soul,
   Let me not name it to you, you chaste stars...
   A balmy breath, that doth almost persuade
   Justice herself to break her sword...

(V,ii,1–4)

By "cause" he must mean the integrity of the Muslim requirement of truthfulness, of which Desdemona's infidelity is the worst possible betrayal. He believes that he is acting in the cause of justice, and has already hinted as much:
Iago Do it not with poison, strangle her in her bed, even the bed she hath contaminated.
Othello Good, good, the justice of it pleases me.

IV,i,203–5)

Earlier, he has said:
Othello I'll see before I doubt, when I doubt, prove,
   And on the proof, there is no more but this:
   Away at once with love and jealousy!

(III,iii 194–6)

Has he really eliminated sexual jealousy from his mind to the extent that he can appoint himself both judge and executioner? Is he really as completely impersonal and impartial as he believes? Why does he reject Desdemona's protestations of innocence? Why does he not remember that he had only married her because he had found her to be as open as he could wish a wife to be, and balance her openness against Iago's "honesty"? Granted that he may have dedicated himself to a lifetime of truthfulness, could he be deluding himself? Is he really one of those souls who, as Emilia says, are "jealous for they are jealous"? If he is not, the only alternative is that his childhood's training in truthfulness and his experience of it in his home were so thorough and permanent as to inhibit the development of a critical sense, thus leaving him unable to compare his own early upbringing with any other, even Desdemona's.

It seems that Muslims are required to be much more pious than Christians, for while the good Christian should go to church at least once a week, the Muslim is required not merely to go to mosque once a week, but to pray to Allah five times a day,[36] kneeling on the ground facing towards Mecca and bowing to touch his forehead on the ground. He must constantly remind himself to submit to the will of Allah, who is kind and merciful to believers. This practice cheers and relaxes him.[37] Evidently the Prophet Mohammed realised that once a week is by no means enough, for the intervening six days allow far too much time for temptation to creep in. This supports the deduction that Othello received so thorough a training in the Muslim cause during his first seven years that the ancient Greek saying "Moderation in all things" plays too small a part in his thinking. His soul is too 'perfect'.

Iago's understanding of his general's religion is remarkable, for he knows that to destroy Othello's happiness in his marriage and perhaps cause him to be executed for killing Desdemona, he only needs to mention—always very hesitantly—Cassio's frequent calls on

---

36   So said the young man in a Muslim Information shop in London, adding, "Out in the street if necessary".

37   The author has long had Muslim neighbours whom he respects highly.

her, and to insert little oblique sexual references and never direct accusations, which will instantly inflame Othello:

Iago   Good my lord, pardon me;
>Though I am bound to every act of duty,
>I am not bound to all that slaves are free to;
>Utter my thoughts? Why, say they are vile and false;
>As where's that palace, where into foul things
>Sometimes intrude not? ...
>
>   ...O beware of jealousy;
>It is the green-eyed monster...
>I know our country disposition well...
>Were they as prime as goats, as hot as monkeys...

(III,iii,137ff.)

In IV,i, Othello reads a letter, strikes Desdemona, angrily sends her out, then speaks to Lodovico:

Othello   Cassio shall have my place, and, sir, tonight
>I do entreat that we may sup together.
>You are welcome, sir, to Cyprus.
>*[His obsessed state now appears in an exploded 'aside'.]*
>   Goats and monkeys!!

(IV,i,257–259)

Iago also knows that to convince Othello of the truth of his insinuations he must meet the Koranic requirement of swearing an oath. It must be a very careful oath, for he does not swear to the truth of his allegations against Desdemona and Cassio, whom he does not mention; he merely reaffirms his total loyalty to Othello:

Othello [He has knelt]   Now by yon marbled heaven,
>In the due reverence of a sacred vow,
>I here engage my words. *(Iago kneels.)*

Iago   Do not rise yet.
>Witness, you ever burning lights above,
>You elements that clip us round about,
>Witness that here Iago does give up
>The excellency of his wit, hand, heart,
>To wrong'd Othello's service; let him command,
>And to obey shall be in me remorse,
>What bloody work so ever.

(III,iii,467–476)

(ix)

Honour killings have long been a feature of the Muslim world:
>Amman: Queen Noor of Jordan has backed a campaign to fight honour killings, the formerly taboo subject of the murders of women in the Arab world for alleged sexual impropriety that claim hundreds of lives every year...
>
>In Jordan alone, a country of 4.6 million people, at least 25 to 30 women are killed annually because of alleged immorality. That represents a quarter of all

murders in the country. Male relations, encouraged by lax laws that can enable them to escape with little or no penalty, take the lives of these women because of their involvement—or alleged involvement—in affairs.

The Times (21 Jan 1999)

"Alleged involvement" suggests that some of these honour killings are committed not on hard evidence but on suspicion only, as is Othello's case.

Since Shakespeare gave him the line "For nought did I in hate, but all in honour" (V,ii,296), the phrase "honour killings" must already have become current in London during his lifetime.

Before the Middle Ages the Moors had overrun Spain and even crossed the Pyrenees and invaded Narbonne, until they were defeated by Charles Martel at Poitiers in 732 A.D.. During the next 700 years Spain was gradually reconquered by Christian forces and eventually united under a single Christian king, and most of the remaining Moors, now called Moriscos, had been driven southward into Granada. Since the Turks, another Islamic nation, remained powerful in the Mediterranean, in 1567 the Moriscos were ordered to desist from their Muslim practices and adopt Christianity. When they refused, there followed over three years of bitter rebellion and bloodshed, at the end of which they were resettled in Northern Spain. There they were only allowed to inhabit houses flanked by Christians' houses. Emigration probably began a few years later, one haven being to London, where Elizabeth I's policy was of total religious tolerance since she desperately needed powerful Islamic allies and revenue.

Topical or contemporary elements in plays give them immediacy to their audiences, and it seems certain that there were mixed-religion marriages in London between the immigrant Moors and English girls, some of whom had been terminated by honour killings, i.e. that honour killings had become a topical theme which would be immediately recognisable to the play's early audiences. Would Shakespeare have made such an un-English theme the centrepiece of his tragedy if it had not become at least moderately familiar to his audiences? Why else would he have chosen it but to illustrate and explain the motivation behind such killings? Why did the late 17th century critic Thomas Rymer (1641–1713) describe the play as "a caution to all Maidens of Quality how, without their Parents consent, they run away with Blackamoors"?

This thought answers the question "What kind of tragedy was Othello intended to be?" Not a "tragedy of character" but simply a tragedy caused by the contrasting religious backgrounds of husband and wife, though none the less an intensely poetic and moving tragedy. Desdemona is indeed the beautiful and dedicated wife and Othello the noble Moor.

Notes:
1) If you are a reader of Shakespeare you will sooner or later encounter every kind of person you would ever meet (my own paraphrase of some other readers).

In peace-time, life in the Forces is usually quiet. On the outbreak of a war, however, their increase in number provides the Regulars with opportunities for promotion. During the first part of my WW II service I briefly met two Regular airmen who had become senior N.C.O.'s, working hard and conscientiously in responsible positions in the hope of eventual promotion to officer-rank.

So, having met him twice (and there would have been many others), I do not see Iago as such an unusual figure except, perhaps, in the completeness of his understanding of his

General's religion! In any case, he has a half-brother, Ancient Pistol in *King Henry V*, who always talks in excessively noble language ("Trailst thou the puissant pike?") in order to appear educated and patronise his associates, i.e. to suggest that he comes from higher up the social ladder, until Fluellen deflates him. Pistol patronises, Iago resents being patronised; their attitudes stem from the same awareness of a limited educational background.

During that war there was much resentment of the fact that only the young men who had received a good education were commissioned. However, it was silent resentment, for overt resentment would have helped no one. It eventually found expression in the result of the first British general election after WW II, a Labour-Socialist landslide.

2) "A stable relationship is almost the most important contributor to quality of life in terms of physical, social and psychological aspects," says Professor John Collings, a psychologist. "In surveys of life fulfilment, people rate being in a stable relationship highly, above having health, money, and adequate housing."

He adds, "Self-esteem comes mainly from interaction with others, and the most important factor seems to be having a partnership of equals, where each tells the other how attractive they are. A person without a partner cannot get to the same heights in terms of self-worth.

> What takes people higher seems to be the more intimate verbal and non-verbal signals in a stable and quite deep relationship. It's a mind-to-mind relationship, not necessarily romantic love, but love between people who are very, very close... Sex...comes much lower down the scale than one would imagine.
>
> John Naish "Marriage Becomes Him" in *The Times* (10 Oct 1998)

Are we now rediscovering something which was known to Shakespeare four centuries ago, and perhaps very much earlier: "It is not good that the man should be alone" (Genesis,ii,18), but now forgotten? Of the 285 entries under "Marriage" in a dictionary of quotations, only five—one being the earlier quoted lines from Sonnet 116—recognise mutual openness as one of the keys to a good married life.

3) An English teacher who taught both *Hamlet* and *Othello* said that her pupils always found the former play much more interesting than the latter. Two possible reasons are: that *Othello* contains fewer psychological subtleties than *Hamlet*; and that it is too explicit, for, as does Gloster in *Richard III*, Iago announces his intentions at the beginning of the play, after which the spectators merely sit and watch him carry them out. In *Hamlet*, all the major events of the plot from Hamlet's lunacy to the fencing match would come to Shakespeare's theatregoers as unpredictable surprises. I find that to the reader—even though he is familiar with it—the play comes more alive if, on re-reading, he visualises such incidents as coming suddenly upon its early audiences and, in conformity with Lope da Vega's principle "Always trick expectancy". Othello does not trick it so often as Hamlet.

30

THE CHARACTER OF MACBETH

Macbeth is the tragedy of an eminent man who has never been in the habit of examining his own motives, has never made the conscious choice between a moral and an immoral or criminal life, and is therefore not as self-aware as he needs to be. When, at a crucial moment in his life, he at last begins to examine himself, he is just a little too slow and a little too late.

A valiant leader in battle and an efficient general, he has long been accustomed to assessing situations and arriving at decisions swiftly; his abilities have brought him commendation and reward. Yet in his preoccupation with success he has never paused to reflect on the kind of man he really is, the kind of life he really wants, and the price he would be prepared to pay for success in his ambitions.

Evidently he is unacquainted with Polonius' advice, "Give thy thoughts no tongue, / Nor any unproportioned thought his act". While the obvious corollary to it is "Let not thy mien betray thine inmost thoughts", he soon reveals both his proneness to unproportioned thoughts and his inability to conceal them when they come into his mind:

1 Witch All hail, Macbeth! hail to thee, Thane of Glamis!
2 Witch All hail, Macbeth! hail to thee, Thane of Cawdor!
3 Witch All hail, Macbeth! that shalt be King hereafter.
Banquo Good sir, why do you start, and seem to fear
  Things that do sound so fair?
[To the Witches]
                          I'th'name of truth,
  Are ye fantastical, or that indeed
  Which outwardly ye show? My noble partner
  You greet with present grace, and great prediction
  Of noble having, and of royal hope,
  That he seems rapt withal.

                                             (I,iii,47–57)

On hearing that he is indeed the Thane of Cawdor as well as Glamis, he becomes even more rapt:

Macbeth [Aside]... Glamis, and Thane of Cawdor:
  The greatest is behind. *[To Rosse and Angus]* Thanks for your pains.
  [To Banquo] Do you not hope your children shall be kings,
  When those that gave the Thane of Cawdor to me
  Promised no less to them?
Banquo   That, trusted home,
  Might yet enkindle you unto the crown,
  Besides the Thane of Cawdor. But 'tis strange:
  And oftentimes, to win us to our harm,
  The instruments of darkness tell us truths,
  Win us with honest trifles, to betray's
  In deepest consequence—
  Cousins, a word, I pray you.

> *Macbeth [Aside]*   Two truths are told,
>   As happy prologues to the swelling act
>   Of the imperial theme. *[Aloud]* I thank you, gentlemen.
>   *[Aside]* This supernatural soliciting
>   Cannot be ill, cannot be good: if ill,
>   Why hath it given me earnest of success,
>   Commencing in a truth? I am Thane of Cawdor;
>   If good, why do I yield to that suggestion
>   Whose horrid image doth unfix my hair,
>   And make my seated heart knock at my ribs,
>   Against the use of nature? Present fears
>   Are less than horrible imaginings.
>   My thought, whose murther yet is but fantastical,
>   Shakes so my single state of man,
>   That function is smother'd in surmise,
>   And nothing is, but what is not.
> *Banquo* Look, how our partner's rapt.
>
>   (I,iii,116–143)

Banquo has instantly begun to suspect the cause of Macbeth's raptness, that the Witches' prophecies have induced in him unproportioned thoughts, and warns him; the behaviour of Macbeth's heart should be another warning He will in fact receive further warnings, the last immediately before he commits his murder, though all will go unheeded.

In I,iv, Macbeth learns that Duncan has appointed his son Malcolm to be his successor:

> *Macbeth [Aside]* The Prince of Cumberland! that is a step
>   On which I must fall down, or else o'erleap,
>   For in my way it lies. Stars, hide your fires;
>   Let not light see my black and deep desires;
>   The eye wink at the hand; yet let that be
>   Which the eye fears, when it is done, to see.
>
>   (I,iv,48–53)

This speech is plain self-deception; it reveals how little he knows himself.

In the next scene, when Lady Macbeth receives his letter, she speaks of "the milk of human kindness" which is in him, and says, "What thou wouldst highly, / That wouldst thou holily", lines which suggest that he has a conscience; how, then, can his desires have become so deep and black so soon after his encounter with the Witches? Has he really succumbed to their temptations as rapidly as that? When did the notion that he might become king arise in his mind? Or was it implanted?

She knows not only that he will need managing but that she can manage him:

> *Lady M.*   Hie thee hither,
>   That I may pour my spirits in thine ear,
>   And chastise with the valour of my tongue
>   All that impedes thee from the golden round
>   Which fate and metaphysical aid doth seem
>   To have thee crowned withal.
>
>   (I,v,25–30)

His wife also knows that he cannot conceal his unproportioned thoughts:

Lady M. Your face, my Thane, is as a book where men
May read strange matters. To beguile the time,
Look like the time; bear welcome in your eye,
Your hand, your tongue; look like the innocent flower,
But be the serpent under't.

(I,v,62–66)

If there is an outstanding trait in Macbeth's make-up, it is his suggestibility. If we are to live in harmony with our fellow humans, we must make a deliberate and conscious choice to live morally; if as criminals, the opposite choice. Now in a high position Macbeth should have made the choice long ago but he has not; otherwise the Witches' prophecies would leave him no more rapt than Banquo (who is contrasted with him), nor would Lady Macbeth speak of her husband as she does. He is wide open to suggestion; and his suggestibility reappears at later moments to the very end of the play.

In I,vi, Duncan and his retinue arrive before Macbeth's castle. One purpose of this scene has been pointed out: to suggest that Macbeth has no need to be as ambitious as he is, since he has won his monarch's favour ("I have begun to plant thee"—I,iv,28), has apparently married an ideal wife, and lives in a most pleasantly situated castle. This also further illustrates both Macbeth's inability to control his thoughts and the degree to which he is dependent on his wife:

Duncan This castle hath a pleasant seat; the air
Nimbly and sweetly recommends itself
Unto our gentle senses.
Banquo This guest of summer,
The temple-haunting martlet, does approve
By his loved mansionry, that the heaven's breath
Smells wooingly here; no jutty, frieze,
Buttress, nor coign of vantage, but this bird
Hath made his pendent bed and procreant cradle:
Where they most breed and haunt, I have observed
The air is delicate.

(I.vi,1–10)

House martins usually build their clay nests on the sheltered side of buildings, under projections such as eaves. In summer the winds in Scotland often come from northwest to southwest, hence this delightful description tells us that Duncan and Banquo are looking at the east or southeast side of Macbeth's castle. We also gather that Banquo is less dominated by ambition than Macbeth, since he apparently spends some of his leisure hours observing nature or, from "temple-haunting", reading the classics:

[Enter Lady Macbeth.]
Duncan See, see! our honoured hostess.—
The love that follows us sometime is our trouble,
Which still we thank as love. Herein I teach you,
How you shall bid God 'ild us for your pains,
And thank us for your trouble.
Lady M. All our service,
In every point twice done, and then done double,

>   Were poor and single business, to contend
>   Against those honours deep and broad, wherewith
>   Your Majesty loads our house: for those of old,
>   And the late dignities heaped up to them,
>   We rest your hermits.
> *Duncan*   Where's the Thane of Cawdor?
>   We cours'd him at the heels, and had a purpose
>   To be his purveyor: but he rides well,
>   And his great love, sharp as his spur, hath holp him
>   To his home before us. Fair and noble hostess,
>   We are your guest tonight.
>
>   (I,vi,10–25)

Where indeed is Macbeth? As host and master of his house, and particularly after being honoured by the gift of the Thaneship of Cawdor, he should certainly have emerged in person to welcome his royal benefactor, but troublesome thoughts have evidently rendered him so incapable of bearing welcome in his eye that his wife has ordered him to remain indoors while *she* greets Duncan. She will have pointed out that he will now have the perfect opportunity to attain their ambition, and the thought has been too much for him.

Duncan's question is unexpected; unable to find a plausible excuse for her husband, Lady Macbeth can only repeat her protestation of service and loyalty:

> *Lady M.*   Your servants ever
>   Have theirs, themselves, and what is theirs, in compt
>   To make their audit at your Highness' pleasure,
>   Still to return your own.
> *Duncan*   Give me your hand,
>   Conduct me to mine host; we love him highly,
>   And shall continue our graces towards him.
>   By your leave, hostess.
>
>   (I,vi,25–31)

And Duncan, a little puzzled but unsuspecting, must be content.

Macbeth later confirms an impression of Banquo which his description of the house-martins suggests:

> *Macbeth*   Here had we now our country's honour roof'd,
>   Were the grac'd person of our Banquo present.
>
>   (III,iv,39–40)

The second line might have read "Were th'respected person of our Banquo present", when "respected" would have told us nothing in particular about Banquo, but since the word is "grac'd", it must suggest that Banquo either naturally possesses or has acquired graces of speech and deportment to a noticeable degree. It was Macbeth who turned the tide of the recent battle; Banquo would have fought no less valiantly if less prominently; perhaps he is less obviously a fighter than Macbeth but more of a courtier. He is certainly more self-aware than Macbeth.

In I,vii, the evening's banquet has begun. Unpracticed in hypocritical concealment, Macbeth has excused himself and left the banqueting hall because he has become ever more uneasy in his duty of playing the welcoming host to the royal guest whom he intends to murder, and needs solitude in which to reflect on his intentions. He emerges into a passage through which waiters ("sewers") occasionally pass, bearing dishes to and from the banqueting hall, and begins to reflect on his own motives for the first time in his life. If he is as much overcome by the Witches' predictions as his "raptness" suggests, it must be the first time. In accordance with his habit of coming to decisions quickly, he begins by attempting to decide on the practical details of the murder in the opening lines and following:

Macbeth If 'twere done—
[He halts, remembers that he has supposedly decided to commit the murder, and corrects himself...]
—when 'tis done—
[...but instantly relapses into the conditional]
—then 'twere well
It were done quickly.

By "quickly" he means "immediately", Duncan's visit to his castle having presented him with an opportunity which may not be offered him again, but this thought throws him back to his real reason for leaving the banquet. Abandoning the attempt to decide on the When and How of the murder, he begins frankly to reconsider the Whether or No and continues:

If th'assassination
Could trammel up the consequence, and catch
With his surcease success; that but this blow
Might be the be-all and the end-all—here,
But here, upon this bank and shoal of time,
We'd jump the life to come.—But in these cases
We still have judgment here; that we but teach
Bloody instructions, which being taught, return
To plague th'inventor: this even-handed Justice
Commends th'ingredience of our poison'd chalice
To our own lips.

[This objection is of a superficial, almost "practical" nature; it is not the kind of argument for which Macbeth is searching. He pauses, then begins to dig deeper:]

He's here in double trust:
First as I am his kinsman and his subject,
Strong both against the deed; then, as his host,
Who should against his murtherer shut the door,
Not bear the knife myself. Besides, this Duncan
Hath borne his faculties so meek, hath been
So clear in his great office, that his virtues
Will plead like angels, trumpet-tongu'd, against
The deep damnation of his taking-off;
And Pity, like a naked new-born babe,
Striding the blast, or heaven's Cherubins, horsed
Upon the sightless couriers of the air,
Shall blow the horrid deed in every eye,
That tears shall drown the wind.

["Judgment here", "deep damnation", and "pity", are leading him towards the argu-

ment he is groping for. He comes nearer to it:]
>   I have no spur
> To prick the sides of my intent, but only
> Vaulting ambition, which o'erleaps itself
> And falls on th'other—

Macbeth, for whom "ambition" once meant the entirely laudable hope of meriting advancement or reward, is just beginning to realise that for him it may have dangerous implications. He will soon see that he has brought himself to a fork in the road and will have to make a deliberate choice between ambition and conscience. He is on the point of asking what for him the crucial question is: "How shall I think of myself if, in cold blood, I murder this saintly king who is now a guest in my house and under my protection—merely from greed for position? Will my conscience be able to withstand the memory of it?" Unfortunately for him, his wife now interrupts:

[Enter Lady Macbeth.]
>   How now!—what news?
> *Lady M.*   He has almost supped. Why have you left the chamber?
> *Macbeth*   Hath he asked for me?
> *Lady M.*   Know you not he has?

Macbeth, having left the chamber, cannot know whether Duncan has asked for him or not; possibly he hasn't, but Lady Macbeth, who in her husband's absence should have remained at table with their royal guest, needs her own excuse for leaving it: she has read her husband's face "as a book", noted his growing unease, and begun to suspect the reason for his long absence:

> *Macbeth*   We will proceed no further in this business:
>   He hath honoured me of late; and I have bought
>   Golden opinions from all sorts of people,
>   Which would be worn now in their newest gloss,
>   Not cast aside so soon.

Macbeth replies with another, even more superficial argument against the murder: "Can we not be content with the advancement we have received?" Evidently Lady Macbeth's sharp "Why have you left the chamber?" has driven his train of thought from his mind, in particular its tentative later stages. He does not tell her that he would rather not have such a murder on his conscience because he has not quite reached the point of thinking in terms of conscience. In any case, he would not dare to speak of conscience to her for fear of appearing weak in her eyes. She now rounds on him and turns him back to his original direction, using well-practised feminine ploys: (1) "You Don't Love Me" and (2) "You Are Nothing but a Coward". They distract him by their falsity and divert his attention to her:

> *Lady M.*   Was the hope drunk,
>   Wherein you dressed yourself? Hath it slept since?
>   And wakes it now, to look so green and pale
>   At what it did so freely? From this time
>   Such I account thy love. Art thou afeard
>   To be the same in thine own act and valour,
>   As thou art in desire? Wouldst thou have that

>   Which thou esteem'st the ornament of life,
>   And live a coward in thine own esteem,
>   Letting "I dare not" wait upon "I would",
>   Like the poor cat i'th'adage?
> *Macbeth*   Pr'y thee, peace.
>   I dare do all that may become a man;
>   Who dares do more, is none.
>
>   (I,vii,1–47)

(3) "You Made Me Do It", or "See What You Made Me Do".

Which of them first suggested that Macbeth should make himself king? It is Macbeth himself who, in I,iii, first betrays his thoughts after the witches' prophecies, and in the next scene describes his "black and deep desires". Lady Macbeth reveals her knowledge of them after reading his letter (I,v), and it may have been she who first planted the suggestion in her husband's mind, then watered and fertilised it. Her comments on his letter reveal her understanding of him; they are a remarkably accurate anticipation of the need to do what she is now doing, chastising him with the valour of her tongue. She further confuses him with some female illogic: she blames him for having raised her hopes, and then repeats the accusation of cowardice and indecision, knowing that since he takes pride in his valour in battle, the accusation will annoy and distract him enough to make him forget why he left the banquet):

> *Lady M.*   What beast was't then,
>   That made you break this enterprise to me?
>   When you durst do it, then you were a man;
>   And, to be more than what you were, you would
>   Be so much more the man. Nor time, nor place,
>   Did then adhere, and yet you would make both:
>   They have made themselves, and that their fitness now
>   Does unmake you.
>
>   (I,vii,47–54)

(4) "I Am Only A Woman, But..." She uses her sex in an ultimate form of the female-to-male appeal. She may be compared with the young women who handed out white feathers on the streets of London to young men who had not yet volunteered for the Army in the early days of World War I: some may have carried babies—a young woman with a baby, a Madonna with Child—being the most appealing of figures. Lady Macbeth, knowing it and totally without scruple, and using a form of emotional blackmail, continues her onslaught without pausing:[38]

>   I have given suck, and know
>   How tender 'tis to love the babe that milks me:
>   I would, while it was smiling in my face,
>   Have plucked my nipple from his boneless gums,
>   And dashed the brains out, had I so sworn
>   As you have done to this.
>
>   (I.vii,54–59)

---

38   The inspiration for the names of these ploys was derived from *Games People Play* by Eric Berne, M.D. (Penguin, 1968).

In fact, he hasn't sworn; on his return at the end of I,v he has merely said "We will speak further", an indication of his inner hesitancy; but no matter! She has now overwhelmed him:

 Macbeth If we should fail?

(5) "Don't you see how easy it will be?" (I,vii,59ff.)
  Lady M.   We fail?
   But screw your courage to the sticking-place,
   And we'll not fail. When Duncan is asleep,
   (Whereto the rather shall his hard day's journey
   Soundly invite him), his two chamberlains
   Will I with wine and wassail so convince,
   That memory, the warder of the brain,
   Shall be a fume, and the receipt of reason
   A limbeck only: when in swinish sleep
   Their drenched natures lie, as in a death,
   What cannot you and I perform upon
   Th'unguarded Duncan? what not put upon
   His spongy officers, who shall bear the guilt
   Of our great quell?

She has swamped his judgment by playing on his hope for children; only after the murder will he discover that his conscience cannot withstand the burden on it: "Glamis hath murthered sleep":

 Macbeth   Bring forth men-children only!
   For thy undaunted mettle should compose
   Nothing but males. Will it not be receiv'd,
   When we have mark'd with blood those sleepy two
   Of his own chamber, and us'd their very daggers,
   That they have done't?
 Lady M.   Who dares receive it other,
   As we shall make our griefs and clamour roar
   Upon his death?
 Macbeth   I am settled, and bend up
   Each corporal agent to this terrible feat.
   Away, and mock the time with fairest show:
   False face must hide what the false heart doth know.

Her "I have given suck" conveys that Macbeth is not her first husband, and explains why she can so easily manipulate him to her purposes; she is the dominant partner. If it was not she who first suggested that he should murder Duncan, why does she speak of Duncan's "fatal entrance under my battlements"? Whether the first or not, she has certainly made the "enterprise" more hers than her husband's: "You shall put / This night's great business into my dispatch". He is evidently unschooled in the ways of women; he cannot have been married before, and is easily fascinated by her ploys.

 He returns to the banqueting hall fortified by his wife's persuasions and able to put on the "fairest show" of the attentive host. Not being in the habit of pausing and thinking, he will not do so again until too late.

In II,i he again receives what he should take as a warning:
Banquo   I dreamt last night of the three Weird Sisters:
   To you they have showed some truth.
Macbeth   I think not of them;
   Yet, when we can intreat an hour to serve,
   We would spend it in some words upon that business,
   If you would grant the time.
Banquo   At your kindest leisure.
Macbeth   If you shall cleave to my consent, when 'tis,
   It shall make honour for you.
Banquo   So I lose none
   In seeking to augment it, but still keep
   My bosom franchised, and allegiance clear,
   I shall be counselled.
                                                    (II,i,20–29)

What the reserved Banquo is thinking of, whether of the Witches' prophecies or Macbeth's "rapt" reaction to them, he does not say, and he cannot say more than he does.

What is the dagger which Macbeth soon sees before him: another of the Witches' machinations? Since it first appears clean, then with gouts of blood "which was not so before", could it not be a warning from a more benevolent Agency? It might well be, for it should certainly make him pause and think, but he does not, until his "hangman's hands" compel him to do so: "To know my deed, 'twere best not know myself." Eventually, he realises that he has given his eternal jewel to the common Enemy of man.

Unaccustomed to considering his motives, he will never pause to reflect on them again, and, instead of attempting to atone for the murder by ruling as wisely and well as he can, will eventually become the tyrant who burdens his conscience ever more heavily.

The knowledge that he has placed an intolerable burden on it which no one can help him to bear makes him independent of his wife as the driving force:
Macbeth   Duncan is in his grave;
   After life's fitful fever he sleeps well;
   Treason has done his worst; nor steel, nor poison,
   Malice domestic, foreign levy, nothing
   Can touch him further.
Lady M.   Come on;
   Gentle my lord, sleek o'er your rugged looks;
   Be bright and jovial among your guests tonight.
Macbeth   So shall I, love, and so, I pray, be you.
   Let your remembrance apply to Banquo:
   Present him eminence, both with eye and tongue;
   Unsafe the while, that we
   Must lave our honours in these flattering streams,
   And make our faces vizards to our hearts,
   Disguising what they are.
Lady M.   You must leave this.
Macbeth   O! full of scorpions is my mind, dear wife!
   Thou know'st that Banquo, and his Fleance, lives.

Lady M. But in them Nature's copy's not eterne.
Macbeth There's comfort yet; they are assailable;
   Then be thou jocund. Ere the bat hath flown
   His cloister'd flight; ere to black Hecate's summons
   The shard-borne beetle, with his drowsy hums,
   Hath rung Night's yawning peal, there shall be done
   A deed of dreadful note.
Lady M.   What's to be done?
Macbeth Be innocent of the knowledge, dearest chuck,
   Till thou applaud the deed.

                                                        (III,ii,22–46)

He has planned his next murder without consulting her. They have now exchanged roles: he takes her "Gentle my lord, sleek o'er your rugged looks" and "You must leave this" as wifely concern for his peace of mind, when in fact she does not want a morose husband at her banqueting table. He even begins to condescend to her with his "Be innocent of the knowledge, dearest chuck." From now on, she will not be his inspiration.

The twice-repeated appearance of Banquo's ghost at their first state banquet should be another warning, but he is long past heeding warnings:

Macbeth (And betimes I will) to the Weird Sisters;
   More shall they speak; for now I am bent to know
   By the worst means, the worst. For mine own good,
   All causes shall give way; I am in blood
   Stepped in so far, that, should I wade no more,
   Returning were as tedious as go o'er...
                    ...My strange and self-abuse
   Is the initiate fear, that wants hard use:
   We are but young in deed.

                                                        (III,iv,132–143)

On learning from the Weird Sisters that his offspring will not inherit the throne of Scotland, he abandons himself to rage and disappointment.

In his last scene he at first fights confidently because he believes himself safe from any man "of woman born", but when he learns that "Macduff was from his mother's womb / Untimely ripp'd", the last trace of his self-confidence vanishes.

31

MACBETH

&

LADY MACBETH

Macbeth is the tragedy of a man who has married the wrong kind of wife: as evidenced, certainly, from his susceptibility to suggestion, her ability to read his face "as a book", the ease with which she manipulates him in I,vii, and her lack of scruple; she is the wrong kind for him. She is not so much evil in its true sense of deliberately malicious as greedy, cunning and short-sighted.

How did they come to be married? It would seem much more likely that she captured such a naïve husband than that he captured her; also, perhaps, that she is older than he.

Lady Macbeth is even more ambitious than her husband. She is conscienceless, or thinks she is, until she finds herself sleep-walking. She knows that her husband has some stirrings of conscience in him: "What thou wouldst highly, that wouldst thou holily," (I,v,20-1) and manipulates him into murdering Duncan with no thought for the possible effects of the crime on him or even herself. Before his crime, she understands him well enough to be able to manage him, but not well enough to foresee that he will become independent of her as the consequence of the irrevocable step of murdering Duncan.

Exactly what is the nature of her ambition? Women's sphere is the running of the home. Even when they have begun a successful career outside the home, they still regard it as their territory, and like to be seen as its efficient manager. If anything, because they are more aware than men of the importance of social gatherings, they like to play the hostess. And while Lady Macbeth may see a future as her husband's guide and mentor when he becomes king, her prime ambition is to become Scotland's principal hostess.

Their first state banquet, to which all Scotland's highest nobles have been invited, begins in III,iv:

Macbeth   You know your own degrees, sit down: at first
    And last, the hearty welcome.
Lords   Thanks to your Majesty.
Macbeth   Ourself will mingle with society,
    And play the humble host.
    Our hostess keeps her state; but in best time
    We will require her welcome.
Lady M.   Pronounce it for me, Sir, to all our friends,
    For my heart speaks, they are welcome...

The First Murderer appears and leaves Macbeth visibly depressed by the news that Fleance has escaped. His wife has to remind him that he must not neglect the formalities which are essential to such an occasion as this:

Lady M.   My royal lord,
    You do not give the cheer; the feast is sold
    That is not given vouch'd, while 'tis a-making,
    'Tis given with welcome. To feed were best at home;

From thence, the sauce to meat is ceremony;
Meeting were bare without it.
Macbeth   Sweet remembrancer!—
Now, good digestion wait on appetite,
And health on both!
Lenox   May it please your Highness sit?
Macbeth   Here had we now our country's honour roof'd
Were the grac'd person of our Banquo present...

As if in response to an invitation, Banquo's Ghost appears and sits in the vacant place. Macbeth, never distinguished for his self-control, now loses his composure completely.
Macbeth   Which of you have done this?
Lords   What, my good Lord?
Macbeth   Thou canst not say I did it; never shake
Thy gory locks at me.
Ross   Gentlemen, rise; his Highness is not well.
[The guests are concerned; Lady Macbeth quickly devises an excuse for him:]
    Lady M.   Sit, worthy friends. My lord is often thus,
And hath been from his youth: pray you, keep seat;
The fit is momentary; upon a thought
He will again be well. If much you note him,
You shall offend him, and extend his passion;
Feed, and regard him not.
[She takes him aside:]   Are you a man?
    Macbeth   Ay, and a bold one, that dare look on that
Which might appal the Devil.
Lady M.   O proper stuff!
This is the very painting of your fear:
This is the air-drawn dagger, which, you said,
Led you to Duncan. O! these flaws and starts
(Impostors to true fear) would well become
A woman's story at a winter's fire,
Authorised by her grandam. Shame itself!
Why do you make such faces? When all's done,
You look but on a stool...

But she cannot see what he sees; apparently he is having hallucinations again, as when he saw the dagger. Though the Ghost disappears, she is unable to shake him in his belief that he saw Banquo. Eventually she returns to her seat; when he does not return to his, she speaks so that all may hear, compelling him to repeat her excuse himself:
Lady M.   My worthy lord,
Your noble friends do lack you.
Macbeth   I do forget.—
Do not muse at me, my most worthy friends,
I have a strange infirmity, which is nothing
To those that know me. Come, love and health to all;
Then, I'll sit down.—Give me some wine, fill full:

> I drink to th'general joy o'th'whole table,
> And to our dear friend Banquo, whom we miss;
> Would he were here!

[Banquo's Ghost instantly responds to this foolish second invitation:]

>   To all, and him, we thirst,
> And all to all.
> Lords   Our duties, and the pledge.
> Macbeth   Avaunt! and quit my sight! let the earth hide thee!
> Thy bones are marrowless, thy blood is cold;
> Thou hast no speculation in those eyes
> Which thou dost glare with...

[Lady Macbeth must again excuse him. The Ghost eventually disappears:]

>   Why so, being gone,
> I am a man again.—

[Already the lords are rising to go:]

>   —Pray you, sit still.
> Lady M.   You have displaced the mirth, broke the good meeting
> In most admired disorder.
> Macbeth   Can such things be,
> And overcome us like a summer's cloud,
> Without our special wonder? You make me strange
> Even to the disposition that I owe,
> When now I think you can behold such sights,
> And keep the natural ruby of your cheeks,
> When mine is blanched with fear.
> Rosse   What sights, my lord?

And now Lady Macbeth, realising that her husband has already betrayed much and may betray more, accepts that her first state banquet, on which as queen and mistress of the palace she had lavished so much care, has turned out to be a disaster:

> Lady M.   I pray you, speak not; he grows worse and worse;
> Question enrages him. At once, good night:—
> Stand not upon the order of your going,
> But go at once.

[And the lords leave, each bowing silently as he goes.]

It is significant that Lady Macbeth, who neither sees the Ghost nor understands the reason for her husband's "infirmity", does not press to know its cause, although she could be expected to demand to know; and before the murder of Duncan she would have. After all, his apparent hallucinations are a very recent "infirmity"; she appears merely to be disconsolate at the failure of her first State banquet:

> Macbeth   It will have blood, they say: blood will have blood:
> Stones have been known to move, and trees to speak;
> Augures, and understood relations, have
> By magot-pies, and choughs, and rooks, brought forth
> The secret'st man of blood.—What is the night?
> Lady M.   Almost at odds with morning, which is which.

In vain has she urged him to exercise some self-control, to play his part as host, and to remember that ceremony is the sauce to meat when guests are being entertained. She has carefully arranged her first royal house-party, only to see it wrecked by the husband whom she had persuaded to lift her to the throne of Scotland by murdering its king and his son. Before the murder, she would have chastised him with the valour of her tongue; if she were angry with him after the failure of her banquet, she would say much more, but this is all she now says.[39]

There will have been an interval after the murder, of what duration the play does not say, but long enough to include Duncan's funeral and Macbeth's coronation, and followed arrangements for the banquet. During the interval Macbeth has become completely independent of her; he now virtually ignores her. She has been compelled to accept that verbal chastisements will be ineffectual.

Although the Hecate scene (III,v,10–13) is not thought to be Shakespeare's, it contains lines which are relevant to the play's theme:

Hecate And, which is worse, all you have done
  Hath been but for a wayward son,
  Spiteful and wrathful; who, as others do,
  Loves for his own ends, not for you.

The Satanist, which is a word which first came into use in the mid-sixteenth century, is one who says, "Evil, be thou my good—Satan, be thou my master". Hecate is rebuking the Witches for wasting their time in such amusements as teasing a sailor's wife, causing her husband to be tempest-tossed, or seducing the easily-tempted Macbeth into committing crimes which will damn him for ever, when they should have been looking for other minds willing to deny conscience and join her as servants of the Evil One. Such a denial can only be made in the full awareness of the meaning of conscience, which Macbeth could not have made because he is not sufficiently self-aware.

His wife could not be a Satanist either; although more self-aware than her husband, she too merely "loves for her own ends".

If she is concerned for his peace of mind, it is not so much from wifely concern as because of the change in her own status; perhaps because she fears that her husband's "Never shake thy gory locks at me" (III,iv,49) has raised suspicions in the lords' minds; perhaps also because the conscience she thought she did not have is already troubling her.

Having become independent of her after the murder of Duncan, he will neglect her from now on. Though she is not as suggestible as he, she is equally short-sighted, since before the murder she too fails to reflect that she might have a conscience. She is not evil; she has merely been greedy for importance in the affairs of the kingdom. After the banquet she drops out of sight until her conscience causes her to sleep-walk; presumably there have been no more state banquets or other occupations which might prevent her memories from tormenting her. She has realised that the blood of Lady Macduff and her children as well as Duncan's is on her hands:

Lady M. The Thane of Fife had a wife: where is she now? —What, will these hands ne'er be clean?

(V,i,40)

---

39   See Note (4) at end of chapter.

Since the Doctor says "This disease is beyond my practice" (V,i,55), and Macbeth later asks him "Canst thou not minister to a mind diseased?" (V,iii,40), she is sick in mind rather than body. The outcry of women (V,v,7) then indicates that her tortured conscience has driven her to end her own life, thus the play's message to its early audiences can be summed in one word: conscience.

In I,vii,53 she uses her sex ("I have given suck") for more than one reason when persuading him to murder Duncan. The image of a child at its mother's breast is not only appealing in itself; it will overwhelm him because she knows he hopes for a child, a desire he instantly confirms:

Macbeth Bring forth men-children only!
For thy undaunted mettle should compose
Nothing but males.

In the classic five-act structure, the first act or exposition sets out the dramatic situation, and the events of the second are its development towards the climax, which normally occurs in the third act. The murder of Duncan, which occurs in the second act, is too early to be the climax; it is therefore Macbeth's visit to the Witches' cave, when he learns that his offspring will not inherit the throne of Scotland, i.e. that he will have no children.[40]

Lady Macbeth's "I have given suck" implies that she has been married before, but an important question is not "How many children had she once had?", but "How many children did she intend to have when she married Macbeth?" Did she intend to have any? Why do she and her husband have none, although his "Bring forth men children only" indicates his hope of a family? Since she wanted to become queen at any price, she can hardly be called a motherly type, nor does she ever express the hope that her dynasty will continue on the throne of Scotland, although, if she really shared her husband's hopes, she would surely do so. Evidently, she thinks solely in terms of her own ambitions.

There is no direct hint in the play as to why she and her husband remain childless, though they do. We may surmise that after the banquet scene , he begins to ignore her completely and that their marriage virtually ceases to be a marriage, although a child or children would prevent its collapse, thus giving Macbeth reason to rule wisely and temperately. Could the cause of their childlessness be partly psychosomatic, i.e. is he no longer able to take any interest in her?[41]

When he is told of her death, all he says is, "She should have died hereafter; / There would have been a time for such a word". He has lost all interest in her as a wife; why? Is it from acute disgust that she persuaded him to murder Duncan in the first place? Or is it his suggestibility that causes the Witches' prophecy—that his heirs will not succeed him on the throne of Scotland—to become self-fulfilling, i.e. does he lose interest in his wife because he immediately accepts it as a true prediction?

Macbeth's continued failure to pause and examine his own motives eventually reduces his life to an empty waste:

Macbeth Tomorrow, and tomorrow, and tomorrow
Creeps in this petty pace from day to day,

---

40 In the usual act-division of the play, the visit is in IV,I, which I feel should be placed at the end of the third act, i.e. that III,vi and IV,i should be interchanged. See Note (1) at end of chapter.

41 See Note (5) at end of chapter.

To the last syllable of recorded time;
And all our yesterdays have lighted fools
The way to dusty death.

(V,v,18–23)

How should Macbeth be acted? The point of some tragedies is that its personages may become changed by the effect of something which happens to or is done to them; or, as in the case of Macbeth, is done by them. If the possibility of change is not recognised, any attempt at character-study will lead to an inconsistent or even puzzling verdict. His crime changes Macbeth drastically; he is anything but the same man at the end of the play that he was at the beginning. In consequence, his appearance will have changed and, since audiences watch as well as listen, should be seen to have changed.

At the beginning of the play he will be as athletic as his prowess on the battlefield suggests, his step will be springy, his skin and eyes clear, his carriage upright, his beard trim, and his dress well-tended. His demeanour will be that of a man with nothing on his conscience: he will stand and walk with a perfectly straight back, looking everyone in the face because there is no reason why he should not.

While he is still the great fighter at the end of the play, he will have developed the slightly rounded shoulders and the more flat-footed walk which come from too many cares, too many sleepless nights and, in his case, a conscience overburdened with murders. From his "Macbeth has murdered sleep" he will have slept badly for some time. In any event he has spent too many of the small hours listening to reports from his spies and planning further crimes, so that his skin will be a little more leathery, any wrinkles deeper, his eyes red-rimmed, and his eyebrows perhaps more bushy. He will now glance at people furtively rather than look them squarely in the face; his royal gown will be carelessly thrown on rather than properly arranged. And from his "Go, bid my mistress, when my drink is ready, / She strike upon the bell" (II,i,31–32) he may have become somewhat dependent on alcohol.

Notes:
1) Play construction:

In the conventional structure of the five-act tragedy, the climax comes in the third act. Duncan's murder occurs in the second act; it is therefore a part of the development to the climax. The text, first printed in 1623 from a prompt-copy or possibly a transcript, has given its editors much trouble. Its shortness has given rise to the suggestion that there was some cutting, perhaps to please King James who is said to have disliked long plays. It is also said to be the worst printed of all the plays.

There may also have been some wrong arrangement of scenes. From the standpoint of the family theme, the climax should be Macbeth's visit to the Witches' house, where the prophecy that his offspring will not inherit the throne of Scotland finally tips the scale and causes him to become the murdering tyrant. In the existing arrangement, the third act ends with the Hecate scene (III,v), followed by the discussion between Lenox and a Lord (III,vi), in which Scotland is already described as "suffering", although at the end of the banquet scene Macbeth has only said, "There's not a one of them, but in his house / I keep a servant fee'd" (III,iv,130–131), i.e he does not appear to have embarked on his numerous murders as yet.

It would seem more logical to reverse the positions of III,vi and IV,i. The visit to the

Witches would then follow the Hecate scene and become the end of a climactic third act. Macbeth's "From this moment, / The very firstlings of my heart shall be / The firstlings of my hand" (IV,I,146–147) would precede and justify Lenox's description of Macbeth as "tyrant" and his country as "suffering".

The Hecate scene III,v ends with the stage direction *[Music. A song within: 'Come away, come away', etc.]*, and since, at the end of Macbeth's visit to the Witches, there is another stage direction: *[Music. The Witches dance, and then vanish, with Hecate]*, the two scenes were probably combined in the original production.

The play has been said to disintegrate in the fourth act, when Malcolm first insists that he is unsuited to the throne, then retracts his words: an episode which interrupts the plot and, as a piece of play construction, seems much below Shakespeare's usual standard. The play's subject would please King James, partly because he was a convinced believer in witches, partly because it depicted an episode in his family history of Banquo and his son Malcolm being James' ancestors. Shakespeare may have decided to follow Raphael Holinshed's *Chronicles* (1587) in order to emphasise that Malcolm also has a conscience. He claims that he commits many sins, but then retracts his words to demonstrate his awareness of the meaning of sinfulness and so contrast himself with the apparently conscienceless Macbeth.

Incidentally, I disagree with those critics who believe that one of Shakespeare's reasons for choosing the plot of *Macbeth* was the Gunpowder Plot, whose circumstances bear only the slightest resemblance to the killing of Duncan. A plot chosen merely because it depicted the killing of a king would hardly have appealed to James or any other king. Had there been no Gunpowder Plot, Shakespeare would still have dramatised the *Macbeth* story.

2) The "cloudy messenger":

Lord ...Thither Macduff
Is gone to pray the holy king, upon his aid
To wake Northumberland and warlike Siward...
...And this report
Hath so exasperate the king, that he
Prepares for some attempt at war.
Lenox Sent he to Macduff?
Lord He did, and with an absolute "Sir, not I",
The cloudy messenger turns me his back,
And hums, as who should say, "You'll rue the time
That clogs me with this answer".

(III,vi,29–43)

As it stands, the Lord's second speech makes no sense. The "holy king" is the king of England who can cure the King's Evil (scrofula, a tuberculous condition of the skin) by the laying-on of hands (IV,iii,141ff.); "the king" in the penultimate line of the Lord's first speech and the subsequent "he's" are Macbeth. "Sir, not I" is Macduff's reply, not the messenger's (if it is the messenger's reply, we do not know how Macduff replied). Since the murders of Lady Macduff and her children soon follow, the person who turns his back and hums threateningly must be Macbeth. A line or lines must have been omitted. As has been surmised, if the Folio was printed from a transcription or second copy of the prompt–copy, the lines may have been overlooked in the copying, or perhaps by the printer. One line suffices:

Lord He did, and with an absolute "Sir, not I",
Macduff sent back; whereat the king upon

The cloudy messenger turns me his back...
3) "Highly and holily":
>...what thou wouldst highly,
>That wouldst thou holily; wouldst not play false,
>And yet wouldst wrongly win; thou'dst have, great Glamis,
>That which cries, "Thus thou must do," if thou have it;
>And that which rather thou dost fear to do,
>Than wishest should be undone.

(I,v,20–25)

This passage is usually so punctuated that it is not at first obvious to the reader that "That which cries" and "That which rather" are both the objects of "Thou'dst have" in a continuous sentence, with the semicolon placed after "have it" being the culprit; it appears in all the editions I have seen. Commenting in his edition of *Hamlet* on "Stand a comma twixt our amities"), said Dr. Johnson (1765), "The Comma is the note of connection and continuity of sentences; the Period is the note of abruption and disjunction." The semicolon, lying between them, implies a much more definite pause than a comma; there is no justification for inserting such a break into what should be a continuous sentence. Editors also vary in their placing of the inverted commas. We try:

>...what thou wouldst highly,
>That wouldst thou holily; wouldst not play false,
>And yet wouldst wrongly win; thou'dst have, great Glamis,
>That which cries "Thus thou must do if thou have it –
>And that which rather thou dost fear to do
>Than wishest should be undone."

4) On the ambitions of hostesses: the older reader may remember *Call Me Madam* (Irving Berlin: music and lyrics, Howard Lindsay & Russel Crouse [1950]), a musical based on the appointment as U.S. Ambassador to Luxembourg for her services to politics, of the lady who had been Washington's leading hostess.

5) On psychosomatic effects: in the late 1980's, when business conditions were deteriorating, there were many bankruptcies and repossessions of mortgaged houses. Soon afterwards newspaper articles on impotence in husbands began to appear.

PART III
THEME OF THE LATER PLAYS: FAMILY

32

KING LEAR

"The greatest of faults, I should say, is to be conscious of none."
Thomas Carlyle (1795–1881)

A family theme appears immediately in the first scene:

Kent   Is not this your son, my lord?

Gloster   His breeding, sir, hath been at my charge: I have so often blushed to acknowledge him, that now I am brazed to it.

Kent   I cannot conceive you.

Gloster   [*Seizing the opportunity for a pun, and letting his amusement show:*] Sir, this young fellow's mother could: whereupon she grew round-wombed, and had, indeed, sir, a son for her cradle ere she had a husband for her bed. Do you smell a fault?

Kent   I cannot wish the fault undone, the issue of it being so proper.

Gloster   But I have a son, sir, by order of law, some year elder than this, who is yet no dearer in my account: though this knave came somewhat saucily into the world before he was sent for, yet was his mother fair; there was good sport at his making, and the whoreson must be acknowledged.—Do you know this noble gentleman, Edmund?

Edmund [Is he choking?—can he only reply briefly?] No.

Gloster   My Lord of Kent; remember him hereafter as my honourable friend.

Edmund   My services to your lordship.

Kent   I must love you, and sue to know you better.

Edmund   Sir, I shall study deserving.

Gloster   He hath been out nine years, and away he shall again.

(I,i,7–32)

All infants arriving in this world must be made to feel totally welcome, which must continue at least to the end of their childhood, and it must be extended equally to all the children in the family. Was Edmund given the same welcome as his elder brother? Every boy wants simply to be his father's son, but Edmund—and his mother—have always been held up to ridicule by his father in his doggish way as "my accidental offspring". He "hath been out nine years"; does this mean that his father sent him away from home in his early adolescence to learn his way in the world? Was Edgar also sent out, or did he remain at home in his father's company? If the children in a family do not receive equal love and encouragement, some, resenting the privileged child, will become jealous and resentful, even feeling that they have been to some degree rejected (the fear of abandonment or rejection in a child can be acute). Yet it seems clear that, in addition to hearing his origin being constantly ridiculed in public, Edmund did not receive the same welcome as his brother, in spite of Gloster's statement that Edgar "is yet no dearer in my account" (I,I,19).

Edmund's later behaviour suggests that there is a vein of treachery and cunning in his nature, which may be the effect of having constantly to dissimulate his feelings; and perhaps putting on an apparently uncaring smile whenever his father introduced him to a stranger. If he does have such a vein, it is not a matter for surprise that he decides to give it full rein, abandon conscience, and advance his fortunes in whatever way he can:

Edmund Thou, nature, art my goddess; to thy law
   My services are bound.

(I,ii,1–2)

There are improbabilities in the plot. Lear's decision to divide his kingdom into three portions is the first, and is the basis of the original story and core of Shakespeare's plot. Gloster's total credulity when he accepts Edmund's letter (I,ii) without allowing Edgar to speak in his own defence is another; but since it is the foundation of the secondary plot, it must also be accepted. He is the other father in the play who displays no understanding of his own children—and without these improbabilities, no play!

While the plots of melodramas must be accepted as they are, mere acceptance is in this case a somewhat superficial approach. Lear is a king of such powerful mind, and so well endowed by nature to wield the authority of a king, that he obscures the true intention of the play, which is to display him as father. If he were merely a wealthy parent who had elected to divide his estate between his daughters and leave to them the cares of its management during his declining years, his action would not seem extraordinary and no one in this first scene appears to find the division unwise or even unusual, even when Kent attempts to reason with Lear, it is because of his rejection of Cordelia, not the partition of the kingdom, and Lear should be regarded as an ordinary father dividing his estate between his heirs.

Lear's mistakes are described by Goneril at the end of the scene:

Goneril You see how full of changes his age is; the observation we have made of it hath not been little; he always loved our sister most; and with what poor judgment he hath now cast her off appears too grossly.
Regan 'Tis the infirmity of his age; he hath ever but slenderly known himself.
Goneril The best and soundest of his time hath been but rash; then we must look to receive from his age, not alone the imperfections of long-ingrafted condition, but therewithal the unruly waywardness that infirm and choleric years bring with them.

(I,i,287–298)

Had Lear always loved Cordelia more than his other children? If he had any understanding of human nature and in particular of children, he would have been careful not to let his preference show even if, as appears to be the case, Cordelia had a softer and more affectionate nature than the others. This is necessarily true; Goneril and Regan may have become what they are as the result of Lear's blindness to the effect of his favouritism on them. He has always let it show, causing her two sisters to become jealous of her and lose much of their regard for their father. Lear being what he is, they have been compelled to distance themselves from him too early in their lives and to see him with the detachment that their words suggest. Some, at least, of their subsequent behaviour is understandable, even excusable. It is not surprising that when he visits them they lose patience with him; might they not have lost it long ago?

His daughters do not turn him out of their houses; he turns himself out into the wild weather because he will not accept the suggested reduction of his hundred knights to twenty-five. His retinue has nothing to do but hunt or joust all day and feast in the evening, as might be expected from knights who are trained as fighters, quarrel and behave riotously, as Goneril later complains (I,iv,198–199 and 238–243). Why must he insist on a hundred merely to maintain his notion of his authority even after he has abdicated? How can his daughters continue with their own lives and duties with such a horde in their houses? Wives insist on running their households themselves. Does he know so little of women as to fail to realise that he must accept living in their houses as a guest, i.e. with them, not over them and at considerable inconvenience to them?

In I,i, when Goneril and Regan hand their father the kind of flattery which his inflated ego demands, they are being hypocritical because they are wiser and more realistic than Cordelia. They have their own viewpoint; it is necessary to think ourselves into their skins, as the playwright must when he is creating his characters. Both turn out to have a vein of cruelty and treachery which appears later, after Lear has cursed and rejected them in even more violent terms than Cordelia. What would be the effect on them of their father's curse and rejection—his final rejection, since his early preference for Cordelia has already amounted to partial rejection? Would they have turned out as they do if Lear had consented to live with them month by month with a small retinue? If he had become more reasonable, might they not have recovered some regard for him and regulated their lives differently? He had never been the kind of father whose advice and support his daughters would welcome, or who would offer advice and support without insisting on dominating them. Advice should be offered preferably having first been requested, then discussed. When did Lear ever brook discussion?

Cordelia is as much her father's daughter and a king's daughter as her older sisters, and will be as much aware of his failings as they. She is more affectionate by nature than either of them. As his favourite child she had received much love from him, which she is quite willing to return. She also knows that as he ages he will need ever more of the filial love and support which all aged parents need. This may be inferred from her remark on her future need to give love to her husband: her loyalty must first be to him, though she would not refuse her father what love he might need.

To such a mind, such exaggerated professions of love as the "pap" from Goneril and Regan are all but impossible; she can only say "I love your Majesty / According to my bond; nor more, nor less" (I,I,91–92), meaning the natural, common bond of "family" (of which women, I find, are more aware than men), i.e. she "loves" in the matter-of-fact, unsentimental way of many, possibly most, women. From this we might suspect that if Lear had come to live with her, she too might have lost patience with his preposterous hundred knights.

Nothing registers with Lear if it does not feed his self-importance, and he rejects her with a speech which, coming from a father to the most affectionate of his children, is hardly believable:

Lear Let it be so! Thy truth, then, be thy dower!
  For, by the sacred radiance of the sun,
  The mysteries of Hecate, and the night;
  By all the operation of the orbs
  From whom we do exist, and cease to be;
  Here I disclaim all my paternal care,
  Propinquity and property of blood,
  And as a stranger to my heart and me
  Hold thee, from this, for ever. The barbarous Scythian,
  Or he that makes his generation messes
  To gorge his appetite, shall to my bosom
  Be as well neighbour'd, pitied, and relieved
  As thou, my sometime daughter.

(I,i,107–119)

Does Lear believe that he really can sever the "tie of blood" which always comes into being between parents and the flesh of their own flesh, and which in the end can never be cut, for the awareness of the tie always remains? Does he imagine himself so far above the common run of humanity as that? What were his children to him—mere extensions of his ego? He turns his back on Cordelia and thinks he can turn it permanently, although she had always been his favourite child with whom he had expected to spend his years of retirement:

Lear   I loved her most, and thought to set my rest
   On her kind nursery.

(I,i,122–3)

Will he really never look back and remember his little daughter in her childhood, or, for that matter, his other daughters, whom he eventually curses even more violently? We must assume that but for the actions of Goneril and Regan, he would not have recalled his memories of Cordelia as he does at the end of the play.

Lear's principal characteristics are: a powerful intellect; innate ability to wield authority; an apparent total lack of insight into human nature; and the habit of self-dramatisation, a habit which eventually becomes self-pity.

Intelligence has been defined as a collection of aptitudes. Few humans have all the aptitudes in equal measure; the very few who have many of them in marked degree are the universal geniuses. The majority of us are born with different aptitudes in varying degrees, and, since it appears to vary considerably from one individual to another, the intuitive understanding of other people appears to be one of them. It does not appear to be scientifically measurable—at least, I have not read of any attempt to measure it. In this Lear appears to be totally lacking; was he born without it? He may have been, but he has both natural authority and the ability to wield it in marked degree; has his natural authority become self-importance to the point where it has swamped any realisation of the need to understand other people, even his own children?

It is difficult to divine Shakespeare's intention, for if Lear was born with no intuitive understanding of other people, he is not quite so culpable as if he possessed some intuition which had let self-importance swamp. To what extent did Shakespeare intend him to receive sympathy from us? The question comes down to "Can Lear help being what he is—was he born with an incurable blind spot?"

Whether it is a question of the ability to understand others or of the willingness to try to understand them, the aptitude seems to be totally absent from his make-up. "He hath ever but slenderly known himself", says Regan, and Goneril replies, "The best and soundest of his time hath been but rash." As king, he must have been dedicated to his duties and won respect, loyalty and obedience, from which we might infer that he should have had sufficient intelligence to see himself with some detachment. But slavish subservience has come to mean far more to him than loyalty, otherwise he would not banish Kent as he does.

Are not his rantings on the blasted heath the screams of a petulant, grown-up spoilt child who has always rejected the slightest suggestion that some of his judgments might just conceivably be the merest trifle in error? Thwarted and frustrated, he takes to raving against the universe.

Richard II has been described as "vain, frivolous, and inconsistent; a dupe of flattery; naturally weak-minded and irresolute" in *Elegant Extracts* ed. Vicesimus Knox (1789). In Shakespeare's play he is a something of a self-dramatiser. At the beginning of the play, he orders that Bolingbroke and Norfolk shall settle their differences with swords and lances at Coventry, waits until the knights are about to fight, then cancels the combat. When his forces desert him, he self-dramatises:

   Richard For God's sake, let us sit upon the ground,
       And tell sad stories of the death of kings.

                                                                         (*Richard II* III,ii,2,155–156)

When trapped in Flint Castle, he self-dramatises again. In spite of Bolingbroke's offer to lay down his arms and end the rebellion, he insists on abdicating and being escorted to London, and then spends what time is left to him in self-pity. Does not Lear do much the same?

Lear's love of drama with himself as the centre of attention causes him to require his daughters to profess their love for him in public; then he rejects his favourite daughter with a consciously dramatic speech ("the mysteries of Hecate" and "the barbarous Scythian" indeed!). In I,iv he rejects the notion that he might have been mistaken in rejecting Cordelia:

   Lear   O most small fault,
       How ugly didst thou in Cordelia show!
       Which, like an engine, wrenched my frame of nature
       From the fixed place, drew from my heart all love,
       And added to the gall.

                                                                         (I,iv,264–268)

He later curses Goneril with a speech so overblown that it could only spring from the ingrained habits of self-righteousness and self-dramatisation:

   Lear Hear, nature, hear; dear goddess, hear!
       Suspend thy purpose, if thou didst intend
       To make this creature fruitful!
       Into her womb convey sterility,
       Dry up in her the organs of increase;
       And from her derogate body never spring
       A babe to honour her! If she must teem,
       Create her child of spleen, that it may live
       And be a thwart disnatured torment to her!

                                                                         (I,iv,273–281)

Having stormed out into the tempest, he at first refuses to take shelter ("Pour on, I will endure"—III,iv,18) before consenting to go into the hovel. Later in the scene, he tears off his clothes. In the farmhouse, his mock-trial of Goneril and Regan (III,vi) is more "drama", followed by self-pity:

   Lear   The little dogs and all,
       Tray, Blanche, and Sweetheart, see, they bark at me.

                                                                         (III,vi,61–62)

Lear convinces himself and, such is his natural authority, all those who remain with him that he is entitled to feel sorry for himself.

We cannot pity Lear even though he is old (he is not senile), nor can we sympathise with him until the end of the play. Has he not deliberately put himself where he is? Can we sympathise with anyone so inflated and unreasonable? He distils the essence of the "unbiddable"; at the end, his family has been destroyed, and he himself has been the principal agent of its destruction.

As some critics have maintained, should we accept that the deaths of Cordelia and the Fool are superfluous horrors? Dr. Johnson regarded them as against "justice"; and so they are, but an important moral of tragedy is that innocent persons may suffer as the result of others' actions.

Does Lear begin to suffer from insanity in the latter half of the play, as Bradley maintains? I dislike this suggestion as much as the notion that there is a vein of true madness under Hamlet's simulation of it. In the most powerful tragedies, the protagonists hold our interest because they are free agents and fully responsible for their actions; if their minds are diseased, the play becomes a kind of medical documentary, little more than a sad-story tragedy. Not that it matters much if Lear's mind does begin to weaken somewhat towards the end of the play; we must assume (and, I feel, do assume) that he is in full possession of his faculties at the beginning; otherwise, the play cannot have its fullest tragic effect. Total belief in one's own rightness in all situations is not in itself insanity; it is occasionally seen, if not to the same exaggerated degree as in Lear. If we accept insanity, we are bound to inquire whether its roots were present in Lear's mind before the play begins; if they were, the play is indeed a mere medical documentary.

Some people develop mannerisms which advance their careers by attracting attention to themselves whenever they speak and impressing their hearers. Lear early discovered that he could impress his followers and subjects by dramatising all his royal decisions. He has practised the mannerism to the point where it has now taken over the whole man: he has become the most successful actor in his kingdom; he no longer remembers that he is a father of children as well as king. In I,i he announces the provisions of his will; should he not first have informed his daughters in private? Private moments have long held no interest for Lear; he is the actor who needs and has long enjoyed a large audience. Goneril's and Regan's overblown professions of love are self-dramatisations of the only kind which could penetrate what Goneril describes as his "long-in grafted condition". Unfortunately for her, Cordelia sees such overblown professions as falsity, and refuses to compete with her sisters in their hypocrisy.

In IV,vi Lear enters "fantastically drest with wild flowers":

Lear   Ay, every inch a king.
When I do stare, see how the subject quakes.
I pardon that man's life. What was thy cause?
Adultery?
Thou shalt not die. Die for adultery? No.
The wren goes to't, and the small gilded fly
Does lecher in my sight.
Let copulation thrive; for Gloster's bastard son
Was kinder to his father than my daughters
Got 'tween the lawful sheets...

(IV,vi,107–116)

This raving against humanity has given rise to the notion of 'madness', but it is merely his usual exhibitionism and self-pity, and no more extreme than the speeches with which he earlier rejects his daughters.

"In his own eyes he must be an Image, a picture in his own imagination", says Luigi Pirandello's Doctor of the madman. This, applied to Lear, is no exaggeration, for he is not aware of being "himself" as well as the Image, he is his Image, he is wholly a role-player.

His exposure on the heath might well cause his wits to wander, but it is self-inflicted. His self-importance has long excluded the sense of proportion which might have enabled him to see himself and his family in perspective, and whose total absence makes him almost a psychopath. However, since as king he must be accepted as intelligent, to whom can the responsibility for his condition be assigned but Lear himself?

Only when he sees that Cordelia is dead does he understand what he has lost; and since he then dies, we cannot know whether he would eventually realise that he must blame himself for the loss of his family. Although his death may signalise the realisation, it is not possible to be sure.

In view of his need to evade capture and execution, Edgar's simulation of lunacy can hardly be called comic relief. Even the Fool's backchat does not lighten the darkness; his outspokenness would earn him more than the threat of the whip from any other royal master, but Lear appears to welcome his verbal liberties because they prove to his own satisfaction that he can find them amusing, i.e. that he is armour-plated against criticism. Nothing the Fool says causes Lear to pause and think; in vain does he suggest that Lear should blame himself for his predicament. Why did Shakespeare choose to dramatise this story? I sometimes think that he wrote *Timon of Athens* because he needed to write a new play for his company, and could find no better plot at the time. He could hardly have created his most intense play for that reason. Incidentally, I do not find that there are no intense moments in his other plays which equal those in Lear; it is his most continuously intense tragedy.

According to John Aubrey (1626–1697), the Elizabethans and Jacobeans had little feeling for children:

> When I recovered [from the smallpox] after Trinity weeke, my father sent for me into the Country again; where I conversed with none but servants and rustiques and soldiers quartred, to my great grief, for in those dayes fathers were not acquainted with their children.
>
> From the time of Erasmus till about 20 years past, the learning was downright pedantry. The conversation and habitts of those times were as stiff and starcht as their bands and square beards, and Gravity was then taken for Wisdome. The very Doctors of those days were but old boies, when quibles past for wit, even in the pulpitts. The Gentry and Citizens had litle learning of any kind, and their way of breeding up their children was suitable to the rest: for wheras ones child should be ones nearest Friend, and the time of growing up should be most indulged, they were as severe to their children as their schoolmaster: and their Schoolmasters, as masters of the House of correction. The child perfectly loathed the sight of his parents, as the slave his Torturor. Gentlemen of 30 or 40 years old, fitt for any employment in the common wealth, were to stand like great mutes and fools bare headed before their Parents: and the Daughters (grown woemen) were to stand at the Cupboards side during the whole time of the proud mothers visitt, unless (as the fashion was) 'twas desired that leave (forsooth) should be given them to kneele upon cushions brought them by the servingman, after they had done sufficient penance standing. The boys (grown young fellows) had their foreheads turned up, and stiffened with spittle: they were to stand mannerly forsooth, thus, the foretop ordered as before, one hand at the bandstring, the other at the breech or codpiece. The Gentlewomen then had prodigious fannes, as is to be seen in old pictures, like that instrument which is used to drive feathers; it had a handle at least half a yard

long; with these the daughters were corrected oftentimes...But fathers and mothers slasht their daughters in the time of that besome discipline when they were perfect woemen.

Intron. Aubrey's *Brief Lives*, ed. Oliver Lawson Dick

It was pointed out earlier that fathers exercised all the authority in their families; they could order sons and daughters to marry a spouse of their choosing whether the spouse was acceptable to the child or not, and this custom persisted till long after Shakespeare's time. As an example from a little later: in Ford's *Perkin Warbeck*, the old Scottish nobleman Huntly assures his daughter Katherine that he will allow her to choose her husband for herself until, to his acute dismay, she chooses the adventurer Perkin! From this it might be inferred that Ford disapproved or felt that his audiences would disapprove of Huntly's policy as too lax.

As an example from the next century: in II,i of Sheridan's *The Rivals* (1775), Sir Anthony Absolute informs his son that he has chosen a wife for him; when Captain Absolute, who has fallen in love with another young woman, begins to voice his objections, his father becomes very angry and threatens to disinherit him:

Sir Anth.   None of your passion, sir!—none of your violence if you please! It won't do with me, I promise you.

Abs.   Indeed, sir, I never was cooler in my life.

Sir Anth.   'Tis a confounded lie!—I know you are in a passion in your heart; I know you are, you hypocritical young dog! but it won't do.

Sir Anth.   So you will fly out! can't you be cool like me? What the devil good can passion do? Passion is of no service, you impudent, insolent, overbearing reprobate!—There, you sneer again! don't provoke me!—but you rely upon the mildness of my temper—you do, you dog! you play upon the meekness of my disposition!—Yet take care—the meekness of a saint may be overcome at last!—but mark! I give you six and a half hours to consider of this...

(The Rivals II,i)

Sir Anthony is a comic version of Lear. Evidently, fathers obsessed by their authority were not uncommon. I do not know of any German play which has a similar passage, but there is such a father-and-son argument in Molière's *L'Avare*.

Children had no escape from or defence against the authority of their parents. From Aubrey's description, everything the child learned was beaten into him: treatment which was hardly educational because it cut off the possibility of sincere communication between parent and child. And the result would be to cause this type of upbringing to continue down the generations, for parents who had had all sensitiveness and all feeling for others beaten out of them early in their lives would become unable to imagine any other kind of upbringing.

Was this parental attitude to children really as general as Aubrey's note suggests? Women had few opportunities outside marriage. It was clearly understood that marriage is not so much love—which all too often means only sexual attraction—as work, the kind of work that the majority of us are born to do and want to do, but still—work. Hence many wives, having created their family, would have become its central pillar, look after the house, the children and their husband the breadwinner. Many marriages must have been harmonious, many parents tolerant and able to bring up their children with the right mixture of discipline and love. Was Aubrey biased by his own early experiences?

Playwrights must base their characters on people they have known and understood and ensure that their audiences will readily understand them; had Shakespeare known excessively authoritarian fathers who had disinherited sons or even turned daughters out of the house for refusing to obey them? Human nature being as fallible as it is, their authority would have gone to some fathers' heads and from Aubrey's description, to some mothers' heads also. Since plays are always written to appeal to and be understood by the audiences of their own time, Shakespeare must have chosen the story of Lear because its theme was familiar to his spectators, and to express his opinion of such extreme authoritarianism. The play would be intended as a topical tragedy, perhaps as a topical warning, in the form of a portrait of an exaggeratedly authoritarian father. Aubrey's description adds some credibility to Shakespeare's picture of Lear.

The argument may also be expressed in terms of the dramatic point that a good play makes to its audiences. Which would have made the more effective principal character, an excessively authoritarian and self-important father who was not unfamiliar to his audiences? Or one who was an extreme rarity (as we today would or should see such a father as Lear), a man so uncommon as to be a mere curiosity?

It is not difficult to imagine Shakespeare choosing a rarity, as did Marlowe with *Tamburlaine the Great* (1587) and *Dr. Faustus* (1604), merely because he would make a spectacular tragic figure, and all Shakespeare's principal tragic figures are outstanding in their various ways. Before he came to write *Lear* he had become fully able to illustrate his insights into human nature with personages that, though great figures who impressed his audiences, were in all other respects recognisably human. I do not believe that when he wrote *Lear* he intended, Marlowe-fashion, merely to offer a spectacularly unusual protagonist to his audiences, i.e. Lear must also have been easily recognisable to them.

If Lear has no wider significance, he is merely spectacular (as, for example, Timon is in his way). His self-importance is certainly spectacular, but I prefer to see him as having contemporary significance arising from the Elizabethan social context and making him familiar to his Elizabethan spectators.

Further justification for this interpretation comes from the fact that Shakespeare deviated from his sources. All the previous versions of the story had happy endings, but Shakespeare's tragic version suggests that he had known or heard of such a father.

While this view may diminish the play in the eyes of some readers, any other explanation of Shakespeare's choice of such a protagonist is difficult to find, for without topical significance its contemporary audiences would have found the play, intense though it is, merely a spectacular tale of a mythical old king.

Why did Lamb say that Lear cannot be acted? It must have been acted convincingly under Shakespeare's direction; in any case, the combination in Lear of high intellect with total belief in one's own rightness—the latter stemming in part from consciousness of the former—is not so uncommon as to be beyond the powers of a perceptive actor.

33
ANTONY AND CLEOPATRA: MISTRESS OR WIFE?

In 1817 William Hazlitt wrote: "She is voluptuous, ostentatious, conscious, boastful of her charms, haughty, tyrannical, fickle." In 1832 Mrs. Anna Jameson continued in the same vein: "She dazzles our faculties, perplexes our judgment, bewilders and bewitches our fancy; from the beginning to the end of the drama we are conscious of a kind of fascination against which our moral sense rebels, but from which there is no escape", and so on. This interpretation, in terms of her "infinite variety", describes merely the surface of Shakespeare's Cleopatra.

That not uncommon figure, the woman who has allowed herself to become a man's mistress and is hoping to become his wife, had already appeared in *Measure for Measure*. At the end of the play Mariana, affianced to Angelo, has played her part in the Bed-trick, now regards him as her husband and pleads for his life:

Duke We do condemn thee to the very block
  Where Claudio stooped to death, and with like haste.
  Away with him.
Mariana   O my most gracious lord,
  I hope you will not mock me with a husband.
Duke It is your husband mocked you with a husband...
            ...For his possessions,
  Although by confiscation they are ours,
  We do instate and widow you with all,
  To buy you a better husband.
Mariana   O my dear lord,
  I crave no other nor no better man.
                    (*Measure for Measure* V,i,411–423)

In spite of the King's offer of Angelo's estate, which as dowry would bring her many offers of marriage, she wants no other man.

After Demetrius and Philo have described her as the "tawny front" and Antony as the "strumpet's fool", Shakespeare's Cleopatra soon reveals what is obsessing her at the beginning of Act I,I,14ff.:

Cleo. If it be love indeed, tell me how much.
Ant. There's beggary in the love that can be reckon'd.
Cleo. I'll set a bourn on how far to be belov'd.
Ant. Then must thou needs find out new heaven, new earth.
[Enter an Attendant.]
Att. News, my good lord, from Rome.
Ant. *[Indifferent]* Grates me; the sum.
Cleo *[At once alert:]* Nay, hear them, Antony:
  Fulvia perchance is angry; or who knows
  If the scarce-bearded Caesar have not sent

>   His powerful mandate to you, "Do this, or this;
>   Take in that kingdom, or enfranchise that;
>   Perform't, or else we damn thee."
> *Ant.* *[Surprised at her sudden insistence on business before pleasure]*
>   How, my love?
> *Cleo.* Perchance? Nay, and most like;
>   You must not stay here longer, your dismission
>   Is come from Caesar, therefore hear it, Antony.
>   Where's Fulvia's process? Caesar's, I would say? Both?
>   Call in the messengers. As I am Egypt's queen,
>   Thou blushest, Antony, and that blood of thine
>   Is Caesar's homager; else so thy cheek pays shame
>   When shrill-tongued Fulvia scolds. The messengers!
> *Ant.* Let Rome in Tiber melt, and the wide arch
>   Of the rang'd empire fall! Here is my space;
>   Kingdoms are clay; our dungy earth alike
>   Feeds beast as man; the nobleness of life
>   Is to do thus: when such a mutual pair
>   And such a pair can do't, in which I bind,
>   On pain of punishment, the world to weet,
>   We stand up peerless.
> *Cleo.*   Excellent falsehood!
>   Why did he marry Fulvia and not love her?
>   *[Wearily sarcastic]*
>   I'll seem the fool I am not; Antony
>   Will be himself.
> *Ant.*   But stirr'd by Cleopatra.
>   Now for the love of love and her soft hours,
>   Let's not confound the time with conference harsh:
>   There's not a minute of our lives should stretch
>   Without some pleasure now. What sport tonight?
> *Cleo.* *[Angrily:]* Hear the ambassadors!
> *Ant.*   Fie, wrangling queen!
>   Whom everything becomes, to chide, to laugh,
>   To weep: how every passion fully strives
>   To make itself, in thee, fair and admired!
>   No messenger but thine, and all alone,
>   Tonight we'll wander through the streets, and note
>   The qualities of people. Come, my queen,
>   Last night you did desire it.
> *[To the ambassadors, who have presumably entered after the Attendant:]*
>   Speak not to us.
>
>   (I,i,14–55)

Cleopatra's references to Fulvia, the wife whom she regards as her rival and of whom she is bitterly jealous, show that thoughts of her take precedence over all others. In line 20, she mentions Fulvia before Caesar, as though news of Fulvia would be more important than news from Caesar. In line 28 she commits a significant slip of the tongue: "Where's Fulvia's process? Caesar's, I would say?" which she then tries to carry off with a further reference to "shrill-tongued Fulvia". Her "Excellent falsehood! / Why did he marry Fulvia, and not love her?" in reply to his profession of love confirms her obsession with Fulvia as a rival.

Next morning she is still angry with him, and leaves as he enters: "We will not look upon him; go with us" (I,ii,84). In I,iii,1ff. she makes clear her intention of venting her annoyance:

[Enter Cleopatra, Charmian, Alexas, and Iras.]
Cleo. Where is he?
Char. I did not see him since.
Cleo. See where he is, who's with him, what he does:
 I did not send you. If you find him sad,
 Say I am dancing; if in mirth, report
 That I am sudden sick. Quick, and return.
[Exit Alexas.]
Char. Madam, methinks if you did love him dearly,
 You do not hold the method, to enforce
 The like from him.
Cleo. What should I do, I do not?
Char. In each thing give him way, cross him in nothing.
Cleo. Thou teachest like a fool: the way to lose him.
Char. Tempt him not so too far. I wish, forbear;
 In time we hate that which we often fear.

Cleopatra's instinct is truer than Charmian's. Octavia, who is contrasted with Cleopatra as completely faithful to her marriage vows, will prove to be the kind of wife who crosses her husband in nothing, but will fail to retain Antony's interest:

[Enter Antony.]
 ...But here comes Antony.
Cleo. I am sick, and sullen.
Ant. I am sorry to give breathing to my purpose,—
Cleo. Help me away, dear Charmian, I shall fall.
 It cannot be thus long, the sides of nature
 Will not sustain it.
Ant. Now, my dearest queen—
Cleo. Pray you, stand farther from me.
Ant. What's the matter?

This is not the 'vapours' or what Antony later calls her "idleness", i.e. her capricious behaviour—it is high female sarcasm! She is saying, "Last evening I urged you four times to listen to the news from Rome, I positively nagged you to hear it, but you insisted on a night of pleasure—and now you come bursting into here full of it!" Her jealousy of Fulvia instantly reappears; it is so strong that she cannot let him defend himself:

Cleo. I know by that same eye there's some good news.
 What, says the married woman you may go?
 Would she had never given you leave to come!
 Let her not say 'tis I that keep you here.
 I have no power upon you; hers you are.

Ant. The gods best know—
Cleo.   O, never was there queen
   So mightily betrayed! yet at the first
   I saw the treason planted.
Ant.   Cleopatra,—
Cleo. Why should I think you can be mine and true
   (Though you in swearing shake the thronèd gods)
   Who have been false to Fulvia? Riotous madness,
   To be entangled with those mouth-made vows
   Which break themselves in swearing!
Ant   Most sweet queen,—
Cleo. Nay, pray you, seek no colour for your going,
   But bid farewell and go: when you sued staying,
   Then was the time for words; no going then;
   Eternity was in our lips and eyes,
   Bliss in our brows' bent; none our parts so poor,
   But was a race of heaven. They are so still,
   Or thou, the greatest soldier of the world,
   Art turned the greatest liar.
Ant.   How now, lady?
Cleo. I would I had thy inches, thou shouldst know
   There were a heart in Egypt.
Ant. *[Now irritated:]*   Hear me, queen:
   The strong necessity of time commands
   Our services awhile; but my full heart
   Remains in use with you. Our Italy
   Shines o'er with civil swords; Sextus Pompeius
   Makes his approaches to the port of Rome;
   Equality of two domestic powers
   Breed scrupulous faction; the hated, grown to strength,
   Are newly grown to love; the condemn'd Pompey,
   Rich in his father's honour, creeps apace
   Into the hearts of such as have not thriv'd
   Upon the present state, whose numbers threaten;
   And quietness, grown sick of rest, would purge
   By any desperate change.
[He is well aware of her obsession with Fulvia.]
                              My more particular,
   And that which most with you should safe my going,
   Is Fulvia's death.
Cleo. Though age from folly could not give me freedom,
   It does from childishness. Can Fulvia die?
Ant.   She's dead, my queen.
   Look here, and at thy sovereign leisure read
   The garboils she awak'd; at the last, best,
   See when and where she died.
Cleo. *[Still quarrelling, or pretending to]*

O most false love!
Where be the sacred vials thou shouldst fill
With sorrowful water? Now I see, I see,
In Fulvia's death, how mine receiv'd shall be.

Ant. Quarrel no more, but be prepared to know
The purposes I bear; which are, or cease,
As you shall give the advice. By the fire
That quickens Nilus' slime, I go from hence
Thy soldier, servant, making peace or war,
As thou affects.

Cleo. *[Still sarcastic]* Cut my lace, Charmian, come;
But let it be, I am quickly ill, and well,
So Antony loves.

Ant. My precious queen, forbear,
And give true evidence to his love, which stands
An honourable trial.

Cleo. So Fulvia told me.

Until now, Cleopatra has been too intent on quarrelling with Antony to reflect on the significance of his news, but it now dawns on her that Fulvia's death enables him to ask her to marry him. Will he?

I prithee turn aside and weep for her,
Then bid adieu to me, and say the tears
Belong to Egypt. Good now, play one scene
Of excellent dissembling, and let it look
Like perfect honour.

[She rises, and throws her arms round his neck, enveloping him in her perfume.]

Ant. You'll heat my blood; no more!

Cleo. *[Archly; clasping him even closer:]*
You can do better yet; but this is meetly.

Ant. Now, by my sword—

Cleo. And target. Still he mends,
But this is not the best.

[He disengages himself.]

Look, prithee, Charmian,
How this Herculean Roman does become
The carriage of his chafe.

Ant. I'll leave you, lady.

[She is still hopeful that he will propose, but quite unable to bring herself to propose to him.]

Cleo. Courteous lord, one word.
Sir, you and I must part, but that's not it:
Sir, you and I have loved, but that's not it;
That you know well, something it is I would—
O, my oblivion is a very Antony,
And I am all forgotten.

Ant. But that your royalty

>   Holds idleness your subject, I should take you
>   For idleness itself.
>
>   (I,iii,1–93)

Even though Antony understands what she is after, he prefers to reply as if his mind is wholly on business. He is not a 'marrying man'. Plutarch says of him that he "disowned anything of marriage". He hadn't much liked being married to Fulvia who, according to Plutarch, had broken him in as a husband, and has already resolved that he "must from this enchanting queen break off" (I,ii,119–125). While Fulvia was alive, his marriage to her confirmed that his roots were in Rome; he will later marry Octavia for that purpose and to ally himself with Octavian. Marriage to Cleopatra would be an act of folly in that he would be enabling his enemies in the Senate to accuse him of forgetting that he was a Roman. He is saying: "Do you not realise this?"

There may also be a hint of contempt in his reply, as there is in some men for women who allow themselves to become their mistresses without insisting on marriage.

By "idleness" he means what Enobarbus later calls her "infinite variety" and which he has already referred to with his "Fie, wrangling queen, / Whom everything becomes" (I,i,48–49), a pretence which she must put on to retain his interest in her, and which she finds infinitely wearisome, and she continues:]

>   *Cleo.*   'Tis sweating labour
>   To bear such idleness so near the heart
>   As Cleopatra this.
> *[She must contain her disappointment as well as she can.]*
>   But, sir, forgive me,
>   Since my becomings kill me, when they do not
>   Eye well to you. Your honour calls you hence,
>   Therefore be deaf to my unpitied folly,
>   And all the gods go with you! Upon your sword
>   Sit laurel victory, and smooth success
>   Be strewed before your feet!
> *[He offers her a few words of consolation as he leaves:]*
>   Let us go. Come;
>   Our separation so abides and flies,
>   That thou, residing here, goes yet with me,
>   And I, hence fleeting, here remain with thee.
>   Away!

Cleopatra is a woman who has allowed herself to become a mistress, then become completely committed to her lover, and now desperately hopes to become his wife:

>   *Cleo.* What, says the married woman you may go?
>   Would she had never given you leave to come!
>   Let her not say 'tis I that keep you here.
>   I have no power upon you; hers you are.

Only too familiar with his pleasure-loving disposition, she tries to compel him to deal with the news from Rome as soon as it arrives and may have done so earlier. Since she is not his wife and has "no power upon him"—the phrase is one of the keys to her—she cannot insist as she would like to.

When Antony says in I,I,33ff.:

Ant. Let Rome in Tiber melt, and the wide arch
Of the rang'd empire fall! Here is my space;
Kingdoms are clay: our dungy earth alike
Feeds beast as man; the nobleness of life
Is to do thus,...

—he is inflating his ego with a splendid-sounding justification of his love of frivolity, and believes himself to be speaking for both of them, but is not, for Cleopatra does not share it:

Cleo. I'll seem the fool *[child]* I am not; Antony
Will be himself.

For her it is "sweating labour". Having taken him as lover and become committed to him, she finds herself trapped: if she is to hold him, she must constantly pander to his addiction to "idleness".

Her behaviour during the rest of the play confirms her commitment to him. In I,v,5–6 she asks for mandragora "That I might sleep out this great gap of time / My Antony is away", eagerly demands news of him from Alexas, and writes to him every day partly—no doubt—to ensure that he, being fickle, is constantly reminded of her. She too is a 'one-man woman':

Cleo. Did I, Charmian,
Ever love Caesar so?
Char. *[Teasing:]* O that brave Caesar!
Cleo. Be choked with such another emphasis;
Say the brave Antony.
Char. The valiant Caesar!
Cleo. By Isis, I will give thee bloody teeth
If thou with Caesar paragon again
My man of men.

(I,v,66–72)

In II,v, she is so maddened by the news of Antony's marriage to Octavia that she vents the fury of a woman scorned upon the Messenger. In III,iii she demands all the details of Octavia's looks, and reveals that she has not lost all hope of attracting Antony back to her:

Cleo. I have one thing more to ask him yet, good Charmian:
But 'tis no matter, thou shalt bring him to me
Where I will write; all may be well enough.

(III,iii,44–46)

The play does not say what she writes but he returns to her before very long.

Antony's desertion tortures her because of her capacity for loyalty and her need of it in return. In II,v she expresses her belief that it is punishment for her disloyalty to the memory of her first lover, Julius Caesar:

Char. Good your highness, patience.
Cleo. In praising Antony, I have dispraised Caesar.
Char. Many times, madam.
Cleo. I am paid for it now.

(II,v,107–109)

She confirms her dearest wish with what are almost her last words:

> *Cleo.* Give me my robe, put on my crown, I have
> Immortal longings in me. Now no more
> The juice of Egypt's grape shall moist this lip.
> Yare, yare, good Iras; quick: methinks I hear
> Antony call. I see him rouse himself
> To praise my noble act. I hear him mock
> The luck of Caesar, which the gods give men
> To excuse their after wrath. Husband, I come:
> Now to that name my courage prove my title!
>
> (V,ii,279–287)

By her loyalty at the end, she is raised from the jealous mistress to the true tragic heroine to her dead lover. Beneath her splendid exterior as queen of the wealthiest country in the Mediterranean basin, she is "No more but e'en a woman, and commanded / By such poor passion as the maid that milks" (IV,xv,73–74).

As for Antony, he is a Triumvir who is "the soldier's pole" and whose legs "bestrid the ocean", he must as be highly intelligent and as self-aware as anyone in such an eminent position needs to be, and his addiction to "idlenesses" must be regarded as deliberate irresponsibility. It is a principal cause of his downfall, the others being his lack of strategic insight before Actium, in which he caused Cleopatra and himself to become besieged and in danger of being starved out; and his allowing her to accompany him in the campaign against Octavian such that both became trapped there. When he fell, he dragged Cleopatra down with him.

This interpretation of Cleopatra should not be taken as diminishing her, for she is in fact two Cleopatras. At times, when she is in the company of Antony, her two women or her other palace attendants with whom she is on intimate terms, she is the private Cleopatra who reveals her inmost hopes. When she is in the company of non-intimates she will display the dignity and authority of the queen of the wealthiest[42] country in the Mediterranean:

> *Alexas*   Good majesty,
> Herod of Jewry dare not look upon you
> But when you are well pleased.
>
> (III,iii,2–4)

At the end of the play she is the defeated queen who can no longer be authoritative; when Octavian and his emissaries come to speak to her she will put on as much of her regal dignity as she can.

As for the pretence of frivolity which she dislikes so much, she can put on an act so persuasively that Enobarbus, the sceptical and irreverent soldier of fortune, finds it convincing:

> *Eno.* Age cannot wither her, nor custom stale
> Her infinite variety: other women cloy
> The appetites they feed, but she makes hungry
> Where most she satisfies.
>
> (II,ii,235–238)

She should therefore be played so as to demonstrate her "infinite variety" with changes

---

42   Food production was then a major industry in all countries, especially since the seasonal flooding of the Nile watered and fertilised its fields and made Egypt a prolific food producer.

of demeanour in accordance with the moment. There are few occasions in the play where she will speak as queen since in creating his own version of her, Shakespeare obviously intended to emphasise the private Cleopatra. She is shown displaying her infinite variety in her first entrance with Antony ("If it be love indeed, tell me how much") and instantly abandons it when the Messenger from Rome enters, again in I,iii when she first "quarrels" with him, then reveals her hope that he will propose to her, but not again, for another such scene would have constituted an out-of-place break in the play's final sequence of tragic events.

Notes:
(1) In his edition of 1765 Dr. Johnson said: "The events of which the principal are described according to history, are produced without any art of connection or care of disposition", and this view of the apparently episodic and disjointed nature of the play has never been challenged. Harley Granville-Barker even said, "In this play there is no dramatically-indicated act-division at all".

Schlegel's comment was more to the point:

> The fullness and variety of warlike and political events, to which the union of the three divisions of the Roman world under one master necessarily gave rise, were too great to admit of being clearly delineated in one dramatic picture. In this consists the great difficulty of the historical drama:—it must be a crowded extract and a living development of history:—the difficulty has in general been satisfactorily overcome by Shakespeare. But here many things, which are transacted in the background, are merely alluded to, in a manner which supposes an intimate acquaintance with the history, and a work of art should contain everything for fully understanding it within itself. Many persons of historical importance are merely introduced in passing, the preparatory and concurrent circumstances are not sufficiently collected into masses to avoid distracting our attention.

So many characters do appear, and so many circumstances are alluded to briefly, that Shakespeare must indeed have assumed a detailed acquaintance with the events of the time, at least among his better-read spectators, and since he was an extremely experienced playwright, he may well have been justified. He either made a historical mistake or changed history with Cleopatra's "If not denounced against us" (III,vii,5), for after the Donations of Alexandria in 34B.C. the Roman Senate declared war on Cleopatra but not on Antony, whom it merely deprived of his position as Triumvir.

What did Schlegel mean by "not sufficiently collected into masses to avoid distracting our attention"? He seems only to have half-realised that the theme of the play is not so much the liaison of Antony with Cleopatra as of how that liaison changed the course of Roman history: the play's theme is as much its political consequences and global consequences at the time as its amorous nature.

Shakespeare's Roman plays are not grouped with his 'histories', although they are as much 'histories' as the earlier plays, with the trivial difference that the historian was Plutarch instead of Holinshed; and the much more important point that the Roman plays are not mere dramatised documentaries but tragedies with emphasis on character or character-defect as the prime cause of the tragic outcome. *Julius Caesar* and *Antony and Cleopatra* are accounts of two episodes which drastically changed the course of Roman history; *Coriolanus* of one which almost caused such a change, and all contain vivid characterisations.

If the play contains a defect in construction or organisation, it is that Shakespeare's picture of Cleopatra absorbs attention to the point where the tragedy becomes her tragedy more than Antony's, although the play is entitled *Antony and Cleopatra*, not merely *Cleopatra*.

As for its framework, a few changes in the act-divisions cause it to fall naturally into the conventional five-act 'masses':

(i) Exposition (I,i to II,i)

We immediately learn that Antony is a "strumpet's fool"; when he and Cleopatra enter, we meet the "strumpet" and learn that Antony is too prone to postpone business for pleasure, in spite of Cleopatra's urging. After an amusing introduction to Charmian and Iras, we hear of Fulvia's "garboils" and of her death, also of Pompey's dominance of the seas round Italy. Antony must leave for Rome. We meet Enobarbus.

In Rome, Octavian and Lepidus discuss Antony's excessive addiction to "sport" and "lascivious wassail"; his presence is required in Rome, particularly because of Pompey and his piratical allies Menecrates and Menas.

For Cleopatra, time goes heavily without Antony.

Pompey and his pirates are introduced; he is perturbed to learn that Antony has left "the lap of Egypt's widow" and is hourly expected in Rome.

We have now met most of the principals.

(ii) Development (II,ii to III,ii)

Antony, Octavian and Lepidus meet, Lepidus being the peacemaker. Octavian states his complaints against Antony, who replies to them. Agrippa proposes that Antony marry Octavia, Octavian's beloved sister, and so unite them in amity; Antony agrees and Octavian gives his assent. Enobarbus describes Antony's meeting with Cleopatra; he does not believe that Antony will "leave her utterly".

Antony meets Octavia and promises that "that to come / Shall all be done by rule". The Soothsayer warns him that his "angel" is "o'erpowered" in Octavian's presence, but that his "demon" is "unmatchable" when he is away from Caesar. Immediately afterwards, Antony says "I'th'east my pleasure lies". He dispatches Ventidius against the Parthians. Lepidus, Maecenas and Agrippa agree to meet at Mount Misenum.

On recalling amusing times with Antony, Cleopatra hears of his marriage and is so enraged that she attacks the messenger.

Antony, Octavian and Lepidus meet Pompey and settle their differences. Enobarbus repeats his belief that Antony "will to his Egyptian dish again".

They celebrate their accord on Pompey's galley; knowing that Lepidus cannot hold his liquor, the others induce him to drink too much. Menas urges Pompey to "cut the cable and fall to their throats" and so make himself the sole master of the Roman Empire; when he refuses, Menas decides to desert his service.

Though Ventidius has defeated the Parthians, he realises that he must give Antony the credit.

Antony and Octavia take their leave of Octavian, Antony promising to "cherish" her.

(iii) Climax (III,iii to III,x)

Cleopatra has got over her rage and is scheming to induce Antony to return to her.

Fresh causes of dissension are arising between Octavian and Antony; to Octavia's sorrow, a confrontation seems imminent. Antony sends her home to Rome from Athens. He is angered that Lepidus has been deposed and Pompey expelled from Sicily, and then murdered. His fleet is "ready for Italy and Caesar".

Octavian recounts Antony's actions to his supporters Agrippa and Maecenas; Antony has returned to Cleopatra and extended her kingdom by giving her three provinces outside Egypt (the Donations of Alexandria), appointed her two young sons (his sons) to six Middle Eastern kingdoms, and allied himself with a number of Middle Eastern monarchs.

Octavia arrives from Athens; Octavian is angered by Antony's treatment of his beloved sister. Her loyalty to Antony is raising Roman feeling against him. Clearly, Antony has given himself and his "regiment" completely to "the Egyptian trull", and is building his own empire in contempt of Rome. Octavian declares war on Cleopatra.

Against better advice, Cleopatra insists on accompanying Antony in his campaign against Octavian. They reach Actium. When Octavian's capture of Toryne takes him by surprise, he agrees, again against better advice, to accept Cleopatra's urging and fight by sea instead of by land. When Cleopatra and her ships flee the battle, Antony flees after her.

(iv) Continuation or Descending Action (III,xi to IV,xiii)
In Alexandria Antony is deeply ashamed, and reproaches Cleopatra for her dominance over him, then relents.

Octavian rejects Antony's appeal through his ambassador; to Cleopatra he will give her requests favourable consideration if she takes Antony's life or drives him out of Egypt. He sends Thidias to Cleopatra; Antony is infuriated by her reception of him, has him whipped, and reproaches her bitterly, then recovers his spirits. Enobarbus, believing that Antony has now lost all judgment, decides to desert him.

Octavian rejects Antony's challenge to single combat. Strange music is heard in the air. Antony arms for battle. He learns that Enobarbus has gone over to Octavian, and sends his baggage after him.

Octavian orders that Antony "be took alive" in the impending battle, but is beaten back to his camp. Enobarbus, learning of Antony's generosity, is ashamed and later dies, consumed by remorse for his desertion.

Next day, Antony decides to fight by sea; the crews defect to Octavian. Enraged by Cleopatra's apparent treachery, he threatens her life. In panic, she flees to the Monument, and has word sent to him that she has slain herself.

On hearing of her death, Antony orders Eros to kill him; instead Eros kills himself. Though he then falls on his sword, he does not die yet. Hearing that Cleopatra is not dead, he has himself brought to her, and dies in her arms. Immediately she begins to think of suicide, but when the Monument is "surprised", she is captured.

(v) Catastrophe (V,i to end)
Refusing to believe Octavian's assurances Cleopatra deceives him as to her intentions by failing to declare half her treasure, as she might if she intended to remain alive. She has already arranged for the asps to be brought in; when Dolabella confirms that Caesar intends to lead her in triumph at Rome, she and her women make use of them. Octavian: "No grave upon the earth shall clip in it / A pair so famous".

While there is a case for placing the Actium scenes at the beginning of the Descending Action, the decision to fight by sea at Actium was the culminating mistake of the three made by Antony after his return to Cleopatra, with the first two being the Donations of

Alexandria and his allowing Cleopatra to accompany her in his campaign against Octavian; and all of them made under her persuasion, and signifying her dominance of him. It appears preferable to keep them together in the Climax.

As for the division between the fourth and fifth acts, it might come before Antony's death so that the last act would depict the tragedy of both equally, but there is a better case for leaving it where it is, as Cleopatra is completely in Antony's power and becomes the helpless victim of his mistakes.

While all this may appear to be of academic interest only, it shows that the play is by no means as 'episodic' as its early editors found, that it is in fact both a history and a tragedy of character. Its canvas is so wide, the scope of its events so world-shaking at the time, its characters so varied and so vivid, its principals so gigantic, its poetry so superb, and its construction proving on examination to be so consistent, that it may be rated as the greatest of Shakespeare's "histories", and second only to *Hamlet* in the order of greatness of his plays.

(2) "Near Actium" (IV,iii).
In the First Folio, the venues of scenes are not given in their preliminary stage directions, and the usual heading given to IV,iii is *[Near Actium. Antony's camp. Enter Cleopatra and Enobarbus]*. The argument between them as to whether Cleopatra should accompany Antony on the campaign against Octavian then follows; however, according to Plutarch, this argument took place in Ephesus during their preparations for the campaign:

> ...and he himselfe with Cleopatra, went unto the citie of Ephesus, and there gathered together his gallies and shippes out of all parts...So Antonius, through the perswasions of Domitius [Enobarbus], commaunded Cleopatra to returne againe into Aegypt, and there to understand the successe of this warre. But Cleopatra, fearing least Antonius should againe be made friends with Octavius Caesar, by the means of his wife Octavia: she so plyed Canidius with money, and filled his purse, that he became her spoken man unto Antonius, and told him there was no reason to send her from this warre.

Cleopatra's "I will not stay behind" fits Ephesus. Shakespeare makes Enobarbus voice his objections in person to Cleopatra, though whether he did is not clear from Plutarch's account, and does not mention Cleopatra's bribing of Canidius to persuade Antony to let her accompany him.

Enobarbus continues with "Nay, I have done, here comes the emperor," Antony and Canidius enter, and now the scene is indeed Actium, for they speak of Octavian's sudden capture of Toryne, which took Antony by surprise and trapped him in Actium, and argue over Antony's decision to fight at sea rather than on land.

In view of Enobarbus' continuation, which apparently confirms that the scene of both conversations is Actium, "I would not stay behind" would be more apt than "I will not stay behind"; even so, the conversation comes too late in the course of events.

Why did Cleopatra insist on accompanying Antony on the campaign against Octavian? She would know that he would have to take with him a large sum from her treasure to pay his men, and that he, being addicted to frivolities, would fritter it away on amusements if she did not go with him and keep the purse-strings in her own hands.

3) An apparent departure from history is Cleopatra's hope that Antony will propose mar-

riage to her, for under Roman law a Roman citizen could only marry another Roman citizen unless he was prepared to forfeit the privileges of Roman citizenship, nor could he marry two wives. The historical Cleopatra would be aware of this law, and would probably have accepted his marriage to Octavia as a political necessity, intended to confirm to Octavian and the Senate that in spite of his long association with her his roots were still in Rome. However, she may have been suffering from jealousy, for about two years before Actium Antony ordered Octavia to leave his house in Rome. This was a mistake because the virtuous and gentle Octavia was so highly regarded that many eminent Romans turned against him. Did he do it under her persuasion?

Plutarch records how, after Octavia had obtained leave from Octavian to travel from Rome to Athens in order to be near Antony while he was preparing for a foray against the Parthians, Cleopatra began to feign the appearance of a mistress who was languishing for her lover, even dieting in order to suggest that she was pining away! Supported by her friends and attendants, so convincing was she that Antony postponed his campaign and left Athens to be with her in Alexandria. This passage may have suggested to Shakespeare that he should emphasise her jealousy.

Why did Antony become so addicted and, in the end, so fatally addicted to Cleopatra's company?

Plutarch describes her as not outstandingly beautiful; it was when she began to speak that the charm of her conversation attracted all near her. She could converse with many ambassadors in their own languages: Plutarch names seven and adds "and many others". When persuading Antony to allow her to accompany him in his campaign against Octavian, one of her arguments was that as ruler of her country she was the equal of any neighbouring male monarch (Herod, confirmed by III,iii,2–4). He may therefore have become so addicted to her not only because she was his "Egyptian dish" but because she could offer him the intellectual companionship of a mind equal in calibre to his own, something that he never encountered in any other woman—and which, of course, was reinforced by high feminine guile.

If she had such a mind, did she really become jealous? She was certainly calculating; she prepared for her first meeting with him on the river Cygnus with great care; and she could be ruthless, as when she persuaded Antony to have her half-sister Antinöe dragged from sanctuary at Ephesus and executed, so eliminating the last possible competitor for the throne of Egypt.

Would a mind capable of such cold rationality also suffer from jealousy? Since Shakespeare's insights into human motives have rarely been equalled, he may well have been correct in displaying her as jealous of both Antony's wives. Her intention was always to consolidate her position as queen of Egypt under the aegis of Rome, and her "jealousy" may have been a deliberate pretence, put on to support her purpose by keeping Antony's attention on her. At the same time, although she was a queen she was also a woman and the mother of three of Antony's children, so she may well have been as jealous as Shakespeare portrays her.

(4) Cleopatra bore a child, Caesarion, to Julius Caesar, then three more to Antony, who were still very young at the time of the final defeat in Alexandria. For this reason and her uncertainty over their fates, her decision to end her own life rather than be led in triumph through Rome must have been made in horror and despair because of her uncertainty over their fates.

In the play the children are only mentioned very briefly:

Oct. ...you shall bereave yourself
  Of my good purposes, and put your children
  To that destruction which I'll guard them from,
  If thereon you rely.

(V,ii,129–132)

Dol. I tell you this: Caesar through Syria
  Intends his journey, and within three days
  You with your children will he send before...

(V,ii,199–201)

Did Shakespeare really intend to suggest that Cleopatra's thoughts in her last moments were all on Antony ("Husband, I come"), although she as their mother would hardly have forgotten her children? Perhaps he remembered them and directed the boy actor playing Cleopatra to display a visible reaction to these somewhat threatening references to them.

(5) *Cleopatra*   Look, prithee, Charmian,
  How this Herculean Roman does become
  The carriage of his chafe.

(I,iii,83–85)

"The carriage of his chafe" might have been a term from horse-riding: a restive horse, disliking its treatment by its rider, might try to throw him. The OED gives an equivalent meaning; after a definition of 'chafe' as 'to inflame the feelings' it gives 'to rub so as to abrade or injure the surface', the example being 'the flap of your saddle chafing you between the confines of the boots and breeches'. While the example is dated 1787, such chafing would long have been a commonplace experience. Thus I conclude that Cleopatra throws her arms round Antony's neck, hoping to heat his blood; he then complains that she is indeed heating it, and pushes her away from him. Alternatively, she is seated when he enters, and he takes a chair; she then goes to him and sits in his lap. Without some such stage business, Antony's "No more, you'll heat my blood" remains unexplained.

(6)   The real historical Enobarbus, who realised that Antony had let himself become trapped in Actium and was facing defeat, deserted him just before the battle. With his typical generosity, Antony had his baggage sent after him, but, being ill, he died a few days later. Shakespeare makes him desert before Antony's final defeat in Alexandria; evidently he decided that grouping the desertion with Antony's other final misfortunes and placing it just before the Catastrophe, would be more dramatically effective than in the Climax.

Which would have been the more effective placing is hard to decide. Shakespeare makes him anticipate his desertion:

Eno.   I'll yet follow
  The wounded chance of Antony, though my reason
  Sits in the wind against me.

(III,x,35–37)

(7) 'Emperor':

Antony is five times called 'emperor' (III,vii,19; III,vii 61; IV,vi,28; IV,vii,4; V,ii,76); Octavian once (V,ii,113). 'Imperator' was a title of honour awarded to generals who had won a notable victory for Rome; applied to the later Roman emperors, it meant 'supreme commander' or 'supreme general' rather than 'ruler ranking above a king'. Rome remained, nominally at least, a republic.

The legions had their own battle standards, hence 'soldier's pole' (IV,xv,65) meant either 'battle standard' or 'Pole star', or perhaps both.

34

THE LAST PLAYS

Coriolanus is regarded by the French critics as Shakespeare's most perfect play, presumably because, being more taut in both style and construction than his other plays, it conforms more closely with the previously mentioned "Rules" of the seventeenth century.

It contains several motifs woven together: the discontent of the common people with their patrician rulers who are "famishing" them, the wars between Rome and the Volsci, the personal rivalry between Caius Martius (afterwards Coriolanus) and Tullus Aufidius the general of the Volsci, and a 'family' motif arising from the nature of Coriolanus himself. This proves to be an equally important theme, perhaps the most important: how has Coriolanus come to be so obsessively convinced of his superiority to all around him that he is now intolerably arrogant, even scorning the praises and thanks offered by his compatriots for his heroism in battle?

He is married to Virgilia, whom he greets as "My gracious silence" (II,i,174), and who is described by John Middleton Murry (1859–1957) as a "neglected heroine of Shakespeare": "In the play Virgilia speaks barely a hundred words. But they are truly the speech of a 'gracious silence'." The appellation suggests that though she is of a submissive nature, she is not, for she steadfastly refuses the urgings of Volumnia and Valeria to leave her house and enjoy a little "mirth" outside it (I,iii) while her husband is fighting. She is another of Shakespeare's dedicated wives; she may be compared to Desdemona, who creates a haven in life for Othello. Coriolanus' excessive arrogance has isolated him from his fellow Romans, but he welcomes Virgilia's unquestioning love and loyalty in his own home.

He has been brought up by his imperious, aristocratic mother Volumnia, who encouraged him to become a fighter and apparently little else as explained in the opening lines of the first act:

Vol. When he was yet but tender-bodied and the only son of my womb, when youth with comeliness plucked all gaze his way, when for a day of king's entreaties a mother should not sell him an hour from her beholding, I, considering how honour could become such a person—that it was no better than picture-like to hang by th'wall, if renown made it not stir—was pleased to let him seek danger where he was like to find fame. To a cruel war I sent him, from whence he returned his brows bound with oak. I tell thee, daughter, I sprang not more in joy at first hearing that he was a man-child than now in first seeing he had proved himself a man.

She does not speak explicitly of encouraging him in any higher ambition, such as to rise to some high position in the government of Rome; he becomes content to fight for his country without thought of reward or even personal prestige:

Mar. (i.e. Coriolanus) I thank you, general,
But cannot make my heart consent to take
A bribe to pay my sword...

(I,ix,36–38)

Only after his defeat of the Volsci does she say:
Vol. ...only
There's one thing wanting, which I doubt not but
Our Rome shall cast upon thee.

(II,i,198–200)

Why, then, has Coriolanus become the grown-up boy with a hyper-inflated ego and no sense of proportion, to the point where he is almost a psychopath? The responsibility does not rest with Volumnia, who has never lost hers, for in III,ii she urges him to dissemble when appealing to the plebs for votes; and at the end of the play pleads with him to return to Rome. It seems likely that he was born without such a sense, and that his supreme prowess in battle has given it no chance to develop:

Vol. Thy valiantness was mine, thou suckst it from me,
    But owe thy pride thyself.

(III,ii,129–130)

His "mammocking" with the gilded butterfly (I,iii,61 on) may even suggest that there is a vein of childish cruelty in him, or at least of indifference to the sufferings of others. He even boasts of the wives he has widowed in Corioli and the children he has rendered fatherless. (II.i,176–178).

In III,iii he is accused of being "a traitor to the people", and is so angered that he decides to desert Rome and bids farewell to his wife and mother (IV,i,20).

At the end, when Volumnia, Virgilia, Valeria and his little son come to plead with him not to remain Rome's enemy, he realises that in letting his arrogance drive him from his roots in Rome he had also severed himself from his life's haven.

Virgilia and Volumnia are both neglected, for after Coriolanus has been killed by the Volsci the play does not remind us that they too have become victims of his arrogance. I imagine a modern production in which the point is made clear at the end by the introduction of a silent episode following the final words of the play:

Aufidius   My rage is gone,
    And I am struck with sorrow...

(V,vi,146–147)

All leave the stage. Re-enter Volumnia and Virgilia, returning because Coriolanus has not followed them. When they see his body, shock overcomes them, they cling together for a few moments as Volumnia realises that she has lost her only child; Virgilia, that she is now a widow with a little son to bring up. They then slowly leave the stage. Re-enter Aufidius and friends:

Aufidius   Take him up...

When nearing the end of his playwriting career, Shakespeare abandoned tragedies and began to dramatise adventure stories; however, he did not completely abandon the "family" theme.

He probably chose to dramatise the story of *Timon of Athens* because he was in need of a plot for his next play, its only passage relevant to the "family" theme being Timon's description of the long-term effects of untreated syphilis, then incurable:

Timon   Consumptions sow
    In hollow bones of man; strike their sharp shins
    And mar men's spurring. Crack the lawyer's voice,
    That he may never more false title plead,
    Nor sound his quillets shrilly: hoar the flamen,
    That scolds against the quality of flesh,

>   And not believes himself: down with the nose,
>   Down with it flat; take the bridge quite away,
>   Of him that, his particular to foresee,
>   Smells from the general weal: make curl'd-pate ruffians bald;
>   And let the unscarr'd braggarts of the war
>   Derive some pain from you: plague all;
>   That your activity may defeat and quell
>   The source of all erection.—There's more gold:—
>   Do you damn others, and let this damn you,
>   And ditches grave you all!
>
> <div align="right">(<i>Tim.</i> IV,iii,154–169)</div>

This passage contributes nothing to our understanding of the situation or of 'character' as it merely confirms Timon's disillusionment, nor does it advance the action—but Shakespeare inserted it.

In *The Winter's Tale*, Leontes begins to suffer from uncontrollable physical jealousy. He and his queen Hermione persuade his boyhood friend and guest Polixenes, who needs to return to his own kingdom of Sicilia, to stay a little longer; then, when he sees Polixenes and Hermione holding hands and "paddling in the palms", he is at once so overcome by jealous suspicion that he even begins to suspect that his little son Mamillius is not his own child.

The "paddling" or "virginalling" in the palms may be no more than a children's' tickling game (perhaps still being played): tickling a playmate's palm by gently scratching it with a forefinger nail, but it is not the only cause of Leontes' suspicions:

> *Leontes*   Is whispering nothing?
>   Is leaning cheek to cheek? Is meeting noses?
>   Kissing with inside lip? Stopping the career
>   Of laughter with a sigh?—a note infallible
>   Of breaking honesty. Horsing foot on foot?
>   Skulking in corners? Wishing clocks more swift?
>   Hours minutes? Noon midnight? And all eyes
>   Blind with the pin and web but theirs, theirs only,
>   That would unseen be wicked—is this nothing?
>
> (I,ii.284–292)

How old is Hermione? Since she has already given birth to Mamillius, who must be five or six, her age is uncertain. Perhaps she was married when very young, as Elizabethan wives could be, and has not yet realised (as Desdemona, who allows Cassio to kiss her, has not—Othello, II,i,99), that after marriage a girl should avoid physical contact with all males other than her husband.

Her second baby is about to arrive; when it does, Leontes is so obsessed by jealous suspicions that he has Hermione imprisoned and the babe exposed on the seacoast of Bohemia, rejecting all assurances of her innocence. Only when Mamillius suddenly dies, and Hermione herself apparently dies, does he realise what he has thrown away.

Posthumus in *Cymbeline* also begins to suffer from physical jealousy. He allows himself to be tempted into a foolish wager on his wife's fidelity; when he becomes persuaded that he has lost it, he too loses all sense of proportion, goes even further than Leontes, and becomes the complete misogynist before he discovers his error:

> *Posthumus* Is there no way for men to be, but women

>   Must be half-workers? We are all bastards;
>   And that most venerable man which I
>   Did call my father, was I know not where
>   When I was stampt; some coiner with his tools
>   Made me a counterfeit; yet my mother seem'd
>   The Dian of that time; so doth my wife
>   The nonpareil of this...
>   ...For there's no motion
>   That tends to vice in man, but I affirm
>   It is the woman's part...
>
>   (II,v,1ff.)

In *Pericles*, Marina is captured by pirates and sold to a brothel-keeper (at age fourteen—IV,ii and iii), but pleads for her chastity, and is eventually rescued.

In *Hamlet* Shakespeare had caused Laertes to warn Ophelia against young men's protestations of love:

> *Laertes* Then weigh what loss your honour may sustain,
>   If with too credent ear you list his songs,
>   Or lose your heart, or your chaste treasure open
>   To his unmastered importunity.
>   Fear it, Ophelia, fear it, my dear sister,
>   And keep you in the rear of your affection.
>
>   (I,iii,29–34)

He had earlier phrased the warning more forcibly in Sonnet 129:

> The expense of spirit in a waste of shame
> Is lust in action; and till action, lust
> Is perjured, murd'rous, bloody, full of blame,
> Savage, extreme, rude, cruel, not to trust;
> Enjoyed no sooner but despised straight;
> Past reason hunted; and no sooner had,
> Past reason hated, as a swallow'd bait,
> On purpose laid to make the taker mad:
> Mad in pursuit, and in possession so;
> Had, having, and in quest to have, extreme;
> A bliss in proof, and proved, a very woe;
> Before, a joy proposed; behind, a dream.
> All this the world well knows; yet none knows well
> To shun the heaven that leads men to this hell.

In *All's Well That Ends Well*, Shakespeare repeated the warning:

> *Mariana* Well, Diana, take heed of this French earl; the honour of a maid is her name, and no legacy is so rich as honesty.
>
> *Widow* I have told my neighbour how you have been solicited by a gentleman his companion.
>
> *Mariana* I know that knave, hang him! one Parolles; a filthy officer he is in those suggestions for the young earl. Beware of them, Diana: their promises, enticements, oaths, tokens, and all these engines of lust, are not the things they go under; many a

maid hath been seduced by them; and the misery is, example, that so terrible shows in the wrack of maidenhood, cannot for all that dissuade succession, but that they are limed with the twigs that threaten them.

(III,v,11–24)

The *Tempest* contains a magician, a fairy, a malicious ugly monster, a beautiful young girl, two villains who provide tense moments, and two characters who provide broad comedy; its plot starts with a disaster and comes to a totally happy ending—again the ingredients of a British Christmas pantomime. It can be summed up in four lines:
    a) plot: very satisfactory to its audience;
    b) characterisation: as much as is needed;
    c) poetic content: extremely high;
    d) serious dramatic content: virtually none.

He now repeated the warning for the last time, emphasising that husbands must not break their marriage vows:

Prospero   O Ferdinand,
   Do not smile at me that I boast her off,
   For thou shalt find she will outstrip all praise,
   And make it halt behind her.
Ferdinand   I do believe it
   Against an oracle.
Prospero Then, as my gift, and thine own acquisition
   Worthily purchased, take my daughter: but
   If thou dost break her virgin-knot before
   All sanctimonious ceremonies may
   With full and holy rite be minister'd,
   No sweet aspersion shall the heavens let fall
   To make this contract grow; but barren hate
   Sour-eyed disdain, and discord, shall bestrew
   The union of your bed with weeds so loathly
   That you shall hate it both: therefore take heed,
   As Hymen's lamps shall light you...
   ...Look thou be true; do not give dalliance
   Too much the rein: the strongest oaths are straw
   To the fire i'the blood: be more abstemious,
   Or else goodnight your vow!

(IV,i,8–25 and 51–54)

Was Shakespeare preaching? I am quite sure that he was, although, since he was the born playwright, I am also sure that he would instinctively understand the rule of the French seventeenth-century playwrights, that plays must point a moral but by naturalness of characterisation rather than by overt moralising. In his last plays he did overtly moralise, but only in brief passages.

Why did Shakespeare turn from tragedies to tales with happy endings? Since he had long intended to buy an estate and house in Stratford and spend his last years there in comfortable and secure retirement, he needed to make money, and may have found that plays with happy endings paid better at the box office than tragedies. Did he also find that he might as well settle for entertaining his audiences instead of preaching to them, because the insights he had built into his tragedies were having no measurable effect on the behaviour of the population around him?

What effect did they have? If the licentiousness of the Restoration is a guide, not to mention the Swinging Sixties of the twentieth century—little or none; to a member of the older generation, a depressing thought.

PART IV
ODDMENTS

35

TWO JACOBEAN SPOOFS
The Revenger's Tragedy
&
The Atheist's Tragedy

> The cynicism, the loathing and disgust of humanity expressed consummately in "The Revenger's Tragedy" are immature in the respect that they exceed the object. Their objective equivalents are characters practising the grossest vices; characters which seem merely to be spectres projected from the poet's inner world of nightmare, some horror beyond words. So the play is a document on humanity chiefly because it is a document on one human being, Tourneur; its motive is truly the death motive, for it is the loathing and horror of life itself.
>
> T.S.Eliot's review of Allardyce Niccoll's edition,
The Works of Cyril Tourneur (1930)

Dead-pan humour may be defined as saying something which you don't or even couldn't possibly mean seriously, but with a straight face as if you did. Appreciation of such humour requires that one must have been sufficiently exposed to it to recognise it instantly for what it is, though the academic outlook is necessarily somewhat literal. Along with some others, Eliot appears to have been too little exposed to it!

Coming nearer the mark, a later critic almost hit it:

> Many authors were writing this kind of tragedy of horrors; it is full of devices (of plot, language and stagecraft) familiar from earlier tragedies; and its fascinations with the corruptions of lust and power seems to have been an obsession of the age...The author in effect declares his awareness that *The Spanish Tragedy* has been performed too often (something asserted more explicitly by other Jacobean authors) and the only viable move remaining is its conversion to black humour through hyperbole.
>
> Robert N. Watson, essay on "Tragedy" in
The Cambridge Companion to English Renaissance Drama

The Revenger's Tragedy is indeed a satire on the plays of this type and on the tastes of the audiences to whom the playwrights were catering; it is a dead-pan spoof of the revenge-tragedy genre. In its exaggerations of style, it spoofs characterisation (even to the names of characters), and situations, to the point where it is almost all black comedy and even farce. By 1606 or 1607, the date to which the play is ascribed, the revenge-tragedy genre was twenty years old and had already reached its peak in *Hamlet*. Thus the author of the play may have decided that the genre was ripe for satirising. It is easy to mistake its intention, for it is superbly dead-pan from beginning to end.

The play opens with Vindice apostrophising the skull of his dead beloved who was poisoned by the old Duke when she refused his advances. We later learn that Vindice's father died in despair because of the disfavour of the old Duke. He has two reasons for desiring revenge, and he has been waiting no fewer than nine years (III,v,121). So he is now very frustrated indeed and quite ready to become the "villainous" avenger: "Brother, I'll be that strange-composed fellow".

He offers himself to Lussurioso in disguise as "Piato", immediately learns that his first task will be to persuade his own sister to become Lussurioso's mistress, and even to approach his mother to help in persuading her. When Lussurioso requires him to swear loyalty to him, he cannot escape doing so.

In conformity with his oath, he approaches his sister, who slaps his face but, to his horror, his mother agrees to help to persuade Castiza because the family is so poor; apparently neither his sister nor his mother recognises him under his disguise! The situation has now been turned upside-down, and it is only the first of a sequence of such inversions. Time after time, things will go unexpectedly wrong for character after character.

Lussurioso invades the old Duke's bedroom on the suggestion of "Piato" that the Duchess is in bed with Spurio, the Duke's bastard son, only to find that she is with the Duke himself, who angrily sends him to prison. Junior, the youngest stepson, who has raped Antonio's wife, is also in prison. The stepbrothers send an order to the prison officers to execute the criminal, intending the victim to be Lussurioso, whom they hope to eliminate as successor to the dukedom, and to bring the head to them in a bag; however, when they open the bag, they find that it is their brother's—very black comedy indeed.

Vindice succeeds in poisoning the old Duke, using a mysterious poison which eats away the Duke's lips, teeth and tongue before killing him. Lussurioso decides that "Piato" was the murderer, so Vindice offers himself to Lussurioso in another guise, and finds that his first task will be to find and kill himself! Lussurioso then orders horsemen to be sent out to scour the countryside for "Piato" while "Piato" is standing next to him.

In IV,iv the brothers enter, propelling their mother by the shoulders and with drawn daggers, and demand that she change her views. She defies them, until Vindice reveals that he had been "Piato":

Vindice   I was the man:
   Defy me now! let's see, do't modestly.
Grat.   O hell unto my soul!
Vindice   In that disguise,
   I, sent from the Duke's son,
   Tried you, and found you base metal,
   As any villain might have done.

Gratiana recants, the two brothers leave, and—remembering that spectators see as well as hear what is happening on the stage—the remainder of the scene may have been played as follows:

Castiza enters, looking like a woman of the streets: she has fluffed out her hair and put a flower in it, her arms are bare and her blouse exposes much of her cleavage, she is wearing a loose and flowing skirt whose lines she accentuates with a swing of the hips as she walks, and she is negligently dangling an upper-body garment with full sleeves from a forefinger.

Cast.   Now mother, you have wrought with me so strongly
   That what for my advancement, as to calm
   The trouble of your tongue, I am content...

She insists until Gratiana, horrified, turns away and hides her face in her hands. Castiza now rapidly tidies her appearance: she smooths her hair and throws the flower away, puts on

the upper-body garment and closes it to the neck, then goes to her mother and gently turns her to face her.
Cast. O mother, let me twine about your neck...

I feel sure that many of the play's spectators who had seen other revenge tragedies were soon asking themselves "What kind of play is this? Would a bare, bony skull really remind anyone of its former owner's beauty? And who is this Old Duke? Could an old man so parched and juiceless really remain so insatiably lustful? And is not nine years a somewhat long time to have been waiting for revenge?" Surely the acting, particularly when characters found themselves discomfited, must have revealed that the play, though nominally on a revenge theme, was all black farce? At appropriate moments towards the end, there are even rolls of thunder, flashes of lightning, and a blazing star.

They may even have asked themselves "Why is it called simply *'The Revenger's Tragedy'*, when all revenge tragedies are revengers' tragedies? Is it the revenger's tragedy to end all revengers' tragedies?"

At the very end of the play, the masked revellers enter, kill Lussurioso and leave, all except—unfortunately for themselves—Vindice and Hippolito. The stepbrothers then kill one another in dispute over who shall inherit the dukedom. The whole court is now clear of corruption; even Antonio, the new Duke, has been revenged for the death of his wife, but when a smirking Vindice reveals that he and his brother had organised it all, Antonio turns on them:

Antonio You two?
Vindice None else i'faith my Lord, nay 'twas well managed.
Antonio Lay hands upon those villains.
Vindice How? on us?
Antonio Bear 'em to speedy execution.
Vindice Heart, was't not for your good my Lord?
Antonio Away with 'em; such an old man as he,
   You that would murder him would murder me.

Not the noblest of reasons, this, is it? Should he not be speaking in terms, not of his personal safety, but of the respect due to law and justice?

Laurel and Hardy, those two old comedy characters, were often seen sometimes sitting in a police cell, blaming one another for whatever disaster had occurred, although, when all is lost, argument over whose fault it was is a fruitless exercise. Still, some minds do it, and the playwright must have known that they do, for he now made the two brothers blame one another, if only briefly:

Vindice Is't come about?
Hipp. 'Sfoot, brother, you begun.
Vindice May we not set as well as the Duke's son?
   Thou hast no conscience, are we not reveng'd?

How was this little episode acted? And did any of the spectators cheer the two brothers off the stage after Vindice's final defiant speech?

Tourneur's tongue was certainly in his cheek when he wrote *The Atheist's Tragedy*, for it is another dead-pan spoof of the revenge-tragedy type of play, also a satire on the

Elizabethan hatred of atheism, but a very quiet sort for, as indicated by the fate of Kyd, overt satire would have been too dangerous.

Some of the names—Levidulcia, Castabella, Languebeau Snuffe, Cataplasma, Soquette, Fresco—indicate a satirical intention, Languebeau Snuffe being a semi-comic satire on the Puritans of the day. The play's ghost is so very different from that in *Hamlet* that it must have been intended as a sideswipe at that play. The Elder Hamlet reveals to its son that it was murdered, and reappears in the closet scene to "whet thy almost blunted purpose", but Montferrer's ghost informs its son that it was murdered, then adds "Leave revenge unto the King of Kings", and later, when forbidding Charlemont to kill Sebastian, repeats the injunction.

Charlemont's behaviour is also the opposite of Hamlet's, for Hamlet displays no repentance for his killing of Polonius and later says "O, from this time forth / My thoughts be bloody, or be nothing worth", whereas Charlemont insists on being arrested and tried for the killing of Borachio, makes no attempt to defend himself although he had acted in self-defence, and even lays his head on the block in readiness for the fatal stroke. When D'Amville raises the axe and "strikes out his own brains", Charlemont then becomes master of three estates (D'Amville's, Belforest's, and Montferrers') along with his wife's.

It even transpires that Charlemont's wife is still "chaste", for Rousard, the son of D'Amville to whom she as D'Amville's ward had been married, was so ill at the time that he could not consummate the marriage before he died. Was Tourneur satirising something else here, or only the preference of audiences for happy endings?

Any spectators who did not realise that the play is blackly comic from beginning to end must have been somewhat simple-minded.

The attribution of *The Revenger's Tragedy* remains uncertain, and Marston and Middleton have been suggested as its author, but when did they or any other playwright of the time build a continuous string of situations turning farcically topsy-turvy into a single play? I therefore ascribe *The Revenger's Tragedy* to Tourneur in the belief that both plays must have emanated from the same satirically inclined, slyly amused, and brilliantly witty mind, one which, in particular, understood the taste and perhaps the need of audiences for fantasy!

36
A SPECIMEN SYNOPSIS OF THE SPANISH TRAGEDY

I found it impossible to understand this play until I had gone through the somewhat tedious process of writing out a synopsis scene by scene, later rewriting it with spaces below each scene in which to record significant lines and my own comments. There proved to be many episodes which were only thinly related to the action or even unrelated to it, all having been inserted, whether they delayed the action or not, because Kyd knew they would entertain or impress his spectators. Only when the frills were stripped away could the framework of the main plot be seen.

While the play is usually classed as a minor Elizabethan tragedy, consider the following facts:

—It was an early effort by a young playwright.
Since no source has been found, its plot must have been original (it was probably based on some real-life episode which Kyd had witnessed or heard of).

—It was written two or three years before 1590, at the beginning of the flowering of the Elizabethan drama.

—It established the revenge-tragedy genre.
Remaining popular for the next fifty years, it was frequently reprinted.

The play contained many plot-elements which entertained the audiences of the day and were therefore adopted, adapted, or imitated by later dramatists. The following list is not claimed to be complete; I am indebted for most of the many points to Professor Thorndike's essay "The Relations of 'Hamlet' to Contemporary Revenge Plays" of 1902:

- A ghost demanding revenge
- Swearing on the hilt of a sword
- Exhibition of a murdered body
- Use of a skull
- Simulation of lunacy
- Actual madness.
- Frustration of the hero
- Delay in obtaining revenge
- Intrigue by, or with, a female character
- Intrigue by the villain
- A play within the play
- Soliloquies
- Premonitions
- Hero enters reading a book
- An army marching by
- Spying on the hero
- Many deaths on stage, by poisoning or stabbing
- The use of mysteriously deadly poisons
- A murder done at dead of night
- Hideous cruelty to someone, on or off the stage

Most of these elements were embodied by Kyd in *The Spanish Tragedy*, and most of them appear in *Hamlet* (the important parallels between the two plays are listed in Chapter 24, "Further Notes on Hamlet"); hence it is hardly apt to call Kyd's play a minor tragedy. It was a quite remarkable play for its time.

I find, in fact, that although Kyd was a less talented poet than Marlowe, he was a more talented dramatist in that he had a superior instinctive understanding of what would entertain his audiences, in particular of the need for variety of episode and for psychological insights. The 'university wits', which included Marlowe, came up to London with their minds dominated by classical models, but Kyd and Shakespeare, who only went to grammar schools, escaped the university education of the time! His style is inferior to Marlowe's, but it is necessary when reading a play to distinguish between the poetry and the drama, the test of a play being its effect on audiences rather than readers. Kyd may have been deliberately writing in a simple style in order to ensure that his meaning would be clear to any illiterate or unsophisticated spectators. If he had not died young, he might have become a major figure in Elizabethan drama.

The additions by some later hand, probably Jonson, are ignored since they merely extend the display of Hieronimo in his 'madness' without advancing the action.

Principal Dramatis Personae

King of Spain
Cyprian, Duke of Castile, his brother
Lorenzo, the Duke's son
Bel-Imperia, Lorenzo's sister

Viceroy of Portugal
Balthazar, his son
Don Pedro, the Viceroy's brother

Hieronimo, Marshal of Spain
Isabella, his wife
Horatio, his son

Alexandro, Villuppo: Portuguese Noblemen

Pedringano, Bel-Imperia's servant
Serberine, Balthazar's servant.

I, i: *[Enter the Ghost of Andrea, and with him Revenge.]* The Ghost's long (85-line) speech describes Andrea's death in battle and his passage through the underworld. Revenge promises him that he shall see his slayer slain in turn by his lady-love Bel-Imperia.]
Comment: Andrea demands revenge because he was slain unfairly and unnecessarily in battle, then describes his passage through the classical rather than the Christian underworld, although Spain was a Christian country.

These two reappear after each act to remind the spectators that the play will be about revenge, and at the end to confirm that it was about revenge, although Andrea's revenge proves to be secondary to Hieronimo's, and his revenge turns out to be Bel-Imperia's, obtained at the cost of her own life. Neither ever speaks to any character in the play, as does the Elder Hamlet's Ghost. They could be omitted without loss to the plot—but ghosts fascinated Elizabethan audiences.

I, ii: *[Enter Spanish King, General, Castile, and Hieronimo.]* The King asks the General to describe the victory over Portugal. He does so at length (in 65 lines!). He mentions that the (Portuguese) Balthazar slew Andrea, but was in turn captured by Hieronimo's son Horatio.]

There has been "A tucket afar off"; the Army now enters and passes by, with Balthazar captive between Horatio and Lorenzo. Hieronimo mentions that Horatio is his son. The army re-enters and then leaves, as do all but Balthazar, Horatio and Lorenzo. Both the two latter claim to have captured him. Balthazar divides the credit between them; the King awards his horse, weapons and armour to Lorenzo, who shall hold Balthazar in guard—Hieronimo's establishment being too small for Balthazar and his train—the ransom to Horatio.

Comment: battles on the stage, or armies marching across it, were forms of spectacle or display, the Elizabethan equivalent of the Hollywood epic with its cast of thousands; compare an army marching across the stage in the fourth act of Hamlet. No doubt the General, who is not seen again, made the most of his description of the battle.

Lorenzo appears to be jealous by nature, their dispute being the first cause of his later enmity towards Horatio.

I, iii: *[Enter Viceroy, Alexandro, Villuppo, and Attendants.]* The Viceroy bemoans his country's defeat and reduction to "tributary" status, and bewails his son Balthazar's death, but is then told that Balthazar is alive and a prisoner.

Vic. Then they have slain him for his father's fault.

Alex. That were a breach of common law of arms.

Vic. They reck no laws that meditate revenge.

And he concludes that his son is dead. In the hope of reward, Villuppo now accuses Alexandro of treacherously shooting Balthazar in the back during the battle and so causing it to be lost. The Viceroy at once condemns Alexandro.

Comment: in a later scene, the Viceroy receives news that Balthazar is alive, immediately releases Alexandro and condemns Villuppo. This episode is apparently unrelated to the main plot, though it would be highly "dramatic" to Kyd's spectators. Its probable purpose was to contrast the haste with which the Viceroy condemns Alexandro with Hieronimo's later caution when seeking evidence of his son's murderers.

It also contains the line "They reck no laws that meditate revenge", an anticipatory hint at the change which will take place in Hieronimo.

I, iv: *[Enter Horatio and Bel-Imperia.]* Horatio relates to her how Andrea was surrounded and wounded, and how he himself had rescued him, but in vain; Andrea died of his wounds. She gives him Andrea's scarf to wear "for both him and me". She says, somewhat ambiguously:

Bel. Yet what avails to wail Andrea's death
From whence Horatio proves my second love?

She decides that she will love Horatio for the sake of obtaining revenge on Balthazar, the slayer of her true love Andrea.

[Enter Lorenzo and Balthazar.] She rejects B.'s advances. On leaving, she lets fall her glove, which Horatio, entering, picks up.

Enter the Banquet, Trumpets, the King, and Ambassador. They sit, and the King asks "Where is Hieronimo?"

[Enter Hieronimo with a drum, three Knights, each his scutcheon: then he fetches three Kings, they take their crowns and them captive.] The three Knights are Robert, Earl of Gloucester; Edmund, Earl of Kent; and John of Gaunt, Duke of Lancaster, who had all defeated kings on the Iberian peninsula. The King professes himself pleased with this "device", and "takes the cup of Horatio" to pledge Hieronimo. They leave for the banquet. Comment: this scene introduces the first though but minor revenge theme, and suggests the reason why Lorenzo and Balthazar will later murder Horatio. Bel-Imperia's exchanges with Balthazar display her as a quick-witted and spirited young lady, and justify her name. Whether she really comes to love Horatio is never certain.

The mimed performance of the three Knights, totally irrelevant to the plot, was a spectacle which would arouse a patriotic response from Kyd's audiences, as in Sheridan's The Critic.

I, v: Andrea and Revenge, who apparently do not leave the stage, give the epilogue to this act; the former is impatient.

II, i: *[Enter Lorenzo and Balthazar.]* Lorenzo urges patience, but Balthazar is lovesick. Lorenzo calls in his servant Pedringano and orders him under threat of death to discover "Whom loves my sister Bel-Imperia?" Pedringano reveals that she loves Horatio. Lorenzo promises him more gold to spy on her.
   Bal. But in his fall I'll tempt the destinies,
        And either lose my life, or win my love.
   Lor. Let's go, my lord, your staying stays revenge...

II, ii: *[Enter Horatio and Bel-Imperia,]* apparently outside her father's house. While they profess their mutual love, "Pedringano showeth all to the Prince and Lorenzo, placing them in secret [above]". Balthazar (aside): "Ambitious villain, how his boldness grows!" (Horatio is not nobly born, as is Bel-Imperia)

II, iii: *[Enter King of Spain, Portingale Ambassador, Don Cyprian, etc.]* The King expresses his approval of Balthazar's proposed marriage to Bel-Imperia and promises her a generous dowry, urging her father "to win your daughter's thought".

II, iv: *[Enter Horatio, Bel-Imperia, and Pedringano]* now in Hieronimo's garden. They retire to the bower, and order Pedringano to keep watch. He leaves—to fetch Don Lorenzo. *[Enter Lorenzo, Balthazar, Serberine, Pedringano, disguised].* They hang and stab Horatio, and drag away the screaming Bel-Imperia.

II, v: *[Enter Hieronimo in his shirt, etc.]* He cuts down the hanged man and then discovers that it is his own son. His wife Isabella enters; both are overcome with grief at the loss of their only child. They bear his body away. Hieronimo is so overcome by rage that he is already speaking of revenge, although he also says:
   Hier. Meanwhile, good Isabella, cease thy plaints,
        Or at the least dissemble them awhile,
        So shall we sooner find the practice out,
        And learn by whom all this was brought about.

II, vi: Andrea complains to Revenge that Horatio has been slain instead of Balthazar. Revenge enjoins patience.

III, i: *[Enter Viceroy of Portingale, Nobles, Villuppo.]* The Viceroy has Alexandro brought in for punishment. He protests his innocence, but is bound to a stake. The Ambassador now enters with the news that Balthazar is alive; Alexandro is released and Villuppo condemned.
Comment: more exciting drama (condemnation and last-minute rescue) for the audience.

III, ii: *[Enter Hieronimo.]* Although he has dedicated his life to the law, he is beginning to feel that his dedication was worthless:
    Hier. O world, no world, but mass of public wrongs,
        Confused and filled with murder and misdeeds;
        O sacred heavens! if this unhallow'd deed,
        If this inhuman and barbarous attempt...
        Shall unrevealed and unrevenged pass,
        How should we term your dealings to be just,
        If you unjustly deal with those who in your justice trust?
        The ugly fiends do sally forth from hell,
        And frame my steps to unfrequented paths.
    [A letter falleth.]
It proves to be from Bel-Imperia, which names the murderers. He realises that he must be cautious.

Enter Pedringano, of whom Hieronimo asks "Where's thy lady"; then Lorenzo, who offers to speak to Bel-Imperia on Hieronimo's behalf, but he refuses the offer, then leaves.

Lorenzo decides that he was betrayed by Serberine and gives Pedringano gold to murder him. He calls his Page, who is to tell Serberine to be at Saint Luigi's Park that evening. He intends to rid himself of both.

Comment: this is the first indication that in spite of the letter, Hieronimo's dedication to the law is weakening.

III, iii: *[Enter Pedringano, with a pistol,]* waiting for Serberine. The Watch enter, wondering why they have been ordered to wait by the Duke's house. Serberine enters; Pedringano shoots him; the Watch seize Pedringano and leave, taking him to Hieronimo the Marshal's house.

III, iv: *[Enter Lorenzo and Balthazar.]* Lorenzo is persuaded that "All's revealed to Hieronimo". Balthazar is ignorant of Lorenzo's machinations. *[Enter Page]* with the news that Pedringano has murdered Serberine and been imprisoned. *[Enter Messenger with a letter]* from Pedringano. Lorenzo sends the Page to Pedringano with a purse and a box which purportedly contains his pardon.

III, v: *[Enter Boy with the box]* which, although forbidden to, he opens, and finds empty.

III, vi: *[Enter Hieronimo and the Deputy.]*
    Hier. This toils my body, this consumeth age,

> That only I to all men just must be,
> And neither gods nor men be just to me.

[Enter Officers, Boy, and Pedringano, with a letter in his hand, bound.] Pedringano admits his guilt, but, sure that he will not be hanged, backchats confidently with the Hangman, until the latter suddenly "turns him off": a stage hanging.

Comment: as mentioned earlier, the latter part of this scene may have inspired Shakespeare to introduce Barnardine and Abhorson in *Measure for Measure*.

III, vii: *[Enter Hieronimo]*, complaining again that the heavens are denying him justice and revenge. *[Enter Hangman with a letter]* found on Pedringano; it confirms that he helped Lorenzo and Balthazar to murder Horatio, and proves that Bel-Imperia's letter was "not feigned". He will "go plain me to my lord the King".

III, viii: *[Enter Isabella and her maid.]* Wild with grief, she "runs lunatic".

III, ix: *[Bel-Imperia at a window]*, complaining that she is "sequestered from the court", and that Hieronimo is "slack in thy revenge".

III, x: *[Enter Lorenzo, Balthazar, and the Page]*, who confirms that Pedringano is dead. *[Enter Bel-Imperia]*, who demands to know why she has been immured by Lorenzo. He speaks of the "old disgrace / Which you for Don Andrea had endur'd" (presumably Andrea was inferior to her in social rank) and of her father's anger. She demands to know why she had no "notice" of it; he *[Whispereth in her ear]*. She rejects Balthazar's advances.

III, xi: *[Enter two Portingales, and Hieronimo meets them.]* When they ask the way to "my lord the duke's", he rants of Lorenzo "bathing him in boiling lead and blood of innocents". They laugh at him as "passing lunatic".

III, xii: *[Enter Hieronimo with a poniard in one hand and a rope in the other.]* He decides not to kill himself, for if he does, no one will avenge Horatio.

[Enter King, Ambassador, Castile, and Lorenzo.] The Ambassador speaks of the Viceroy's pleasure at the proposed marriage of Balthazar to Bel-Imperia; he brings Balthazar's ransom to Horatio. Hieronimo at once demands "Justice, O justice!", but when Lorenzo interrupts with "Hieronimo, you are not well advis'd", he becomes so distracted that he *[diggeth with his dagger]*, and the King judges him to be deranged. Lorenzo suggests to the King that Hieronimo resign his office as judge.

Comment: this scene contains the first hint that Lorenzo is baulking Hieronimo's attempts to obtain justice although Kyd's spectators were probably suspecting as much by now.

III, xiii: *[Enter Hieronimo with a book in his hand.]* He begins by quoting "Vindicta mihi"—"Vengeance is mine, saith the Lord"—but as he reads Seneca he soon decides not to rely on Heaven:

> Hier. And to conclude, I will revenge his death!
> But how? not as the vulgar wits of men,
> With open, but inevitable ills,
> As by a secret, yet a certain mean,
> Which under kindship will be cloaked best...

No, no, Hieronimo, thou must enjoin
Thine eyes to observation, and thy tongue
To milder speeches than thy spirit affords,
Thy heart to patience, and thy hands to rest,
Thy cap to courtesy, and thy knee to bow,
Till to revenge thou know, when where, and how.
[Enter a Servant], who announces "a sort of poor petitioners":
First Citizen...So I tell you this, for learning and for law
There's not any advocate in Spain
That can prevail, or will take half the pain
That he will, in pursuit of equity.

And he tears their papers, then runs out. He re-enters to the Old Man, who too has lost his only son by murder, but only offers to comfort him.

Comment: this is the crucial scene in the play, the moment when Hieronimo finally decides that his former dedication to law and justice was a futility, and that he will obtain revenge himself by underhand means. His tearing of the suppliants' papers indicates his loss of faith in the law.

"Hero enters reading a book" was imitated by other playwrights, including Shakespeare and Ford, though the reading was not crucial to their plots.

Until now, the play has been somewhat tedious and to the reader at least, though probably not to Kyd's spectators, but from now on the action gathers momentum.

III, xiv: *[Enter King of Spain, the Duke, Viceroy, and Lorenzo, Balthazar, Don Pedro and Bel-Imperia.]* Bel-Imperia and Balthazar are to be married tomorrow; the Viceroy is delighted. *[Exeunt all but Castile and Lorenzo.]* The Duke demands to know the origins of the report that Lorenzo is thwarting Hieronimo; Lorenzo replies evasively that Hieronimo has "misconstered" him; the Duke says, "Go one of you and call Hieronimo". *[Enter Balthazar and Bel-Imperia].* The Duke has forgiven the "disgrace" of her love for Andrea. *[Enter Hieronimo and a Servant.]*

Hieronimo denies that he has any complaint against Lorenzo, and embraces him: his first deception.

Comment: here we might ask, "Why have we heard no more of the letters which prove that Horatio's murderers were Lorenzo and Balthazar and that Bel-Imperia was a witness?" Has Hieronimo torn them up too in his distraction and frustration? His hypocritical profession of friendship to Lorenzo suggests that he is not as distracted as all that. Does his desire for personal revenge rather than public justice now dominate him?

III, xv: *[Enter Ghost and Revenge.]* Andrea complains that Revenge is asleep; Revenge says "Content thyself". *[Enter a Dumb Show.]* Hymen blows out the nuptial torches and quenches them with blood.

Comment: unnecessary to the action, but entertaining to the spectators.

IV, i: *[Enter Bel-Imperia and Hieronimo.]* She rebukes him for his apparent inaction; he now mentions her letter (but not Pedringano's?) and craves pardon for not believing it.

They will join forces.
   [Enter Balthazar and Lorenzo.] The latter asks Hieronimo to put on a show for the King and Ambassador. Hieronimo is ready with a tragedy he had written in his younger days; it is to be "in unknown languages":
   Hier.   I'll play the murderer, I warrant you,
      For I have already conceited that.
[Balthazar is suspicious; he would prefer a comedy, but Lorenzo decides that "We must resolve to soothe his humours up."]
   Hier.   And if the world like not this tragedy,
      Hard is the hap of old Hieronimo.
Comment: the first two lines are superb dramatic irony; the second two were echoed by Shakespeare in *Hamlet*:
   Hamlet   For if the king like not the comedy,
      Why, then, belike—he likes it not, perdy.

IV, ii: *[Enter Isabella with a weapon.]* She cuts down the arbour, then stabs herself and exits, presumably to die off-stage.

IV, iii: *[Enter Hieronimo; he knocks up the curtain. Enter the Duke of Castile.]* Hieronimo asks the Duke "That when the train are passed into the gallery, You would vouchsafe to throw me down the key".
Comment: "Knocks up the curtain" appears to mean "create a temporary curtain" behind which Hieronimo can hide the body of his dead son. "Throw me down the key": Hieronimo intends to lock the courtiers in the gallery so as to have time to hang himself (the gallery must have been a large upper stage).

IV, iv: *[Enter Spanish King, Viceroy, the Duke of Castile, and their train.]* The play is performed but presumably not in "sundry languages". Hieronimo stabs Lorenzo; Bel-Imperia stabs Balthazar, then herself. Hieronimo now exposes his dead son's body and in a long half-hysterical speech explains the reason for these stabbings but forgets to mention the letters or Isabella's suicide. The courtiers break in before he can hang himself. He bites out his tongue to prevent himself from speaking under torture; Castile points out that he can still write; he makes signs for a knife to mend his pen, and with it stabs the Duke, who is presumably trying to prevent him from stabbing himself; then stabs himself.
Comment: the depiction of Hieronimo's gradual descent from judge and protector of the law to criminal has continued to the last scene, the slaying of the Duke of Castile being totally out of character for the Hieronimo of the beginning of the play.
   The disappearance of the incriminating letters is an apparent weakness in the plot; however, when Hieronimo discovers his son's body, Kyd makes him speak of justice and revenge in the same breath, possibly a hint that Hieronimo will eventually take his revenge without troubling to produce actual evidence. Was Kyd suggesting that in a society where private revenge was often the only way to obtain redress, rage at an injury might overcome respect for law and order even in a judge?

IV, v: In the epilogue, Andrea and Revenge summarise events, and outline punishments and rewards.
   "To place thy friends in ease, the rest in woe."

37
WHO WAS THE AUTHOR OF SHAKESPEARE'S PLAYS?

The principal candidates for the title are Shakespeare himself, Francis Bacon, and the Earls of Oxford, Derby, and Rutland.

The style of Bacon's essays is among the finest English prose ever written; it could hardly be more precise, concise, and penetrating. I quote a few openings:

> Of Death: Men fear death as children fear to go in the dark; and as that natural fear is increased with tales, so is the other.

> Of Marriage and Single Life: He that hath wife and child hath given hostages to fortune.

> Of Great Place: Men in great place are thrice servants; servants of the Sovereign or State, servants of fame, and servants of business.

More to the present purpose are the following:

> Of Revenge: Revenge is a kind of wild justice, which the more man's nature runs to, the more ought law to weed it out. For as for the first wrong, it does but offend the law, but the revenge of that wrong putteth the law out of office.

> Of Love: The stage is more beholding to love than the life of man.

> Of Masques and Triumphs: These things are but toys, to come amongst such serious considerations.

Revenge tragedies were a popular genre of the time, but the first extract suggests that Bacon would not have taken advantage of their popularity by writing one himself; the second and third, that Bacon was looking at the stage not as a member of the acting profession but with the detachment of an outside observer.

His main interests were the law, education, and natural philosophy. His style was formed during his legal training: terse, analytical, detached, and far too matter-of-fact for a poet. I find his later writings too erudite and wordy; they are so prolix that it is hard to imagine him writing in the taut, dynamic style which is essential for stage dialogue and ideally is in character for each individual speaker. He appears never to have attempted to write dialogue even as a method of illustrating his meaning. He is always the observant moraliser and philosopher, never a poet. Though he did publish a volume of poetry, he is not remembered as a poet.

As for the earls: if any one of them had possessed the innate playwriting genius of a Shakespeare, he would have devoted a large proportion of his active life to writing plays, and since the secret of their authorship would sooner or later have leaked out, would then have been acknowledged by his contemporaries as an outstanding playwright. None of them was.

I remain a Stratfordian.

For me, the important question is: what was Shakespeare doing in the 1570's between his departure from Stratford and his arrival in London? As the style of his first play *Henry VI Part I* shows, when he reached London he was already on his way to becoming an excellent poet and playwright.

* * * * *

BIBLIOGRAPHY

Alexander, Peter, *Shakespeare's Life and Art* (Nisbet, 1939)
Agate, James, *Brief Chronicles* (Cape, 1943)
Bentley, Eric, *What is Theatre?* (Dennis Dobson, 1957).
Bentley, Gerald Eades, *Shakespeare, a Biographical Handbook* (Yale, 1961)
Berne, Eric, M.D., *Games People Play* (1964; Penguin, 1969)
Bevington, David (ed.), *20th Century Interpretations of Hamlet* (Prentice-Hall Trade, 1968)
Boulton, Marjorie, *The Anatomy of the Novel* (Routledge and Kegan Paul, 1975)
Bowers, Fredson, *Elizabethan Revenge Tragedy* (Princeton U.P., 1940)
Bradbrook, Muriel C., *Shakespeare the Craftsman* (Chatto and Windus, 1969). *Themes and Conventions of Elizabethan Tragedy* (1969). *The Living Monument* (C.U.P., 1977)
Bradley, Andrew C., *Shakespearean Tragedy* (Macmillan, 1969)
Braunschvig, Marcel, *Notre Littérature Etudiée dans les Textes*, Vol 1 (Librairie Armand Colin, 1931)
Brown, John Russell, *Shakespeare's Dramatic Style* (Heinemann, 1970). *Antony and Cleopatra: a Casebook* Casebook Series (Macmillan, 1968)
Bullough, Geoffrey (ed.), *Narrative and Dramatic Sources of Shakespeare*, Vol.VII. (Routledge and Kegan Paul, 1973)
Caudwell, Hugo, *Introduction to French Classicism* (Macmillan, 1931)
Chute, Marchette, *An Introduction to Shakespeare* (N.Y., 1951)
Clemen, Wolfgang, *Shakespeare's Dramatic Art: Collected Essays* (Methuen, 1972)
Cook, Judith, *Women in Shakespeare* (Harrap, 1980)
Conklin, Paul S., *A History of Hamlet Criticism* (1601–1821)
Corneille, Pierre, *Le Cid* (1637). *Horace* (1640)
Cotton, Charles (trans.), *Horace* (1671)
Danby, John F., *Shakespeare's Doctrine of Nature—A Study of King Lear* (Faber, 1948)
Davis, Norman (ed.), *The Paston Letters and the Papers of the Fifteenth Century* (Oxford Clarendon Press 1977)
Deschamps, Pierre, *Procès du Méchant et Détestable Ravaillac* (1855).
Procès, Exament, Confessions et Negations du Parricide. Ravaillac
Dick, Oliver Lawson (ed.), *Aubrey's Brief Lives* (Secker and Warburg, 1960)
Draper, John W., *The Hamlet of Shakespeare's Audience* (1938). *Queen Gertrude* (1934)
Duthie, George I., *Shakespeare* (Hutchinson, 1951). *The "Bad" Quarto of Hamlet* (1951)
Dutton, Richard, *William Shakespeare* (Macmillan, 1989)
Eliot, Thomas S., *Selected Prose* (Peregrine Books, 1963)
Elliot, George R., *Scourge and Minister: a Study of Hamlet as Tragedy of Revengefulness and Justice* (Duke University Press, 1951)
Encyclopaedia Britannica (1956 edn.), various articles
Evans, Sir Ifor: *A Short History of English Literature* (Pelican, 1963). *A Short History of English Drama* (Pelican, 1948)
Evans, T.F. (ed.), *Shaw: The Critical Heritage* (Routledge and Kegan Paul, 1976)
Frost, David L., *The School of Shakespeare* (C.U.P., 1968)
Frye, Roland Muskat, *Shakespeare and Christian Doctrine* (Princeton U.P., 1963)

Gardner, Richard A., *Psychotherapy with Children of Divorce* (Jason Aaronson Inc, N.Y.)
Grant, Michael, *Cleopatra* (Weidenfeld and Nicholson, 1972)
Granville-Barker, Harley, *Prefaces to Shakespeare* (Batsford)
Greer, Germaine, *Shakespeare* (Oxford Paperback, 1986)
Halliday, F.E., *A Shakespeare Companion*, 1564–1964 (Penguin, 1964). *The Life of Shakespeare* (Pelican, 1963)
Harrison, George B., *Introducing Shakespeare* (Pelican, 1962)
Hart, Roger, *Witchcraft* (Wayland Publishers, 1973)
Hayter, Alethea, *Horatio's Version* (Faber and Faber, 1972). Hinchliffe, Arnold P. (ed.), *Drama Criticism: Developments since Ibsen*, Casebook Series (Palgrave Macmillan, 1979)
Honigmann, Ernst A.J., *Shakespeare: Seven Tragedies* (Macmillan, 1976)
Hooker, Elizabeth Robbins, Essay "The Relation of Shakespeare to Montaigne" (1902)
Horne, Richard H., *Was Hamlet Mad?* (1871)
Hughes, Pennethorne, *Witchcraft* (Pelican, 1963)
Hunter, G.K., *Dramatic Identities and Cultural* Tradition (Liverpool U.P.)
Hope, Alec D., *Dunciad Minor: An Heroick Poem,* extract (Melbourne University Press, 1970)
Jump, John D. (ed.), *Shakespeare: Hamlet* (Macmillan, Casebook Series, 1968)
Harrison, George B. (ed.) *King James I Daemonologie of 1597* (Bodley Head, 1924)
Kitto, Humphrey D.F., *Form and Meaning in Drama* (Methuen, 1956)
Knights, Lionel C., *Hamlet and Other Shakespearean Essays* (C.U.P.).
Some Shakespearean Themes (Chatto and Windus, 1959)
Lee, Sir Sidney, *A Life of William Shakespeare* (John Murray, 1925)
Lemmon, Jeremy & Watkins, Ronald, *In Shakespeare's Playhouse—Hamlet* (David and Charles, 1974)
Leavis, Frank R., *Anna Karenina and Other Essays* (Chatto and Windus, 1967)
Levi, Peter, *The Life and Times Of William Shakespeare* (Papermac, 1988)
Levin, Harry, *Shakespeare and the Revolution of the Times* (O.U.P, 1976). *The Question of Hamlet* (Oxford University Press, 1970)
LeWinter, Oswald (ed.), Shakespeare in Europe (Penguin, 1963)
Lloyd Evans, Gareth and Barbara, *Everyman's Companion to Shakespeare* (Dent, 1978)
Long, Michael, *The Unnatural Scene* (Methuen, 1976)
Lough, John, *Seventeenth Century French Drama: the Background* (Oxford, 1979)
Lucas, Frank L., *Literature and Psychology* (Cassell, 1951). *Tragedy* (Hogarth Press, 1971)
Mangan, Michael, *A Preface to Shakespeare's Tragedies* (Longman, 1991)
Mangan, Roscoe (trans.), *Horace* (1881)
Margeson, J.M.R., *The Origins of English Tragedy* (O.U.P., 1967)
Masefield, John, *Shakespeare* (Williams and Norgate 1924).Masson, Georgina, *A Concise History of Republican Rome* (Thames and Hudson, 1973)
May, Robin, *Who Was Shakespeare?* (David and Charles, 1974)
MacLure, Millar (ed.), Marlowe: *The Critical Heritage*. (Routledge and Kegan Paul, 1979)
McEvedy, Colin, *The Penguin Atlas of Medieval History* (Penguin, 1961)
McClellan, Kenneth, *Whatever Happened to Shakespeare?* (Vision, 1978)

Matthews, Brander (ed.), *Papers on Playmaking* (Books for Libraries Press, 1957)
Mehl, Dieter, *The Elizabethan Dumb-Show* (Methuen, 1965)
Michell, John, *Who Wrote Shakespeare?* (Thames and Hudson, 1999)
Miles, Rosalind, *The Problem of Measure for Measure* (Vision Press, 1976)
Mornet, Daniel, *Histoire des Grandes Oeuvres de la Littérature Française* (Librairie Larousse, 1925)
Muir, Kenneth & Schoenbaum, Samuel, *A New Companion to Shakespeare Studies* (C.U.P., 1971)
O'Connor, Gary, *William Shakespeare* (Hodder and Stoughton, 1991)
Olivier, Laurence, *On Acting* (Weidenfeld and Nicholson, 1960).
Confessions of an Actor (do. 1980)
Onions, Charles T., *A Shakespeare Glossary* (O.U.P.)
Parker, Patricia & Hartmann, Geoffrey, *Shakespeare and the Question of Theory* (Routledge N.Y. and London, 1985)
Pepper, Frank S., *Dictionary of Biographical Quotations* (Sphere, 1985)
Pickthall, Muhammad M., *the Glorious Koran* (trans.) (TaHa Publishers Ltd.)
Plutarch, *Lives. Opera Moralia*
Pocock, Gordon, *Corneille and Racine* (C.U.P., 1973)
Quiller-Couch, Sir Arthur, Notes on *Shakespeare's Workmanship* (N.Y., 1917)
Rackin, Phyllis, *Shakespeare's Tragedies* (N.Y., 1978)
Raleigh, Walter, *Shakespeare* (Macmillan, 1916)
Johnson *On Shakespeare (O.U.P., 1965)*
Rattigan, Terence, *Collected Plays*
Razzell, Peter, *William Shakespeare, The Anatomy of an Enigma.* (Caliban, 1990)
Ribner, Irving, *Patterns in Shakespearean Tragedy* (Methuen, 1960)
Richardson, William, *A Philosophical Analysis of Some of Shakespeare's Characters* (J. Murray, 1774)
Robertson, John M., *The Problem of Hamlet* (Allen & Unwin, 1919)
Rose, Mark (ed.), *Twentieth Century Interpretations of Antony and Cleopatra* (Prentice Hall, 1977)
Rowse, Alfred L., *Prefaces to Shakespeare's Plays* (Orbis, 1984). *William Shakespeare* (Harper and Row, 1963. *My View of Shakespeare* (Duckworth, 1996)
Salgado, Gamini, *Eyewitnesses of Shakespeare* (Sussex U.P.)
Scot, Reginald, *The Discoverie of Witchcraft (1584):* reprint of first edition, (ed.) Brinsley Nicholson, M.D. (1886); also 1964 edition.
Scott, Sir Walter, *Letters on Demonology and Witchcraft*
Scullard, Howard H., *From the Gracchi to Nero* (Methuen, 1959)
Southern, Pat, *Cleopatra* (Tempus, 1999)
Scullard, Howard H. & Cary, Max, *A History of Rome* (Macmillan, 1979)
Spurgeon, Caroline, *Shakespeare's Imagery* (C.U.P., 1939)
Squire, Sir John, *Shakespeare as a Dramatist* (Cassell, 1935)
Stewart, John.I.M, *Character and Motive in Shakespeare* (Longman, 1949)
Stoll, Elmer E., *Art and Artifice in Shakespeare* (Methuen, 1963)
Stratford-upon-Avon Studies, *Hamlet* (1963)
Styan, John L., *The Shakespeare Revolution* (C.U.P., 1977)
Terrell, Hull, *Was Shakespeare a Lawyer?* (Longman, 1871)

Thorndike, Ashley H., Essay *The Relations of Hamlet to Contemporary Revenge Plays* (1902)
Tillyard, Eustace M.W., *Shakespeare' Problem Plays* (Chatto and Windus, 1971). *Shakespeare' History Plays* (do. 1944)
Traversi, Derek, *An Approach to Shakespeare* (Hollis and Carter, 1969)
Vial, Francisque et Denise, Louis (ed.s), *Idées et Doctrines Littéraires du XVIIe Siècle* (Librairie Delagrave, Paris, 1925)
Vickers, Brian (ed.), *Shakespeare: The Critical Heritage*, (6 volumes, 1974–81)
Waldock, Arthur J.A., *Hamlet: A Study in Critical Method* (Sydney U.P.)
Watts, Newman, *Was Hamlet Mad?* (1888)
Weitz, Morris, *Hamlet and the Philosophy of Literary Criticism* (Faber, 1972)
Wells, Stanley, *Literature and Drama* (Routledge and Kegan Paul, 1990)
Williamson, G., (ed.), *Readings on the Character of Hamlet* (Anthology) (Allen and Unwin, 1950)
Williamson, James A., *The Tudor Age* (Longman, 1953)
Willson, David H., *King James VI and I* (Jonathan Cape, 1956)
Wilson, Edwin (ed.), *Shaw on Shakespeare* (Penguin, 1969)
Wilson, Frank P., *The English Drama*, 1485–1585 (O.U.P., 1969)
Wilson, Ian, *Shakespeare, the Evidence* (Headline, 1993)
Wilson, John Dover, *What Happens in Hamlet* (C.U.P., 1959). *Life in Shakespeare's England* (Pelican, 1944)
Wilson Knight, G., *The Wheel of Fire: Interpretations of Shakespearian Tragedy (1930). Shakespeare's Dramatic Challenge: on the Rise of Shakespeare's Tragic Heroes* (Barnes & Noble, 1977)
Wilson, Mona, *Queen Elizabeth* (Daily Express Publications)
Wrightson, Keith, *English Society: 1580–1680* (Hutchinson, 1982)

PLAYS

SHAKESPEARE: Complete Works

Hamlet
    First Quarto (facsimile)
    Second Quarto (facsimile)
    First Folio (facsimile)
    A.W. von Schlegel (trans.) (c.1800)
    Samuel Johnson (ed.) (1765)
    M.Mull (1885)
    H.N.Hudson (1879)
    C.H.Herford (1900)
    H.Morley (1903)
    Sir A.Quiller-Couch (1910)
    G.S.Gordon (1912)
    D.C.Somervell (1923)
    J.Q.Adams (1929)
    J.Dover Wilson (1936)
    A.W.Verity (1966)
    *B.Lott (1968)
    P.Abrahams and A.Brody (1968)
    A.Barton (1984)
    H.Jenkins (1982)
    G.R.Hibbard (1987)
    Susanne L. Wofford (1994)

Othello
    Arden, (ed.) M.R.Ridley (1958)
    *Arden (2), (ed.) M.R.Ridley (Methuen & Co., 1984)
    Arden (3), (ed.) E.A.J.Honigmann (1987)
    Signet Classics, (ed.) Alvin Kernan (1963)

Antony and Cleopatra
    H.N. Hudson (1881)
    T.Henshaw (1953)
    E.Jones (1977)
    *M.R.Ridley, (Methuen & Co. 1954; & 1981)
    A.E.Morgan & W.S.Vines (undated)

Troilus and Cressida
    T.Tonson (1734)
    H.Morley (1889)
    K.Palmer (1982)
    *David Bevington (Bloomsbury 1998)

Marlowe, Christopher, *Plays,* introduced by Edward Thomas (1950)
Kyd, Thomas, *The Spanish Tragedy*, (ed.s) T.W. Craik (1974) & P.Edwards (1959)

Other Plays: various Arden editions

* * * * *

Editor referencing (*):
**All's Well That Ends Well,* (ed.) G.K.Hunter (1962, repr.Routledge 1994)
**Coriolanus,* (ed.) P Brockbank (1976, repr. Routledge 1988)
**King Lear,* (ed.) K.Muir (1972. repr. Routledge 1992)
**Measure for Measure,* (ed.) J.W.Lever (1965, repr. Bloomsbury 2015)
**Macbeth,* (ed.) K.Muir (Thomas Nelson & Sons, 1951 & repr. 1999)
&
*The Arden Shakespeare: *Shakespeare Complete Works* (Revised edition, (ed.s) R. Proudfoot, A. Thomson, D.S.Kastan (Bloomsbury, 1998, repr. 2011)

Lightning Source UK Ltd.
Milton Keynes UK
UKOW01n1325210917
309633UK00003B/193/P